Playing with the Past

PRAISE FOR
PLAYING WITH THE PAST

"*Playing with the Past* is a serious cultural contemplation on a media genre that forever changed the way a generations thinks. An engaging exploration into the way media engages and redefines history, *Playing with the Past* is a groundbreaking work in Media Studies and an essential text for the study of video games and the history of ideas."

C. JASON SMITH, *Professor of English,*
The City University of New York-LaGuardia, US

"Elliott and Kapell have gathered a remarkable collection of contributions—engaging deep issues about what history IS, and how one can present its issues in a vital contribution within contemporary studies. The scope is compendious, from Rome to Native America, from Japan to Colonial America; this book just might become the basis for up-to-the-minute narrative/historical/digital mediations, and should be of interest in the many fields of the superior college or university."

WILLIAM G. DOTY, *Professor Emeritus,*
University of Alabama, US

"*Playing with the Past* is an innovative, lucid and engaging collection that strikes a number of carefully constructed and rewarding balances. The tone is both serious and playful. Its analysis and findings are simultaneously rigorous, illuminating and entertaining. *Playing with the Past* provides a neat summation of the previous work which has explored the relationship between digital games and their interaction with history as a foundation to establish, with great sophistication and clarity, the critical and conceptual terrain for the current and future debates."

STEPHEN McVEIGH, *Associate Professor,*
Department of Political and Cultural Studies, Swansea University, UK

"*Playing with the Past* is a far-reaching volume, guiding readers through ancient civilizations, modern wars, and futures premised upon counterfactual pasts. In this reflexively-organized array of essays, game scholars will find both a primer on historiographic inquiry and a series of cogent analyses that are not simply conversant with issues driving the field but also bring new depth and insight to their examination."

GERALD VOORHEES, *Assistant Professor of Digital Media*
and Communication, University of Waterloo, Canada

Playing with the Past

Digital games and the simulation of history

Edited by
MATTHEW WILHELM KAPELL
and
ANDREW B.R. ELLIOTT

B L O O M S B U R Y

NEW YORK · LONDON · NEW DELHI · SYDNEY

Bloomsbury Academic

An imprint of Bloomsbury Publishing Inc

1385 Broadway	50 Bedford Square
New York	London
NY 10018	WC1B 3DP
USA	UK

www.bloomsbury.com

Bloomsbury is a registered trademark of Bloomsbury Publishing PLC

First published 2013

© Matthew Wilhelm Kapell, Andrew B.R. Elliott and Contributors, 2013

All rights reserved. No part of this publication may be reproduced or transmitted in any form or by any means, electronic or mechanical, including photocopying, recording, or any information storage or retrieval system, without prior permission in writing from the publishers.

No responsibility for loss caused to any individual or organization acting on or refraining from action as a result of the material in this publication can be accepted by Bloomsbury or the author.

Library of Congress Cataloging-in-Publication Data

A catalog record for this book is available from the Library of Congress.

ISBN: HB: 978-1-6235-6614-2
PB: 978-1-6235-6728-6
ePDF: 978-1-6235-6387-5
ePub: 978-1-6235-6824-5

Typeset by Integra Software Services Pvt. Ltd.
Printed and bound in the United States of America

For our wives

Sara Maghini
Who forgave Andrew for buying an Xbox
and then not talking to her for the next two weeks.

And

Amy Kapell
Who once put everything she owned into a pickup truck
and drove 2,298 miles just to be with Matthew.

As well as
Zoe Sluka-Kapell
Jedi Knight

And

For our students, past, present, and future.
It is shocking how much you can learn from people
you are supposed to be teaching.

Contents

Acknowledgments

The editors have accrued many debts during this process. Most importantly, we need to thank our wives, Sara Maghini and Amy Kapell, for putting up with us, and for letting us love them back.

Katie Gallof, our editor at Bloomsbury, was the perfect person to support this project on a number of levels. She is, simply, a superhero. With a cape, even. Indeed, the entire creative team at Bloomsbury deserves huge thanks. From design, to layout, to the cover, we can only hope as editors that this book is as good as it looks.

The staff at the consulting firm Closed Loop, Amy Kapell's company, was supportive on many technical issues when we needed to understand a number of computer-related issues. They are exactly as they claim: Rock Stars.

Shane Hill, once a student of Matthew Kapell's at the University of Michigan–Dearborn, kept in touch over the years in part to simply demand repeatedly that this project eventually be undertaken. He is exactly what every teacher hopes for in his or her best students, so, Shane: here it is. Hope you like it.

Andrew Elliott's colleagues at the University of Lincoln have been incredibly helpful and supportive, from the Game Studies group who let him gatecrash a session to their fantastic lecturers, Dr. Patrick Dickinson, Dr. Conor Linehan, Dr. Ben Kirman, Dr. Grzegorz Cielniak, and Dr. Nicola Bellotto, who patiently explained to him which way around to hold the controller and where the batteries go. Likewise Dr. Sarah Barrow and Professor Ann Gray, who allowed him to disappear to Portugal at short notice in the middle of teaching, bailed him out of marking, and were immensely forgiving when he missed important deadlines as he and Matthew tried to bring a ridiculously ambitious project together. Last but not least, the numerous students who have helped Andrew not only by tolerating his busy schedule but by talking to him about games and history, most especially the FTV class of 2013, who allowed Andrew to derail his Heroes and Villains sessions to talk about their favorite video games.

Matthew owes a rather large and ongoing debt to Dr. Stephen McVeigh of Swansea University, who taught Matthew more than he knows. Professor Lynn Medeiros at Sierra College, Dr. Ace Pilkington at Dixie State University, Professor C. Jason Smith at CUNY–LaGuardia, Professors Emeriti John

Shelton Lawrence and William G. Doty, Professors Greg Gassman and Jennifer McCabe of Woodland Community College, and a host of really amazing students all offered insight, support, or simply the right words at the right time.

The three editors of the series *Approaches to Digital Game Studies*, Gerald A. Voorhees, Katie Whitlock, and Josh Call, laid out a way to consider this topic in their excellent volumes. And Voorhees and Whitlock were also helpful personally—or more directly via email with encouragement and insights. We thank them with great sincerity.

Too many other colleagues to name them all have offered sage advice on this project, but we would like to acknowledge just some of them. In no particular order, then, Danielle Kinsey and Shawn Graham at Carleton University, Filipe Penicheiro of Coimbra University, Karl Hardy of Queens University, and Kathryn Tomasek of Wheaton College, all provided encouragement, interest, and thoughtfulness. There are more, but we'll stop by thanking those named with the caveat that the thanks also go to many unnamed.

We would be remiss if we did not also offer a huge Thank You to Guernsey B. T. Kapell, Esquire, III, and Mia. Both were instrumental in making sure we both knew that our work was at once important and, well, not *that* important.

All of the contributors here have done their best with limited word counts available, a time frame that demanded a blue police box time machine, and editors who kept demanding more of them. As editors we accept responsibility for any issues readers might have with this book, but are immensely pleased to offer the contributors total credit for all that is good in this volume.

1

Introduction: To Build a Past That Will "Stand the Test of Time"—Discovering Historical Facts, Assembling Historical Narratives

Andrew B.R. Elliott
University of Lincoln

Matthew Wilhelm Kapell
Sierra College

What's in a name?

The book you now hold in your hands went through a number of iterations before it, and the ideas contained within it, began to grow into something book-shaped. Not least among our concerns, almost from the outset, was the title, which went through several suggestions until we settled on *Playing with the Past*. What is more revealing than what we eventually decided as the title for the collection, however, are the reasons for which we disregarded others, since they speak volumes about the book's main concern: the relationship between video games and their complex, changing, and multifaceted association with history. *Digital History* (one early option) seemed implicitly to suggest that our central argument was that video games could *do* history in a similar vein to Marc Ferro's early claims that cinema could act as a historian—which was not necessarily the point of this book.[1] *Video Games and Historical Engagement* not only loses the (in our view, important) nuances of "playing," but also unwittingly suggests an overwhelmingly academic approach to the subject, one which plays on stereotypes of the historian as a fusty, fussy pedant who emerges from dusty archives to scowl at all things popular with the audacity to demean their noble pursuit. Such a stereotype of course no longer fits the modern history department (if ever it did), but more importantly, the specificity of the title betrays an overly academic approach implying that the only way of engaging with the past is by traditional academic study, an image of historical inquiry that no longer holds in an era in which subscriptions to dedicated history channels, visitors to genealogical websites, and box-office receipts for films set in the past are soaring.

Video games and history

So it was, then, that we settled on *Playing with the Past*, and the volume you hold in your hands; a title that encapsulates several of the major issues with which this book is engaged—what is "the past" and how does it relate to "history"? How do we "represent" both of those ideas? Actually, many of those themes came from an already classic 2005 article by William Uricchio, discussing the simulation of history through video games. There he observed that the opportunities for mediation through play pose new and difficult questions about narrative authority and representation. "What happens," he asked,

> if we push the notion of mediation beyond language, to the domain of game, enactment, or simulation? Does this allow us to slip out of the well-critiqued trap of representation? And if so, where does it land us?[2]

Amid a world of SIMs (Simulations), first-person warfare games, strategy, MMO (Massive Multiplayer Online games) and MMORPGs (Massive Multiplayer Online Role Playing Games) in which players can influence the outcome of past battles, campaigns, and even entire civilizations, such questions about the means by which history is delivered to new generations gain increasing importance. When history can be simulated, re-created, subverted, and rewritten on a variety of levels, new questions arise about the relationship between video games and the history they purport to represent, questions that traditional historical approaches cannot properly address.

It is, then, the issue of representing history, and the wider questions about the representation of history, that this book aims to address by looking at several major issues concerning the ways in which digital games approach the past. One such issue is the conception of history not as an academic or exclusive field of study (what Rosenstone famously terms "History with a capital H"[3]) but as "the past," a more inclusive and inviting concept that embraces all aspects of our history and implicitly refers to its relationship to the present. Another important term is, of course, "playing," which has largely been replaced in Game Studies with the more technical term "ludic." That term, from the Latin *ludus*, has come to mean "play," and we choose to use it this way even though it also carries with it the implication of spontaneous or aimless play that does not fit neatly with the notion of playing the "historical games" studies here. However, we use the term since it recognizes both the ludic nature of digital games—the sense that games are not designed as artifacts only to be looked at or understood narratively like films or television, but to be played, thus their ludic nature obliges us to understand them differently—but it also recognizes the importance of play as a human activity, which according to Huizinga, has the ability to "promote the formation of social groupings,"[4] and which Suits, building on Caillois, suggests as being "the voluntary effort to overcome unnecessary obstacles."[5] It is this conception of play—and that built up in later studies of ludology—which is of significance to our understanding of engagement with history.

When we talk about playing with the past, however, or engaging with history through games, it is first and foremost important to be specific about precisely what is meant here. Questions about the ways in which video games can have a serious impact on learning have already been addressed before in a variety of ways. Steven Johnson, for example, offers an important defense of popular culture's ability to encourage critical and complex thinking, based on what he terms a "sleeper curve."[6] Recognizing that although much of the mainstream discussion of video games is dominated by violent games like *Quake* or *Doom* (or, recently, *Grand Theft Auto*), he argues that in fact the "two genres that historically have dominated the charts are both forms of complex simulation: either sport sims, or GOD games like *SimCity* or *Age of Empires*," the kind of games that, he argues, "require the most thinking."[7] Thus, he continues, "in this age of attention deficit disorder and instant gratification, in this age of gratuitous violence and cheap titillation, the most intellectually challenging titles are also the most popular."[8]

In fact, research into games' potential for education has broken significant ground over the last decade, reaching a tipping point in recent years, as indicated by James Paul Gee's classic *What Video Games Have to Teach Us about Learning and Literacy*, as well as David Williamson Shaffer's *How Computer*

Games Help Children Learn, alongside Kurt Squire's work on *Civilization III* and learning about history, which we discuss below.[9] Likewise, judging by the number of students passing through our offices recently who want to do research on history and games, as well as the enormous response to this collection, all of the indications hint that, if anything, this scholarly interest is likely only to grow. In this book we aim to build on this existing work and to approach what is an old question (about historical representation in modern popular culture) from a new perspective, using a methodology drawn from both of our earlier works on the depiction of history in popular culture—that is from the perspective of history rather than that of games studies proper, on the grounds that this approach raises new questions that take us away from discussions about accuracy or nostalgia, which have dominated some of the earlier work in this area.

When we ask about how games engage with history, it seems to us that we need to specify precisely what we mean by these terms:

1   First of all, what do we *mean* by history? What *kind* of history?

2   What do we mean by games? Can games be treated as one and the same thing in their relationship with history? Do different kinds of games engage with history in different ways?

3   What about intentions? Before trying to evaluate whether games can teach history, we also need to establish whether a historically themed game is even *trying* to do so in the first place.

So in beginning to ask these sorts of questions, a number of parameters emerge. Of critical importance here is what kind of history, or indeed what kind of historical engagement, we are talking about. Jerome de Groot, for example, in his excellent study of public history, has a somewhat pessimistic view of the potential for historical engagement through video games. Commenting on the ludic uses of the past in general, he argues that: "Game shows, pub quiz nights, and board games present history as a set of facts which are correct, the right answer. [...] Historical knowledge in these manifestations is the command and recall of a set of facts–generally dates, leaders, events or places."[10] Even in the video games sector, which emphasizes play over knowledge recall and thus should better fit his arguments about public history, he argues that their "underlying ludicness, [... have] little innate value outside of the game structure."[11] For our purposes, however, these two claims—one about the use of facts, and the other about processes that we might otherwise call historical contingence—both emerge as interesting and debatable issues, and consequently form the starting point for our discussion.

To reduce it to its most basic elements (and, in fact, to remove the idea of history as an academic practice altogether), we can see that when it comes to public history, the notion of history covers two contradictory ideas. As J.L. Gorman writes, "History is an ambiguous word ... it can refer to the historical past itself, to the subject matter about which historians write. Second, it can refer to the study of that past, to the practices and writings of historians."[12] Thus, on the one hand we have the study of the past as a series of facts and movements, and on the other we have a concept of the past considered as a whole, in which those facts, movements, and events have combined in a certain way to lead us to the present day. The first is a type of flat "names, dates, facts, and figures" conception of history, while the second is the narrative produced from the first—whether by a professional historian or not.

Historiography, or the history of history

In fact, a great deal of ink has been spilled over the last half-century describing the historiographic issues that this sort of division engenders. Historiography, though a term often restricted to scholarly use, is in fact a straightforward idea that recognizes the fallibility of the historical record and tries to separate out the historian from the history she or he retells.[13] In one telling (and oft-cited elsewhere as well as in the following pages) description of historiography by E.H. Carr, the divisions outlined above between facts and processes are already there, lurking beneath the surface meaning. In a key passage from his now-classic *What Is History?*, Carr claims that

> History consists of a corpus of ascertained facts. The facts are available to the historian in documents, inscriptions, and so on, like fish on a fishmonger's slab. The historian collects them, takes them home, and cooks them and serves them in whatever style appeals to him.[14]

If we can unpack this a little, we will see that Carr's argument that history consists of a corpus of ascertained facts means that there is an element of selection of the facts (which implies that not all facts can be used), that they form a corpus (so are woven together according to modern taste) and, implicitly, that there must be someone to choose them (who may be liable to distort them in all kinds of ways). This process of selection, assembly, and presentation—as Andrew Elliott has discussed elsewhere—means that the history that emerges would depend on: (1) which facts are chosen, and (2) how they are put together again (the process).[15]

Thus, from the very outset, any claims about the relationship between popular culture's representations of history are obliged immediately to recognize the inherent fallibility of history as a discipline itself—or at the least the recognition of its lack of objectivity. This is not to launch an internecine attack on scholarly history, of course, since it is an issue that is widely acknowledged by historians themselves, and which also explains why some historians bristle at being placed not in the humanities but in the social sciences.[16] Here, then, historiography—that is, the study of creating history that recognizes its own limitations—can help us by acknowledging that there are at least three elements in play in shaping a historical narrative.

First, the selection of facts, which concedes that here we are limited not only by those facts selected by the historian, but also by which facts are *available* in the first place, which ones are known, and which facts are assumed. In video games, as with film, given that it is impossible to show everything, any simulation of the past is of course constructed to a great degree by which facts or details are selected, which leads to new issues. As Paul Veyne suggests, somewhat provocatively, "if everything is historical, then history becomes that which we choose."[17] In any case, a fact-based approach (what Rosenstone endearingly calls "Dragnet history")[18] also assumes that accuracy is the objective of video games, when in fact the debate is, as we will see, far more complex. To give only one example, Stephen Poole argues somewhat counterintuitively that excessive realism can often get in the way of authenticity, since "you don't *want* it [the game] to be too real. The purpose of a video game is never to simulate real life, but to offer the *gift of play*."[19] In film, too, we find that changes to the facts are made not to make better history, but to make a better film; here again Rosenstone neatly summarizes the position in his observation that, "you do not have to see many films to know that such [a fact-based] approach is ridiculous in the extreme. Films that have been truest to the facts [...] have tended to be visually and dramatically inert, better as aids to sleep than to the acquisition of historical consciousness."[20] For the same reasons, anachronisms and inaccuracies are not always evidence of ignorance on the designer's part, but can sometimes be intended to enhance the gameplay. Thus in these cases we see a conflict between the rules of the game and the rules of history: history is designed with the goal of knowledge, understanding, and enlightenment in mind; video games are designed to be won or lost, but their ludic nature—the playing—is the key.

The second element is the assembly of those selected facts to form a narrative, which is less widely acknowledged, and therefore more difficult to detect. It is the assembly of facts (which Carr compares to cooking the fish, and which White calls "shaping a narrative") that in fact governs the kind of history on offer, and here again theories of narrative make it clear that different historians will tell histories in different ways. Various prominent thinkers over the past century have come to doubt a scientific approach to history, recognizing that in the piecing together of facts the resulting historical narrative is precisely that: one way, among several, to tell a given story with a given ending. One of the corollaries of this is that very often, when explaining or exploring the past, we are liable to impose upon those events modern values, meanings, and motivations in order to make sense of the actions of our distant forebears, which Droysen argues is to drag the past into the present, or else the present into the past.[21] Moreover, because we are writing at the endpoint of all of these facts, it is uncomfortable to think that we are merely the byproducts of a series of accidents and chance encounters, so we very often (albeit unconsciously) impart a sense of teleology into the narrative—a sense that we are the inevitable end result of things that were meant to be (which risks a pseudo-scientific historical determinism). As Erin Evans defines it in her essay, "*télos* is Greek for 'consummation' or 'completion'; it is the final end of a process." In historical terminology, then, teleology describes a goal, objective, or endpoint, so a teleological narrative is simply the presentation of something as an inevitable conclusion, and thus recounting a tale as though that outcome was the only possible one, a position termed "determinism". Now, while this may sound like an obscure and complex issue, we all in fact understand the concept of teleology a lot better than we think. A student, for instance, who has just completed her degree and immerses herself in a difficult job market, will understand intimately what this means; her résumé or CV will almost certainly have been written, edited, rewritten, and re-edited time and again in order to suggest that all of her electives, extra credits, placements, and decisions made in the past were made on the basis that they led her to be an ideal candidate for the job on offer and no other. Thus, in one sense, the successful candidate for the job is the one who understands teleology the best .... Just as a person's past can be rewritten in any number of ways (selecting different facts each time), so too can the historical past be rewritten to construct the present as an inevitable progression from the "then" to the "now," which is why in recent years the idea of counterfactual history has achieved a certain (sometimes begrudging) acceptance in many quarters, since as Ferguson eloquently argues, "virtual history is a necessary antidote to determinism."[22] So the ways in which we assemble the selected facts is in many ways as important as the selection of the facts themselves.

The third element, hinted at but not explicitly voiced by Carr, is the shopper, the "we" that present, select, and assemble the history in the first place. The big question here, of course, concerns the credentials, qualifications, and perspective of the historian him- or herself to put together that history in the first place. This is, for instance, the sort of question that we examine in Part II of this book, in which we examine the role of Western triumphalism—what Edward Said memorably terms "Orientalism" (but which has been extended well beyond studies of just the "Orient")—in assembling narratives about the past, but it also has ramifications for the trend of "modding," that is for players themselves to alter narratives about the past in order to enhance our ability to engage with it.[23]

It is important to remember, then, that these arguments about historiography and the ways in which we write history, despite being wrapped up in academic and scholarly terms, are by no means limited to scholarly historical inquiry. These are exactly the same issues faced in the real world by museum curators (who try to assemble a narrative linking the past to the present), filmmakers (who try to tell an engaging and entertaining narrative about the past), and game designers (who must permanently bear in mind both accuracy to the past and playability in the present). Such problems have already been discussed at length by noted scholars such as Jeremy Black, Raphael Samuels, and Jerome de Groot in the field of public history, and in the field of historical film by a long pedigree of scholars ranging from Marc Ferro in the late 1970s to Robert Rosenstone and Jeffrey Richards, all of whom have used their solid historical training to tackle difficult questions about the possibility of communicating history through public—and non-academic—media.[24] Among these discussions, a number of scholars have broached precisely the difficult questions with which this book is embroiled—about the depiction of history in modern media, which leads us not only to question the reliability of these historical representations, but also the nature of historical representation in the first place.

While it is impossible to synthesize what has, over the course of some four decades, become a contentious and potentially divisive issue, there is broadly speaking a general agreement among scholars that, once we move away from the tiresome discussion of accuracy, the most interesting questions about history in popular culture concern historiography; it is less interesting to note where and whether a given product *deviates* from the historical record, but rather for *what reason it does so* and what effect this might have. Ubisoft, for example, when putting together *Assassin's Creed III*, were no less mindful of historical constraints than many historians themselves, even if the end product may not be described unproblematically as "history." In one interview the game's creative director, Alex Hutchinson, claims that he sought to produce a piece of historical fiction that struck a balance between playability and fun on the one hand and historical accuracy on the other, claiming that "the official tagline is 'history is our playground' and we take it very, very seriously. We do a lot of research; we have historical advisors on staff."[25] In a later interview with *GameInformer*'s Matt Bertz, Lead Writer Corey May admitted, revealingly, "we try to be as historically accurate as possible, technology and fun-factors allowing [....] When we do diverge from the historical record it's almost always because … it makes the game a better game."[26] Such an emphasis on historical accuracy is thus intended, as one AP report observes, to reflect the historical approaches of some academic historians, such as François Furstenberg of the University of Montreal, who worked as a consultant for *Assassin's Creed III*, whose interests were "less in making sure names and dates were perfect, but more in the game's overarching narrative [...] the game's creators shared his desire to depict the war in a nuanced way that avoided portraying one side as the good guys and vice versa."[27]

What this means in simple terms, then, is that the question of historical accuracy is no longer *whether* it is possible to engage with history in popular culture, since any video game that challenges our past is bound to engage with history on some level. Instead, the question is *what kind of engagement* this is, what it means, who is doing this engagement (the designer, writer, player, modder), and what it means for our subsequent understanding of the past.

The problem of intention and agency

Thus, before we can even begin talking about historical video games and whether they are able to play with the past while respecting historical accuracy, we see that there are distinct problems—even among academics—of accepting the concept of historical accuracy as a single, unassailable concept. When we broach the question of historical engagement through video games, as the above has shown, we instantly face those same unresolved questions about *which* facts to select, *how* to present them, and the *influence* of the present on the past; and if these questions are yet to be resolved in history itself, it seems markedly unfair to expect game designers (or filmmakers, or novelists) to answer them.

Furthermore, one of the most difficult questions that need to be broached here revolves around the question of intention. If a games designer has no intention of providing an accurate representation of the past, as with *Prince of Persia* or *Legend of Zelda*, it seems churlish and unnecessarily pedantic to criticize them for misunderstanding a past with which they were not trying to engage in the first place. Film scholars' responses have traditionally been to give those examples a "pass," either by shunting them off to the realm of fantasy, or else by not mentioning them at all—Andrew Elliott's book on medieval film, for example, deals with the significant problem of Tolkien's medievalism by the cowardly route of steadfastly refusing to discuss

Lord of the Rings in any depth at all. However, such a pass is significantly more difficult in the field of video games for one specific and important reason, which is that the video game player is markedly more active in the production of meaning than the moviegoer; as Thomas Apperley asserts, "interactivity–the way in which the game is played, rather than watched–is a nonrepresentational feature common to all video games."[28] Espen Aarseth goes even further to describe this interactivity as integral to gameplay itself, claiming, "since a game is a process rather than an object, there can be no game without players playing."[29] That is not to suggest, of course, that film audiences are passive consumers of content, but that is to say instead that the nature and technological setup of video games is predicated precisely on an interface with the game. Uricchio terms play "the *sine qua non* of games generally," which makes the hypothetical "passive" consumer an untenable concept since all action (with the obvious exception of cutscenes) is a direct consequence of the player's input.[30] As Allison terms it, "in the case of the video game the 'viewer' becomes a 'player' [so ...] the relationship between the user and the media changes. The interactivity of the video game appears to promise a different relation to the narrative and experience of the game, as well as a different relation to history."[31]

In a game like *Call of Duty* or *Medal of Honor*, wherein a player is in direct control of a historically situated agent, it is clear that all actions of the player are interpreted through a variety of means to become virtual actions in the historical past—which seems to be an almost textbook definition of historical engagement, or engagement with the past.

Indeed, a closer examination of historical games reveals at least three further levels of historical engagement that closely resemble what Espen Aarseth describes as the "three dimensions that characterize every game." These are, in Aarseth's terms,

1 The gameplay (the players' actions, strategies, and motives);

2 The game world (fictional content, topology/level design, textures, etc.), and

3 The game structure (the rules of the game, including the simulation rules).[32]

The first takes place at the level of interaction with environment, with the "facts" of the game, by which we mean the fifteenth-century buildings to be climbed in *Assassin's Creed II*, or the D-Day landings of *Medal of Honor*. This level of engagement with the environment of the game allows a player to engage with a simulated past in much the same way as the historian encounters facts or evidence about the past, and is exploratory in nature, so it does not necessarily teach players about history, and in any case we have seen above the problems with fact-based approaches.

The second level of engagement comes as a consequence of this first level, and it involves the ways in which a player's actions change the narrative of the game, allowing history to unfold as a process, so that killing Montezuma in *Colonization* affects the outcome of the Aztec's battle with the Spaniards, or (not) assassinating Fidel Castro in *Call of Duty: Black Ops* affects later gameplay within the game world. This is an important means of engaging with the past, as it offers the potential to understand history as a process; it is at this level that Harry Brown argues historical games offer their most powerful lessons about history, since "by constructing a virtual past and granting the player agency within it, video games have become the ideal medium for teaching the lesson of contingency [the effect of past actions on present realities]."[33]

The third level of engagement concerns the player's agency within the established rules of the game, since it teaches players that actions that may be perfectly possible *now* were not available in other time periods, and thus explains why certain historical events unfolded as they did. This is often seen in simulations, wherein—as Wackerfuss demonstrates in his essay in this volume—a World War I airplane simulation can be played according to difficulty settings that become more or less strict according to historical accuracy; heightened accuracy (such as the inclusion of the possibility of a stalled engine if climbing too suddenly) would therefore affect the rules of the game and the possibilities (or affordances, as Chapman terms them in Chapter 4) are limited as a consequence.

This separation has, in fact, important ramifications for the ways in which video games engage with history, since we can immediately see that the level of details (largely the designers' area of interest) allows for a different kind of engagement than the level of actions (which reveals teleology or contingency in putting together the narrative). An important passage from a 2005 article on this subject is worth quoting in full, in which Uricchio calls for us to view historical games not as a genre, but to imagine instead

a spectrum of historical computer games as sites to tease out the possibilities and implications of historical representation and simulation. These two extremes [representation and simulation] have different historiographic appeals. One sort, such as the 1967 *Grand Prix Legends* game or the *Battle of the Bulge*, is specific in the sense that it deals with a particular historical event–a race, a battle–allowing the player to engage in a speculative or "what if" encounter with a particular past. In these games, efforts are usually taken to maximise the accuracy of historical detail, allowing the setting and conditions to constrain and shape gameplay. At the other extreme are games that deal with historical process in a somewhat abstracted or structural manner. *Civilization III* and *The Oregon Trail* typify these historically situated games in which a godlike player makes strategic decisions and learns to cope with the consequences, freed from the constraints of historically specific conditions. Although games of this sort also elicit speculative engagement with the past, they tend to be built upon particular visions or theories of long-term historical development.[34]

However, while resolving the disparity between types of games and historical intentions, the acceptance of the agency of the player raises new questions. Even if, for example, the game designers' intentions in engaging with history are wholly innocent, and they have genuinely tried to construct a past world as authentically as possible, when "freed from the constraints of historically specific conditions" a player who is navigating the game structure is playing for different reasons—she or he is not playing to faithfully reproduce the past, but is playing to win. As Galloway, Myers, and Apperley note, the rules of the game mean that the player is not necessarily playing to understand history, but to beat the algorithm: "To play the game means to play the code of the game. To win means to know the system."[35] Myers, writing on strategy games, talks about this in terms of the player's knowledge and competence, claiming that expert players "contextualize relationships between certain values within the game-world in order to obtain the best possible outcomes."[36] In this case, Myers continues, "the strategic play of the expert player comes from a combination of knowing the various options available and being able to correctly value them within the game context. This process is ongoing, as the player learns more about the values of the variables."[37]

Consequently, even with a game like Muzzy Lane's *The Calm and the Storm*—a game designed for pedagogical purposes—the designers are nevertheless trying to create a game with appeal to players, which causes a friction between the rules of the game world and their effects in the real world. As Jesper Juul outlines in *Half-Real*, while we win or lose the game in the real world, our actions take place and have effects only within the game world, meaning that designers' priorities ought logically to privilege playability over accuracy.[38] Speaking of the various anachronisms in the *Total War* series, Brown acknowledges: "Although the Creative Assembly, like Gearbox, relies on careful historical research, they sacrifice accuracy for playability."[39] And finally, Poole recognizes the priority of playability in his claim that "Generally, the world-building philosophy of video games is one in which certain aspects of reality can be modeled in a realistic fashion, while others are deliberately skewed, their effects caricatured of dampened according to the game's requirements."[40]

The anachronisms and inaccuracies are designed to enhance the game mechanic, and thus in these cases we see a conflict between the rules of the game and the rules of academic history—history is designed with the goal of knowledge, understanding, and enlightenment in mind; video games are designed to be played. As a result, playability can be seen to overpower historicity.

Video games and learning

Such a paradox might thus lead us to conclude, resignedly, that when it comes to digital games, the possibilities of engaging with history seem to be at best incompatible with playing the games, and at worst downright impossible, since even the most accurate simulation of the past on the first level (the level of details) is potentially doomed to failure by granting players the freedom (agency) to explore, expand, contradict, or subvert the historical realities. Expertise in *Three Kingdoms*, argues Hyuk-chan Kwon, allows a player the freedom to choose a minor character rather than an aristocrat and to rise from commoner to supreme ruler, not by understanding history but by playing along with the counterfactual history of the game. In these examples, the "facts" of the game may well be designed according to accurate selection (to use Carr's terminology), but by relinquishing control of the assembly (Carr again) to the player, the gameplay ultimately undermines the historicity of the video game as a whole. It is in this sense that de Groot is right to lament the reduction of history to such depictions of the past world that "... are not authentic [... but] are clearly part of an intertextual culture in which history is one of a number of fetishised discourses that can be used to market commodities ..."[41]

However, set against de Groot's (often justified) objections, the element of gameplay often comes to the rescue, in which the ludic capacity of historical video games allows for an in-depth understanding not just of facts, dates, people, or events, but also of the complex discourse of contingency, conditions, and circumstances, which underpins a genuine understanding of history. Indeed, one of us (Kapell) notes a recent very positive student evaluation of his history teaching that began with "I used to think 'history' was boring, but I now see that it is just that most history teachers are boring." If digital games allow players to interact with a past that, if not wholly accurate, is at least *authentic*,[42] and if this enables the player to actually enjoy the process and find the events of the past to be fascinating, we must ask a simple question that far too few history teachers ever ask: what is wrong with helping people enjoy history? Or, what is wrong with finding a way to make history more exciting for students—or just everyday people—by providing them a playground of the past? Our answer to such questions is simple: not only is nothing wrong in this, but also it is a process that is to be encouraged.

As this book attests, it is also a process that should also be the subject of study.

If history is a process of selection *and* assembly, it is the latter process in which historical video games (as the following essays show) demonstrate their greatest capacity to engage players actively in constructing meanings and understanding history as a process rather than a master narrative of Great Men and their actions or acknowledged Social Forces and their effect. Thus, our first thought when a professional historian objects to games that engage with history is, simply, that the objection is mostly about allowing a non-professional to do her or his own "assembly" of the past. That is to say, the objection is a conceit because every historian is fully aware that the assembly process is the most subjective part of the historical project. To us this is not only an example of an overly prideful position for such a historian but it risks embracing a rather poor philosophy of teaching—or pedagogy. And, pedagogically, any historian should encourage the kind of play allowed in digital games if it carries the possibility to expand the understanding of past events—not only in their students, but also in every member of society.

Speaking of another pedagogically oriented game, *The Oregon Trail*, Brown observes that it is not the facts that involve players-as-learners, but the understanding of the effects of individual actions in a wider process of historical contingency. In *The Oregon Trail*,

> the game does not offer a clear path to victory. Every option bears its own risks, and even the wisest player can be undone by chance. Its structure, though uncomplicated compared to current historical simulations, illustrates a fundamental approach to thinking about the past, one that informs more advanced video games as well as serious historical research: history is contingent upon decisions, and while some are more consequential than others, they all add up to what we know as history.[43]

In this sense, then, the agency granted to the player, together with the game mechanic that privileges a successful expansion, inculcates in the player a deep understanding of the number of possible alternatives that any given historical event might have resulted in, implanting in the player a deeper understanding of causality; as Brown concludes, "by constructing a virtual past and granting the player agency within it, video games have become the ideal medium for teaching the lesson of contingency."[44] Indeed, no person who has ever played *The Oregon Trail* has avoided the common way of losing the game that is also a very real emphatic statement about historical contingency: "You have died of dysentery" the game declares, often seemingly randomly, as the player loses. Such contingency is central to any understanding of history—and it is central as well to any kind of "Playing with the Past." This is why the title of this introduction, cognizant of such contingency, quotes from another game franchise—*Sid Meier's Civilization*—in which players must understand how to use such contingent events in an effort to "Build an Empire to Stand the Test of Time."

It is, in fact, this question of contingency and causality, underpinning some of the very best research in historical engagement through popular culture and *Civilization*, that can offer insight into that question on many levels. Kurt Squire, from the University of Wisconsin, conducted an extensive study on teaching world history through *Civilization III*, in which he observed that "*Civilization III* represents world history not as a story of colonial domination or western expansion, but as an emergent process arising from overlapping, interrelated factors .... Successful students [playing the game] developed conceptual understandings across world history, geography, and politics."[45] Likewise Sam Wineburg, from Stanford University, has led a number of studies into the possibilities of learning through video game simulations that examine "the differences between history as traditionally taught in school and as practiced by historians."[46] As a result of one study about the Battle of Lexington, Wineburg concluded that playing games with the past allowed students to learn to think like historians by replicating professional historical practices:

> [W]hat distinguished the high school students from the historians was not the number of facts that they knew about the American Revolution. Instead, the difference was in their understanding of what it means to think historically. For the students, history is what is written in the textbook, where 'facts' are presented free of bias. For the historians, historical inquiry is a system for determining the validity of historical claims based on corroboration of sources in conversation with one another rather than an appeal to a unitary source of truth—it is a way of knowing based on using specific evidence to support claims rather than trying to establish a set of facts that exist without bias.[47]

Other video games dealing with history have uncovered similar findings that further corroborate Squire and Wineburg's studies; these include MIT's innovative Education Arcade, which includes projects such as *Revolution*, a Multiplayer Role Playing Game, which replicates a living museum like Colonial Williamsburg but which allows the players themselves to "assume the role of the colonials, controlling their actions and observing their consequences. The game proposes to teach American history by giving students the opportunity to experience the daily social, economic, and political lives of the town's inhabitants."[48]

Games such as *Revolution* and *The Calm and the Storm* thus allow players agency within the narrative that in turn offers a unique way of engaging with the past by understanding the individual facts and their relationship to one another as processes that make up the overall historical record. "In this way," Brown continues, "strategy games pose distinct advantages over role-playing games, emphasizing an interdisciplinary understanding of human events as well as the lesson of historical contingency, two of the greatest benefits that historians identify in counterfactual speculation."[49] Shaffer argues that this freedom to explore and play underpins the ability to learn. About one simulation game he argues that, though unable wholly to replace rote-learning of facts and dates, the simulations can replicate such processes of thinking about assembly that are of great use in the real world: "the rules of the imaginary world of the [debating] game do a better job of representing what it means to think like a historian than the traditional text-lecture-and-recitation of many history classes."[50]

In this way, games that engage in historical contingency are structured around two fundamental ontological processes (facts and processes) working in tandem. These create an unparalleled means of engaging with the past by involving the player within an open-ended story of the past that can be changed by decisions made in the gameworld. Thus, the two fundamental ontological processes eschew master narratives that portray history as an *inevitable* causal sequence of events in favor of a counterfactual narrative that allows players to understand the importance of circumstances and decisions. As Squire discovered, allowing students to play with that world in a counterfactual spirit allows them to see how things might have turned out otherwise, if the Aztecs had horses, if Britain had no navy, etc., which are an integral part of understanding history on the grounds that in historical thinking there "is a *logical* necessity when asking questions about causation to pose 'but for' questions, and to try to imagine what would have happened if our supposed cause had been absent."[51] This mode of thinking thus empowers players to select, assemble, and manipulate narratives by entertaining what historians term counterfactuals, or what Ferguson (in an ironic choice of words given our present concerns) terms "virtual history." As Ferguson argues, the business of imagining such counterfactuals is a vital part of the way in which we learn. Because decisions about the future are-usually-based on weighing up the potential consequences of alternative courses of action, it makes sense to compare the actual outcomes of what we did in the past with the conceivable outcomes of what we might have done.[52]

On "playing" within a historical narrative

Thus, as much as "history" is represented as a narrative—that is, a "story" of "events"—digital games would seem to be an excellent medium to approach through various forms of the study of narrative or, as scholars would call it, "narratology." To put this in another way, it would seem that the study of digital games could be profitably approached through various schools of thought born out of the study of literature or, more recently, film and television—as well as the discipline of history itself. Games scholars in what was, just a few short years ago, categorized as an "emerging" field, have already had within their ranks this very argument. Some, with a background in literature, film, or media studies saw digital games as a realm that could be approached with the already well-established paradigms of those disciplines.[53] From this perspective digital games could be seen and studied as part of a larger ecology of media that involve, at their very base, storytelling as a key aspect.[54] However, this leaves out a single, major aspect of the gaming experience. As digital games scholar Gonzalo Frasca put it as early as 1999, "there is another dimension that has been usually almost ignored when studying this kind of computer software: to analyze them as games."[55]

This desire to analyze digital games as exactly that—games—gave rise to a paradigm called "ludology." From the work of scholars such as Frasca, Aarseth, and Murray, the study of games needed to be approached not as extensions of storytelling traditions but, rather, through their representation of ritualized and formalized rules within the game itself.[56] For Game Studies scholars who call themselves ludologists the games in question should be examined as created formal systems that the player engages with. Alice Henton has described such an approach as seeing games as "elaborate constructs dependent upon systems of rules, objectives, and strategic behaviors."[57] A result of this approach is, simply, that a ludic study of games represents a way of examining digital games as something that a player interacts with, and the true value of the study of such a system requires continual recognition of the primacy of both the "rules of the game" and the "player's behavior" within those rules.

The approach of a narratologist is thus through the story. For a ludologist, though, the play's the thing.

We approach *Playing with the Past* as editors and authors from a position that varies from that of both narratology and ludology. This is not because of a desire on our part to offer something new simply for the sake of *being new*, however. The examinations in these pages are all predicated on various games that carry one common denominator: they are games that deal, in one fashion or another, with *history*. This is not always an obvious thing—some of the chapters in what follows are about "histories" that never happened and are imaginary in the sense that they present alternate pasts or imagined futures. But, in each chapter there is an aspect of history—or historiography—that the player must engage with.

In other words, what a player of the games discussed in this book must deal with is, precisely, a history that is selected, assembled, and played. And history, by its very nature, is a narrative. But in engaging with a historical narrative the gamer is playing with that narrative. Thus, the ludic approach, which specifies the rules and systems of rules, is valuable because those rules exist in a common approach to an understanding of what a player understands history, itself, to be. At the same time, history (as noted above) is very much a narrative of things that have happened. *Playing with the Past*, then, is a book that suggests a middle way through the debates that approach digital games as narratives and those that approach them from the perspective of gameplay. This is because the formalized "systems of rules" inherent in the games are, by necessity, external as are the popularly understood narrative rules of history, itself.

This is not to say that we simply suggest a collapse of the ludic approach into the narrative inherent in history as represented in the games under discussion. Indeed, the relationship is far more complex—and far more usefully complex at that. The game player does work within a system of rules when playing a historical game, but those rules are at least in part defined not by the programmer or the game (or even the player of the game) but through an understanding of the generally accepted rules of causality within the discipline of history and a common understanding of *history* itself. Thus, in historical games the ludic rules are at least somewhat—and often largely—external to the programmed "system of rules" of the game itself.

But, importantly, a player's success is not determined necessarily by following those "rules of history" or "rules of historical change." Indeed, in games such as *Sid Meier's Civilization* franchise, for example, the gameplay is only somewhat predicated on "fitting the historical narrative," and the player can have an equally satisfying experience by purposely creating counterfactual histories. Indeed, that is precisely the point of such games, as Squire and others have demonstrated. Varying the accepted historical narrative is often the exact purpose of such games. At the same time, following the historical narrative does increase the likelihood of success. Within *Civilization*, again, with sufficient skill it is just as possible to succeed in the game by playing the Ottoman Empire, the Aztecs, or the Japanese as it is by playing the British or Americans—but success remains possible only in as far as the player accepts certain understandings of what "historical progress" means.[58]

As a result, the relationship between the two aspects of contemporary Game Studies can be uniquely approached through an examination of games that use history and historiography as a basic approach. The distinctions between the ludic and narrative approaches, each quite necessary in games that are *played* within a historical *narrative*, can be uniquely highlighted to see which perspective is of primary importance and which is, instead, secondary. Though, of course, the answer will vary from game to game, it is the question that each contributor here finds fascinating—and important.

As we noted above, for narratologists the point is about the story while for ludologists the "play's the thing." In digital games that begin from within a historical narrative, however, the thing is the *play* within the *narrative*.

About this book

Finally, then, having established some of the rules of engagement that dictated the central approach of the book, we turn to the book itself, and make a final note on its makeup. We have divided the work into five separate parts, which each deal, broadly speaking, with one or another aspect of historical engagement as we have described it above. Part I takes on the concept of causation and teleology to explore the ways in which history is constructed as a process. Beginning with Peterson, Miller, and Fedorko's essay, which takes on the issue of historical representation head on, their examination of the *Total War*, *Civilization*, and *Patrician* franchises offers a solid overview of what historical simulation means for our purposes. Daniel Reynolds then takes up the gauntlet to question the issue of temporal planes, by fundamentally questioning what we mean by "old" in the first place, followed by Adam Chapman who uses the ecological theories of James Gibson to explore the tension between our actions in the game world and our ability to engage with the past outside of it.

In Part II we explore the issue of Western triumphalism by examining a series of games that challenge Western-oriented approaches to the past, according to which "the United States is made the ultimate inheritor of all the human advancement and elevated to the position of the most perfect and most 'civilized' state of all."[59] Beginning with Emily Bembeneck's analysis of the Barbarian as a convenient Other by which Romans were able to externally locate the Self, Rebecca Mir and Trevor Owens move on to explore the ideological fault lines running through *Sid Meier's Colonization*, a game that provoked outrage on its release because of its perceived implicit endorsement of European domination of indigenous peoples. These two essays lead up to Joshua Holdenried and Nicolas Trépanier's essay, which looks in more depth at strategies of representing the Aztec people in *Age of Empires II* and *Medieval: Total War II* and the ways in which the non-white Other can be "played" to understand historical contingency during a period of European colonization. Finally, the part ends with two essays on Asian history: Hyuk-chan Kwon's essay explores the significance of *Three Kingdoms* to players in China, Korea, and Japan in constructing the past through play. This is followed by Kazumi Hasegawa's study of *otome* games, in which Japanese girls are able to "date" historical personages in a process of "queering history" that represents a challenge to the Great Men approaches to history, and runs counter to the heterosexual and masculine depictions of the past in other cultural products.

Part III examines the question of assembling a narrative by looking more closely at the user as the one who assembles the historical narrative in the first place. In their essay on Brand WW2, Andrew J. Salvati and Jonathan M. Bullinger examine the selection of those facts with deep resonance outside the game to generate a sense of authenticity that they dub "selective authenticity." This question of authenticity further informs Josef Köstlbauer's study of authenticity and simulation in other wargames, situating the subgenre within a broader tradition of *kriegspiel*—that is, tactical war games. The last two essays examine the phenomenon of "modding," the ability for players to alter the code of the game to enhance gameplay, which tackles head on some of the complex tensions outlined above between the rules of the game and the rules of history. Thomas Apperley's essay looks at the ways in which modders and modding communities tweak the games they play in order to achieve enhanced verisimilitude creating what we might genuinely term a "usable past." Likewise, Gareth Crabtree looks at the *Battlefield* series in particular to compare the process of fan-based modding to historical re-enactment as an "active form of consumption and production" of historical meaning.

Part IV adopts a different interpretation of authenticity, examining a number of situations in which strict factual accuracy is implausible or even impossible, for reasons of playability and narrative. In Douglas N. Dow's study of *Assassin's Creed II*, Dow examines the issue of authenticity in re-creating fifteenth-century Florence to demonstrate that in fact strict accuracy would run counter to the objective of the game, and in any case the player's agency and freedom allows for a different—and more resonant—engagement with the past than its alternative. Likewise, Andrew Wackerfuss examines the limitations of technology in depicting realistic flight SIMs based in World War I, with the powerful argument that limitations of processing power have led modern players to exaggerate the importance of the aerial combat in WWI. The two essays that follow both take on more recent history, looking at the ways in which games have explored counterfactuals and realism in depicting the Cold War, representations that deal as much with politics as with history, but that each demonstrate problems of authenticity in terms of memory politics. Clemens Reisner discusses *Call of Duty: Black Ops* as a way of "shaping the public view of the Cold War as a historic period"; Marcus Schulzke then extends this to discuss what he calls "speculative history" in which the politics of representing the Cold War inform our imagined future geopolitics, suggesting that a hypothetical Third World War would logically follow the same course. "In doing so," Schulzke argues, "they attempt to make sense of the threats presented by the ongoing War on Terror by reframing them in terms of the more familiar Cold War threats."

Finally, Part V looks at the more explicit counterfactual scenarios as embodied in depictions of nuclear war and devastation in games such as the *Fallout* series. William K. Knoblauch looks at the last throes of the Cold War and the threat of Mutually Assured Destruction and its influence on games trying to make sense of the shadow of nuclear war—in this sense, such games can be seen as a counterfactual process in which fears are exorcised or exacerbated, and possibly fostered support for the controversial Strategic Defense Initiative (SDI) of the Reagan era. Joseph A. November's essay continues with the idea of a nuclear holocaust, but examines *Fallout* as a means of "accessing and communicating complex ideas about the mid-20th century U.S." Such an approach, November argues, allows players to question the importance of decisions taken in the mid- to late 1940s and their effects on the alternative future that *Fallout* offers. Tom Cutterham takes a similar approach in his analysis of *Fallout 3*, too, using the game to explore further questions about counterfactual history, placing the game in a tradition of anxiety about endings that contains a paradoxical dual appeal—the reinforcement of the status quo and fantasies about destruction of society, offering, as he terms it, "a window on the way we imagine the American past." Robert Mejia and Ryuta Komaki use the *Biohazard/Resident Evil* franchise as unwitting revelations of historical responses to disease epidemics, which they situate in a broader climate of fear surrounding AIDS, disease, and terrorism. Finally, Erin Evans's essay takes us far, far into the future and way back into our past at the same time in her analysis of the *Xenosaga* series as a means of understanding ancient religions, which structure our present.

No conclusions

Playing with the Past, then, is a book about play and a book about narrative. It is an exploration into digital games that confronts questions concerning accuracy and authenticity, the past and the present. It is also a book that confronts existing dichotomies in other ways.

As editors we remain wholly uncomfortable with the notion that history is something *done by historians* with the simple declaration that what historians might do will not become "history" unless it is eventually accepted as a useful narrative by people who are, themselves, *not* historians. People who are playing games that engage with the past are thus experimenting with notions of history in ways that may make some professional historians uncomfortable, but they are also doing so in ways—regardless of the factual accuracy of the games they play—that make them better equipped to engage with the actual work of those professional historians.

We also find ourselves uncomfortable with the idea that the examination of digital games needs to be approached from the perspective of either the narrative or the play. In *Playing with the Past* we come to the conclusion that both of these approaches are required to understand fully the cultural importance of games themselves—and of the history they represent. While it may be an obvious statement, as we note above, that in games that require *play* within a historical *narrative* both halves of this Game Studies paradigm must be accommodated, we also remain convinced that this is not merely a way of looking at historical games, but one that would bear fruit for those studying other games as well. As Gerald Voorhees, Josh Call, and Katie Whitlock describe their approach to another genre of games—First Person Shooters—we also suggest that the following pages are "ultimately an open world for the reader to explore."[60] The intent of *Playing with the Past*, then, is very much the same as the intent of the games we study here: not to limit exploration, but to encourage it.

One of us (Kapell) wrote about the fan interaction with the narratives of *Star Wars* by claiming something that we also believe should apply to a book such as this—or any book that suggests a popular engagement with history. Stealing that idea we end this introduction by noting that the intent is to wonder what these games "tell us about ourselves, and our own past and present, and may even help shape our future in ways about which we can only begin to speculate."[61]

In other words, *Playing with the Past* is about the past. But it is also about much more, as the past—by necessity—always is.

Notes

1 Marc Ferro, *Cinema and History*. Detroit, MI: Wayne State University Press, 1988.

2 William Uricchio, "Simulation, History and Computer Games," in Ed. Joost Raessens and Jeffrey Haskell Goldstein, *Handbook of Computer Game Studies*. Cambridge, MA: MIT Press, 2005, 327–338.

3 Robert A. Rosenstone, *Film on History/History on Film*. Harlow: Longman/Pearson, 2006, 2.

4 Johan Huizinga, *Homo Ludens: A Study of the Play Element in Culture*. London: Routledge, 2008, 13.

5 Bernard Suits, *Grasshopper: Games, Life and Utopia*. Boston, MA: David R. Godline, 1990), 41.

6 Stephen Johnson, *Everything Bad Is Good for You: How Popular Culture Is Making Us Smarter*. Harmondsworth: Penguin, 2006, xi–xii.

7 Johnson, *Everything Bad Is Good for You*, 135–136.

8 Johnson, *Everything Bad Is Good for You*, 136.

9 James Paul Gee, *What Video Games Have to Teach Us about Learning and Literacy*. New York: Palgrave Macmillan, 2003; David Williamson Shaffer, *How Computer Games Help Children Learn*. New York: Palgrave Macmillan, 2006; Kurt Squire, "Replaying History: Learning World History through Playing *Civilization III*," Ph.D. Thesis, Indiana University, 2004. For more on this subject, see also Harry J. Brown, *Video games and Education*. Armonk, NY: M.E. Sharpe, 2008; Beavis, Catherine, Joanne O'Mara and Lisa McNeice, Eds. *Digital Games: Literacy in Action*. Kent Town, SA: Wakefield Press, 2012.

10 Jerome de Groot, *Consuming History*. London: Routledge, 2008, 7.

11 de Groot, *Consuming History*, 7–8.

12 J.L. Gorman, *Understanding History: An Introduction to Analytical Philosophy of History*. Ottawa, ON: University of Ottawa Press, 1992, ix.

13 For a full explanation and study of historiography, the classic text still remains Hayden White, *The Content of the Form*. Baltimore, MD: Johns Hopkins Press, 1990. See also E.H. Carr, *What Is History?*. Harmondsworth: Penguin, 1964; Mark T. Gilderhus, *History and Historians: A Historiographic Introduction*, Harlow: Longman/Pearson, 2009.

14 Carr, *What Is History?*, 9.

15 Andrew B.R. Elliott, *Remaking the Middle Ages: The Methods of Cinema and History in Representing the Medieval World*. Jefferson, NC: McFarland, 2010, Chapter 1; see also Rosenstone, *Film on History/History on Film*.

16 John Clive, *Not by Fact Alone: Essays on the Writing and Reading of History.* Boston, MA: Houghton Mifflin, 1989, 12.

17 Paul Veyne, *Comment on écrit l'histoire.* Paris: Éditions du Seuil, 1971, 42, our translation.

18 Robert A. Rosenstone, *Visions of the Past: The Challenge of Film to Our Idea of History.* Cambridge, MA: Harvard University Press, 1995, 7.

19 Steven Poole, *Trigger Happy: The Inner Life of Video games.* London: Fourth Estate, 2000, 77; emphasis added.

20 Rosenstone, *Visions of the Past,* 7.

21 Johann G. Droysen, *Outline of the Principles of History.* New York: H. Fertig, 1967, 219.

22 Niall Ferguson, Ed. *Virtual History: Alternatives and Counterfactuals.* Basingstoke: Papermac, 1997, 89.

23 Edward W. Said, *Orientalism.* New York: Doubleday, 1979.

24 Marc Ferro, *Cinéma et histoire.* Paris: Denoël, 1977; Rosenstone, *Visions of the Past;* Jeffrey Richards, *Visions of Yesterday.* London: Routledge & Kegan Paul, 1973.

25 Reported in *Albion Pleiad,* http://www.albionpleiad.com/2012/11/history-is-our-playground-using-assassins-creed-iii-and-other-video games-for-education/, accessed 2 February 2013.

26 Interview on *GameInformer's* YouTube channel, http://www.youtube.com/watch?v=hRiiCJa1P_o, uploaded 9 March 2012.

27 Associated Press report printed in *The Oregonian,* 30 October 2012.

28 Thomas H. Apperley, "Genre and Game Studies: Toward a Critical Approach to Video Game Genres," *Simulation Gaming,* 37, no. 6 (2006), 7.

29 Espen Aarseth, "Playing Research: Methodological Approaches to Game Analysis," *Game Approaches/SPil-veje. Papers from Spilforskning.dk Conference,* 2004, 2.

30 Uricchio, "Simulation, History and Computer Games," 329. For more on agency and narrative, see Janet Murray, *Hamlet on the Holodeck: The Future of Narrative in Cyberspace.* New York: Simon & Schuster, 1997; Henry Jenkins and Kurt Squire, "The Art of Contested Spaces," in Ed. Lucien King, *Game On: The History and Culture of Video Games.* London: Lawrence King, 2003, 64–75; Gonzalo Frasca, "Ludology Meets Narratology: Similitude and Differences Between (Digital) Games and Narrative," *Ludology.org* (1999).

31 Tanine Allison, "The World War II Video Game. Adaptation and Postmodern History," *Literature Film Quarterly,* 38, no. 3 (July 2010), 183–193: 183.

32 Aarseth, "Playing Research," 2.

33 Brown, *Video games and Education,* 118.

34 Uricchio, "Simulation, History and Computer Games," 328.

35 Alexander Galloway, *Gaming: Essays on Algorithmic Culture.* Minneapolis, MN: University of Minnesota Press, 2006, 90–91.

36 David Myers, *The Nature of Computer Games: Play as Semiosis*. New York: Peter Lang, 2003, 44.

37 Apperley, "Genre and Game Studies," 13.

38 Jesper Juul, *Half-Real: Video Games between Real Rules and Fictional Worlds*. Cambridge, MA: MIT Press, 2005.

39 Brown, *Video games and Education*, 131.

40 Poole, *Trigger Happy*, 61.

41 de Groot, *Consuming History*, 8.

42 For more in-depth discussion of this division between authenticity and accuracy, see Elliott, *Remaking the Middle Ages*, Chapter 9; Robert Burgoyne, "Memory, History and Digital Imagery in Contemporary Film," in Ed. Paul Grainge, *Memory and Popular Film*. Manchester: Manchester University Press, 2003, 220–236; A. Keith Kelly, "Beyond Historical Accuracy: A Postmodern View of Movies and Medievalism", *Perspicuitas* (February 2004).

43 Brown, *Video games and Education*, 118.

44 Brown, *Video games and Education*, 118.

45 Squire, "Replaying History."

46 Cited in Shaffer, *How Computer Games Help Children Learn*, 30.

47 Shaffer, *How Computer Games Help Children Learn*, 31.

48 Brown, *Video games and Education*, 122.

49 Brown, *Video games and Education*, 127.

50 Shaffer, *How Computer Games Help Children Learn*, 29.

51 Ferguson, *Virtual History*, 87.

52 Ferguson, *Virtual History*, 2.

53 See Part II, "Ludology," in Eds. Noah Wardrip-Fruin and Pat Harrigan, *FirstPerson: New Media as Story, Performance and Game*. Cambridge, MA: MIT Press, 2004.

54 Henry Jenkins, "Games as Narrative Architecture," in Ed. Wardrip-Fruin and Harrigan, *FirstPerson*, 118–130. See also Jenkins and Squire, "The Art of Contested Spaces"; Patrick Crogan, "Gametime: History, Temporality and Narrative in *Combat Flight Simulator 2*," in Ed. Mark J.P. Wolf and Bernard Perron, *The Video Game Theory Reader*. London and New York: Routledge, 2003, 275–330; and Chris Crawford, "Interactive Storytelling," in the same volume, 259–273.

55 Frasca, "Ludology Meets Narratology."

56 See Jesper Juul, "Are Games Telling Stories? A Brief Note on Games and Narratives," *Games Studies*, 1 (2001); Murray, *Hamlet on the Holodeck*; Espen Aarseth, *Cybertext: Perspectives on Ergodic Literature*. Baltimore, MD: Johns Hopkins University Press, 1997; Markku Eskelinen, "Towards Computer Game Studies," in *FirstPerson: New Media as Story, Performance and Game*, 36–44; Ian Bogost, *Unit Operations: An Approach to Video Game Criticism*. Cambridge, MA: MIT Press, 2006.

57 Alice Henton, "Game and Narrative in *Dragon Age: Origins*: Playing the Archive in Digital RPGs," in Ed. Gerald A. Voorhees, Joshua Call, and Katie Whitlock, *Dungeons, Dragons, and Digital Denizens: The Digital Role Playing Game*. New York: Continuum, 2012, 68.

58 Matthew Wilhelm Kapell, "Civilization and Its Discontents: American Monomythic Structure as Historical Simulacrum," *Popular Culture Review*, 13, no. 2 (2002): 129–136.

59 Kacper Poblocki, "Becoming-State: The Bio-Cultural Imperialism of *Sid Meier's Civilization*," *Focaal—European Journal of Anthropology*, 39, 163–177: 166.

60 Gerald A. Voorhees, Joshua Call, and Katie Whitlock, "Introduction: Things That Go Boom: From Guns to Griefing," in Ed. Gerald A. Voorhees, Josh Call, and Katie Whitlock, *Guns, Grenades, and Grunts: First-Person Shooter Games*. New York: Continuum, 2012, 1–21: 19.

61 Matthew Wilhelm Kapell, "Conclusion: Finding Myth in the History of Your Own Time," in Ed. Matthew Wilhelm Kapell and John Shelton Lawrence, *Finding the Force of the Star Wars Franchise: Fans, Merchandise and Critics*. New York: Peter Lang, 2006, 285.

Works cited

Aarseth, Espen. "Playing Research: Methodological Approaches to Game Analysis," *Game Approaches/SPil-veje. Papers from Spilforskning.dk Conference* (2004).

Aarseth, Espen. *Cybertext: Perspectives on Ergodic Literature*. Baltimore, MD: Johns Hopkins University Press, 1997.

Allison, Tanine. "The World War II Video Game. Adaptation and Postmodern History," *Literature Film Quarterly*, 38, no. 3 (July 2010): 183–193.

Apperley, Thomas H. "Genre and Game Studies: Toward a Critical Approach to Video Game Genres," *Simulation Gaming*, 37, no. 6 (2006): 6–23.

Beavis, Catherine, Joanne O'Mara, and Lisa McNeice, Eds. *Digital Games: Literacy in Action*. Kent Town, SA: Wakefield Press, 2012.

Bogost, Ian. *Unit Operations: An Approach to Video Game Criticism*. Cambridge, MA: MIT Press, 2006.

Brown, Harry J. *Video games and Education*. Armonk, NY: M.E. Sharpe, 2008.

Burgoyne, Robert. "Memory, History and Digital Imagery in Contemporary Film," in Ed. Paul Grainge, *Memory and Popular Film*. Manchester: Manchester University Press, 2003, 220–236.

Carr, E.H. *What Is History?*. Harmondsworth: Penguin, 1964.

Clive, John. *Not by Fact Alone: Essays on the Writing and Reading of History*. Boston, MA: Houghton Mifflin, 1989.

Crawford, Chris. "Interactive Storytelling," in Ed. Mark J.P. Wolf and Bernard Perron, *The Video Game Theory Reader*. London and New York: Routledge, 2003, 259–273.

Crogan, Patrick. "Gametime: History, Temporality and Narrative in *Combat Flight Simulator 2*," in Ed. Mark J.P. Wolf and Bernard Perron, *The Video Game Theory Reader*. London and New York: Routledge, 2003, 275–301.

de Groot, Jerome. *Consuming History*. London: Routledge, 2008.

Droysen, Johann G. *Outline of the Principles of History (Grundriss der Historik)*. New York: H. Fertig, 1967.

Elliott, Andrew B.R. *Remaking the Middle Ages: The Methods of Cinema and History in Representing the Medieval World*. Jefferson, NC: McFarland, 2010.

Eskelinen, Markku. "Towards Computer Game Studies," in *FirstPerson: New Media as Story, Performance and Game*, Ed. Noah Wardrip-Fruin & Pat Harrigan, Cambridge, MA: The MIT Press, 2004, 36–44.

Ferguson, Niall, Ed. *Virtual History: Alternatives and Counterfactuals*. Basingstoke: Papermac, 1997.

Ferro, Marc. *Cinéma et histoire*. Paris: Denoël, 1977.

Ferro, Marc. *Cinema and History*. Detroit, MI: Wayne State University Press, 1988.

Frasca, Gonzalo. "Ludology Meets Narratology: Similitude and Differences Between (Digital) Games and Narrative," *Ludology.org* (1999), http://www.ludology.org/articles/ludology.htm/, accessed 24 May 2013.

Galloway, Alexander. *Gaming, Essays on Algorithmic Culture*. Minneapolis, MN: University of Minnesota Press, 2006.

Gee, James Paul. *What Video Games Have to Teach Us About Learning and Literacy*. New York: Palgrave Macmillan, 2003.

Gilderhus, Mark. *History and Historians: A Historiographic Introduction*. Harlow: Longman/Pearson, 2009.

Gorman, J.L. *Understanding History: An Introduction to Analytical Philosophy of History*. Ottawa, ON: University of Ottawa Press, 1992.

Henton, Alice. "Game and Narrative in Dragon Age: Origins: Playing the Archive in Digital PRGs," in Ed. Gerald A. Voorhees, Joshua Call, and Katie Whitlock, *Dungeons, Dragons, and Digital Denizens: The Digital Role Playing Game*. Approaches to Digital Game Studies. New York: Continuum, 2012, 66–87.

Huizinga, Johan. *Homo Ludens: A Study of the Play Element in Culture*. London: Routledge, 2008.

Jenkins, Henry. "Games as Narrative Architecture," in Ed. Noah Wardrip-Fruin and Pat Harrigan, *FirstPerson: New Media as Story, Performance and Game*. Cambridge, MA: MIT Press, 2004, 118–130.

Jenkins, Henry and Kurt Squire, "The Art of Contested Spaces," in Ed. Lucien King, *Game On: The History and Culture of Video Games*. London: Lawrence King, 2003, 64–75.

Johnson, Stephen. *Everything Bad Is Good for You: How Popular Culture Is Making Us Smarter*. Harmondsworth: Penguin, 2006.

Juul, Jesper. *Half-Real: Video Games between Real Rules and Fictional Worlds*. Cambridge, MA: MIT Press, 2005.

Juul, Jesper. "Are Games Telling Stories? A Brief Note on Games and Narratives," *Games Studies*, 1 (2001).

Kapell, Matthew Wilhelm. "Civilization and Its Discontents: American Monomythic Structure as Historical Simulacrum," *Popular Culture Review*, 13, no. 2 (2002): 129–136.

Kapell, Matthew Wilhelm. "Conclusion: Finding Myth in the History of Your Own Time," in Ed. Matthew Wilhelm Kapell and John Shelton Lawrence, *Finding the Force of the Star Wars Franchise: Fans, Merchandise and Critics*. New York: P. Lang, 2006, 269–276.

Kelly, Keith A. "Beyond Historical Accuracy: A Postmodern View of Movies and Medievalism," *Perspicuitas* (February 2004), http://www.gamestudies. org/0101/juul-gts/, accessed 24 May 2013.

Murray, Janet. *Hamlet on the Holodeck: The Future of Narrative in Cyberspace*. New York: Simon & Schuster, 1997.

Myers, David. *The Nature of Computer Games: Play as Semiosis*. New York: Peter Lang, 2003.

Poblocki, Kacper. "Becoming-State: The Bio-Cultural Imperialism of Sid Meier's *Civilization*," *Focaal—European Journal of Anthropology*, 39 (2002): 163–177.

Poole, Steven. *Trigger Happy: The Inner Life of Video games*. London: Fourth Estate, 2000.

Richards, Jeffrey. *Visions of Yesterday*. London: Routledge & Kegan Paul, 1973.

Rosenstone, Robert A. *Film on History/History on Film*. Harlow: Longman/ Pearson, 2006.

Rosenstone, Robert A. *Visions of the Past: The Challenge of Film to Our Idea of History*. Cambridge, MA: Harvard University Press, 1995.

Said, Edward W. *Orientalism*. New York: Doubleday, 1979.

Shaffer, David Williamson. *How Computer Games Help Children Learn*. New York: Palgrave Macmillan, 2006.

Squire, Kurt. "Replaying History: Learning World History through Playing *Civilization III*," Ph.D. Thesis, Indiana University, 2004, http://www.perspicuitas. uni-essen.de/, accessed 24 May 2013.

Suits, Bernard. *Grasshopper: Games, Life and Utopia*. Boston, MA: David R. Godline, 1990.

Uricchio, William. "Simulation, History and Computer Games," in Ed. Joost Raessens and Jeffrey Haskell Goldstein, *Handbook of Computer Game Studies*. Cambridge, MA: MIT Press, 2005, 327–338.

Veyne, Paul. *Comment on écrit l'histoire*. Paris: Éditions du Seuil, 1971.

Voorhees, Gerald A. Joshua Call, and Katie Whitlock, Eds. *Guns, Grenades, and Grunts*. New York: Continuum, 2012.

Wardrip-Fruin, Noah and Pat Harrigan, Eds. *FirstPerson: New Media as Story, Performance and Game*. Cambridge, MA: MIT Press, 2004.

White, Hayden. *The Content of the Form*. Baltimore, MD: Johns Hopkins Press, 1990.

Games cited

Age of Empires II. Tokyo, Japan: Ensemble Studios, Konami, 2000.

Assassin's Creed II. Montreal, Quebec: Ubisoft Montreal, 2009.

Assassin's Creed III. Montreal, Quebec: Ubisoft Montreal, 2012.

Battlefield (Multiple titles). Redwood City, CA: DICE, Electronic Arts, PC, 2002–2009.

Call of Duty. Santa Monica, CA: Infinity Ward, Activision, 2003.

Call of Duty: Black Ops. Santa Monica, CA: Infinity Ward, Activision, 2010.

Calm and the Storm, The. Newburyport, MA: Muzzy Lane, 2007.

Doom. Richardson, TX: id Software, 1993.

Fallout (Multiple titles). Beverley Hills, CA: Interplay Entertainment, 1996–2008.

Grand Theft Auto: San Andreas. Edinburgh: Rockstar North, 2004.

Legend of Zelda. Kyoto: Nintendo, 1986.

Medal of Honor. Redwood City, CA: Dreamworks Interactive, Electronic Arts, 1999.

Medieval II: Total War. Tokyo, Japan: The Creative Assembly, Sega, 2007.

The Oregon Trail. Brooklyn Center, MN: Rawitsch et al., Minnesota Educational Computing Consortium (MECC), 1971.

Patrician (Multiple titles). Worms, Germany: Gaming Minds Studio, Kalypso Entertainment (formerly Ascaron Entertainment), 1992–2010.

Prince of Persia. San Rafael, CA: Brøderbund, 1989.

Quake. Richardson, TX: id Software, 1996.

Romance of the Three Kingdoms. Yokohama, Japan: Koei, 1985.

Sid Meier's Civilization III. Paris, France: Firaxis, Infogrames, 2001.

Sid Meier's Civilization IV: Colonization. Novato, CA: Firaxis Games, 2K Games, 2008.

PART ONE

History as a Process

This opening part begins by analyzing some very familiar problems for historians and students of history, but which also cut across the disciplines to affect games designers too: namely the issues of teleology, contingency, and understanding history as a process, rather than an accumulation of facts. First, Peterson, Miller, and Fedorko broach the issue of historical contingency—the ways in which historical narratives produce historical knowledge, not by teaching dry facts, but by simulating the process over time to understand how history is formed by decisions and their effects. Next Reynolds questions these narratives themselves by asking what we mean by "old": looking at these narratives as processes, he shows how video games, unlike films or television programs, offer a range of potential narratives based on decisions taken at each stage of a game. These decisions—the narrative possibilities—then form the basis of Chapman's discussion of "affordances," which are the various options allowed ("afforded") to players at different stages of the game.

Thus, overall, this part argues that games-as-history piece together a narrative of the past, which may well not be accurate by traditional historical measures of facts, but which forces players to understand the role of contingency, and to learn about history as a dynamic process and not events, dates, people, and places to learn by rote.

Recommended books to understand more about counterfactual/virtual history and history as a process:

Arnold, John H. *History*. New York: Sterling Publishing Company, Inc, 2009.

Bloch, Marc. *The Historian's Craft*. Manchester: Manchester University Press, 1954.

Cannadine, David, Ed. *What Is History Now?* London: Palgrave Macmillan, 2004.

Carr, E.H. *What Is History?* Harmondsworth: Penguin Group, 2008.

Gilderhus, Mark T. *History and Historians: A Historiographical Introduction*, 5th ed. Upper Saddle River, NJ: Prentice Hall, 2003.

Jenkins, Keith. *Rethinking History*. London and New York: Routledge, 2012.

White, Hayden. *The Content of the Form: Narrative Discourse and Historical Representation*. Baltimore, MD: Johns Hopkins University Press, 1990.

Woodfield, Andrew. *Teleology*. London and Cambridge, UK: Cambridge University Press, 2010.

2

The Same River Twice: Exploring Historical Representation and the Value of Simulation in the *Total War, Civilization,* and *Patrician* Franchises

Rolfe Daus Peterson
Mercyhurst University

Andrew Justin Miller
Erie County Public Library, Pennsylvania

Sean Joseph Fedorko
Indiana University, Bloomington

No man can step in the same river twice, for the second time it's not the same river, and he's not the same man.

HERACLITUS, FRAGMENT 41; QUOTED BY PLATO IN *CRATYLUS*

Heraclitus's meaning is often interpreted as a statement on the inevitability of mortality, the ever-changing nature of man, and the frequent frustration with our inability to alter the past. We use it here to motivate an analysis on the viability of video games as a form of media allowing players to cultivate historical thinking by actively engaging with a simulated past. Video games that employ historical artifacts, characters, settings, or events, either as a mode of storytelling or as a function of play, create a unique opportunity to affect historical understanding and improve its conventional interpretation. In essence, games can provide a means to step into the same river twice, to make meaningful use of counterfactuals, and to learn broad concepts about past events that help explain where the river of our past has been, our current place within it, and to consider where it may be going and why.

Like radio and television before it, video games have encountered increased scrutiny as society develops divergent views on the value of this new media. Some portray games as merely innocuous entertainment, while detractors caution that video games desensitize players to violence and withdraw them from healthier community engagement.[1] Others praise their capacity to elicit emotion, to stir up imagination, and to immerse people in a participatory experience.[2] As a medium for learning, video games carry the potential to stimulate problem solving and critical thinking, from nascent educational games like *Oregon Trail* (published in 1971) to the critically acclaimed and popular *Minecraft*.[3] Whatever the contention, there is no denying the prominence of video games in modern life with 49 percent of households in the United States that currently have one or more dedicated game consoles, with nearly every home having some form of access to a console, computer, or smart phone.[4] Examining specific points of value within this medium is becoming increasingly important as it expands in use and variation.

No longer limited to arcade machines or single-purpose game consoles, video games have become ubiquitous in the new era of digital devices. Moving ahead of single-purpose gaming devices, video games are increasingly becoming available on devices for which gaming is an accessory feature, such as tablets, cell phones, and computers.[5] As the hardware-specific barrier to access has been overcome, many new game genres, such as casual-gaming, have created a video game library with easy access and wide appeal. As a result it is important to broaden our perspective and identify the place of video games in social discourse.

William Uricchio aptly points out that games are only the latest manifestation of human culture's innate propensity to "play."[6] Connecting games to the work of Johan Huizinga, Uricchio adopts the term "*Homo ludens*" to describe humans as having cross-cultural, universal proclivity to play. As Huizinga originally phrased it, civilization "arises in and as play, and never leaves it."[7] Anthropology also supports the cross-cultural significance of narrative, storytelling, and imaginative reenactment in how humans understand their world, culture, and common past using archetypes and common mythology.[8] Thus, games fulfill a greater cultural and societal function than mere entertainment, and increasingly, video games are central to our modern form of play. A growing number of scholars, in particular, are exploring the value of video games for historical understanding and learning.[9]

The debated value of video games in relation to history concerns historical representation (the historical accuracy of games) and simulation (the structure of games enabling experimentation in historical settings). While the rigorous standards of representation are seldom met by video games, historical simulation is attainable. The goal of this chapter is to introduce readers to the debate on historical representation and take the argument further by addressing questions central to video games and history: Can true historical scholarship be transmitted through games as it has been through other formats? In what new ways can this media be used to inform and educate? If video games do not impart the *product* of scholarship, can they teach the *tools* of historical scholarship?

Ultimately we argue that, while commercial historical video games cannot function as a medium for true historical representation, they are effective at teaching invaluable tools for acquiring and producing historical knowledge. While historically themed video games are, by their nature, ahistorical, their unique seat at the table of historical learning is their ability to provide a rich simulation environment to foster necessary conceptual models. After outlining our theoretical perspective, we define three specific components of historically contextualized simulation games, which facilitate the understanding and construction of historical representations: the *context* of historical artifacts and events, the *subjectivity* of actors making decisions within their unique historical context, and the *concepts* that either describe or explain historical events. Examples from the *Civilization, Total War,* and *Patrician* franchises will illustrate the functions we claim video games to have generally. We begin with a discussion of historical representation, historical simulation, and how video games enhance history.

Historical representation

History is the analysis of human action in past events, the circumstances surrounding their occurrence, and their implications for other people and subsequent events. Bernard Bailyn describes history as having two meanings, "one is simply *what happened* ... the other is history *as knowledge of what happened*."[10] The first is *historical fact*. These are names, dates, and events whose occurrence can be proved without a doubt. An example of this type of history might be: "Napoleon existed, and he lost the Battle of Waterloo." The second facet Bailyn describes is *historical analysis*, which leads to the creation of a *historical representation,* which assembles facts into a reasonable causal narrative. A historian may take the preceding historical fact and ask, "Why did Napoleon lose the battle of Waterloo, and how did this defeat affect European and world history?" The product of this inquiry would be a historical representation. This representation would be subject to review of other historians, and if found to be reasonable, added to accepted historical knowledge.

In a technological era of objective, empirical science, the study of history is often confronted by questions of authenticity and accuracy. However, history is a thoroughly subjective discipline; different historians given the same set of data can often produce vastly different interpretations.[11] Without the ability to observe the event they are describing, and often at the mercy of incomplete or unreliable sources, historians are tasked with creating reasonably objective, evidence-based interpretations of the past. Historians have full prerogative over their representation, and they set it in a narrative structure so that it can be reviewed easily by their peers. These representations of the past are not definitive: no historian can claim complete knowledge of a person or event. Unlike crime investigators, historians "must assume, at one and the same time, the function of the public prosecutor, council for the defense, and the jury" critiquing alternative interpretations and defending their own.[12]

The Western tradition of historical inquiry and the creation of historical representations have gone through many evolutions. Humanistic Greeks like Thucydides and Herodotus attempted to write objective accounts of past action based on eyewitness testimony. "But as to the facts of the occurrences of the war," wrote Thucydides in his introduction, "I thought my duty to give them, not as ascertained from any chance informant, nor as seemed to me probable, but only after investigating with the greatest possible accuracy of every detail."[13] In this statement, Thucydides identifies the trajectory of historical representation for centuries to come: that he aims to represent the past as objectively as possible. These two basic ideas—that the historical representation is codified in writing and that it aims to be as objective as possible by being based on factually informed causal interpretations—continue to be the foundations of historical study today.

Despite fundamental agreements on process, modern historical representations have varied. Romanticist historians such as Thomas Carlyle wrote popular and embellished histories, while Positivist historians like Leopold von Ranke attempted to rationalize the discipline with empirical methods and close adherence to archival sources.[14] The Marxist tradition, itself an early-modern school of history, attempted to frame all historical events as contests between conflicting socioeconomic classes. These and other attempts to apply universal theoretical models to all of history ultimately failed to provide convincing representations. Unbounded by a universal model, historical inquiry has diversified to address areas ignored by previous historians, such as gender and family history. These new substantive questions and research approaches have become increasingly multidisciplinary and have experimented with new tools for cultivating historical interpretation. One of the most powerful of these tools is historical simulation.

Historical simulation

By incorporating other disciplines into historical inquiry, historians have the opportunity to improve the accuracy, breadth, and clarity of their interpretations of the past. Simulation in particular has been advocated as improving historical inquiry by providing "interactivity, representation of complex processes in a dynamic, visual, and integrated manner, and presentation of the past as it was by those who lived it."[15] However, by using the methods of other disciplines, historians are now confronted with larger, epistemological questions: just what methods can they include in their study of history and have it still be the study of "history"?

Simulation can be an effective multidisciplinary tool for this purpose. Historians have classically conveyed their knowledge through fixed oral, written, or performed narratives. The experience for learners by these means has been passive. Simulation, on the other hand, is neither fixed nor passive. A simulation is an imitation of real-world situations or processes as they function over time. A participant in the simulation operates within the confines of a modeled process, with mechanisms that are not perfectly known to the player, meaning that the effects are not perfectly predictable.[16] As in any real-life decision, there is experimentation and both intended and unforeseen consequences. After each step, the resultant new circumstances are evaluated and new choices made, always attempting to achieve the objective, while being confronted with unforeseen events and consequences. A simulation is an interactive medium, and when created as a historical model, as in the cases of the *Crusader Kings II, Port Royale, Europa Universalis, Total War, Civilization,* and *Patrician* series, it affords a unique way of interacting with history.

For a game to be a proper vehicle for historical representation "it must maintain the hallmarks of scholarly history: the use of empirical evidence; the absence of an appeal to rhetoric; the application of a narrative structure; and the requirement of a truth attribute."[17] Simulations necessarily fail as tools of legitimate historical representation because simulations are defined by player interaction. From the moment the player makes their first decision, they are no longer seeing actual *history*. Instead, they are acting within a counterfactual—an expression of what has not happened but might have under different conditions—which most historians view as having limited use in established historical practice and some rebuke altogether as "a mere parlour game, a red herring."[18] However, counterfactuals are helpful for understanding causality across the social sciences because they enable the investigator to test processes, which may explain outcomes or how outcomes would change given different choices, events, and stimuli.[19] But a distinction should be made between the concern with the *outcome* of a counterfactual, which has little utility, and that of the *process* of counterfactuals, which enables illustrative simulation. While commercial simulation video games fail to act as genuine historical representation, we argue that they successfully model the conceptual frameworks necessary to understand and construct historical representation better than alternate media.

The place at the table

Context

Historical representation strives for the construction of a causal narrative, using explanatory concepts, relevant to a particular context, to provide objective knowledge of what has happened in the past and subjective understanding of why it happened. The counterfactual nature of simulations makes historical representation implausible through video games. Nevertheless, they allow players to learn facts, processes, and perspectives, all of which are components of historical knowledge.

To create context, simulations present the artifacts of historical representation in rich detail. Textual descriptions of the Acropolis, a battle between formations of musket men, or navigation of a sixth-rate frigate, do not convey as much understanding of the process as a video demonstration. This is the power of film as a representation. The context of people, places, and things can be depicted in greater detail by more densely descriptive and demonstrative media.

Video games use this advantage of film, introducing cutscenes or animations during gameplay for their demonstrative and narrative capacity in setting the context of the simulation. Video games also incorporate the advantages of other media. *Civilization*, for example, has included a game-specific encyclopedia that provides information about the rules of the simulation but also incorporates the historical context of people, places, and artifacts relevant to the model. Game events in *Civilization V* and the *Total War* series frequently trigger the presentation of informative text or quotations recounting real histories related to events in the game. Video games are uniquely suited to provide the advantages of all other media within their own. However, simulation advances beyond simple demonstration and allows actual interaction with artifacts, to "play" with the components of historical representations.

Interactivity is the unique means of understanding artifacts and context that video games enable. Most traditional media used for historical representation are passive; learning of a trebuchet being used against a fortified position may be done by reading a book, hearing a lecture, or watching a film. However, in a video game the player can personally investigate a question about an artifact: how effective would a trebuchet be against cavalry? Through simulation, the function of an artifact can be experimented with as well as understood through textual description and visual demonstration. Simulation then goes beyond demonstration by approximating experiential knowledge of the actual characteristics of people, places, and circumstances as they are or may have been in the real world.

Subjectivity

In his introductory book on historiography, Mark Gilderhus defines historicism as the attempt to imagine the perspective of historical actors themselves as a "methodological means to fathom the meaning of the past ... it pointed to the diversity of human experience and claimed that different peoples quite literally view the world differently. To comprehend the past, scholars had to enter the mental universe of past actors emphatically and reconstruct their picture of reality."[20] Simulations are uniquely situated to allow students to achieve a level of historicism. By allowing a student to engage with a set of rules and variables that are reasonably historic in nature, those students *comprehend the historical actor* in his or her own historical circumstances. This unique utility is the subjective experience of history.

A difficulty that frequently occurs in history is enabling the learner to understand the mindset of actors in their time. The confident, frantic, and sometimes blind choices of historical figures appear as necessary consequences due to our foreknowledge of the outcomes. To understand the processes that led to history outcomes, we need to understand more than the order of causes and their historically significant effects. We need to understand the choices that were being made without full knowledge of what their effects would be. The subjective mindset also extends to the fragility of the outcomes and events in history as well. As Huizinga argues, "The historian must ... constantly put himself at a point in the past at which the known factors will seem to permit different outcomes."[21] Simulations put players into that role by creating context and model concepts so as to create the kind of tension between choices that historical actors have experienced. Being able to understand an era, event, or actor from a comparable experience is a unique value of simulation.

Concepts

Simulations not only present students with challenges similar to those faced by historical actors in their appropriate context, but also model the concepts necessary to assemble historical facts into historical representations. Concepts are generalized models of processes that operate in the real world. Autocratic government, mercantile economics, or strategies of war are all concepts about how people take action or organize systems. Concepts are what allow us to infer patterns from particular events. Military A may surround military B inside a city. A waits for B to run out of supplies while B attempts to make the costs of waiting high enough that A withdraws. This event has happened often enough and is unique enough that it is now a common concept of war: laying siege. Unlike linear text, simulations provide more than a definition for readers to conceptualize, they demonstrate a concept in operation by allowing interactive experimentation. The degree of success and failure of alternative processes can be evaluated and compared by the players themselves.

Simulations allow players to form concepts from these experiments and draw conclusions without being taught the concepts beforehand. Without formally learning about siege warfare, a player may unintentionally develop a robust understanding of its function by playing a game. Complex relationships can be better understood through subjective experience and active participation. "Rather than a what-if simulation with a known case study as a referent," says Uricchio, "nonspecific simulations provoke a wider range of interrogations, encouraging more abstract, theoretical engagement of historical processes."[22] In simulations, players are discovering the function and utility of complex concepts through problem solving and experimentation. For example the evolutionary game *Spore* has been used to demonstrate and critique conceptual models of evolution.[23] Classes played *Spore* to experiment with processes of evolution and to critique the particular model of evolution presented in the game. Similar to *Spore* modeling the important scientific concept of evolution, historical video games such as *Total War*, *Patrician*, and *Civilization* model concepts are vital to historical understanding.

Case studies in imperial mercantilism, market demands, and geopolitics

We do not claim that all video games are historically instructive simulations merely because they are historically contextualized. To this point, we first provide a counter-example. Consider the popular first-person-shooter series, *Call of Duty*. The game design includes places, people, and conflicts that take place during a historical event. However, the contextualization is merely thematic. These are not simulation games because they do not model real-world processes or real subjective experiences. The options, actions, and motivations are not representative of those that the corresponding historical actors faced. The objective and structure of the multiplayer mode especially, which is to get the highest competitive score exclusively through perpetual combat, is not an objective of historical actors. The game uses trappings of history to create a fiction, and the fiction created does not simulate any genuine historical concept. As discussed in the introduction to this volume, this is a case of a game mechanic rewarding skillful competition set to a theme, not eliciting subjective experiences or modeling historically relevant processes.

Imperial economics and mercantilism in *Total War*

Creative Assembly's *Total War* series is a blend of turn-based strategy played on an overview map, which transitions into a real-time war simulator when battles are initiated by the player or the computer. Iterations of the series present a specific time period: the Roman Empire, medieval Europe, seventeenth-century Europe, and feudal Japan. Each game attempts to incorporate era-appropriate geography, political motivation, military technology, key actors, and scientific achievements.

In *Empire Total War*, the player assumes the role of leading a seventeenth-century European power during the era of imperialism. Players quickly learn that not all nations have the same motivations. While England begins with its defensive island position and in possession of overseas colonies, the Netherlands sit above multiple hostile nations on the continent. Successful players must assess their country's position and note the most significant pressures that they face. They then must determine what course to take in the following areas: researching technological innovation, establishing overseas trade routes or colonies, building national infrastructure, maintaining beneficial diplomatic interaction, and changing the forms of governance.

Immersed within context, players learn how a nation like England may utilize its colonies to keep economies afloat in the face of mounting challenges in Europe. For example, why not raise taxes on far-away colonies to finance pressing wars at home? Seeing unrest build because of a player's chosen tax policy reinforces the importance of national fiscal decisions and demonstrates economic class bias for particular policies. By considering these concepts within an established framework of the game's historical constraints, players can achieve a basic level of historicism. As the game progresses and the players' choices build into wider outcomes, the game still attempts to anchor players in the time period, either with static notifications of historical events or by constraining the player's progress in science and technology.

Supply and demand in *Patrician*

In Ascaron Entertainment's *Patrician* series, the player becomes an apprentice Hanseatic League merchant in the early-modern period. Players are tasked with devising profitable trade routes among accurately placed historical trading ports in northern Europe. As the player amasses trade wealth, they can begin to build their own commercial ventures, influence and participate in local governance, and hinder competing traders via less-than-respectable methods. The game's simulated economy is dynamic: as the player and the computer (or human) controlled opponents buy and sell goods, supply and demand change accordingly.

Instead of considering many different macro-concepts and motivations from a leader's standpoint as in the *Total War* games, *Patrician* players participate in the historical simulation from the ground up. Attempts at ground-level historical representation are not new; many historians write micro histories concerning one person or a small group of people. These historians attempt to answer the large questions of historical inquiry by focusing their study to the smallest possible point, whether it is an individual, family, event, or place. In the same fashion, simulations like *Patrician* can introduce large questions by way of small focus: behind the seemingly simple supply and demand economics simulation, *Patrician* players are able to draw connections between wealth and power, trade and politics, religion and society—all within the context of the early-modern period.

The geopolitics of *Civilization*

The *Sid Meier's Civilization* series has been criticized as merely having the trappings of history to enhance gameplay. We, however, draw a distinction between games like *Call of Duty* (to which this criticism applies) and games such as the *Civilization* series. *Civilization* offers a significantly greater degree of historical context, going so far as to provide a literal encyclopedia of relevant knowledge. The "Civilopedia" includes encyclopedic entries on all artifacts (buildings, people, tools, technologies, etc.) and links their factual historical context to their functional representation within the simulation. Further, the leniency of historical circumstance enables a broad exploration of historically important concepts. While a loose argument could be made for the subjective experience of evaluating state decisions, we concede that the experience of subjectivity is thin at best.

The strength of *Civilization*'s contextual information is not in how closely it adheres to actual circumstance but in the associations it creates. While the historical context of concepts is entirely inaccurate (Native Americans may implement a democracy in 400 CE), the nature of the simulation allows for the widest possible experience with and implementation of a vast array of concepts. Consider a player who elects to play the Greek civilization and chooses Alexander the Great as the leader. Already, the player can associate Alexander the Great, unique military units known as "hoplites" and "companion cavalry," and the first city the player constructs, Athens, with the Greek civilization. The player goes on to build several cities, develop amicable relations with some civilizations, engage in war with others, discover technologies and the new systems or tools they enabled, and go through alterations in the form of government. All of which are simulated concepts relevant to understanding similar real historical events.

Geopolitics, for example, studies how geographic location in relation to other states, especially in regard to resources, economies, and demographics, affect politics. During gameplay, the player is confronted with geopolitical decisions: cities built on rivers receive more initial trade; cities built on hilltops are more defensible; the proximity of natural resources will influence growth rate, economy, and maximum population, perhaps even religious beliefs; and the location relative to other players will influence relations with that civilization. Unknowingly, the player is evaluating complex geopolitical tensions modeled after the real world. Interacting with all these systems, the player is not being "taught" concepts about geopolitics, government, or economics, but he or she will use them for problem solving and develop an abstract understanding of their function.

The value of simulating history

This chapter makes the case that historical video games engage players by simulating the artifacts and context of historical periods, the concepts relevant to historical systems, and the perspectives of historical actors. These simulations provide a unique opportunity for students to experience and play through historical thinking, rather than passively receiving historical representations. While we present a few cases to emphasize the practicality of current games to accomplish these objectives, the above examples only scratch the surface of the potential for games to cultivate experiential understanding. A video game acts as more than a medium for entertainment, it provides the tools and information necessary, within a controlled environment, for players to generate rich conceptual knowledge through simulation.

Such rich concepts are required for the comprehension and creation of historical knowledge. Consider the various conceptions of politics (the study of who gets what, when, and how),[24] the study of power (the means by which one entity may cause another to make choices it otherwise would not make),[25] or the study of economics (how scarce resources are allocated among competing demands that exceed supply). Much historical interpretation will rely on the various, sometimes competing, concepts of these and many more subjects to represent our past accurately. While none of these concepts may be explored completely, games do provide the most dynamic, engaging, and natural means of learning them —through the act of play.

We are *Homo ludens*, a playing creature. Play socializes us, educates us, and satisfies us at all ages. During play, the systems and simulations embodied in particular video games foster learning through action within the system but also through the critique of it. For example, critical consideration of *Civilization* reveals a bias toward representing all of history as inevitable and constant scientific advancement and social progressivism. The absence of complex systems of slavery in *Total War* forces us to ask why the system marginalizes slavery and if any economy prior to emancipation can be understood without consideration of slavery's influence. Playing *Patrician*, a person might wonder what enabled merchants to trust one another in an era with little government oversight to secure and stabilize trade. With any simulation, the structure necessitates a reduction in complexity to enable player interaction with core concepts, and still be fun. Simulations fail to address all possible aspects of the actors and events they portray. Nevertheless, that absence affords room for critical thinking and critique, as any particular representation of history must invite.

Historiography can draw on a diverse and evolving toolset, often utilizing concepts from related fields. Modern economic studies influence the interpretation of historic economic events such as The Great Depression. Studying the causes of stability and disunity in modern governments informs the historical interpretation of revolutions and civil wars. New philosophical, sociological, and psychological thinking improves how the motivations of individuals and societies are understood. All these fields can contribute to the historical challenge of explaining where we have been and how we arrived at where we are. Video game simulations can cultivate in players the multidisciplinary knowledge necessary for investigating, understanding, and critiquing representations of the past. In an era when many possibilities exist for integrated multimedia learning, the relevance of video games should be recognized and capitalized on as a vehicle for historical knowledge.

Notes

1   Media as varied as movies, television, and comic books faced similar questions about negative effects on consumers. For a discussion of limits of the "effects" research, see Justin Lewis, *The Ideological Octopus: An Exploration of Television and Its Audience*. New York and London: Routledge, 1991, 7–11.

2   See, for instance, James Paul Gee's, *What Video Games Have to Teach Us about Learning and Literacy*. New York: Palgrave Macmillan, 2003; David Williamson Shaffer, *How Computer Games Help Children Learn*. New York: Palgrave Macmillan, 2006.

3   Lisa Guernsey, "An 'Educational' Video Game Has Taken Over My House," *Slate*. http://www.slate.com/articles/technology/future_tense/2012/08/minecraft_teachers_love_the_game_but_as_a_parent_i_m_worried_my_kids_are_addicted.single.html

4   Entertainment Software Association, "Essential Facts about the Video game Industry." http://www.theesa.com/facts/pdfs/ESA_EF_2012.pdf, 2.

5   See also Jesper Juul, *A Casual Revolution*. Cambridge, MA: MIT Press, 2010.

6   William Uricchio, "Simulation, History, and Computer Games," Chapter 21, in *Handbook of Computer Game Studies*. Cambridge, MA: MIT Press, 2005, 327–338.

7   Quoted in Uricchio, "Simulation, History, and Computer Games," 329.

8   Joseph Campbell, *The Hero with a Thousand Faces*. Novato, CA: New World Library, 2008.

9   For example Kevin Kee "Computerized History Games: Narrative Options," *Simulation & Gaming*, 42, no. 4 (2011); Uricchio, "Simulation, History, and Computer Games," and Jerremie Clyde, Howard Hopkins, and Glenn Wilkinson, "Beyond the 'Historical' Simulation: Using Theories of History to Inform Scholarly Game Design," *Loading ... The Journal of the Canadian Game Studies Association*, 6, no. 9 (2012): 3–16.

10 John Clive, *Not by Fact Alone: Essays on the Writing and Reading of History.* New York: Alfred A. Knopf, 1989, 7. (Emphasis in the original.)

11 E.H. Carr, *What is History?* London: Penguin, 1987, 23.

12 Gaetano Salvemini, *Historian and Scientist.* Freeport, NY: Books for Library Press, 1969, 50.

13 Thucydides, *Peloponnesian War.*

14 G.P. Gooch, *History and Historians: History and Historians in the Nineteenth Century.* New York: Peter Smith Co., 1949, 78.

15 Tom Taylor, "Historical Simulations and the Future of the Historical Narrative," *Journal of the Association for History and Computing,* 6, no. 2 (September 2003): 1–5.

16 Barry L. Nelson, et al. *Discrete-Event System Simulation.* New Jersey: Prentice Hall, 2001.

17 See Clyde, Hopkins, and Wilkinson, "Beyond the 'Historical' Simulation," for a discussion on the development of a video game as a historical representation, as opposed to the use of commercial games.

18 Niall Ferguson, Ed. *Virtual History: What Could Have Been.* New York: Fall River Press, 1997, 4.

19 Gary King, Robert Keohane and Sidney Verba. *Designing Social Inquiry: Scientific Inquiry in Qualitative Research.* Princeton, NJ: Princeton University Press, 1994.

20 Mark T. Gilderhus, *History and Historians: A Historiographical Introduction,* 5th ed. Upper Saddle River, NJ: Prentice Hall, 2003, 45–46.

21 Ferguson, Ed. *Virtual History: What Could Have Been.*

22 William Uricchio, "Simulation, History, and Computer Games," in *Handbook of Computer Game Studies.* Cambridge, MA: MIT Press, 2005, 330.

23 Dorothybelle Poli, et al. "Bringing Evolution to a Technological Generation: A Case Study with the Video Game SPORE," *The American Biology Teacher,* 74, no. 2 (2012): 100–103.

24 Harold Dwight Lasswell, *Politics: Who Gets What, When, How.* New York: Meridian, 1960.

25 Peter Bachrach and Morton Baratz, "An Analytical Framework," *American Political Science Review,* 57, no. 3 (1963): 632–642.

Works cited

Bachrach, Peter and Morton Baratz. "An Analytical Framework," *American Political Science Review,* 57, no. 3 (1963): 632–642. *JSTOR.* Web. 9 April 2012.

Campbell, Joseph. *The Hero with a Thousand Faces,* 3rd ed. Novato, CA: New World Library, 2008.

Carr, E.H. *What Is History?* London: Penguin, 1987.

Clive, John. *Not by Fact Alone: Essays on the Writing and Reading of History*. New York: Alfred A. Knopf, 1989.

Clyde, Jerremie, Howard Hopkins, and Glenn Wilkinson. "Beyond the 'Historical' Simulation: Using Theories of History to Inform Scholarly Game Design," *Loading . . . The Journal of the Canadian Game Studies Association*, 6, no. 9 (2012): 3–16.

Entertainment Software Association. "Essential Facts About the Video game Industry." http://www.theesa.com/facts/pdfs/ESA_EF_2012.pdf/, accessed 21 January 2013.

Ferguson, Niall, Ed. *Virtual History: What Could Have Been*. New York: Fall River Press, 1997.

Gee, James Paul. *What Video Games Have to Teach Us about Literacy and Learning*. New York: Palgrave Macmillan, 2003.

Gilderhus, Mark T. *History and Historians: A Historiographical Introduction*, 5th ed. Upper Saddle River, NJ: Prentice Hall, 2003.

Gooch, G.P. *History and Historians in the Nineteenth Century*. New York: Peter Smith Co, 1949.

Guernsey, Lisa. "An 'Educational' Video Game Has Taken Over My House," *Slate*. http://www.slate.com/articles/technology/future_tense/2012/08/minecraft_teachers_love_the_game_but_as_a_parent_i_m_worried_my_kids_are_addicted.html/, accessed 4 October 2012.

Juul, Jesper. *A Casual Revolution*. Cambridge, MA: MIT Press, 2010.

Kee, Kevin. "Computerized History Games: Narrative Options," *Simulation & Gaming*, 42, no. 4 (2011): 432–440.

King, Gary, Robert Keohane, and Sidney Verba. *Designing Social Inquiry: Scientific Inquiry in Qualitative Research*. Princeton, NJ: Princeton University Press, 1994.

Lasswell, Harold Dwight. *Politics: Who Gets What, When, How*. New York: Meridian, 1960.

Lewis, Justin. *The Ideological Octopus: An Exploration of Television and Its Audience*. New York and London: Routledge, 1991.

McMichael, Andrew. "PC Games and the Teaching of History," *The History Teacher*, 40, no. 2 (February 2007): 203–218.

Nelson, Barry L., John Carson, Jerry Banks. *Discrete-Event System Simulation*. Prentice-Hall International Series in Industrial and Systems Engineering, NJ: Prentice Hall, 2001.

Poli, Dorothybelle, Christopher Berenotto, Sara Blankenship, Bryan Piatkowski, A. Geoffrey "Bringing Evolution to a Technological Generation: A Case Study with the Video Game SPORE," *The American Biology Teacher*, 74, no. 2 (2012): 100–103.

Salvemini, Gaetano. *Historian and Scientist*. Freeport, NY: Books for Library Press, 1969.

Shaffer, David Williamson. *How Computer Games Help Children Learn*. New York: Palgrave Macmillan, 2006.

Taylor, Tom. "Historical Simulations and the Future of the Historical Narrative," *Journal of the Association for History and Computing*, 6, no. 2 (September 2003): 1–5.

Thucydides, *Peloponnesian War*. 22, no.1.

Uricchio, William. "Simulation, History, and Computer Games," in Eds. Joost Raessens and Jeffrey Goldstein *Handbook of Computer Game Studies*. Cambridge, MA: MIT Press, 2005.

Games cited

Call of Duty: World at War. Santa Monica, CA: Treyarch, Activision, 2008.
Crusader Kings II. Stockholm, Sweden: Paradox Development Studio, Paradox Interactive, 2012.
Empire Total War. Tokyo, Japan: Creative Assembly, Sega, 2009.
Europa Universalis III. Stockholm, Sweden: Paradox Development Studio, Paradox Interactive, 2007.
Minecraft. Stockholm, Sweden: Mojang Studios, Notch Enterprises, 2011.
The Oregon Trail. Brooklyn Center, MN: Rawitsch, et al., Minnesota Educational Computing Consortium (MECC), 1971.
Patrician IV. Worms, Germany: Gaming Minds Studio, Kalypso Media (formerly produced by Ascaron Entertainment), 2010.
Port Royale 3. Worms, Germany: Gaming Minds Studio, Kalypso Media, 2012.
Sid Meier's Civilization V. Novato, CA: Firaxis Games, 2K Games, 2010.
Spore. Redwood City, CA: Maxis, Electronic Arts, 2008.

3

What Is "Old" in Video Games?

Daniel Reynolds
Emory University

I declare I am interested in this story, and wish I had been there.

TRISTRAM SHANDY[1]

I used to joke about my nostalgia for video games. My memory of the "Overworld Theme" music from *The Legend of Zelda* (Nintendo, 1987), I would say, was as moving to me as was any childhood memory; the irony was that I was experiencing nostalgia for an environment, a time, a series of events that did not really happen. Now, I am not so sure. These things *did* happen, and though they left no significant traces in the real world, the nature of video games means that they could happen again.

Video game time has something like a present tense with a progressive aspect. It exists as a potential that can only be activated through the exploratory engagement of a player; to play a game is to create a history not only for oneself and for one's in-game character, but also for the game's world. Because games can be replayed, they provide opportunities to rebuild, or to rewrite, their diegetic *and* their extradiegetic histories. This capacity troubles games' relationships to the basic language we use to describe our experience of time and history and provides new opportunities for thinking about how we create history by living it.

What can be described as "old" in video games? In asking the question, I set aside the word "old" in quotation marks because I want to consider it as a conceptual category with roughly defined boundaries, to ask how the term, in any of its connotations, can be applied to video games. A video game can be old because it was designed a long time ago, as was *Tennis for Two*

(Willy Higinbotham, 1958), possibly the first action-based video game ever made. A video game can be old because it was played a long time ago: the first time I played through *The Legend of Zelda*, for instance, is an old series of actions; in this sense of the term, an "old" video game is imbued with meaning as an event in a player's personal history. A saved-game file is old: I have been slowly making my way through *Shenmue 2* (Sega, 2001) for many years, and when I go back to my game, I am certainly picking up and working with something old. Almost any used console memory card or computer hard disk has a few old saved-game files on it, their narratives suspended and their outcomes undetermined. These stories exist as parameters for events, but their narratives, and their narration, are undetermined until the games are played.

The phrase "What is 'old' in video games?" is intentionally ambiguous in another way: "in video games" can mean "in the field of video games," as in the previous examples, or it can mean "in the worlds of video games." The diegetic worlds of video games have their own histories, but the worlds of video games, unlike those of conventional films, are constructed from scratch rather than derived, though chemical or digital photographic processes, from the real world. The automatic transcription that occurs in photography (and filming) creates a historical record of the things photographed, writes André Bazin:

> For the first time, between the originating object and its reproduction there intervenes only the instrumentality of a nonliving agent. For the first time the image of the world is formed automatically, without the creative intervention of man … Photography affects us like a phenomenon in nature, like a flower or a snowflake whose vegetable or earthly origins are an inseparable part of their beauty.[2]

While Bazin's claims here about the effects of photography may overemphasize the "naturalness" of the photographic image, the image's production through automatic transcription does mean that it has a limited indexical relationship to the objects and events that it depicts. A camera works via a process of photographic transcription; the events depicted in a conventional film once occurred in front of a camera, and a film is a physical index of their having taken place. The images with which we are confronted in video games, on the other hand, are computer-rendered representations of coded geometries. Until we boot up a game and play it, these worlds exist only as code; they are realized as spaces through our play, and the form that that play takes affects how the game world is depicted. Thus, while a photograph is a technological transcription of a certain place at a certain time, viewed from a certain angle, and a film is the same extended over a span of time, a game is not a record but a set of rules and conditions that facilitate the creation of a virtual space and time. Films come after the events that they index; they refer *back* to their images' own production, which is necessarily in the past. Games as physical artifacts instead precede the depictions they enable.

The concept of the "old" within gameplay is similarly complicated. Any game creates a virtual world of a greater or lesser degree of complexity, and the impression that these worlds preexist the player's "entry" into them is of varying importance. In abstract games such as *Tetris* (Alexey Pajitnov, 1985) and *Klaax* (Atari, 1989), the game world's preexistence is not much of an issue, as it is not depicted as being inhabited by sentient beings. In marginally narrative games like *Pac Man* (Namco, 1980), the appearance of a player avatar in the virtual world implies a world with preexisting boundaries and rules that can be discovered through navigation of game spaces. In games with more complex worlds, such as *Grand Theft Auto: San Andreas* (Rockstar, 2004), a past may be manifest in the textures of the diegetic world: there can be "old" things there. The details of the game world, and of the events that transpire there, work to obfuscate the fact that this rendered environment, in its present state, did not preexist the player turning on the system *this time*. Structures and limits—physical, social, behavioral—can seem to preexist the player's arrival, and events from the past can be revealed, either through recounting (as in cutscenes of "cinema scenes," non-interactive vignettes that are often used to advance and give texture to game narratives) or through enactment of earlier events. Enacted flashbacks are a major part of the structure of *Eternal Darkness: Sanity's Requiem* (Silicon Knights, 2002), and the bulk of *Prince of Persia: The Sands of Time* (Ubisoft, 2003) is staged as one long flashback that is both recounted through voice narration and enacted through gameplay. In his discussion of cinematic history, Pierre Sorlin writes:

> The positivist history of cinema ... leaves the films themselves to one side ... This is where I see the main divergence between history and cinematic history. The latter, unlike the former, cannot be a memory in absentia. The films remain. Materially they still exist ... Their physical permanence emphasizes the unbridgeable distance between what is no longer—the past—and what still exists.[3]

As with films, old video games still exist in their physical manifestations. But the "past" of gameplay is not like the historical past depicted in films: game narratives unfold in a perpetual now.

Present progressive

Any fiction has a narrating "voice," expressed in the form given to the story being recounted. This voice is a tool that allows its user to, among other things, bend the representation of time, whether for convenience or dramatic effect, or to signal points of major importance in a narrative. Jacques Tati can seamlessly compress an entire evening's revelry into forty-five minutes of screen time in *Playtime* (1967) without the film's temporal structure intruding into our comprehension of the events depicted or interrupting the story's "flow."[4] Nearly all films bend time in one way or another, but it is usually the effects achieved by the bending, and not the bending itself, that are the point. Continuity editing emphasizes relative invisibility over noticeable temporal articulations. Noel Burch calls this the "zero point of cinematic style," a paradigm that has kept film from attaining "formal autonomy."[5]

Compare this emphasis on continuity to a moment of temporal shock such as a point toward the end of Virginia Woolf's *Orlando: A Biography* in which the title character, who has had a centuries-long shifting perceptual and physical relationship with the flow of time, snaps suddenly into the present:

> [Orlando] saw everything more and more clearly and the clock ticked louder and louder until there was a terrific explosion right in her ear. Orlando leapt as if she had been violently struck on the head. Ten times she was struck. In fact it was ten o'clock in the morning. It was the eleventh of October. It was 1928. It was the present moment.
>
> No one need wonder that Orlando started, pressed her hand to her heart, and turned pale. For what more terrifying revelation can there be than that it is the present moment? That we survive the shock at all is only possible because the past shelters us on one side and the future on another. But we have no time now for reflections; Orlando was terribly late already.[6]

Woolf here expands "the present moment," both in its psychological magnitude and in her treatment of its duration. When the present moment catches up with Orlando, it comes as a shock to her, and to the narrating voice, which has to regain its composure and restate its intentions. Orlando being "terribly late" puts temporal pressure not only on her but also on the narration itself. Suddenly, it is not free to recount Orlando's story at its own pace; it must focus its energies on keeping up with her activities in "the present moment."

Even in stories being told in the linguistic present tense, there is a necessary remove from the events at hand, a feeling that their endings are predetermined—which, in conventional novels and films, they are. Holding a half-finished novel in our hands, we hold its unknown conclusion, so that even if we imagine that its story is unfolding as we read it, its very nature cannot help but remind us otherwise, both in the form it takes as a physical object and in its narration, which, even if its voice is in the present tense, has an implicit perfective aspect. The story cannot change as it goes along, as it is a construction that was assembled in the past. "In perfective aspect," writes Payne, "the situation is viewed in its entirety, independent of tense."[7]

In conventional film, the necessity of the past is reflected in every frame. Each is a photograph of something that happened before. In our comprehension of film, too, our understanding of events in the diegesis is filtered through their presentation to us, as Edward Branigan observes:

> [W]hat we are constructing when we see a shot on the screen is decidedly nonlocal and nonvisual in nature—namely, patterns and connections that give underlying form to an event ... No image appears simply in a "present-time" removed from thought, memory, and expectation, at least in narrative discourse ... do we see an image that is being presented by a higher-level, implicit narration in order to reveal information and advance the plot? But, when we look again, don't we see that this higher-level narration is itself being presented ... by a still more powerful narration in order to delay and hide developments in the story so that the plot will not just halt, but will continue, and in due course will have a proper end?[8]

We are aware that a film has a runtime, and that it has a narrative in which a certain amount of diegetic time will be depicted as passing during the runtime of the film. We may not assume that the story will reach a decisive conclusion, but we can reasonably expect that at some point during the next few hours, the telling will end. We may not know where a film is going, but we know *that* it is going, and we know that its destination is determined before we join it on its way. A film is at once perceptually present to us, its events unfolding before our eyes and ears, real things happening to us, and at the same time an artifact from the past, in which "the image of things is likewise the image of their duration."[9]

The events that unfold in a video game are less determined. A game may have a rough narrative structure, and most games with stories have single narrative conclusions toward which players progress, but the details of that progress are dependent on the enactive decisions made by the player of a game. Gameplay is limited only by the rules that constitute the virtual world and the control scheme of the game, and not by the conventional expectation of a "proper end" nor by the perception that we are negotiating our way through a physical object, as is the case with a book's pages or with a film's passage, foot by foot, though a projector.

A video game is difficult to locate as an object. We can point to a strip of celluloid and say "that is a film," and we can identify the physical limits of a book, but it is harder to say precisely where a game is. Not all video games are contained on cartridges, nor in arcade cabinets, nor on discs. To "have" a game is instead to have access to a set of conditions that facilitate its play. Today, I could play *The Legend of Zelda* with an original cartridge on a Nintendo Entertainment System; through hardware emulation on the computer on which I am now typing this sentence; or on the Nintendo Wii's virtual console, which makes older games available for download and play. In any of these cases, it would be true that I would "have" the game, but only in the first would I be able to point at a physical object and say, "there it is."

While many games have narrative arcs with conclusions, there is less of a feeling with games than there is with non-interactive fictions that those conclusions are inevitable. Even if a game has only one possible narrative ending, how we get there is entirely up to us, within the parameters of play that the game allows. If the narration of books and films can unfold in a variety of possible tenses, with a medium-inherent perfective aspect, most video games occur in something more like a present tense with a progressive aspect, in that characters' actions are initiated by player actions and do not precede them: "progressive aspect," writes Payne, "implies an ongoing, dynamic process."[10] No matter how long ago a video game was made nor how long we have "had" it, gameplay always happens *now*. If other commercial media seem to be reeling in the wake of video games' ascent to popularity, perhaps it is because they are feeling the shock of narrative representation snapping into "the present moment."

Video games and the diegetic past

In *Shadow of the Colossus* (Sega, 2005), the player's character, Wander, enters a barren and unfamiliar landscape. He is told that he must battle sixteen zoomorphic colossi, and that killing them might bring his late beloved back to life. While this series of tasks provides the game's narrative a framework, most of the time spent in the game is not in battling the colossi but in exploring the game's vast environments, searching for the colossi and gathering clues about the nature of the place. The environment seems empty of life but for Wander, his horse, the colossi, and a few small fauna. A tall abandoned temple sits in the middle of the map, and smaller moss-covered shrines can be found throughout the landscape. As Wander makes his way through this world, he encounters occasional evidence of a long-ago forgotten society: the ruins of a castle, underground areas supported by seemingly man-made beams, artificial light sources. The narration of *Shadow of the Colossus* is apparently chronological, and the game never explicitly reveals the origins of these structures. These clues to the ancient history of the game environment encourage us to wonder about the nature of the world in which we find ourselves and to hypothesize about the processes that have shaped it. In other words, they cue historical thinking.

A chief appeal of the massively popular *Grand Theft Auto* games, especially those released since *Grand Theft Auto III* (Rockstar, 2001), has been their immersive urban and occasionally rural environments, which are much more densely populated than is the landscape of *Shadow of the Colossus*. The emphasis in the *Grand Theft Auto* games has been less on investigation of the remnants of the history of the virtual world than on adapting to and functioning in a dynamic environment. As the series has progressed, increasing effort has been made to portray the game environments as lived-in spaces, built up and occupied long before the player "arrived." In *Grand Theft Auto: San Andreas*, this means that minor characters have complex past relationships with one another that can be discerned and sometimes only barely inferred; that recounting of events set before the opening of the game figures heavily in the unveiling of the game's conspiracy-heavy narrative, especially since the game aligns us with the consciousness of the sometimes naïve main character, Carl "C.J." Johnson, and that observation of the daily behavioral tendencies of the people in the world could give the player advantages in the gameplay. If *Shadow of the Colossus* provides the option of speculating about the history of the diegetic world, *San Andreas* asks us to be everyday historians, recognizing patterns, positing causal relationships, and making pragmatic decisions based on the predictive capacities that these inferences grant us.

In short, *San Andreas*, through the complexity of its diegetic world, illustrates games' engagement with what Carl Becker calls "history [at] its lowest terms,"

> defining it as the memory of things said and done, [and] showing concretely how the memory of things said and done is essential to the performance of the simplest acts of daily life ... Mr. Everyman does not wish to learn the whole truth or arrive at ultimate causes ... he wishes to adjust himself to a practical situation, and on that practical level he is a good historian precisely because he is not disinterested: he will solve his problems, if he does solve them, by virtue of his intelligence and not by virtue of his indifference.[11]

Becker's conception of "Mr. Everyman" as a practical, and "good," historian seems to apply, really, to all gameplay; for what is gameplay if not adjustment to a practical situation?

Dropped into the world of a video game, we must adjust first to its control scheme (as Adam Chapman describes in Chapter 4), then to its physics model, then to its modeled environment and cause–effect simulation, to the behavioral patterns of its non-player characters and environmental threats, and finally to the specifics of the goals that the video game sets for us within its virtual environment. Understanding and adapting to games' necessary abstraction and to their modeling of physical relationships is an aspect of all gameplay (not just play in video games; board games, sports, and games of make-believe, draw upon the similar processes). Anybody who plays a game is engaging with history merely by adapting to the unique behavioral demands that games put on their players.

Video games that model the passing of time in their worlds as independent of character action add another level of complexity. *Shadow of the Colossus* and the *Grand Theft Auto* games, and environmentally complex games like them, can create an impression that time is always passing in their virtual worlds. There are always radio broadcasts going on in *Grand Theft Auto: San Andreas*, for instance, whether the player is listening to the radio or not. When C.J. gets into a car and turns the radio on, he often joins the station's program already in progress. Jesper Juul points out that "one of the more interesting developments in recent years" is games providing expository information through the implied histories of in-game objects. "This is the basic detective game model," Juul writes. Items in the game world can "inform the player of events that happened prior to the time of the playing, or at least outside the time that you can interact with."[12] The relationship between in-game objects and the inferred history of game worlds is more fundamental still; it is not limited to detective games, nor is it so recent a development, at least not if history is thought of in Beckerian terms. It is manifested in the structures and the processes of virtual worlds. We engage with historical thought from the moment we pick up a controller.

The Sands of Time

Games often fill in their narrative backstories through clues, character recountings, and cutscene enactments. But, as Juul writes, "an *interactive* flashback leads to the time machine problem: the player's actions in the past may suddenly render the present impossible. This is the reason why time in games is almost always chronological."[13]

Prince of Persia: The Sands of Time, a game that engages with history on many of the levels that I have mentioned here, is built around an interactive flashback structure. As the game begins, the player's avatar, the eponymous prince, stands on a balcony outside a brightly lit, curtained room. The player is free to move the prince about the balcony, but an attempt to move him through the curtains and into the room cues the game to backtrack and tell the story of the events that led to this point. The backstory is filled in through interactive action along with occasional cutscenes and voiceover narration by the prince. The prince is established as an unreliable narrator and an unabashed narcissist, so that his voiceover accounts of events often directly contradict the actions that the player performs in the game's reenactment. This feature of the game's flashback narration allows the game to resolve the "time machine problem": if the prince is killed or falls to his death, the game presents the opportunity to backtrack a little bit and continue playing, an option that is accompanied by a voiceover of the prince saying, "Wait, no, that's not how it happened." If the player chooses to continue, the prince says, "Let me tell you how it *really* happened," and the narrative resumes from a few moments before his demise.

Through its creative scripting, *Prince of Persia: The Sands of Time* allows its players to engage with historical and causal structures in ways that remain rare in video games. The game's overall narrative structure—its recounting of the prince's history—is, like the "history written by historians" described by Becker, "a convenient blend of truth and fancy."[14] The game also deals with historical mutability on a more local level. The "sands of time" of the game's title allow the prince to reverse the flow of time for a moment and to retry risky jumps that he has miscalculated or to reconsider his approach to a battle situation. Once it is integrated into a player's enactive repertoire, this becomes an invaluable tool for the navigation of the game space. The freedom to move backward and forward in time can affect the way a player moves through space. A trial run is possible, for instance, to see if a gap can be jumped. If the leap proves impossible, the player can merely reverse time to before the jump. The (possible) future becomes past, and the player is free to try to find another way across the gap; pragmatic historical thought can become a form of contingency planning.

The Sands of Time deals with history on still another level, one that blends the diegetic and the extradiegetic. The game is an installment in a series that began with the computer game *Prince of Persia* (Brøderbund, 1989). At one point in *The Sands of Time*, as the player moves through a passageway deep inside a palace, the voiceover narration intones, "It's said they built this palace on the ruins of another." This line hints at a hidden feature of the game. Near where the prince stands when this narration is cued is a weak wall that can be knocked down with repeated sword blows. A nearby crank can then be turned, opening a gate that was concealed behind the wall. By passing through the gate, the player can enter the world of the original *Prince of Persia*. That game is hidden, in its entirety, within the palace of *The Sands of Time*. The game *The Sands of Time* establishes a temporal connection between itself and the original *Prince of Persia*, refers to its own lineage in video game history, and gives players who were familiar with the original game an opportunity to play it again in a new context—to engage in the strange combination of nostalgia and reenactment that attends the revisiting of old games.

Nostalgia

Video games do not only afford us a limited form of Tristram Shandy's desired "being there" in a story, but they allow us (also like Shandy) to revisit those stories that we find compelling, and always to find something new there. Nostalgia for old games is, in a way, like nostalgia for places that are old to us, in that we can long to go back, both in space and in time, to something we knew, something we experienced, earlier in our lives. As John Berger has written, the cinema "takes us away from where we are to the scene of action ... [it] transports us elsewhere."[15] Video games, likewise, transport us to an "elsewhere"; both media also transport us to an else-*when*. With old films, we can revisit a nested set of times in the past—the time of filming, the time depicted by the film, our own experience of previously viewing the film—that is relatively crystallized in its forms. To play old games is to revisit else-wheres and else-whens, and also to reactivate prior enactive conditions; in addition to elsewhere and else-when, video games provide access to an else-*how*.

As Becker writes, "History is the memory of things done."[16] The nostalgia for *The Legend of Zelda* about which I used to joke is, in fact, no joke, but it is, rather, a legitimate and productive mode of historical thought. My younger self did, in fact, guide the hero Link on a journey through the land of Hyrule to fell the evil king Gannon many times, taking a number of different routes to get there and learning something a little bit different each time. When I recently downloaded *The Legend of Zelda* to my Wii's virtual console, I reactivated "the history that does work in the world ... living history, that pattern of remembered events"[17] that, in this case, did simultaneous work in the real world, guiding my gameplay, and in the virtual world, leading Link on his quest (which is proving more difficult than I remembered).

"Nietzsche," Sorlin writes, "tries to imagine the dazzling sensation of freedom that would seize man if he managed only for a moment to erase his past."[18] This amounts to a fantasy about an impossible erasure of memory. But what if we could retry the past, knowing then, as the saying goes, what we know now? Old video games—and perhaps all video games—collapse the past and the present tenses; most relevant is their progressive aspect, their persistence in reality, and the persistence *of* their realities, realities that we have the option of revisiting. To go back and to try again, whether through the diegetic manipulation of the sands of time in *Prince of Persia* or through blowing the dusts of time off from a long-untouched game cartridge, is to revisit an elsewhere and an else-when, to wind back an else-how and to ask: How else?

Notes

1 Laurence Sterne, *The Life and Opinions of Tristram Shandy, Gentleman*. New York: The Modern Library, 2004, 404.

2 André Bazin, "The Ontology of the Photographic Image," in trans. Hugh Gray, *What is Cinema? Vol. I*. Berkeley, CA: University of California Press, 1967, 13.

3 Pierre Sorlin, "Cinema: An Undiscoverable History?" trans. Keith Reader, *Paragraph*, vol. 15, 1992, 6.

4 David Bordwell, *Narration in the Fiction Film*. Madison, WI: University of Wisconsin Press, 1985, 82.

5 Noël Burch, "Spatial and Temporal Articulations," in Eds. John Orr and Olga Taxidou, *Post War Cinema and Modernity: A Film Reader*. Edinburgh: Edinburgh University Press, 2000, 75.

6 Virginia Woolf, *Orlando: A Biography*. San Diego, CA: Harcourt, Inc., 1956, 289–299.

7 Thomas Payne, *Describing Morphosyntax*. Cambridge: Cambridge University Press, 1997, 239.

8 Edward Branigan, *Projecting A Camera*. New York: Routledge, 2006, 176–177.

9 Bazin, "Ontology," 15.

10 Payne, *Describing Morphosyntax*, 240.

11 Carl Becker, "Everyman His Own Historian," in Ed. Stephen Vaughn, *The Vital Past: Writings on the Uses of History*. Athens, GA: University of Georgia Press, 1985, 25–28.

12 Jesper Juul, *Half-Real*. Cambridge, MA: MIT Press, 2005, 148.

13 Juul, *Half-Real*.

14 Becker, "Everyman," 31.

15 John Berger, "Ev'ry Time We Say Goodbye," in *Keeping a Rendezvous*. New York: Vintage International, 1992, 14.

16 Becker, "Everyman," 22.

17 Becker, "Everyman," 34.

18 Sorlin, "Cinema," 7.

Works cited

Bazin, André. "The Ontology of the Photographic Image," in trans. Hugh Gray, *What is Cinema? Vol. I*. Berkeley, CA: University of California Press, 1967, 9–16.

Becker, Carl. "Everyman His Own Historian," in Ed. Stephen Vaughn, *The Vital Past: Writings on the Uses of History*. Athens, GA: University of Georgia Press, 1985, 20–36.

Berger, John. "Ev'ry Time We Say Goodbye," in *Keeping a Rendezvous*. New York: Vintage International, 1992, 10–24.

Bordwell, David. *Narration in the Fiction Film*. Madison, WI: University of Wisconsin Press, 1985.

Branigan, Edward. *Projecting a Camera*. New York: Routledge, 2006.

Burch, Noël. "Spatial and Temporal Articulations," in Eds. John Orr and Olga Taxidou, *Post War Cinema and Modernity: A Film Reader*. Edinburgh: Edinburgh University Press, 2000, 66–74.

Juul, Jesper. *Half-Real*. Cambridge, MA: MIT Press, 2005.

Payne, Thomas E. *Describing Morphosyntax*. Cambridge: Cambridge University Press, 1997.

Sorlin, Pierre. "Cinema: An Undiscoverable History?" in trans. Keith Reader, *Paragraph*, vol. 15, 1992, 1–18.

Sterne, Laurence. *The Life and Opinions of Tristram Shandy, Gentleman*. New York: The Modern Library, 2004.

Woolf, Virginia. *Orlando: A Biography*. San Diego, CA: Harcourt, Inc, 1956.

Games cited

Eternal Darkness: Sanity's Requiem. St. Catharines, ON: Silicon Knights, 2002.

Grand Theft Auto III. Edinburgh: Rockstar North, 2001.

Grand Theft Auto: San Andreas. Edinburgh: Rockstar North, 2004.

Klax. Milpitas, CA: Atari Games, 1989.

The Legend of Zelda. Kyoto: Nintendo, 1987.

Pac Man. Tokyo: Namco, 1980.

Prince of Persia. San Rafael, CA: Brøderbund, 1989.

Prince of Persia: The Sands of Time. Montreal: Ubisoft Montreal, 2003.

Shadow of the Colossus. Tokyo: Team Ico, 2005.

Shenmue 2. Tokyo: Sega AM2, 2001.

Tennis for Two. Higinbotham, Willy, 1958.

Tetris. Pajitnov, Alexey, 1984.

4

Affording History: *Civilization* and the Ecological Approach

Adam Chapman
University of Hull

Historical video games are one of the prime points of confluence in the attempt to give traditional game structures more meaning and depth and many are amongst the most successful popular histories of recent years.[1] There seems to be increasing acceptance of the idea that games can be historical.[2] However, there is still relatively little academic work that forgoes privileging the content of individual games in favor of trying to understand how they make meaning as histories and invite players to do the same.[3] This leads us to the question of how best to analyze these histories.

Whilst historical theory can provide a lot of answers, using traditional methods also risks reducing these games to nothing more than poor facsimiles of our other forms. Such a closed perspective ignores the unique aspect of this new form of historical expression and the precise reason why it is so popular in the first place: gameplay. Accordingly, we need a broader theory of action—I propose the ecological approach of my title—to understand how historical video games seek to explore past action by offering opportunities for present action. Consequently, in this chapter I will use the ecological approach to digital games in order to illustrate some of the potential of games for making arguments about history. I will do this by analyzing *Sid Meier's Civilization* series, a turn-based strategy game in which the player is given the task of leading a particular "civilization" (e.g. Roman, English, Chinese) from prehistory to beyond the present day. The player must choose the path of the civilization by making decisions about technology, culture, government, diplomacy, military strategy, and urban development, as well as a number of other factors that the game highlights as historically significant.

The ecological approach

The ecological approach originates from the work of James Gibson and has been developed in its application to games by Linderoth.[4] This framework, "address[es] the reciprocal relation between humans (as well as other animals …) and the environment … [which] *offers* the individual different ways of acting. These offers are called affordances and … are relative to an organism (relative between species as well as between individuals)."[5] In the case of video games we can understand the controller, software, and screen as things that are part of the environment of the player and afford particular gaming actions.

"Although many basic affordances are of such nature that they can be acted upon by a majority of the animals in a species, there are individual differences."[6] Thus affordances are based on a number of factors including training and "Humans, at least, must learn to use affordances."[7] It is also important to note that some actions will transform the affordances of a situation allowing new ones to emerge: "Thus, the environment can be said to have affordances for gaining other affordances. We do not only adapt the environment [often through the use of tools], we also reveal information about affordances through action."[8] It is therefore possible to *develop* expertise in particular affordances through a process of differentiation, by "becoming attuned to our environment, being able to make finer distinctions" in the available information.[9]

Historical video games afford players particular actions. First, this is in the most mundane sense, the hardware/control pad allows particular actions. For example, buttons afford pressing. Second, and most relevant in a historical context, the game affords the player (normally through an avatar) particular actions in affecting the historical game world and the screen will produce a particular (normally audio-visual) perceptual information in response to the actions of players. In video games these affordances are determined by developers with a desire to create fun-to-play products, by the limitations of the commonly available technology and also the pressures and conventions of the video game form as it has developed. However, in historical video games, these affordances are also likely to be determined by their reference to something that—though now inaccessible—once existed (the past), by historical evidence and the historian/developer's interpretation, epistemological approach, and story/content decisions.[10] Thus, whilst fun may be a primary determiner of the affordances that make up the game, the desire to create believable historical representations is also important.[11] Accordingly, in historical first-person shooter games such as *Brothers in Arms*, we are afforded actions that represent our avatar running, jumping, and crouching but not floating or flying. Conversely in *Civilization*, we do not have an explicit fictional representative/avatar and can move the camera as if floating above the map. However, the actions of the historical agents depicted within (and thus the affordances of the player) are in some way determined referentially. So, for instance, cavalry can move further, faster than infantry but cannot cross deep water as ships can. Thus, the actions afforded to players often represent intrinsic physical capabilities, training, and skills of a particular historical agent or group of agents (in relation to a given environment) and how these capabilities are/were extended by various tools. In this way, the affordances of historical video games make particular arguments about past action and afford particular opportunities for historical meaning-making and discovery to players. Despite the obvious abstractions of the historical actions into gameplay actions, we can still potentially learn what actions (according to the games historical representation) were afforded particular historical agents (or groups) and why these actions were useful or necessary, by what is afforded us as players.[12]

Civilization makes two significant connections with the ecological approach. First, the game, through the actions it affords players, makes a number of ecological arguments that seem to function as an example of Reed's proposition that "ecological psychology also makes important contact with the discipline of history. The basic material of history is our human ability to transform ourselves collectively, itself a function of our incessant collective efforts after meaning and value."[13] Second, by using the ecological approach to analyze *Civilization*, we can see that it affords the player actions in relation to the practice of historians. What Munslow, drawing from Greg Dening, refers to as "historying."[14]

Ecological arguments

Civilization is a history of human affordances, particularly those that the game posits as integral to the concept of "civilization." The player's historical identity is more complex than in many games as she or he does not have a direct avatar representative in the game space. Instead of gaining the affordances of a particular represented historical agent, the player instead explores the affordances of a represented historical collective, essentially, a group of organisms that in relation to the environment can be viewed as a collective organism with *shared affordances*. This possibility is seemingly supported by Gibson who states that a post box "affords letter mailing to a letter writing human in a community with a postal system."[15] Thus, Gibson opens the idea of affordances beyond the organism as an individual. Though the affordance of posting itself is available to the individual, it is only meaningful as communication because it is part of a shared system of affordances by the collective. Other games, though less focused on this aspect, can also do essentially the same thing. For example, the *Brothers in Arms* series makes this argument about WWII combat through its team command mechanic, which in a (seemingly) collaborative effort opens up new affordances unavailable to the individual (player/avatar). *Civilization* makes a similar argument: often the sharing of particular technologies or knowledge throughout a collective organism opens up new affordances not available to the individual (what I term "macro-affordances"). Thus, whilst agriculture affords an individual the opportunity to survive efficiently within their environment, it affords an entire civilization population growth and urbanization. *Civilization* also demonstrates that sharing these newly realized affordances can occur rapidly and efficiently within human groups because this knowledge can be *mediated*. The game demonstrates the role of social and cultural structures and institutions in extending the availability of these affordances within a given society. For example, a barrack affords the training of veteran troops. The institution functions as a knowledge tool that rapidly reveals new affordances.

Similarly, there are systemic changes brought about by the occasional occurrence of "great persons" who are defined by the game as such by their ability to transform the affordances of the entire collective. This can be seen as an argument for Carlyle's great man theory.[16] However, the fact that these great persons (or rather their effects) are only afforded players whose civilization meets certain criteria also seems to indicate that the game accounts for Spencer's famous criticism of said theory by showing great persons as a product of and dependent on, the affordances of the collective in which they occur.[17] The game also echoes this debate in what it affords the player. Accordingly, because it naturally implicates an "interactivity dilemma, that is the question how much and which parts of the game can be influenced by players, and, conversely, which ones cannot, [the historical video game] resembles greatly the heated nineteenth-century debate on the relation between free will and necessity in history."[18] Poblocki notes that Meier (and indeed *Civilization* itself) seems to support Plekhanov's assumption that "influential individuals can change the *individual features of events and some of their particular consequences*, but they cannot change their general trend . . . [for] *they are themselves the product of this trend.*"[19] In this way both form and historical content are linked and the game cannot help but emphasize that "the force behind many of the [collective] transformations comes from the tension between individuals discovering facts about their relationship to their environment and culturally selected patterns of properties."[20] The ecological approach allows us to bridge an understanding of these different affordances (the represented historical and gameplay), which nonetheless are connected through the tensions of discipline and adaptation, and to see that in *Civilization* (as well as many other games) the power of the individual is explored in tangible ecological terms through action. Thus, by focusing on the transformation of affordances in its gameplay, *Civilization* makes basic arguments about cultural diffusion.

Approaching *Civilization* from an ecological perspective can also allow us to reflect upon how we construct particular historical identities for collectives, in terms of their *shared altered relations* to the environment. For instance, in popular history at least (and in the *Civilization* series) the Celts tend to be grouped together as one culture because of their similar languages and iron working. But in reality these were many different cultural groups (e.g. the Insular Celts, Gauls, Celtiberians, Galatians) with often distinct cultural practices. Within the game, some affordances are often characterized as intrinsic to the civilization and are given to the player as bonuses. For instance, in *Civilization V* the Americans have a bonus called "Manifest Destiny" (all land military units have +1 sight and there is a discount when purchasing territory). *Civilization* accordingly makes an argument for the intrinsic affordances of particular cultures through what is immediately afforded the player that chooses them. These civilization-specific affordances granted to players can be seen as an argument for culture being the most important factor in determining a collective's capabilities. However, conversely, the broader trend of the games' rules make an argument about how the environment is the defining feature in what is afforded particular collectives, particularly in terms of resources, movement, and strategy. Therefore, *Civilization* also argues for an understanding of historical affordances as determined environmentally by what the game environment affords the player.[21] Thus the game puts forward two arguments about the nature and origins of collective affordances: one which suggests that the individual culture is the major factor, and the second which privileges the environment. However, it appears from work by Squire that the second tends to be more widely recognized by students (and thus perhaps all players).[22] This second argument not only makes a strong historical and politically relevant point but also actually supports the ecological perspective itself by highlighting how what is afforded an organism is always dependent on the nature of, and thus its relation to, its environment.

Accordingly, we can see that the game makes ecological arguments by what it affords the player as a unified collective. Also, importantly, the game represents sources (social groups, institutions, sub-collectives, and technologies), which it depicts as enabling these affordances. By doing so, the game also argues the importance of the division of labor (where skill does not have to be distributed evenly) in the development of collective affordance. For example, though fighting with swords may benefit a whole collective, blacksmiths and warriors may be different roles performed by different people. *Civilization* manifests this in its many different unit types.[23] Specialization and mediation such as this allowed the attaining of affordances that would be a huge task (or more likely impossible) for a single agent to achieve. *Civilization* emphasizes this and accordingly, the importance of understanding *collective action*, in terms of the larger movements of history.

Civilization's core argument about history rests on the idea that the ability to not only *utilize* but *transform* affordances (particularly through technology) was the key variable in the progression (or not) of civilizations. Perhaps the most obvious example of this focus is the technology tree, which is a tree diagram of the various "techs" that can be researched by the player's civilization during the game and that shows which combinations of technology are required to unlock further technologies (Figure 4.1).

The tech tree is an excellent representational tool in this context because it takes as its very basis (and superbly demonstrates) how certain affordances afford the discovery of others, how new affordances make old ones obsolete, and how the relationship between the organism and environment is rarely stable and thus dependent (for humans at least) on technology and the adaptive discovery of new affordances. This is particularly important because the environment is also made up of enemy civilizations whose affordances are also constantly adapting. Through play, the tech tree (as well as the various

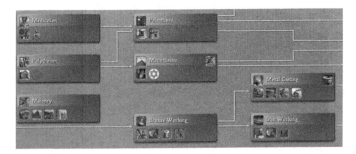

FIGURE 4.1 *"Technological Tree" from the early stage of* Civilization *showing the relationship between various technological advances. Screen capture courtesy of Trevor Owens and Rebecca Mir*

religious, political, and ideological "trees") serves as more than just a visual map and becomes a procedural map of the links between particular tools, knowledge and, most importantly, *collective action*, in the games history of human civilization(s). Accordingly, the tech tree is a core aspect of the game's ecological arguments.

Because of these arguments the games make significant connection with Reed's aforementioned proposition that ecological psychology has important contact with the discipline of history. This, combined with the intrinsic focus (as a game) on action, which includes taking as its primary focus of discourse "affordances," *Civilization* (and other games like it) could even be interpreted as a new approach to the past: "ecological history." Such games link technology, knowledge, progression, dominance, and power through an understanding of these themes in terms of what they afford(ed). What is unique is that they do so in a form that uses a, arguably, naturalized descriptive rhetoric of historical action by affording the player (as a civilization) actions within a challenging interactive experience. Again, this is done within an environment with sufficient pressure to encourage us to learn the significance of what particular elements afford if we are to win. In *Civilization* the abstraction of performatory action becomes less important because the game does not try to represent the historical actions of singular agents but collectives; there is therefore, often no direct equivalent for the player actions to abstract from.

Affording history

Perhaps more important than the game's interesting arguments about past affordances is the second layer of player affordances. *Civilization* also functions as a knowledge tool that extends the affordances of the player by giving them *some* of the affordances of the academic historian. This only really works because being a historian is an exploratory challenge rather than a performatory one (though many tired historians might disagree).[24] From a historical perspective, *Civilization* allows the player actualized (i.e. beyond interpretation) agency within the historian/developers' virtual "story space."[25] This is a space made up of selected evidence, arguments that are found convincing, interpretation, theory, understandings of causation, epistemological assumptions, biases, preferences, resonances, and what is imagined. Consequently, this is essentially linked to the historian's historical understanding and knowledge, which can often take years to develop. True agency (i.e. beyond interpretation) in this story space is normally the sole preserve of the author who creates the historical narrative within it, which is eventually narrated to the audience. However, in all historical video games, but particularly those like *Civilization*, the player is given an actualized share in authoring within the virtual story-space. This is because, as Reynolds argues above, the final historical narrative remains uncertain until the game is played and the player configures it from the mass of historical elements that make up the virtual story space. This indicates a subtle shift from receiving historical narratives toward producing them.

Thus, in *Civilization*, the player is given a *structured* representational environment (virtual story space), within the bounds of which they are free to rearrange and configure various elements. This is structured in that much of the groundwork is already done and the boundaries of the story space established. Therefore, the player is equipped with the knowledge tools of underlying theory work, methodology, pre-selected evidence, ideology, epistemology, and a theory and network of causal relationships (perhaps best indicated by the tech tree). These tools and choices are commonly the reserve of those who are experts in differentiating this information: historians. Accordingly, *Civilization* works as a system that affords players opportunities for playfully writing historical narratives, basic historical inquiry, and "counter histories" and thus, *limited* engagement in the expert practice of the historian. Consequently, there is a move from receiving history to "historying."

Expanding upon these ideas allows us to see *Civilization* as a simulated explorative-discourse system. In such a system there is information to be gained but we can also negotiate and question the limits of the games' representation more actively than with a similar discourse in a book through the gameplay actions we, as both the player and represented collective, are afforded. For instance, let us look at the last of these practices (counter history, or counterfactual history).[26] Counter-history is a useful form of inquiry that seeks new understanding by examining the "simulation gap" between the past as we understand it and a "what if?" scenario.[27] Historians, in fact, do this all the time; it is a natural part of constructing an historical narrative (e.g. an idea of what did happen always constructed in opposition to an idea of what did not happen). Sometimes these thought processes even become full and valuable narratives.[28] When a historian considers a counterfactual scenario, they construct it against their existing knowledge of what did happen but also against their understanding of the variables that could affect such a scenario according to their historical understanding and therefore form a story space. *Civilization* provides a system whereby these variables and their causal links are already accounted for and yet in which multiple stories can be told by players.

Though this is in an admittedly limited capacity, *Civilization* does allow practices like "counter history" to become available without the player spending the years it would normally take to train these affordances to competency by accruing knowledge of evidence, methodology, and theory. In these ways *Civilization* can function as a knowledge tool, extending the player some of the affordances of discourse that are normally the reserve of the historian. It does this by providing a structured causal network of selected and interpreted evidence, thus creating a shared virtual story space that still allows the player to playfully configure historical narratives and counterfactual scenarios.

Conclusion

The ecological approach gives us a solid theory of action with which to analyze historical video games because it allows us to explore history in terms of the actions through which the game cannot help but operate. Thus, in return, the approach allows us to see what particular titles afford both as games and histories. Naturally, therefore, the ecological approach also emphasizes that meaningful historical representations can be produced and received in experiential forms like video games.

The analysis here using the ecological approach has allowed us first to explore how historical video games produce meaning within a compelling ludic framework that challenges players to differentiate historical information as it relates to particular actions. Second, it allows us to examine how games as action-led texts are well-suited to making ecological arguments about the past, can represent macro-affordances as systems of collective action, and (due, partly to the focus on fairness) make arguments that focus on environmental factors and the transformation of affordances through technology or tools. Lastly, the ecological approach shows how the video game (perhaps uniquely) can extend the affordances of players and afford them some of the discursive practice (actions) of the historian. Each of these aspects is dependent upon particular game structures that there is simply not enough room to discuss here. However, in each there is the presentation of opportunities for players to take historically meaningful action.

Games therefore represent past actions through present ones and it could even be argued that this is perhaps the most natural form of rhetoric to describe past action. First, in that functioning as a visual form the "image makers can arouse in us an awareness of what they have seen, of what they have noticed, what they recall, expect, or imagine, and they do so *without converting the information into a different mode.*"[29] Second, by also allowing action, a second layer of information is created and audiences are afforded actively testing some of what they perceive against the arguments of the historian/developer as communicated by the affordances of the system. Lastly, using (even different) actions to represent action infers a somewhat lesser degree of abstraction than using spoken or written language. This means that the video game as a form may be better suited to some kinds of historical representation than written history (and of course vice versa). It could then well be that video games will provide new and interesting ways to explore our relationship with the past and that the Gibsonian ecological approach will prove crucial to both understanding, and perhaps even creating, these games that represent the past. From this perspective we can approach historical video games as texts of action, skill, and challenge and simultaneously systems of representation, exploring how these representations are constructed audio-visually, and importantly, *ludically*.

Notes

1 Historical games here are defined, not by their ludic (game) genre (e.g. racing, roleplaying, or first-person shooter), but by their concern with creating representations of the past. "Thus we wish to define a historical game outside the parameters of 'activity' (shoot, manage, take a turn), and within that of its world setting." (Esther MacCallum-Stewart and Justin Parlser, "Controversies: Historicising the Computer Game," *Proceedings of DiGRA 2007 Conference* (2007): 203–210.) The historical games genre's popularity is immediately apparent when we consider that (according to vgchartz.com) *Call of Duty: World at War* has now sold over thirteen million copies worldwide.

2 See my arguments for this in Adam Chapman, "Is Sid Meier's *Civilization* History?" *Rethinking History* (forthcoming, 2013).

3 Similarly, read my arguments for how we should approach these games by privileging analysis of form in Adam Chapman, "Privileging Form Over Content: Analysing Historical Video games", *The Journal of Digital Humanities*, 1, no. 2 (2012): n.p. http://journalofdigitalhumanities.org/1-2/privileging-form-over-content-by-adam-chapman/.http://journalofdigitalhumanities.org/1-2/privileging-form-over-content-by-adam-chapman/

4 James J. Gibson, *The Ecological Approach to Visual Perception*. New Jersey: Lawrence Erlbaum Associates, 1986; Jeffrey Linderoth, "Why Gamers Don't Learn More: An Ecological Approach to Games as Learning Environments," *Journal of Gaming and Virtual Worlds*, 4, no. 1 (2012): 45–62; Jeffrey Linderoth, "Beyond the Digital Divide: An Ecological Approach to Gameplay," *Proceedings of DiGRA 2011 Conference: Think, Design, Play 4* (2011): 1–15; Jeffrey Linderoth and Ulrika Bennerstedt, "This is Not a Door: An Ecological Approach to Computer Games," *Proceedings of DiGRA Conference 2007* (2007): 600–609.

5 Linderoth, "Beyond the Digital Divide," 4.

6   Linderoth, "Beyond the Digital Divide," 4. Linderoth uses the example of a stone that affords, "being thrown for someone with a hand and an arm of certain strength ... [but this] is not an affordance for an infant or someone with a disability in their arms or hands" (Linderoth, 2011, 4).

7   Eleanor J. Gibson and Anne D. Pick, *An Ecological Approach to Perceptual Learning and Development*. New York: Oxford University Press, 2000, 16.

8   Linderoth, "Beyond the Digital Divide," 5.

9   Linderoth, "Beyond the Digital Divide," 5.

10 For more on these ideas surrounding historical narrative creation, see Alun Munslow, *Narrative and History*. Basingstoke: Palgrave Macmillan, 2007.

11 It should be noted that Gibson pointed to the flaw in representation as a concept and as a term: "There is no such thing as a literal re-presentation of an earlier optic array" (Gibson, 1986, 279). However, it is not necessary to relinquish the word when using a postmodernist perspective (as I do here) whereby the flaws of representation are always consciously acknowledged and the term is used to imply the subjective and constructed relationship between historian, history, and past.

12 This may be as simple as being able to move the camera to gain information about an in-game character's actions. It should also at this point be noted that we can only really talk about opportunities for action that exist within the games for a typical player but of course the ability to perceive or utilize these depends on the capabilities of individual players.

13 Edward S. Reed, *Encountering the World: Toward an Ecological Psychology*. New York: Oxford University Press, 1996, 188.

14 Alun Munslow, *The Future of History*. Basingstoke: Palgrave Macmillan, 2010, 8.

15 Gibson, *The Ecological Approach*, 139.

16 Thomas Carlyle, *On Heroes, Hero-Worship, and the Heroic in History*. New York: Cosimo Inc, 2010.

17 Though Spencer argues his ideas using problematic examples, even contemporarily his refutation of Carlyle's ideas has some validity: "the genesis of a great man depends on the long series of complex influences which has produced the race in which he appears, and the social state into which that race has slowly grown .... Before he can remake his society, his society must make him" (Spencer, 1896, 30–31).

18 Kacpar Poblocki, "Becoming State: The Bio-Cultural Imperialism of Sid Meier's *Civilization*," *Focaal*, 39 (2002): 167.

19 Niall Ferguson, *Virtual History*. London: Papermac, 1998, 41. Emphasis in original.

20 Reed, *Encountering the World*, 188.

21 This environmental determinism argument is of the type infamously made by Jared Diamond, *Guns, Germs and Steel*. London: Chatto & Windus, 1997.

22 Kurt Squire, "From Content to Context: Video games as Designed Experience," *Educational Researcher*, 35, no. 8 (2006): 19–29.

23 For example, both workers and warriors benefit the civilization though each affords the player different things.

24 Exploratory challenges are where "it is a challenge for the assumed player to know what action to take but executing the action is more or less trivial" (Linderoth, 2011, 10). Games such as chess, poker, and monopoly emphasize this type of challenge.

25 "[T]he authored model of what, how, when, why and to whom things happened in the past, which the reader/consumer enters into when they read, view or 'experience' the past, constituted as history" (Munslow, 2007, 6).

26 This idea was first explored by Atkins who noted that *Civilization* made counter-history, normally the reserve of professional historians, available to a popular audience.

27 Ian Bogost, *Persuasive Games*. Massachusetts: MIT Press, 2007, 43.

28 Such as those in Ferguson's edited collection, *Virtual History*.

29 Gibson, *The Ecological Approach*, 262. Original emphasis. This is even more important in realist games such as the aforementioned *Brothers in Arms*.

Works cited

Atkins, Barry. "History is bunk?: Historiographic barbarism in Civilization", English language preprint, published as "La storia è un'assurdità: Civilization come esempio di barbarie storiografica?" in Ed. Matteo Bittanti, trans. Valentina Paggiarin, *Civilization: Storie Virtuali, Fantasie Reali*. Milan: Costa & Nolan, 2005, 65–81.

Bogost, Ian. *Persuasive Games*. Massachusetts: MIT Press, 2007.

Carlyle, Thomas. *On Heroes, Hero-Worship, and the Heroic in History*. New York: Cosimo Inc, 2010.

Chapman, Adam. "Is *Sid Meier's Civilization* History?" *Rethinking History* (forthcoming, 2013). http://www.tandfonline.com/doi/abs/10.1080/13642529.2013.774719#.UZ9I79ggtOQ.

Chapman, Adam. "Privileging Form Over Content: Analysing Historical Video games," *The Journal of Digital Humanities*, 1, no. 2 (2012): n.p. http://journalofdigitalhumanities.org/1-2/privileging-form-over-content-by-adam-chapman/, accessed 24 May 2013.

Diamond, Jared. *Guns, Germs and Steel*. London: Chatto & Windus, 1997.

Ferguson, Niall. *Virtual History*. London: Papermac, 1998.

Gibson, Eleanor J. and Anne D. Pick. *An Ecological Approach to Perceptual Learning and Development*. New York: Oxford University Press, 2000.

Gibson, James J. *The Ecological Approach to Visual Perception*. New Jersey: Lawrence Erlbaum Associates, 1986.

Linderoth, Jeffrey. "Why Gamers Don't Learn More: An Ecological Approach to Games as Learning Environments," *Journal of Gaming and Virtual Worlds*, 4, no. 1 (2012): 45–62.

Linderoth, Jeffrey. "Beyond the Digital Divide: An Ecological Approach to Gameplay," *Proceedings of DiGRA 2011 Conference: Think, Design, Play*, 4 (2011): 1–15, http://www.digra.org/dl/db/11307.03263.pdf, accessed 10 August 2012.

Linderoth, Jeffrey and Ulrika Bennerstedt. "This is Not a Door: An Ecological Approach to Computer Games," *Proceedings of DiGRA Conference 2007* (2007): 600–609.

MacCallum-Stewart, Esther and Justin Parlser. "Controversies: Historicising the Computer Game," *Proceedings of DiGRA 2007 Conference* (2007): 203–210, http://www.digra.org/dl/db/07312.51468.pdf, accessed 5 June 2011.

Munslow, Alun. *The Future of History*. Basingstoke: Palgrave Macmillan, 2010.

Munslow, Alun. *Narrative and History*. Basingstoke: Palgrave Macmillan, 2007.

Poblocki, Kaspar. "Becoming state: The Bio-Cultural Imperialism of *Sid Meier's Civilization*," *Focaal*, 39 (2002): 163–177.

Reed, Edward S. *Encountering the World: Toward an Ecological Psychology*. New York: Oxford University Press, 1996.

Spencer, Herbert. *The Study of Sociology*. New York: D. Appleton, 1896, http://www.questia.com/read/96277756/the-study-of-sociology, accessed 15 September 2012.

Squire, Kurt. "From Content to Context: Video games as Designed Experience," *Educational Researcher*, 35, no. 8 (2006): 19–29.

Games cited

Brothers in Arms. Montreal: Ubisoft, 2005/2005/2008.

Call of Duty: World at War. Santa Monica, CA: Infinity Ward, Activision, 2008.

Sid Meier's Civilization. Alameda, CA: MicroProse, 1991.

Sid Meier's Civilization II. Alameda, CA: MicroProse, 1996.

Sid Meier's Civilization III. Paris, France: Firaxis, Infogrames, 2001.

Sid Meier's Civilization IV: Colonization. Novato, CA: Firaxis Games, 2K Games, 2005.

Sid Meier's Civilization V. Novato, CA: Firaxis Games, 2K Games, 2010.

PART TWO

History Written by the West

This part tackles an important and very serious issue, for both historians and gamers (as well as a number of others, too). This issue is the tendency to focus on those histories and concerns of Western, predominantly white European, societies. Such a tendency tends to privilege particular perspectives and ways of seeing the world, which assume a Western perspective and thus divides the world into categories of Self and Other. In part this is historically understandable, since history as a discipline has traditionally relied on the reconstruction of a past through material evidence, which privileges a particular understanding of what constitutes evidence and thus, without realizing it, history comes to mean what Western societies define it to be. However, such an approach tends to reimagine history from the perspective of the West, taking ownership in the process of those cultures deemed to be "without history."

Bembeneck first examines the use of the barbarians as Other, a concept that was used by the Romans (and the Greeks before them) to define the Self. Looking at games set in Ancient Rome, she argues that games have tended unconsciously to adopt this perspective that overlooks differences in the Other to provide a homogeneous depiction of the Self. Mir and Owens then take this concept forward to look at the implicit assumptions of *Sid Meier's Colonization*, which they argue perpetuate such beliefs in the ways in which they represent European colonization of the so-called "New World" (itself a negation of the history of the indigenous population) as an inevitable "march of progress." Holdenried and Trépanier, too, look at the Colonization of the Americas to assess the power structures of games attempting to depict the same period, focusing on the problematic concept of "dominance" in relations between European invaders and Aztec populations. Making the traditional Other central to a historical narrative, Kwon then turns from the West to the East, looking at the hugely successful novel and game series *Three Kingdoms* to ask whether the game normalizes national experiences and images of the nation on which modern national identities are sometimes founded. Finally, in Hasegawa's essay this geographical Other is examined as a doubly marginalized concept in Japanese girls' *otome* games, in which adolescent girls can "play" at falling in love with historical figures as a way both of viewing their past and therefore themselves.

Recommended books to understand more about non-Western history and Orientalism:

Rorato, Laura and Anna Saunders. *The Essence and the Margin: National Identities and Collective Memories in Contemporary European Culture*. Amsterdam, NY: Rodopi, 2009.

Said, Edward W. *Orientalism*. Toronto, ON: Knopf Doubleday Publishing Group, 1979.

Sardar, Ziauddin. *Orientalism*. Maidenhead: Open University Press, 1999.

Todorov, Tzvetan. *The Conquest of America: The Question of the Other*. Norman, OK: University of Oklahoma Press, 1984.

Wolf, Eric R. *Europe and the People Without History*. Berkeley and Los Angeles, CA: University of California Press, 2010.

5

Phantasms of Rome: Video Games and Cultural Identity

Emily Joy Bembeneck
University of Michigan

The term "barbarian" has a rich history of meanings. In modern English, it typically signifies an uncouth or even savage behavior. In a game like *Everquest*, barbarian is a particular race of large, Saxon-looking humans with a great deal of blunt force but limited intelligence.[1] For the ancient Greeks, the term "barbarian" referred to a people whose language sounded like gibberish. They were the antithesis of Greek: a non-Greek by definition. The barbarian was the Other against which the Greeks could define what it meant to be Greek.[2] It is this notion of barbarian, denoting a lack of cultural identity, that we will be looking at here, particularly in terms of barbarians in the Roman arena and in video games with a Roman presence.

Video games often use the figure of the barbarians to address the question of cultural identity by placing notions of a cultural Other in an idealized past, often that of the Roman past in which anonymous and inferior barbarians act as a foil to the civilized and superior Romans. In truth, even this is somewhat historical. Just as video games for us are a fantastical experience in a virtual space inherently separate from reality, the Roman arena was a space set apart from the everyday experiences of the Roman population, a space in which notions of cultural identity were ideologically presented against a cultural Other. Within its walls, the lowest member of society was free to speak to the emperor, and the wildest creatures from the extreme reaches of the empire were present at the center of the city.[3] Monsters of men and beasts raged at each other, acting out the violent forces of empire on the nature surrounding it. This focal point of Rome, the place of the arena games, was a center where identities were forged in the collisions of near and far, of high and low, and of Self and Other.

In this chapter, we will see how Roman fantasies of identity are reimagined in video games today. I will argue that the various representations of barbarians in three video games are closely related to the understanding of a cultural Other as ideologically presented in Rome's arena. Further, we will see how this representation is sometimes used as a cultural myth in modern times for our own understanding of cultural identity as a fantastical homogeneity amidst the reality of diversity. But first, let us briefly consider the Roman understanding of barbarians as presented in the arena and thus construct a framework from which to critique and compare our game examples.

The Roman understanding of the barbarians as cultural Other

Although the Roman Empire, and the city of Rome itself, were both characterized by a particularly diverse cultural ecosystem, the arena was a place where cultural identity was forged through ideological representation of barbarians as Other. Although the games of the arena involved a variety of activities and representations, those most applicable to our study here are those of the gladiators themselves.[4]

Gladiators originally were drawn from conquered prisoners of war and thus embodied the notion of the frontier, of the barbarian, of the threatening Other on the periphery.[5] Even after the Italic tribe the Samnites, for example, were long part of the Roman Empire, some gladiators were still organized under that name.[6] The name "Samnite" implied a separation from Rome due to its implicit reminder of war with outside tribes of Italians and helped mark barbarians as a non-Roman Other. Later, gladiators also came from the ranks of criminals, slaves, and even volunteers who saw the chance of fame and fortune on the arena floor.

Gladiators projected the identity of the Other, not only through their inherent status as either non-Roman or sub-Roman, but through their very appearance. Gladiators often wore helmets that covered their faces, which served the double purpose of ensuring anonymity to the crowd and also to their opponent who may have been a comrade in their gladiatorial school. They were separated into particular armor and fighting classes and, as we see in the tale of the martyr Perpetua, were easily recognizable as non-Roman.[7] This particular appearance, coupled with the knowledge that they were outcasts, prisoners of war, or former Romans who had volunteered to forego that privilege of identity, created a recognizable Other whose gruesome defeat could be cheered and relished.

In the everyday experience of a Roman, however, visual diversity would have been extreme, particularly in the late Republican and Imperial eras. Individuals from Gaul, Britain, and the far eastern provinces would have been seen on a regular basis. However, this kind of everyday encounter in which those who were once barbarians but were later recognized as Romans would be seen in juxtaposition with the depiction of barbarians as inferior, conquered peoples on monuments such as the pillars of Trajan and Marcus Aurelius.[8] At the time in which these pillars were constructed, Rome had extended its borders as far as it ever would and thus had acquired peoples from the far stretches of the Mediterranean. Thus Romans, even those with non-Roman ancestry, were accustomed to viewing themselves on various monuments as well as in the arena as visually homogeneous versus a barbarian Other.[9] This was a very different experience from their diverse reality and it further highlights the problem of understanding Roman-ness or any cultural identity in the midst of extreme heterogeneity.

Even on the arena floor, gladiators mirrored this complex reality when they managed to embody the Roman ideals that could conquer and overwrite the former identity of Other. In the case of some gladiatorial matches, the winning gladiator could affirm the ideals of the crowd and thus join into that identity against his opponent, sometimes achieving his freedom in the process.[10] A gladiator who performed admirably and showcased the ideals of Roman society could no longer serve as an Other in the arena. Through his strength and courage, he had identified himself as a member of the Roman crowd, as part of the Self, and the crowd reacted by crying for his freedom since he no longer belonged on the floor, but in the stands.

Through the complex fantasies brought to life in the space of the Roman arena, the games of the gladiators were able to simultaneously represent not only the barbarian Other as uncultured subhuman and the elevation of Roman martial ideals as the uniting force of society, but also the periphery of the Empire being subsumed into the center. In this magic circle that started past the arena entrance, actors on the arena floor engaged in a representational metamorphosis of unrealistic ideals into fantastic reality.[11] The power of this ideological fantasy was great enough to influence even the actions of the emperor Vespasian soon after he rose to power. Having come from the East, he wanted to emphasize his Roman-ness and thus held extravagant games at Rome.[12] He realized that the Eastern periphery was fearful and unknown, so to avoid this stigma, he chose to bring himself to the center and incorporate himself in Rome by putting on games. Not only did Vespasian realize the cultural capital available in the arena, but so did the conquered people themselves. The amphitheater came to stand for Roman ideals to such an extent that it was a prime tool in cities' attempts to be more Roman than their neighbor, especially in the provinces.[13] Before an individual even set foot in the amphitheater, he was already being presented with a declaration of Roman identity and its ideals.[14]

The arena was not only a passive representational space though; the spectators in the audience were actually active participants in this fantasy game. As Augustine writes, an individual in the arena "was not the man who came, but one of the crowd."[15] The images and actions on the arena floor were able to be so powerful because of the homogeny imposed through crowd participation.[16] Even ancients recognized this collective membership in the arena fantasy. Ovid remarked that, in the arena, "he who saw the wounds, had a wound."[17] Although class lines were still a reality in the very seating arrangements of the arena, everyone was yet equal in the sense that anyone could approach the Emperor in the arena and everyone was of higher status than those on the arena floor.[18] This sense of class equality was another part of the fantasy of the arena, but one which aided in the rest of the imaginative act and strengthened the understanding of cultural identity presented by the representations of the games. In fact, the very possession of class itself, whether low or high, was a mark of Roman-ness because it was one of the most important traits lacking in those on the arena floor.[19]

Similarly, in video games, the player is invited to take part in an act of fantasy in which he or she projects his identity or a portion of it into the game through the activity of play.[20] In the process of playing, the player takes part, not just as a spectator, but as an interactive member of a particular group. In the games we are looking at, this group is either the Romans as a cultural group or else some other singular civilization. For the duration of the play experience, the player is a member of the cultural Self versus one or more separate groups that play the role of either a barbarian Other or a separately defined culture that emphasizes its difference from the player's civilization through their unique features and simultaneously affirms the player's homogeneous cultural identification.

Let us begin by looking at *Civilization V* and its treatment of barbarians not as a separate culture, but as an inferior, culture-deprived population, bereft of any group identity aside from that of the Other.[21]

A *Civilization* like no other

As we have seen in Chapter 4, the *Civilization* franchise is a series of turn-based strategy games in which the player builds a civilization from ancient times into the future of space colonization. Players choose a single civilization to play throughout an instance of the game, and progress their civilization by founding cities via Settler units, discovering new technologies through the scientific output produced by cities, and conquering enemies with military units trained within cities.

In *Civilization V*, the difference between the player's cultural group and the Other(s) is primarily represented through the visual characteristics of the units and cities belonging to each group. Each civilization in a game has a particular color that is represented on the banner that each of their units carries. Further, it is this same color that frames their city names on the world map and is represented on a coat of arms when the game communicates to the player some event in which the civilization has partaken, such as a declaration of war. Although they are not a civilization as the Romans or Americans are, barbarians also have a distinct color in the game to mark them as a separate population group. Their banner and coat of arms is always red, but there is no red framework to their cities' names because they have no cities.

Barbarians in *Civilization V* neither build cities nor take cities, and neither do they have the possibility of either because they are unable ever to attain the status of civilization. From the early ancient era through to the future beyond the present day, barbarians only have thatched huts located in remote locations of the world map. While the cities of other civilizations have built skyscrapers and spaceships, barbarians may have the technology to build modern military units, but are never given the capability of building cities and thus truly progressing as a group. Instead, their primitive huts can still be found even late in the game, still granting the same small economic bonus upon conquest as they did in the early years of history. Barbarians become less and less relevant throughout the game because the game's rules inherently limit them from progressing as other populations do. Further, even if barbarians were to capture an enemy Settler unit, the unit will change to a generic Worker upon capture and lose the "Build City" ability. Barbarians cannot even own the units with which to found cities, let alone cities themselves.

Civilizations in the game are distinguished not only by their color but also by particular units and buildings that only they can construct. For example, the French are the only civilization that has access to the Musketeer unit, and Persians are the only group who can build Immortals. As such, various unique units will make an appearance throughout any given game, underlining the separate cultural identities and unique status of the civilizations in play. Barbarians, however, have no such units. Instead, they build a predictable set of units, the limited possibilities of which are coded into the game files. These units are closely related to the state of technological progress in the game, and usually, barbarians build units that are inferior to those available to other civilizations.[22] Thus, when a barbarian attacks a player's city, it is rarely a force to be reckoned with. Rather, barbarians serve only to provide a nuisance along the frontiers; there is no great Attila the Hun, and no marauding Visigoths, to bring down the greatest empire ever known. Such a barbarian threat would be inconceivable in *Civilization V*'s generic game rules.[23]

Despite the differences between separate civilizations in this game, internally, a single civilization is always visually homogeneous, even immediately after an act of integration whether on the part of the player or the AI. Throughout a game session, a player will typically use her military units to conquer a different civilization's city or will suffer a conquest at the AI's hands. In real-world circumstances, such a case of occupation would not lead to an immediate cultural assimilation, nor even necessarily an eventual one. In *Civilization V*, however, a conquered city suffers from civil unrest for a short while but otherwise takes on the appearance of every other city in the empire. Thus, when the Romans take over Tokyo (in one random example), the name Tokyo may remain, but any outward trappings of Japanese civilization are instantly erased. Military units that had defended Tokyo are destroyed and civilian units immediately change to Roman civilians. Although barbarian units are typically destroyed in battle as well, one civilization has a unique ability that allows more. If a player has chosen to play as Bismarck, leader of the Germans, she is able to flip barbarian military units to her side. When this occurs, the barbarian unit immediately changes from carrying a red banner to carrying a silver banner, the color of Bismarck's troops. There is no outward sign that the members of this particular squadron are not German at all and the game does not allow for desertion or reversion.[24] Once Bismarck conquers them, it is as if they were never barbarian at all.

Barbarians are a lesser group of players; the players of named civilizations, whether human or artificial players, have the opportunity to build cities, expand their empire, and eventually win the game. Barbarians do not have the option to have a capital, found cities, or participate meaningfully in the game. They do not exist in any diplomatic form unlike the other civilizations, and thus cannot be partnered with, allied with, extorted, betrayed, or defended. Although barbarians do make an appearance in city-state negotiations, it is only as a potential target for destruction. Throughout the game, independent city-states will ask the player to complete tasks or acquire resources for which they offer a bonus in reputation. Barbarians do appear in some of these tasks, but only as an annoyance to be eliminated. Thus, rather than a complex diplomatic relationship between two groups of people, barbarians are only a means to an end. There is no potential of raising reputation with barbarians because they are incapable of such a level of human interaction. They attack or are attacked, and typically, overwhelmingly conquered in the process.

This treatment of barbarians versus civilizations and city-states is the representation of a culture-less Other. Beyond just an affirmation of a player's own civilization and cultural identity through a barbarian counter-example, barbarians serve to define culture itself (and civilization) through their lack of it. *Civilization V* suggests, through this representational choice, that civilization is the same as culture and, more subversively, that those without it cannot attain it and have no social or economic potential of their own, but rather exist only to serve the interests of those superior to them.[25]

Slaving away in *Grand Ages: Rome*

Grand Ages: Rome is a city-building simulation that uses the narrative of the Roman Republic in the first century BC to provide a framework for missions and objectives. The player chooses a Roman family as their identity and plays as a provincial governor completing tasks for a superior in the hopes of political advancement. Each mission asks the player to reach some level of city development and/or military victory over competing Roman politicians.

In *Grand Ages: Rome*, this visually distinct representation of barbarians and Romans continues, while furthering the argument that barbarians have no societal purpose, but are instead only useful as slight economic bonuses for the player.[26] As we saw in *Civilization V*, barbarians in *Grand Ages: Rome* also assume a single appearance through all scenarios and all maps versus a varied cast of alternate civilizations. In this game, various Roman factions and leaders are distinguished by contrasting flags and correspondingly colored uniforms, but barbarians universally carry a somewhat anonymous banner of gray. Further, barbarians do not congregate or form distinct cities or empires of their own. Rather, they are only present as small villages on a map. These villages may either be subjugated in order to extract resources or they may be razed in which case the barbarians are killed except for those the player chooses to take as slaves.

This game's use of barbarians as inconsequential slave labor stands in contrast to the game's representation of Roman classes as strictly demarcated groups with particular crucial functions in the economic machine of a Roman city. As such, while different classes of Romans need to be recruited actively and somewhat equally as all strata are necessary for a successful city, barbarian slaves—whether acquired through battle or more passively—are a dispensable form of cheap labor that is not necessary to a city's survival.[27] As such, they are marked as inferior to Romans, not simply due to their lack of culture or fine clothes, but due to their inability to contribute usefully to society. As with the function of class within the Roman arena discussed above, class in *Grand Ages: Rome* becomes a signification of Roman-ness.[28] Together, everyone in the arena, whether high or low, is equal in the sense they can speak to the Emperor and have the status of being a spectator rather than a class-less participant on the arena floor. In *Grand Ages: Rome*, all humans, regardless of Roman faction, are part of some class and thus have a role to play in society—except for barbarians. In fact, one of the forms of labor for which a player may use barbarian slaves is as gladiators in their city's arena!

Admittedly, this game's focus is on the factional squabbles of first century BC Rome and not on the marauding barbarian tribes of the later centuries. However, the presence of barbarians as a subclass of people is a representational choice, one which reiterates the underlying narrative framework of civil war by contrasting the cultural identity of the factions against a weak backdrop of anonymous barbarians. Further, the focus on barbarian weakness betrays the game's inherent judgment that the only significant culture is that of the Romans, a perspective designed to affirm the player's temporary fantasy identity as a Roman noble. However, historically in the first century BCE, the barbarians that Rome encountered, particularly those of Gaul and Britain, were of distinct cultural groups with unique appearances, practices, and fighting styles. They were real enemies in their own right, not just weak villages to burn and enslave. Further, the barbarians of Gaul and Britain were not simply conquered and pillaged for use as slaves in Roman mines. The Gauls were Romanized and able to achieve citizenship in the Empire and even political positions of authority in Roman cities.[29] In *Grand Ages: Rome*, by contrast, the highest status a barbarian can hope to achieve is that of a slave.

Although *Grand Ages: Rome* provides a fantastical but mostly faithful representation of the events leading to Augustus' reign, its depiction of barbarians as merely inferior villagers vastly simplifies the actual array of cultural diversity and diplomatic interests during the time period. Barbarians in this game are a mythical construct that serve to emphasize Roman-ness at the expense of realistic diversity.

Attack of the diverse Others in *Rome: Total War*

Rome: Total War is a strategy game with both real-time and turn-based elements that invites players to construct and recruit various kinds of soldiers and then organize them strategically on the field with the aim of winning pitched battles. The game offers various missions and objectives in its main campaign that incorporate administrative duties, diplomacy, and population management along with the primary military aspect of the game.

These somewhat simplistic views of Roman versus Barbarian in the game examples above are quite different from the depiction of these distinct groups in the game *Rome: Total War*, particularly in its expansion entitled "Barbarian Invasion."[30] The representation of barbarians in this game provides a striking counter-example to those we have seen earlier in this chapter and allows us to better understand the use of a generic, inferior barbarian as a particular cultural myth that is a reconstructed fantasy, unrelated to the actual experience and status of barbarians in the ancient world. Further, it allows us to see our own usage of this myth to provide an idealistic cultural Other against which we can define a notion of an easily distinguishable cultural Self, purged of diversity and simplified to a clinically clean image that presents a sterilized picture of cultural identity, detached from reality. These representations of the barbarian are not simply misguided understandings of the past, but rather evidence of our own struggles to reconcile diversity and cultural identity in our global culture outside the game.

Rome: Total War: "Barbarian Invasion" differs in its presentation of barbarians in that it specifically/explicitly names the barbarians within the game. Although the title of the expansion is in fact "Barbarian Invasion," within the game, each "barbarian" group is a named culture in its own right. Thus, instead of using the anonymous term "barbarian," the game separates them and names them, and in so doing, elevates them to an equal status with Rome. Not only do these groups now have unique names, but also the player's option to choose one of these diverse barbarian groups as their cultural identity in a play session shows an implicit reinforcement of individuality inherent in the game's architecture. Whereas in our other game examples, barbarians were an anonymous subculture that placed no threat on the player, in this game the player is able to choose whether to play as Roman or as one of the barbarian cultural groups. Each barbarian culture has its own particular strengths and fighting styles, its own starting location, and its own particular flag. Further, each barbarian cultural group has the ability to enter into diplomatic negotiations with other cultures on the map. Barbarians are able to take cities and expand their holdings, constructing in the process a cultural and geographical base that can and often will rival the Romans or other groups on the map.

In this game, there are no generic and inferior barbarians of the kind we saw in the *Civilization V* and *Grand Ages: Rome*. There are no anonymous villages waiting to be destroyed and pillaged with no diplomatic alternative. In effect, *Rome: Total War*: "Barbarian Invasion" does not actually incorporate this breed of mythical barbarian at all. It has uniquely identifiable cultures that are "barbarian" only in the sense that they are not Roman. However, as playable cultures, these "barbarians" must be able to offer a unified identity for the player to assume, unique from the other players in the game, both Romans and other barbarian groups. As such, every cultural group in this game is defined on its own merits regardless of their relationship to the Romans. Here, there is no inherent value structure that automatically denotes Romans as a superior group over the generic barbarian masses. Barbarians as an anonymous, inferior cultural Other do not exist here. Rather, every group in the game serves as an Other to everyone else and thus the term "barbarians" has been stripped of its negative meaning, at least within the game.

Despite this refreshing change in the representation of barbarians, the inherent diversity of the Romans is still sanitized in favor of strict lines marking Roman as one thing and Celt/Hun/Saxon as another. The truth that the Roman arena was composed of a variety of these groups is ignored.

Conclusion

The depiction of barbarians in the first two game examples is a mythical construct representing a cultural Other that provides a vastly inferior foil for the idealistic notion of a homogeneous and easily identifiable cultural Self. In *Rome: Total War: "Barbarian Invasion,"* however, every group is different from every other and must be defined by its own strengths and weaknesses rather than against a weak and inferior Other. The representation of barbarians in this last example shows us a more realistic view of barbarians as cultures in their own right, but still avoids any internal diversity in each group.

Much as the Romans themselves attempted to negotiate the problematic lines of cultural identity through the fantasies of the arena—which perhaps constitutes their own way of imposing making sense of the world through "play"—so too do we in our video games. The fascination with easily identifiable cultural groups is not some aspect of design limitations, but rather evidence of issues related to cultural diversity and integration in the world outside the game. Struggles to identify the meaning of American, for example, are easily solved in a context like *Civilization V*, where Americans all carry a blue flag and look like little blue, cloned soldiers. The difficulty that some individuals may have in identifying a Muslim as American in New York or a Hispanic as American in Arizona is no longer an issue when visual diversity has been removed in favor of a generic "American" appearance. There is no multiculturalism in this fantasy game space; there exist only Us and Them.[31] Further, there is no gray space between the two categories even when those groups are equals. In most cases, there is no question of which group is superior.

Games are a place where the rules of reality are constructed as temporarily separate from the world outside the game, much like the experience within the walls of the Roman arena. Barbarians as a conquered or conquerable Other remain today a powerful object reflecting back to us an idealistic and easily identifiable opposite that affirms our own sense of cultural identity and belonging. The myth of the barbarian Other is a comforting fantasy that temporarily removes the beautiful diversity that defines culture in this global age.

Notes

1 Sony Online Entertainment, *Everquest*. San Diego, CA: SOE, 1999.

2 See, for example, Edith Hall, *Inventing the Barbarian: Greek Self-Definition through Tragedy*. Oxford: Clarendon Press, 1991.

3 The arena is sometimes even referred to as the Roman "parliament," though this may be a little too generous. Keith Hopkins, "Murderous Games," in Ed. Keith Hopkins, *Death and Renewal*. Cambridge: Cambridge University Press, 1985, 1–30: 16. See also David S. Potter, "Performance, Power, and Justice in the High Empire," in Ed. W.J. Slater, *Roman Theater and Society*. Ann Arbor, MI: University of Michigan, 1996; Traugott Bollinger, *Theatralis Licentia*. Winterthur: Hans Schellenberg, 1969, 24–73.

4 There is a rich history of scholarship on the Roman games and on Roman gladiators specifically. A good place to start is David S. Potter, "Spectacle," in Ed. David S. Potter, *A Companion to the Roman Empire*. Malden, MA: Blackwell Publishing, 2006, 385–408.

5 Carlin A. Barton, *Sorrow of the Ancient Romans*. Princeton, NJ: Princeton University Press, 1993, 13.

6 The Thracians were another group of gladiators named for an ethnic group and distinguished from other gladiators by his armor. For further discussion of gladiatorial groups, see Eckart Köhne, Cornelia Ewigleben, and Ralph

Jackson, *Gladiators and Caesars*. Berkeley, CA: University of California Press, 2000.

7 *The Passion of Saints Perpetua and Felicity*, 3.2. For an English translation, see Shewring, W. H.*The Passion of SS Perpetua and Felicity Together with the Sermons of Saint Augustine on These Saints*. San Francisco: Ignatius Press. 2002.

8 The column of Trajan celebrates his two victories over the Dacians, a population of Thracians living in the Danube region. Marcus Aurelius' column celebrates similar military victories also in the region of the Danube. For more information and general reference, see Mark Wilson Jones, *Principles of Roman Architecture*. New Haven: Yale University Press, 2000.

9 For a more comprehensive discussion of the barbarian figure in Roman art, see I.M. Ferris, "The Pity of War," in Ed. Erich S. Gruen, *Cultural Identity in the Ancient Mediterranean*. Los Angeles, CA: Getty Publications, 2011, 185–201.

10 Suetonius, *Tiberius*, 47; Cassius Dio, *Historia Romana*, 57.11.6.

11 Paul Plass, *The Game of Death in Ancient Rome*. Madison, WI: University of Wisconsin Press, 1995, 27.

12 Thomas Wiedemann, *Emperors and Gladiators*. New York: Routledge, 1992, 42.

13 Wiedemann, *Emperors and Gladiators*, 41.

14 Katherine E. Welch, *The Roman Amphitheatre*. Cambridge: Cambridge University Press, 2007.

15 Augustine, *Confessions*, 6.8.

16 Garrett G. Fagan, *Lure of the Arena: Social Psychology and the Crowd at the Roman Games*. Cambridge: Cambridge University Press, 2011.

17 Ovid, *Ars Amatoria*, 1.165–166. Ovid is here speaking of the arena as a location where people fall in love. He remarks that while spectators watch gladiators get wounded, they themselves get wounded by Cupid's arrow. A few lines later, he says that after someone has felt Cupid's dart, he "becomes a part of the show he sees." Ovid is able to successfully use the arena and its effects on a spectator as part of this metaphor because the power of spectator engagement in the events of the arena was a real and familiar thing.

18 See Wiedemann, *Emperors and Gladiators*, 130–ff.

19 See Barton, *Sorrows of the Ancient Romans*, 14–ff; Wiedemann, *Emperors and Gladiators*, 28–ff, for further discussion on the debasement of even volunteer gladiators. On their damaged status in society outside the arena boundaries, see Hopkins, "Murderous Games," 23. See also Tertullian, *De Spectaculis*, 22. Those emperors who appeared in the arena, Caligula, Nero, and Commodus, were "a threat to established morality" and later reviled as poor emperors. See Wiedemann, *Emperors and Gladiators*, 131.

20 Group identity with which the player can temporarily merge in play is one of the main ways to create emotion in game design according to David

Freeman, *Creating Emotion in Games: The Craft and Art of Emotioneering.* Topeka, KS: Sagebrush Education Resources, 2003, 169–170.

21 Firaxis Games, *Civilization V.* Novato, CA: 2K Games, 2010.

22 In previous iterations of the series, barbarians were unable to advance beyond medieval technologies. *Civilization V* allows them later technologies but still limits their rate of technological progression.

23 The *Civilization* series is known for its active modding community. There could be many individual barbarian civilizations represented as true civilizations and barbarians as they stand could be removed from play, but there is currently no method in *Civilization V* for modders to change the abilities of barbarians as such to evolve into a kind of civilization on their own (for more on modding, see Apperley, Chapter 12, and Crabtree, Chapter 13).

24 The flipped unit will have no upgrades available to it because it was not produced in a city with a barracks. Of course, it would be impossible for barbarian troops to be produced in a barracks because barbarians have no cities.

25 Much more could be said about *Civilization V*'s use of culture as a game mechanic to provide social policies and the means of government to a civilization. Less culture means less advanced social policies. Obviously, barbarians have no hope of any form of government or social advances because culture as a game mechanic is not available to them.

26 Haemimont Games, *Grand Ages: Rome.* Worms, Germany: Kalypso Media, 2009.

27 Only after there are both Plebs and Equites in the player's city, and only when they are both reasonably happy, will Patricians be inclined to settle. These high-class citizens are employed in civic areas such as temples, and require luxuries that are produced by Equites with resources acquired by Plebs. Thus, city management and progression in the game can only be achieved through very close attention to each of the three levels of society.

28 cf. Roland Barthes: "Everyone is reassured, installed in the quiet certainty of a universe without duplicity, where Romans are Romans thanks to the most legible of signs: hair on the forehead," *Mythologies.* New York: Random House, 1993, 26.

29 For more discussion on the Romanization process of Gaul, see Greg Woolf, *Becoming Roman.* Cambridge: Cambridge University Press, 2000.

30 The Creative Assembly, *Rome: Total War: "Barbarian Invasion."* Santa Monica, CA: Activision, 2005.

31 There is of course a vast amount of scholarship on multiculturalism and cultural identity. One recent volume that addresses these topics and may provide helpful bibliography for further reading is Montserrat Guibernau and John Rex, Eds. *The Ethnicity Reader: Nationalism, Multiculturalism, and Migration.* Cambridge: Polity Press, 2010.

Works cited

Barthes, Roland. *Mythologies*. New York: Random House, 1993.

Barton, Carlin A. *The Sorrows of the Ancient Romans*. Princeton, NJ: Princeton University Press, 1993.

Bollinger, Traugott. *Theatralis Licentia*. Winterthur: Hans Schellenberg, 1969.

Fagan, Garrett G. *The Lure of the Arena: Social Psychology and the Crowd at the Roman Games*. Cambridge: Cambridge University Press, 2011.

Ferris, I.M. "The Pity of War," in Ed. Erich S. Gruen, *Cultural Identity in the Ancient Mediterranean*. Los Angeles, CA: Getty Publications, 2011, 185–201.

Freeman, David. *Creating Emotion in Games: The Craft and Art of Emotioneering*. Topeka, KS: Sagebrush Education Resources, 2003.

Guibernau, Montserrat and John Rex, Eds. *The Ethnicity Reader: Nationalism, Multiculturalism, and Migration*. Cambridge: Polity Press, 2010.

Hall, Edith. *Inventing the Barbarian: Greek Self-Definition through Tragedy*. Oxford: Clarendon Press, 1991.

Hopkins, Keith. "Murderous Games," in Ed. Keith Hopkins, *Death and Renewal*. Cambridge: Cambridge University Press, 1985, 1–30.

Jones, Mark Wilson. *Principles of Roman Architecture*. New Haven: Yale University Press, 2000.

Köhne, Eckart, Cornelia Ewigleben, and Ralph Jackson, Eds. *Gladiators and Caesars*. Berkeley, CA: University of California Press, 2000.

The Passion of Saints Perpetua and Felicity. Translated by W. H. Shewring, http://www.indiana.edu/~shopkow/b204/perpetua.htm, accessed 29 September 2012.

Plass, Paul. *The Game of Death in Ancient Rome*. Madison, WI: University of Wisconsin Press, 1995.

Potter, David S. "Performance, Power, and Justice in the High Empire," in Ed. W.J. Slater, *Roman Theater and Society*. Ann Arbor, MI: University of Michigan, 1996, 129–160.

Potter, David S. "Spectacle," in Ed. David S. Potter, *A Companion to the Roman Empire*. Malden, MA: Blackwell Publishing, 2006, 385–408.

Welch, Katherine E. *The Roman Amphitheatre*. Cambridge: Cambridge University Press, 2007.

Wiedemann, Thomas. *Emperors and Gladiators*. New York: Routledge, 1992.

Woolf, Greg. *Becoming Roman*. Cambridge: Cambridge University Press, 2000.

Games cited

Civilization V. Novato, CA: Firaxis Games, 2K Games, 2010.

Everquest. San Diego, CA: Sony Online Entertainment, 1999.

Grand Ages: Rome. Worms, Germany: Haemimont Games, Kalypso Media, 2009.

Rome: Total War "Barbarian Invasion." Santa Monica, CA: Activision, The Creative Assembly, 2005.

6

Modeling Indigenous Peoples: Unpacking Ideology in *Sid Meier's Colonization*

Rebecca Mir
New-York Historical Society

Trevor Owens
United States Library of Congress

The 2008 release of *Sid Meier's Civilization IV: Colonization* (hereafter *Colonization*) sparked an immediate controversy due to the game's subject. Its players have the ability to colonize the Americas turn-by-turn, in the style of traditional *Civilization* games. Ben Fritz wrote in a blog post for *Variety* that in allowing the player to do "horrific things ... or whitewash some of the worst events of human history," the game *Colonization* was offensive.[1] Firaxis Games' president Steve Martin responded to the controversy, stating, "As with all previous versions of *Civilization*, the game does not endorse any particular position or strategy—players can and should make their own moral judgments."[2] We disagree with both perspectives.

Colonization interprets the history of the American colonial encounter. While players can and do make their own moral judgments about the game and the history of colonial encounter, the model of the world in the game comes with a "procedural rhetoric," an argument expressed in the computational logic and design that drives the game.[3] The game's model inherently suggests certain strategies and positions and thus shapes player agency and action. We identify these positions and strategies by closely analyzing how design decisions shape players' interpretations of Native American cultures and the history of colonial encounters. Through a critical reading of the player experience and the game's art, rules, and internal encyclopedia (the "Civilopedia"), we explore tensions between potential player agency in interpretation and the boundaries placed on that agency. In short, this game (like all games) presents a particular ideological model of the world. Specifically, *Colonization*'s model restricts potential readings to a limited and Americanized colonialist ideology.

The colonialist ideology represented in *Colonization* mixes the idea of glorified conquest with a range of dull, mechanical components that in turn undermine that glorification. The central activity of *Colonization* is managing the logistics of gathering, training, and putting people or "units," to work in your settlements, turning raw resources into commodities, and selling finished goods back in Europe. As we became mired in the banality of logistical shuffling, we were struck with the ennui of the bureaucratic evil at the core of the game. The game's box cover art shows men (and only men) of action ready to conquer the New World, but your "glorious" conquest is rewarded by endless project management and accounting: a spreadsheet of cultural domination.

The way in which simulations put players in control of a set of competing values in its algorithms is novel. As media scholar Alexander Galloway suggests, these kinds of games are always an "ideological interpretation of history" or the "transcoding of history into specific mathematical models."[4] In this case, the game's model is similar to the way that states "see." Like states, these kinds of games turn people and landscapes into resources and commodities. Galloway's "allegories of control" in games are similar to what anthropologist and political scientist James C. Scott discusses in his book *Seeing Like a State: How Certain Schemes to Improve the Human Condition Have Failed*. Through a series of examples of failures in governance, Scott explores the way governments make nature, cities, and people legible through categorical and numerical simplification. Games like *Colonization* allow players to see the world in the same ways a state sees the world. This is one way in which *Colonization* succeeds at representing an ideological vision of the world from a colonialist viewpoint.

Our goal is to unpack how an ideology is created and works in a historical simulation, not to chastise the designers. We firmly believe that as games mature as a medium, we will be able to appreciate the ones that ask us to explore painful parts of our history. Games can and *should* challenge our preconceived notions of the world by evoking guilt or highlighting causal relationships. While there are games that come with this kind of gravitas, components of *Colonization* point toward the expressive potential of games as historical arguments. For example, Trevor first played a copy of the original version of *Colonization* (released in 1994) when he was in the sixth grade. He played the game repeatedly, first learning the basic rules and then trying out different play styles. At first he played as the French and the Dutch. The French get bonuses in interacting with Native peoples and the Dutch get bonuses in trade. In both cases, Trevor would try to rewrite history and coexist with Native peoples. After exploring that side of the game, Trevor eventually played as the Spanish, who receive extra gold from destroying Native cities. These bonuses remain in the 2008 version of *Colonization*, called *Civilization IV: Colonization* because it was made using the *Civilization IV* engine. Exploring the different possibilities provided by the game was always engaging for Trevor, but they were not all necessarily "fun." The interactivity and agency that players experience in games make playing from disturbing points of view possible and thus provides the ability to provoke feelings of guilt in players. The power of this guilt suggests a potential for games that portray disturbing points of view as potent vehicles for exploring the past and understanding a more nuanced history.

Indigenous peoples according to *Colonization*

So what would the indigenous peoples of the Americas look like in *Colonization* if the game did not endorse a particular position or strategy? What would the game's model be like? We do not know (nor are we sure it is possible!). The game is called *Colonization*, and the very premise of the game requires the player to colonize. Consider the cover of the game, which shows a group of European men wading ashore from their boats, guns and flags in hand. These men represent both the idea that colonization is inevitable, and the American myth of progress of the expanding the frontier, as discussed by Matthew Kapell in "*Civilization* and its Discontents."[5] Having dismissed the question of whether the game endorses a position, we can now take up the more interesting question: does *Civilization IV: Colonization* at least give players enough agency to make their own decisions about reenacting the history of colonial encounter?

When considering how disease affected Native populations in combination with the advanced technology of the colonial powers, it might seem to players that European domination over Natives was a foregone conclusion. However, a great benefit of simulations is the ability to explore alternate histories through a series of choices.[6] One of the biggest strengths of other games in the *Civilization* series is that players can create radically different pasts and play out counterfactual events. What if Africa had experienced a Renaissance, instead of Europe? What if India took over Great Britain? What if the Iroquois colonized Europe? These kinds of questions are possible to pose and play in the *Civilization* series because of the open-ended nature of the game. But *Colonization* has a strict and problematic win condition: players *must* be a colonial power, *must* rebel against their motherland, and *must* fight in a war for independence. Instead of reaching terms of peace with the homeland, or paying the homeland for freedom, players are thus compelled to reenact the colonial history of the United States of America. While players cannot avoid this win condition, can they avoid the assumption that Native Americans had to be pushed west and onto reservations? In order to answer this question, we need to explore more deeply what rules *Colonization* has used to define what both players and Native game units can and cannot do.

Making Native cultures playable

Colonization players do not have the option of playing as any of the Native American cultures in the officially published version of the game. It is relatively easy to change that, and through a slight modification to the game's source code, players can choose to be a Native American culture in the beginning of the game. After this modification of the game's code, however, Natives are not really playable in the same sense as the colonial powers because the game was designed for players to act as colonizers. (When we refer to "Europeans," "colonial powers," "Native Americans," and "indigenous peoples," we are, of course, referencing the multiple cultures represented in the game, not trying to promote the idea of monolithic cultures.) As user Androrc the Orc explains on the Civilization Fanatics online forum:

> It is very easy to make natives playable (you just have to change the "bPlayable" field in CIV4CivilizationInfos.xml to 1), but the gameplay is uninteresting ... almost no buildings, little options for play, etc. ... That having been said, things could be done to improve them, perhaps to the point of making playing them be interesting, but a way for them to sell their goods, among other issues, would have to be thought out.[7]

For the sake of comparison, below are two images: one of the city management interface while playing as a European culture, and one of the city management interface while playing as a Native culture with bPlayable on (Figures 6.1 and 6.2).

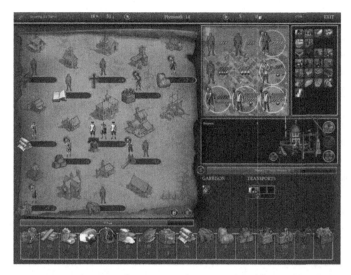

FIGURE 6.1 *A working settlement in the New World emphasizing European settler's activities*

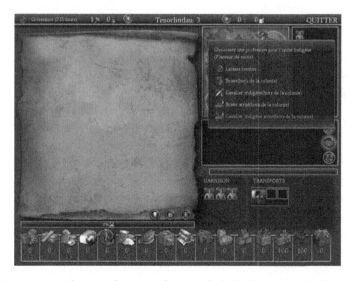

FIGURE 6.2 *A settlement of Natives showing the lack of activity of such settlements*

The screenshot of Tenochtitlan was taken by Robert Surcouf, who quite eloquently captures the sentiment (Figure 6.2) of the situation in his comment: "There is not much in Tenochtitlan, but it belongs ... to me."[8] The ghost town in Surcouf's Aztec settlement explicitly shows the limitations placed on different Native cultures in the game. Many things would have to be changed in the game to make Native cultures fully playable in a way equal to that of the European cultures in the game.

It is important to briefly explain a little about how this game was made. *Civilization IV: Colonization* is written using the *Civilization IV* engine. As a result, instead of being programmed from scratch, the 2008 version of *Colonization* was written as a series of addenda to the original game. Much of these addenda are visible by simply opening up a range of uncompiled text files that make up much of the source code of the game, which players download to their computers when they install the game. Anyone can look through the directories of their copy of the game and find CvPlayer.app, which includes governing rules and functions for the game. Throughout this CvPlayer file there are a range of statements that provide peoples in the game with particular abilities (determined elsewhere in the games code). From the perspective of the game's source code there are normal peoples (colonial units controlled by the player), Native peoples (controlled by the computer), and Europeans (also controlled by the computer). Normal peoples come with a range of abilities and characteristics that make the game playable and fun, and the game's code takes many of those abilities away from peoples who are flagged as "isNative". Native peoples are defined within the game's procedural rhetoric, *at the functional level of the code*, to be the "Other."

What should we make of the fact that what defines Native peoples in *Colonization* is a limitation of abilities? We can "read" the model of the game from our own gameplay experience but we can also open the game's files and start looking at how the game's model was actually written to function. In modifying and editing the game's code and playing an altered version of the game, we learn how those rules are enacted in gameplay and how the game models the world. While it is easy to turn bPlayable to 1, the game resists our ability to make Natives playable in a robust sense, and thus the process of trying to make Native peoples playable exposes the game's logic. There is no way around it: at the level of the scripts the game systematically and explicitly restricts things like civic development from Native cultures. In this sense we could say that the ideology of colonialism of the game is represented in the code. To what extent does it matter how the rules of colonialism are enacted in the scripts? It is clear that this is a relatively efficient way to write code (i.e. make the game work) and what we interpret in the code is a result of functionality in enacting game design decisions. Therefore, we can understand how restrictive certain design decisions are by analyzing the code and by understanding how the game functions. In this case, it is clear that despite our best wishes to modify *Colonization* to play as a Native American culture, the model of society represented in the code itself resists our actions.

Even though developers at Firaxis encourage players to modify *Civilization* games, there are still limitations on how drastically fans can alter games. Any player can make Natives playable somewhat easily, but then the player is faced with a range of rules that make the game problematic. If we overwrite basic rules for trade and settlement building, we discover that the game cannot be won unless we can trade goods with Europe. The models in the game's code, while rewritable, carry with them extensive inertia. This inertia, powered by rules for winning the game and the exceptions placed on Natives in the code, resists our desire for a revisionist experience of *Colonization* in which Natives are robust playable people. Attempting to modify the game further thus exposes the game designers' intentions and the underlying colonialist ideology that resulted from the game's design.

How Natives and Europeans interact in *Colonization*

Cultural exchange plays a major role in understanding the history of interactions between Europeans and the indigenous peoples of the Americas. In works like Richard White's *The Middle Ground* or Karen Kupperman's *Indians and English*, historians have developed rich discussions about the interactions between Native peoples and colonials. The functional and visual modes through which *Sid Meier's Colonization* models exchange and interaction between cultures offer an interesting place to further interpret the game.

In order to win a game of *Colonization*, you must successfully manage relationships with other colonial powers and Natives. Some player strategies and game reviews suggest keeping amicable relations with as many Native cultures as possible because raising a rebel army is difficult enough without waging wars with your neighbors.[9] Other strategies suggest raiding Aztec and Incan settlements for gold, since they have an assigned trait that increases gold yielded from captured settlements by 300 percent.[10] At first players may think managing peaceful economic relationships with Natives is easy; they are a good source of trade and give gifts to the player upon first contact. Trading with Natives seems straightforward, but most of their settlements consistently request guns and horses, and once the player trades these items with Native settlements, the items will be used to upgrade Native military units.

Of course the player can use this trade mechanic to his or her advantage by selling guns and horses to Natives with whom he or she is allied or with Natives at war with other colonial powers. Once the player (or another colonial power controlled by the computer) starts trading these items with Natives, it is clear that their cultures have been directly influenced by these European technologies. This is not historically off base; the horse made its way back to its continent of origin and into Native cultures thanks to Spanish colonization efforts. Horses used by the Spaniards were taken and subsequently moved through a series of Native trade routes and undeniably shaped Native cultures, most famously the semi-nomadic cultures of the Great Plains.[11] Guns, along with many other material goods, similarly traveled between and within Euro-American and Native American groups. It is refreshing to see an example of direct cultural influence in a core (but subtle) mechanic of a Sid Meier game. *Civilization* games have previously been critiqued because trading supplies and technologies with other cultures for centuries produces no messy hybridized identities or beliefs.[12]

Absent from *Colonization* is the exchange of germs between Natives and colonials. Native Americans had no previous contact with, and therefore no immunological defenses against, European diseases. And while diseases are not artifacts that can be traded, or a set of beliefs that can be learned, they were transmitted between, and had a huge impact on, both colonists and Native Americans. Smallpox, measles, chickenpox, influenza, typhus, typhoid, cholera, bubonic plague, scarlet fever, and malaria were all unstoppable post-contact. What would a game of *Colonization* be like where over the course of a few turns, 80–90 percent of the Native American units were wiped out, or where entire villages the player meant to trade with simply no longer existed? What if players could sabotage villages with smallpox-ridden blankets, or if colonial units started to weaken and die from contracting syphilis after sleeping with Native Americans?[13] The inclusion of disease in *Colonization* would certainly be more "accurate" historically speaking, but such a mechanic would limit a player's control and possible choices and might worsen player experience. We also understand that coding for the exchange of diseases might overly complicate an already complex game and that it would be a natural decision on the part of designers to avoid another controversial issue in a game about colonization. However, a game that depicts the offensive history of colonial encounter and a colonialist ideology *should* include disease.

Cultural cross-dressing, education, and assimilation on the frontier

Another benefit in maintaining good relationships with Natives in *Colonization* is the ability to establish missions and generate "Converted Native" units, pictured here in the game's Civilopedia (Figure 6.3). He (and all Natives in the

FIGURE 6.3 *Converted Native Unit*

game, whether converted or not, are male—another problematic issue) wears a waistcoat, breeches, stockings, and pilgrim buckle shoes, while the feather in his hair signifies his Indian-ness. Wearing certain clothing was, as Ann M. Little explains, "central to the discourse of status, power, and identity on the frontier."[14] As a cultural cross-dresser, the Converted Native represents the messy hybridization that the Sid Meier games typically avoid. However, there is no Euro-American equivalent to the Converted Native, even though exchange and cultural cross-dressing were not limited to Natives. Euro-Americans were inevitably influenced by their neighbors both ideologically and in the production and use of their material goods.[15] While Free and Indentured Servant Colonist units can be educated in Native settlements and learn master trades (e.g. farming, cotton planting, etc.), they emerge from those settlements in colonial clothing, their cultural identity unaltered by their contact with Natives. The Converted Native, in contrast, will change into a Free Colonist unit if he graduates from a school within one of the player's settlements. Essentially, assimilation occurs through Western education, which removes all visual identifiers that this unit used to be Native, and this is true for his skin color as much as his clothing. In *Colonization*, culture is transmitted in one direction: Natives can actually *become* European, but Europeans do not take on *any* Native cultural traits (Figure 6.4).

The fact that Converted Natives become white after being educated in a colonial settlement might be excused as a technical detail; it was probably easier to make Converted Natives become white Colonists instead of creating

FIGURE 6.4 *Various Stages of "Converstion" of the "Native" unit*

another specialized unit (i.e. The Educated Converted Native). However, this detail is particularly problematic in the historical context of colonial powers' attempts to educate Native Americans. The process of cultural assimilation in the game is deeply resonant with the educational theories of Captain Richard H. Pratt, founder and longtime superintendent of the Carlisle Indian Industrial School, who often mentioned that Native American education should "Kill the Indian, and save the Man."[16] His attempts to systematically eradicate any traces of native culture, in requiring individuals to stop using their Native American names, forbidding anyone from speaking Native languages, and explicitly forcing individuals to look more like "Whites" by cutting off their long hair, represent a similar model of cultural assimilation via education enacted in *Colonization*. This is not to suggest that the functionality of the game condones this educational pedagogy, but education in *Colonization* does function in a way that fits this troubling ideology.

There is no option for the player to keep Converted Natives from becoming European once they have graduated from school. If this makes the player uncomfortable, then his or her only option is to keep the penalties (and rewards) inherent to the Converted Native and refuse to "educate" them. But since Converted Natives are easier to get than any other unit, and since many units are needed to generate rebel sentiment, to amass an army, and to sell manufactured goods, the game's design encourages players to educate these Converted Natives in order to win the game.

Do the Natives exist to be used as a means to an end?

The various traits that Native American leaders possess assume that the player would only play as a colonial power. There is less variation in the Native cultures' traits, and all of their traits intentionally benefit the player. Natives are described primarily not by internal characteristics but by characteristics by which a colonial power could use or manipulate them.[17] For example, one of the traits Native American leaders possess is "Impressionable," meaning that missionaries can convert Natives at an increased rate. Compare with one of the European leader traits, "Tolerant," which causes immigrants to come to the colonies at a faster rate. Other traits follow this pattern: Native leader traits help the colonial powers and the player and European leader traits help the player and colonial powers. The exception to this general rule is that Natives can promote their mounted, melee, or gunpowder units to a specific status for "free" (i.e. they do not need gold to "purchase" the upgrade as the player normally does) (Figure 6.5).

The Sioux, for example, have a free promotion called "Grenadier I" that allows mounted, melee, and gunpowder units to have increased power when attacking settlements. As previously mentioned, however, Natives must first acquire guns and horses through trade with the player or other colonial powers. These militaristic bonuses could still be beneficial to the player if he or she were allied with the Natives possessing guns and horses. If players

FIGURE 6.5 *Leader traits for Sitting Bull in the Civilopedia*

tried to play a game of *Colonization* as the Sioux (or Apache, Arawak, Aztecs, Cherokee, Incas, Iroquois, or Tupi), they would quickly realize how much the Native cultural traits benefit colonial powers. Not only would players have to wait for the colonizers to trade guns and horses to make use of the one helpful bonus Natives possess, but the Sioux players would also lose units to religious conversions more quickly than other Native cultures!

Authentic or beautiful *Colonization*?

There are many things that could be done to create a game that more accurately models the history of colonial encounter. Interestingly, members in the "modding" community are trying to do exactly that.[18] These "modders" alter the game in order to include various features that they believe would improve gameplay. Modders discuss the inclusion of controversial features in their own modifications ("mods") of *Colonization*, such as disease or the slave trade. A particularly large mod claimed to represent the "authentic colonization" while refusing to include disease or the slave trade due to the heated disagreements between modders on the creation team.[19] Player Tigranes questioned this decision, stating:

> Why is it so hard to include Slave unit? Why is it so hard to include a Plague mechanics [sic] which would wipe up entire (and very useful) villages of Natives? If the mod would call itself—Beautiful Colonization—I would agree. But Authentic? Make things ugly, please … or change the name.[20]

If unpleasant and difficult mechanics such as the exchange of germs or slaves have been sterilized out of gameplay, should there not at least be more winning options available to the player than starting a revolution? In forcing the player to relive the American colonial experience, *Colonization* systematically denies the player a series of interesting choices and opportunities to create a radically different past. Removing the players' ability to dramatically change the past locks them into the ideological model of the game and limits their interpretations. With this said, features like misrepresenting acculturation and assimilation and representing Native peoples in terms of how they can be manipulated are actually in keeping with the idea that a game called *Colonization* should be offensive.[21] If we think about the purpose of *Colonization* as modeling a disturbing moment in history, then the most problematic point is that the game does not include the devastating role that disease played during colonization and nearly avoids the history of slavery altogether.

Wrongs and rights in *Colonization*

In *Colonization*, Native peoples are simply a resource to be managed in the spreadsheet of cultural domination. At the level of code they are the "Other," limited in actions and cultural traits that specifically benefit their colonizers.[22] Aside from acquiring things from the West, Native peoples are trapped in time, unable to advance by their own means. If players chose to educate Native peoples, the game eradicates any sense that they were once indigenous. Even if players chose to simply leave Native peoples alone, they stagnate, failing to develop any technologies, to change, to adapt, or to do any of the things that peoples do. Although they can be powerful allies and/or resources in earning money, declaring independence, and fighting the mother country for freedom, Native Americans are not directly relevant to winning the game.

Colonization is undoubtedly offensive, but it would be impossible to create a value-free simulation of the colonial encounter. The redeeming qualities of the game are found within the notion of the banality of evil and the feelings of guilt that come from thinking about what histories have been whitewashed and what evils have been wrought throughout the course of each game. In the end, if there is something regrettable about the game in its current state, *it is that it is not offensive enough.* While the game lets you do some rather evil things, those evil things are nevertheless sanitized versions of the events that actually took place in reality. We would love to see a Eurocentric, colonialist representation of colonialism in which Native Americans are robust, playable peoples, because it would allow players to experience the ugly, authentic colonization that so radically changed and shaped our world.

Notes

1 Ben Fritz, "Civilization IV: Colonization … Wow That Looks Offensive," *The Cut Scene - Video Game Blog on Variety.com*, 25 June 2008.

2 Ben Fritz, "Firaxis Responds to my Colonization Post," *The Cut Scene - Video Game Blog on Variety.com*, 27 June 2008.

3 Ian Bogost, *Persuasive Games: The Expressive Power of Video games.* Cambridge, MA: MIT Press, 2007.

4 Alexander R. Galloway, *Gaming: Essays On Algorithmic Culture*. Minneapolis, MN: University of Minnesota Press, 2006, 102–103.

5 Matthew Kapell, "*Civilization* and its Discontents: American Monomythic Structure as Historical Simulacrum," *Popular Culture Review*, 13, no. 2 (Summer 2002): 129–136.

6 For more on this, see Holdenried with Trépanier's argument in Chapter 7.

7   Androrc the Orc, 13 December 2011 (2:26 a.m.), comment on malcolm01234's "Native Mods?" *Civilization Fanatics' Center*, 1 December 2011, http://forums. civfanatics.com/showpost.php?p=11117645&postcount=6.

8   Robert Surcouf, 12 December 2011 (11:21 p.m.), comment on malcolm01234's "Natives Mods?" *Civilization Fanatics' Center*, 1 December 2011, http://forums. civfanatics.com/showpost.php?p=11117478&postcount=5.

9   Allen 'Delsyn' Rausch, "Sid Meier's Civilization IV: Colonization," *GameSpy*, 21 August 2008, http://pc.gamespy.com/pc/civilization-game- untitled/901363p1.html; David Craddock, "Hands-on: Sid Meier's Civilization IV: Colonization," *Big Download*, 3 July 2008, http://news.bigdownload. com/2008/07/03/hands-on-sid-meiers-civilization-iv-colonization/.

10 Acornoil, "Trading with Natives," *Civilization Fanatics' Center*, 27 December 2008, http://www.civfanatics.com/civ4/colonization/strategy/nativetrade/, accessed 14 February 2013.

11 Pekka Hämäläinen, "The Rise and Fall of Plains Indian Horse Cultures," *The Journal of American History*, 90, no. 3 (December 2003): 833–862.

12 Ted Friedman, "*Civilization* and Its Discontents: Simulation, Subjectivity, and Space," in Ed. Greg Smith, *On a Silver Platter: CD-ROMS and the Promises of a New Technology*. New York: New York University Press, 1999, 132–150.

13 Nathan Nunn and Nancy Qian, "The Columbian Exchange: A History of Disease, Food, and Ideas," *Journal of Economic Perspectives*, 24, no. 2 (Spring 2010): 163–188: 2.

14 Ann M. Little, " 'Shoot That Rogue, for He Hath an Englishman's Coat On! ': Cultural Cross-Dressing on the New England Frontier, 1620–1760," *The New England Quarterly*, 74, no. 2 (June 2001): 238–273: 269.

15 James Hanson, "Laced Coats and Leather Jackets: The Great Plains Intercultural Clothing Exchange," in Eds. Douglas H. Ubelaker and Herman J. Viola, *Plains Indian Studies: A Collection of Essays in Honor of John C. Ewers and Waldo R. Wedel*. Washington, D.C.: Smithsonian Institution, 1982, 105–117: 116.

16 Richard Pratt, "The Advantages of Mingling Indians and Whites," in Ed. Francis Paul Prucha, *Americanizing the American Indians: Writings by the "Friends of the Indian" 1880–1990*. Cambridge, MA: Harvard University Press, 1973, 260–271.

17 PolyCast, "Focus: 'Civilization IV: Colonization' with Firaxis Games," [Podcast] Season 2, 15 August 2008, 32:00–36:40, http://civcomm.weplayciv.com/ polycast/polycast/season2.php#focus_civ4col.

18 See chapters 12 and 13 for more on modding and its effects on historical representation.

19 Ronnar, 26 January 2012 (1:15 a.m.), comment on Writing Bull's "[Mod] The Authentic Colonization," *Civilization Fanatics' Center*, 18 September 2011, http://forums.civfanatics.com/showpost.php?p=11217076&postcount=124.

20 Tigranes, 25 January 2012 (4:19 p.m.), comment on Writing Bull's "[Mod] The Authentic Colonization," *Civilization Fanatics' Center*, 18 September 2011, http://forums.civfanatics.com/showpost.php?p=11216316&postcount=123M.

21 Initially approached by Trevor in a blog post on playthepast.org, this idea was consequently developed in a series of posts written by both of us. We sincerely appreciate the conversations the posts generated, all of which contributed to this book chapter: Trevor Owens, "*Colonization*: Is It Offensive Enough?" *Play the Past*, 23 November 2010; Trevor Owens and Rebecca Mir, "If (!isNative()){return false;}: De-People-ing Native Peoples in Sid Meier's *Colonization*," *Play the Past*, 1 March 2012; Rebecca Mir and Trevor Owens, "Guns, Germs, and Horses: Cultural Exchange in Sid Meier's *Colonization*," *Play the Past*, 13 March 2012; "Playing at Slavery: Modding *Colonization* for Authenticity," *Play the Past*, 24 May 2012.

22 See Chapter 5 for a full discussion of the creation of the Self and Other through foreignness.

Works cited

Bogost, Ian. *Persuasive Games: The Expressive Power of Video games.* Cambridge, MA: MIT Press, 2007.

Civilization Fanatics' Center, http://www.civfanatics.com/, accessed 3 December 2012.

Craddock, David. "Hands-on: Sid Meier's Civilization IV: Colonization," *Big Download*, 3 July 2008, http://news.bigdownload.com/2008/07/03/hands-on-sid-meiers-civilization-iv-colonization/, accessed 3 December 2012.

Friedman, Ted. "*Civilization* and Its Discontents: Simulation, Subjectivity, and Space," in Ed. Greg Smith, *On a Silver Platter: CD-ROMS and the Promises of a New Technology*. New York: New York University Press, 1999, 132–150.

Fritz, Ben. "Civilization IV: Colonization ... Wow That Looks Offensive," *The Cut Scene–Video Game Blog on Variety.com*, 25 June 2008, http://web.archive.org/web/20110501080422/http://weblogs.variety.com/the_cut_scene/2008/06/civilization-iv.html, accessed 3 December 2012.

Fritz, Ben. "Firaxis Responds to my Colonization Post," *The Cut Scene–Video Game Blog on Variety.com*, 27 June 2008, http://web.archive.org/web/20080729211300/http://weblogs.variety.com/the_cut_scene/2008/06/firaxis-respond.html, accessed 3 December 2012.

Galloway, Alexander R. *Gaming: Essays On Algorithmic Culture.* Minneapolis, MN: University of Minnesota Press, 2006.

Hämäläinen, Pekka. "The Rise and Fall of Plains Indian Horse Cultures," *The Journal of American History*, 90, no. 3 (December 2003): 833–862.

Hanson, James. "Laced Coats and Leather Jackets: The Great Plains Intercultural Clothing Exchange," in Eds. Douglas H. Ubelaker and Herman J. Viola, *Plains Indian Studies: A Collection of Essays in Honor of John C. Ewers and Waldo R. Wedel*. Washington, D.C: Smithsonian Institution, 1982, 105–117.

Kapell, Matthew. "*Civilization* and its Discontents: American Monomythic Structure as Historical Simulacrum," *Popular Culture Review*, 13, no. 2 (Summer 2002): 129–136.

Kupperman, Karen Ordahl. *Indians and English: Facing Off in Early America*. Ithaca, NY: Cornell University Press, 2000.

Little, Ann M. " 'Shoot That Rogue, for He Hath an Englishman's Coat On! ': Cultural Cross-Dressing on the New England Frontier, 1620–1760," *The New England Quarterly*, 74, no. 2 (June 2001): 238–273.

Mir, Rebecca and Trevor Owens, "Guns, Germs, and Horses: Cultural Exchange in Sid Meier's *Colonization*," *Play the Past*, 13 March 2012, http://www.playthepast.org/?p=2531, accessed 3 December 2012.

Mir, Rebecca and Trevor Owens. "Playing at Slavery: Modding *Colonization* for Authenticity," *Play the Past*, 24 May 2012, http://www.playthepast.org/?p=2856, accessed 3 December 2012.

Nunn, Nathan and Nancy Qian. "The Columbian Exchange: A History of Disease, Food, and Ideas," *Journal of Economic Perspectives*, 24, no. 2 (Spring 2010): 163–188.

Owens, Trevor. "*Colonization*: Is It Offensive Enough?" *Play the Past*, 23 November 2010, http://www.playthepast.org/?p=278, accessed 3 December 2012.

Owens, Trevor and Rebecca Mir. "If (!isNative()){return false;}: De-People-ing Native Peoples in Sid Meier's *Colonization*," *Play the Past*, 1 March 2012, http://www.playthepast.org/?p=2509, accessed 3 December 2012.

Pratt, Richard H. "The Advantages of Mingling Indians and Whites," in Ed. Francis Paul Prucha, *Americanizing the American Indians: Writings by the "Friends of the Indian" 1880–1990*. Cambridge, MA: Harvard University Press, 1973, 260–271.

Quick, Daniel "DanQ", Locutus, and Impaler [WrG]. "Focus: 'Civilization IV: Colonization' with Firaxis Games," *PolyCast* [Podcast], 15 August 2008, http://civcomm.weplayciv.com/polycast/polycast/season2.php#focus_civ4col, accessed 3 December 2012.

Rausch, Allen. "Sid Meier's Civilization IV: Colonization," *GameSpy*, 21 August 2008, http://pc.gamespy.com/pc/civilization-game-untitled/901363p1.html, accessed 3 December 2012.

Scott, James C. *Seeing Like a State: How Certain Schemes to Improve the Human Condition Have Failed*. New Haven: Yale University Press, 1998.

White, Richard. *The Middle Ground: Indians, Empires, and Republics in the Great Lakes Region, 1650–1815*. Cambridge: Cambridge University Press, 1991.

Games cited

Sid Meier's Civilization IV: Colonization. Novato, CA: Firaxis Games, 2K Games, 2008.

7

Dominance and the Aztec Empire: Representations in *Age of Empires II* and *Medieval II: Total War*

Joshua D. Holdenried with *Nicolas Trépanier*
University of Mississippi

The fall of the Aztec Empire to a small expeditionary force of conquistadors appears, to the casual observer, to be an unlikely outcome. Understanding what brought it about requires a broad perspective and the use of key concepts, chief among which stands the concept of *dominance*, defined for the purposes of this chapter as the unequal relationship between separate parties where one is subjugated to another. Dominance permeates much of Aztec history, from their arrival on the Mesoamerican scene in the early fourteenth century through the apex of their power and, half a century later, their defeat at the hands of Spanish conquistadors in 1519.[1]

The rise and fall of the Aztecs has attracted the attention of a community of academic historians, but these events have also been represented through many different media, from popular nonfiction books to feature films and, in recent years, video games.[2] The Aztec case therefore also allows us to put in parallel the work of historians and the relatively new medium of video games.

The meeting of history and video games has obvious limitations. For one, as discussed in the introduction to this volume, the centrality of gameplay (games, as commercial products, *must* be fun if they are to find any success) can lead game designers to overlook or even contradict the consensus conclusions of historians, and in almost all cases brings about an oversimplification of the historiography. Furthermore, game designers often integrate, willingly or not, myths and inaccuracies into products that are sold as "historically accurate."

But the video games also display unique strengths as a medium of historical representation. For example, whereas the linear narratives of other media suggest predetermined outcomes, video games can convey uncertainty and contingency by creating an interactive environment where the player can play and replay through countless variations on a given scenario.[3] They can also convey aspects of history without addressing them through abstract discussion, therefore affording players an *experience* of history much closer than that which historians' academic articles and monographs ever could offer.

As this chapter will show, the Aztec experience of dominance is one such aspect of history that has been efficiently represented in video games. Dominance is particularly well suited to being conveyed in video games, insofar as a very large proportion of video games designate the establishment of relationships of dominance with rivals, be they human or simulated, as the primary criterion to evaluate the success of the player.[4]

In the following pages, we will first survey the multiple ways dominance appears in the historiography of the Aztec Empire, going from the foundation myths to the zenith of an Empire dominating its neighbors to the downfall that Spanish conquerors brought about by redefining the cultural modalities of dominance. We will then move on to the representations of the Aztec Empire in two games that are both part of critically and commercially successful franchises, *Age of Empires II: The Conquerors* and *Medieval II: Total War: Kingdoms*. As will become clear, both of these games manage to integrate the diverging Spanish and Aztec cultural understanding of the concept of dominance into the game mechanics in very different but fairly successful ways.

Aztec origins

While historians remain uncertain of the details surrounding the earliest origins of the Aztecs, it seems that the tribe had originally moved into the region that would become the site of their capital, Tenochtitlan, around 1325 CE.[5] Much better established is the fact that, in the sixty years or so that preceded contact with the Spaniards in 1519, the Aztec elite effectively "developed and imposed a new tradition conveying an image of the past that would fit the requirements and ideals of the group whose dominance was in the process of rapid expansion."[6] Central to this origin myth was the status of subordinates, which they attributed to their own ancestors, whom they portrayed as serving and paying tribute to the tribes that dominated them.[7] Accompanying this vision of a humble past was a prophecy promising that freedom and dominant status would soon belong to the Aztecs, and imparting upon them "the cult of the gods, human sacrifice and the fighting of wars to obtain captives and impose Aztec rule," a prophecy that would eventually be fulfilled in their regional political domination.[8]

The first step toward this regional expansion took the shape of "an extraordinary strengthening of [Aztec] military powers," which, "combined with their conviction about their own destiny, resulted in continued political and economic expansion."[9] However, beyond their capital city of Tenochtitlan, Aztec rule remained mostly indirect, operating through a powerful "Triple Alliance" with the neighboring Tlacopan and Texcoco tribes.

In this alliance, aimed at gaining access to various forms of tribute from subordinates, the Aztecs always remained the dominant partner. They maintained their status through the militarized character of a society that placed a very high value on warfare and sacrifice (and therefore served as a deterrent to rebellion), as well as marriage alliances with partner tribes and an inflow of tribute from surrounding regions.[10] Tribute-paying tribes, however, "remained independent, and usually notably disaffected, despite the conquering city's conviction of the legitimacy of their supremacy."[11] Growing financial resources provided not only for war expenses, but also to support the poor and farmers and, increasingly over time, maintenance of the ruler and his court. In short, military dominance brought about political and economic dominance as well.[12]

These various forms of dominance were mirrored in a number of symbolically loaded rituals.[13] Chief among those were arranged battles known as "Flowery Wars" in which, through the fighting skills of its warriors, "each side [had a chance] to demonstrate its valor and the opportunity to take appropriate captives for sacrifice."[14] Those involved in the "Flowery Wars" understood the event as "a sacred contest, the outcome unknown but preordained, revealing which city, which local deity, would rightfully dominate another."[15] But the Aztecs, unwilling to leave any ambiguity about their legitimacy, would go as far as sending "food and weapons [...] to the selected target city as a part of the challenge, there being no virtue in defeating a weakened enemy."[16] More often than not, the Aztec warriors prevailed in these Flowery Wars. In fact, "the Aztecs were to become notorious among their neighbors for their mass ceremonial killings, and for the extravagant theatricalism in which those killings were framed."[17] The Flowery Wars, in short, offered a prime arena of expression of symbolic dominance.

It is in such a political context that Spanish commander Hernán Cortés arrived in 1519. A little over two years later, the fall of capital city Tenochtitlan (the largest city in the Americas, with a population between 150,000 and 200,000) to a force that reportedly amounted to "86 horsemen, 118 musketeers and crossbowmen, and 700 foot soldiers, as well as perhaps another 400 men who manned the ships he built to sail on the lake" brought about the final collapse of the Aztec empire.[18]

Given such unlikely odds, how could this conquest take place at all? Much of the answer resides in the weaknesses inherent in the system of Aztec dominance. More specifically, it was Hernán Cortés, the leader of the Spanish conquest, who made use of these weaknesses by exploiting the hatred harbored by surrounding tribes, forcing Aztec ruler Montezuma into subservience, and subverting the Aztec conception of warfare.

Even before he first met the Aztec leaders, Cortés had encountered the neighboring Tlaxcala tribe. Though the contact was at first hostile, he soon learned of the existence of Tenochtitlan and of the pre-existing enmity between the Tlaxcala and the Tenochtitlan, which he used to bring the Tlaxcala to the Spanish side.[19] This allowed Cortés to develop an understanding of the Aztec Empire and how it had hitherto maintained its dominion over central Mexico. Realizing that the Tlaxcala's negative feelings toward the Aztecs were far from unique, he was savvy enough to manipulate this product of years of Aztec dominance over the region.

Another important building block for the rising Spanish fortunes lay in their military culture and technology. Although highly sophisticated from a political and economic perspective, the Aztec empire relied on technology (military or otherwise) that essentially placed them in the Stone Age: "Metallurgy was limited, the wheel had no practical applications, there were no large beasts of burden, and other technologies known in the Old World like the milling of grain by mechanical means were unknown in the Americas."[20]

Compounding the Aztecs' technological inferiority was a cultural approach to warfare that stood in contrast with that of the Spaniards and was exploited by the latter. For the Aztecs, war was a sacred contest where warriors were to meet on an equal playing field so that the best man might win. Furthermore, the ideal outcome was not to kill on the battlefield, but to stun or disable the opponent enough to grab him by the "warrior lock" of hair (thus symbolizing dominance) and bring him back for sacrificial purposes.[21] The Spaniards, by contrast, measured military success "in terms of body counts, territory controlled, and evidence of decay in the morale of the 'enemy,' which included all warriors, actively engaged in battle or not, and all 'civilians' too."[22] The Aztecs never really adapted to this ruthless understanding of warfare, which relied on musket and crossbows and the "capacity to pick off selected enemies well behind the line of engagement."[23] Cortés and his captains, realizing that these "great men painted for war" were high-value targets in terms of demoralizing the enemy, frequently ordered their men to kill these warriors first. The tactic consisting in putting in front of Aztec eyes the tableau of "those sudden, trivializing deaths of great men painted for war, but not yet engaged in combat [...] such deaths at a distance, without putting one's own life in play" proved devastatingly efficient.[24]

The Aztecs managed to build a massive empire resting on a sophisticated system of dominance. However, the byproduct of this process was an accumulation of resentment, which, together with a massive imbalance in the military technologies used and deeply contrasting cultural attitudes to war, Cortés very efficiently exploited to dominate the Aztecs. Through its rise and fall, the Aztec story can therefore be understood as defined by relationships of dominance.

Themes of dominance

The theme of dominance is structurally part of any game that contains an element of competition between rivals, be they human or simulated. But the modalities of its implementation can vary widely. Such variations are particularly interesting when depicting historical events in which dominance played an important role. In this respect, the contrast between *Age of Empires II* and *Medieval II: Total War* offers an interesting sample of the range of choices available to game designers wishing to maintain a balance between entertainment value and reasonable historical accuracy.

In *Age of Empires II: The Conquerors*, the campaign entitled "Montezuma" consists of six levels organized along a narrative that reveals itself through a series of cutscenes. While this narrative mirrors the history of the conquest for most of the campaign, counterfactual components appear, especially in the later levels, in order to make an Aztec victory against the Spaniards feasible. This is a necessity because the game would be devoid of interest if the player, who always controls the Aztec side, was destined to lose.[25] The campaign, in which the theme of dominance appears both explicitly and implicitly, does not fully cover the origins of the Aztecs, but some references are made to the pre-Contact period as a means of explaining the unfolding of events.

The first level in the campaign, entitled "Reign of Blood," conveys important components of Aztec dominance pertaining to the extent and nature of the empire they ruled before the arrival of the Spanish and the way its structure created for them numerous enemies. The cutscenes prefacing this level give the player a sense of the Aztecs' observance of human sacrifice, albeit slightly exaggerating its importance. While it is true that the Aztecs offered the many captives they acquired through conquests as sacrificial gifts to their gods, it was not the sole reason for conquest as the narrator of the cutscene suggests when stating that "much of our empire ... has been conquered in the name of sacrifice. The magicians tell us that we must make a sacrifice every single day for the sun to continue to rise."[26] Obtaining financial tribute was in fact also very important for the Aztecs. This choice of downplaying tribute in favor of human sacrifice can be ascribed to the fascinating character of human sacrifice and its widespread association with the Aztecs, whereas mere tribute might have appeared much less exotic and, therefore, much less appealing.

In the second level of the campaign, "Triple Alliance," the game designers attempt to illustrate the political relationship of dominance that the Aztecs maintained through the Triple Alliance. Just as they ignore financial tribute as an imperial purpose behind the Triple Alliance, here again they simplify the facts and present the purpose of the Alliance as, quite simply, "to attack our long-time enemies, the Tlaxcala."[27] The player's objective in this level is to deliver summons of war to the Texcoco and Tlacopan town centers. Dominance is obvious in this representation: when the player's Aztec unit arrives at the town center, he does not request but rather *demands*, on behalf of Montezuma, that Tlacopan and Texcoco go to war with the Tlaxcala. The responses are equally revealing: the Tlacopan replies by saying that "Montezuma oversteps his authority, but we will comply," while the Texcoco point out that "Montezuma asks us to do much for the Aztecs, but we will do his bidding ... for now."[28]

Later in this second level, the player then has to defeat the Tlaxcala by destroying most of their units and buildings, with the aid of the alliance partners. However, once the Tlaxcala are defeated, the player's allies suddenly revolt against the Aztecs, and must be defeated as well. This is historically inaccurate, as the Aztecs did not have open war against the other members of the Triple Alliance before the arrival of the Spaniards. But in a context where gameplay centers on military rather than political maneuvers, this inaccuracy allows the game to convey both the tensions and the dominance of Tenochtitlan within the Triple Alliance by collapsing a more complex political process into a metonymic event. Besides illustrating the way in which the Aztecs treated their allies, this design choice also helps the player understand why, later in the campaign, Cortés so easily manages to recruit local allies, and why patterns of dominance lead the former members of the Triple Alliance to defect to the enemy camp.

In creating a campaign that concludes with an Aztec victory, it is difficult to ignore the main factors that led to the Aztecs' historical defeat, namely the technological gap and different cultural perceptions of warfare between the Aztecs and the Spanish. The most interesting game design challenges for this campaign of *Age of Empires II* may well be the need to reconcile these factors with the presentation of an Aztec victory as a plausible outcome.

That challenge was only partially met. The clash in cultural perceptions of warfare was all but ignored by the designers, probably because of those technical limitations in the game mechanics, which Mir and Owens categorize (drawing on Bogost) as "Procedural Rhetoric."[29] The natural way to represent the effects of the Spanish approach to warfare would have been to introduce a morale modifier similar to the one found in *Medieval II: Total War*, as discussed below. In the absence of such a modifier, any encounter between two units is simply resolved by the victory of the unit with the most hit points, in a way that closely follows the Conquistadores' conception of military success and almost entirely ignores its Aztec counterpart.

The game designers tackled more directly the second possible alteration: uneven access to military technology. As the narrator points out in the cutscene preceding level five, "Boiling Lake," "Although our Aztec warriors fought well that day, my men were frightened by the beasts that the Spanish rode into combat, and by the noise of their exploding weapons."[30] Through this statement, the designers underline the disadvantage of having neither horses nor firearms. However, counterfactualism ensures that the possibility of victory still remains within reach for the Aztecs. Thus, after defeating some Spanish conquistadors on the run, the player receives a message stating "We captured a Spanish horse! Perhaps if we return it to our town center we can learn how to ride it."[31] Later, in the same level, once the player's forces close in on the Spanish base, horse-drawn trade carts appear that can be converted into one of the player's units. Another message then pops up, explaining that the Spanish trade cart carried gunpowder, and if the player brings it back to the town center, "there is no reason we [Aztecs] cannot learn to use the gunpowder to make cannons of our own."[32] Through this radical elision of the process of technological acquisition, the player can produce musketeers, artillery units, and cannoned guard towers, which offer the only way to defeat the better equipped Spanish units. While this game mechanic constitutes a grossly simplified and, ultimately, counterfactual representation of historical reality, it nevertheless allows the game designers to convey the full importance of military technology in establishing dominance, whereas it remains impossible for them to portray the contrast efficiently in military cultures.

The *Montezuma* campaign in *Age of Empires II* follows a very linear structure, in which cutscenes play a central role not only in structuring the narrative, but also in representing historical events from the Aztec point of view. This historical representation is, overall, fairly close to what can be found in academic historiography, although the accuracy falls short when it runs against some gameplay mechanics (such as in the representation of differing cultural attitudes to warfare) and, obviously, insofar as the game provides for alternative outcomes for the campaign.

Medieval II: Total War

Medieval II: Total War, the other game examined here, does much better at representing this clash of cultural perceptions of warfare. The *Total War* franchise shares with its *Age of Empires* counterpart a focus on historical confrontations on the battlefield. It also offers some predetermined "scenario battles." However, unlike *Age of Empires*, the campaign mode of *Medieval II: Total War* follows a nonlinear structure, in which battles are brought about by the player's turn-based actions on a broader strategic map rather than by a predetermined scenario. In *Medieval II: Total War*'s "Americas" campaign, the player is given the option to choose from the various factions present in America during the early sixteenth century and, regardless of which faction the player chooses, the goals and progression throughout the game are essentially the same.

While the game designers do not enjoy the degree of control over the player's experience that a linear scenario could offer, they manage to integrate specific elements of historical accuracy in a number of ways. For example, when Cortés is one of the player's generals, his unit possesses extra strength, thereby echoing a frequent—if outdated—historiographical trope praising Cortés's individual qualities.[33] This is something that *Age of Empires II* cannot represent.

Yet the value in *Medieval II: Total War*'s historical representation of dominance first and foremost resides in battlefield tactics. The best example can be found in the preset single-battle scenario "Battle of Otumba," where, returning from his first expulsion from Tenochtitlan, Cortés arrives to meet a massively assembled Aztec army. Before the battle, the player has the option to review the strengths and weaknesses of the combatants on either side. Thus the Spanish have "excellent infantry, cavalry, and missile troops," but a "small number of men [and they] must rely on native mercenaries."[34] The Aztecs, on the other hand, are "brave, zealous, and vast in numbers," but "completely lacking in armor and weapon technology."[35] This assessment, as it turns out, aligns neatly with the consensus among historians, as do the comments of the narrator who introduces the battle: "The Aztecs, without knowledge of horses in battle, have chosen to meet the Spaniards on Otumba's open plains, rather than amongst the crags and forests that would have negated the awesome power of Cortés's cavalry."[36] All of these considerations allow the game designers to highlight the Spanish dominance in an elegant and relatively accurate fashion.

Furthermore, one particular feature pushes the accuracy even further by integrating the contrast in cultural approaches to warfare, which Cortés used to establish his dominance, into the game mechanics. Thus as the camera pans over the Aztec army before the battle begins, the narrator singles out a number of Aztec "chiefs," wearing easily identifiable feathers and decorations. These are the prime targets of the player, who by the rules of the scenario must lead the Spanish troops, as the death of this handful of warriors brings about the collapse of the Aztec army. Through this mechanic, the game designers very efficiently replicate the observation of Clendinnen who, as we already noted above, points out that "[t]he psychological demoralization attending those sudden, trivializing deaths of great men painted for war, but not yet engaged in combat, must have been formidable."[37] Despite the nonlinear nature of their game, the designers of *Medieval II: Total War* thus manage to integrate factors underlying the relationship of dominance on the battlefield in one of its most important tactical incarnations, contrasting cultural perceptions of warfare.

Unequal relationships and Aztec history

Dominance, as an unequal relationship between two parties, played a central role throughout the history of the Aztecs, starting with their origin myth. It defined their self-perception and framed the relationships with surrounding tribes, through which they rose to prominence in Mesoamerica. When Cortés arrived in central Mexico, he quickly understood and exploited the weaknesses of this system and turned the tables on the Aztecs.

Dominance is likewise a central component of many video games, making the latter an ideal medium to convey this aspect of the historical Aztec experience. But video games are subject to a number of unique constraints, beginning with the basic requirement of being fun and understandable for their target audience. As the examples of *Age of Empires II* and *Medieval II: Total War* demonstrate, the gameplay structure that characterizes a given franchise also offers unique challenges and opportunities for those seeking representations of history that are reasonably aligned with the conclusions of scholarly historians.

The designers of *Age of Empires II* consequently managed to convey the relationship of dominance even in their portrayal of an alternative history. They did so, for example, by retaining the association between technological superiority and military dominance, even if they withdrew the Spanish monopoly over such technological superiority from their counterfactual universe. The designers of *Medieval II: Total War* opted for an entirely different yet complementary approach that fills many of the gaps left by *Age of Empires II*, specifically in the representation of differing cultural perceptions of warfare and their concrete effects. More generally, in the absence of a linear structure to the game's campaign, elements of historical accuracy in *Medieval II: Total War* are concentrated at the battlefield level, whereas the designers of *Age of Empires II* make extensive use of narrative elements, especially in the shape of cutscenes.

Every medium has strengths and weaknesses when it comes to its ability to convey a given aspect of reality, and video games are no different. Many point out that this medium has a tendency to oversimplify its representation of reality, a weakness that largely derives from technological limitations that are slowly but surely fading away, and from the need to connect with a non-specialist audience. This medium is also liable to present historical myths and misconceptions as fact, even when historical accuracy is central to the game's presentation and marketing. However, it is important to remember that none of these shortcomings is unique to video games, which should therefore be compared to other popular representations of history such as trade books, television programs, and films.

Much more importantly, as discussed in earlier chapters, academic historiography itself is not free from medium-specific limitations either, and indeed an extensive literature exists that discusses the shortcomings of academic historical writing.[38] Whether or not they accept the premises of postmodernist and postcolonial approaches, historians should acknowledge that the very format of the academic articles and monographs they write is fundamentally different from the experience of the historical characters they discuss. The Aztecs did not approach dominance as an abstract concept, they *lived* it, they exerted it, and they suffered it. And this is the point where video games can excel: both *Age of Empires II* and *Medieval II: Total War* manage, through a variety of gameplay mechanics, to convey dominance without ever naming it, and therefore mimic the experience of historical actors more accurately than almost any scholarly monograph or article.

Notes

This chapter is based on a research paper by Joshua Holdenried in the undergraduate honors seminar *Representations of History in Video games*, taught by Nicolas Trépanier (University of Mississippi, Spring 2011). Nicolas Trépanier has rewritten and revised the text in order to make its publication possible.

1 Mesoamerica was, before European contact, a culturally coherent region that encompassed, roughly speaking, the southern half of modern-day Mexico, as well as Belize, Guatemala, Salvador, and parts of Honduras and Nicaragua.

2 A quick search for the keyword "Aztecs" on Amazon.com brings up approximately 3,700 items under "Books," and over two hundred under "Movies & TV."

3 For more on this, see Reynolds's discussion of potential narratives in Chapter 2.

4 Or, as Jesper Juul would put it, an outcome with a more desirable value. *Half-Real: Video Games between Real Rules and Fictional Worlds*. Cambridge, MA: MIT Press, 2005, 6–7.

5 Miguel León-Portilla, "Mesoamerica before 1519," in Ed. Leslie Bethell, *The Cambridge History of Latin America. Volume I: Colonial Latin America*. Cambridge: Cambridge University Press, 1984, 14.

6 *Idem*. See also Mir and Owens's discussion of the aftermath of European colonization in Chapter 6.

7 León-Portilla, "Mesoamerica before 1519," 14–16.

8 León-Portilla, "Mesoamerica before 1519," 14–15, 25.

9 León-Portilla, "Mesoamerica before 1519," 17.

10 Stuart B. Schwartz, *Victors and Vanquished: Spanish and Nahua Views of the Conquest of Mexico*. Boston, MA: Bedford/St. Martin's, 2000, 5–6; Michael E. Smith adds that the stability of the uneven "alliance" also rested to a considerable extent on the willing collaboration of Tlacopan and Texcoco elites, co-opted "through marriage alliances, preferred trade agreements, and other mechanisms," especially since "the burden of tribute fell on provincial commoners, not the elite" ("The Role of Social Stratification in the Aztec Empire: A View from the Provinces," *American Anthropologist*, 88, no. 1 (1986): 71).

11 Inga Clendinnen, " 'Fierce and Unnatural Cruelty': Cortés and the Conquest of Mexico," *Representations*, 33, special issue: the new world (Winter 1991): 78.

12 Friedrich Katz, "The Evolution Of Aztec Society," *Past and Present*, 13, no. 1 (1958): 18–19; León-Portilla, "Mesoamerica before 1519," 17–18; Ross Hassig, *Trade, Tribute, and Transportation: The Sixteenth-Century Political*

Economy of the Valley of Mexico. Norman, OK: University of Oklahoma Press, 1985, 103–110.

13 Inga Clendinnen, "The Cost of Courage in Aztec Society," *Past and Present*, 107, no. 1 (May 1985), 53–54.

14 Schwartz, *Victors and Vanquished*, 12.

15 Clendinnen, "Fierce and Unnatural Cruelty," 78.

16 Clendinnen, "Fierce and Unnatural Cruelty," 78.

17 Clendinnen, "The Cost of Courage in Aztec Society," 50.

18 Schwartz, *Victors and Vanquished*, 14. This does not, however, mean that Spain held complete and permanent control of the region afterwards. On this subject, see Matthew Restall, *Seven Myths of the Spanish Conquest*. Oxford and New York: Oxford University Press, 2003, 64–76.

19 Clendinnen, "Fierce and Unnatural Cruelty," 74 and 89.

20 Schwartz, *Victors and Vanquished*, 14.

21 Clendinnen, "The Cost of Courage in Aztec Society," 62.

22 Clendinnen, "Fierce and Unnatural Cruelty," 81.

23 Clendinnen, "Fierce and Unnatural Cruelty," 80.

24 Clendinnen, "Fierce and Unnatural Cruelty," 80.

25 As Juul points out (*Half-Real*, 7), this ability to influence the outcome in fact is a necessary condition to call this a "game" in the first place.

26 *Age of Empires II: Reign of Blood.*

27 *Age of Empires II: Triple Alliance.*

28 *Age of Empires II: Triple Alliance.*

29 See Mir and Owens, Chapter 6.

30 *Age of Empires II: Boiling Lake.*

31 *Age of Empires II: Boiling Lake.*

32 *Age of Empires II: Boiling Lake.*

33 Clendinnen, "Fierce and Unnatural Cruelty," 65–66. The same author makes a detailed portrait of the man as intensely ruthless and energetic, but also theatrical, rational, and calculative in his methods, manipulative in almost all of his human interactions, and driven by self-interest above and beyond anything else (72–75).

34 *Medieval II: Total War.*

35 *Medieval II: Total War.*

36 *Medieval II: Total War.*

37 Clendinnen, "Fierce and Unnatural Cruelty," 80.

38 One can mention Edward Said, *Orientalism*. New York: Pantheon Books, 1978, and Hayden White, *The Content of the Form: Narrative Discourse and Historical Representation*. Baltimore, MD: Johns Hopkins University Press, 1987, just to name the harshest critics. See also the introduction to this volume and Peterson, Miller, and Fedorko's discussion of historiography in Chapter 1.

Works cited

Clendinnen, Inga. "The Cost of Courage in Aztec Society," *Past and Present*, 107, no. 1 (May 1985): 44–89.

Clendinnen, Inga. " 'Fierce and Unnatural Cruelty': Cortés and the Conquest of Mexico," *Representations*, 33, special issue: the new world (Winter 1991): 65–100.

Elliott, John Huxtable. "The Spanish conquest and settlement of America," in Ed. Leslie Bethell, *The Cambridge History of Latin America. Volume I: Colonial Latin America*. Cambridge, UK: Cambridge University Press, 1984, 149–206.

Hassig, Ross. *Trade, Tribute, and Transportation: The Sixteenth-Century Political Economy of the Valley of Mexico*. Norman, OK: University of Oklahoma Press, 1985.

Hicks, Frederic. " 'Flowery War' in Aztec History," *American Ethnologist*, 6, no. 1 (February 1979): 87–92.

Juul, Jesper. *Half-Real: Video Games Between Real Rules and Fictional Worlds*. Cambridge, MA: MIT Press, 2005.

Katz, Friedrich. "The Evolution of Aztec Society," *Past and Present*, 13, no. 1 (1958): 14–25.

León-Portilla, Miguel. "Mesoamerica before 1519," in Ed. Leslie Bethell, *The Cambridge History of Latin America. Volume I: Colonial Latin America*. Cambridge, UK: Cambridge University Press, 1984, 3–36.

Restall, Matthew. *Seven Myths of the Spanish Conquest*. Oxford and New York: Oxford University Press, 2003.

Schwartz, Stuart B. *Victors and Vanquished: Spanish and Nahua Views of the Conquest of Mexico*. Boston, MA: Bedford/St. Martin's, 2000.

Smith, Michael E. "The Role of Social Stratification in the Aztec Empire: A View from the Provinces," *American Anthropologist*, 88, no. 1 (1986): 70–91.

Games cited

Age of Empires II: The Conquerors. Tokyo, Japan: Ensemble Studios, Konami, 2000.

Medieval II: Total War: Kingdoms. Tokyo, Japan: The Creative Assembly, Sega, 2007.

8

Historical Novel Revived: The Heyday of *Romance of the Three Kingdoms* Role-Playing Games

Hyuk-Chan Kwon
City University of Hong Kong

Introduction

This essay discusses how *Sanguozhi yanyi* 三國志演義 (*Romance of the Three Kingdoms*; hereafter *Three Kingdoms*), a Chinese historical novel, has survived the downfall of traditional narratives by transforming itself into a historical role-playing game. In this essay, I will first discuss readers' engagement with the novels and their uses in a host of areas such as Japanese corporate culture, followed by a discussion of progress of the novel's readership. These observations will be followed by a discussion of fandom and transmedia engagement with *Three Kingdoms*, and will be concluded with a discussion of how these failed aspirations of the traditional readers of the novel are realized virtually in the *Three Kingdoms* role-playing games.

Three Kingdoms is a Chinese historical novel whose attributed author is Luo Guanzhong. There being many debates regarding its authorship and date of publication, its oldest complete printed edition was published no later than 1522 in the Ming dynasty. *Three Kingdoms* has been hugely important within China, where it has been avidly read and studied by scholars since its appearance in 1522, but it also achieved classic status in Korea, Japan, Vietnam, and other areas within the Chinese cultural sphere.[1]

Moss Roberts, who translated the work into English, introduces it as follows in the inner cover of his book.

> *Three Kingdoms* tells the story of the fateful last reign of the Han dynasty (206 B.C.–A.D. 220), when the Chinese empire was divided into three warring kingdoms. Writing some 1,200 years later, the Ming author Luo Guanzhong drew on histories, dramas, and poems portraying the crisis to fashion a sophisticated, compelling narrative that has become the Chinese national epic. The novel offers an intimate and unsparing view of how power is wielded, how diplomacy is conducted, and how wars are planned and fought. As important for Chinese culture as the Homeric epics have been for the West, this Ming dynasty masterpiece continues to be widely influential in China, Korea, Japan, and Vietnam, and remains a great work of world literature.[2]

Three Kingdoms is a work often described as "seven parts truth and three parts fiction" (*qishi sanxu* 七實三虛), which was brought to completion by Luo Guanzhong's meticulous comparisons with and investigations of *Sanguo zhi* (*Chronicles of the Three Kingdoms*) by Chen Shou 陳壽. It chronicles the lives of feudal lords and their retainers, who tried to replace the declining Han Dynasty. Whereas the novel features hundreds of heroes, the main focus is on the three states of (1) Shu, led by Liu Bei; (2) Wei, led by Cao Cao; and (3) Wu, led by Sun Quan and the struggles of these states to reunite China for nearly 100 years.

Moreover, the popularity noted by Moss Roberts shows no signs of abating. *Three Kingdoms* remains one of the most widely read Chinese novels in Korea and Japan in particular. For example, Yi Munyŏl's translation of *Three Kingdoms* (1984) alone has sold some seventeen million copies (and counting), making it the number one Korean best seller of all time; needless to say, numerous other translations and adaptations of *Three Kingdoms* also circulate in the Korean book market. Among the numerous heroes in the original work, some heroes were favored more by different types of readers in different periods. For example, compared to readers in China, for many decades Japanese readers have shown a tendency to favor Cao Cao, the greatest antihero against Liu Bei, upon whom many Confucian historians such as Sima Guang bestowed historical legitimacy in terms of Neo-Confucian ideology. Guan Yu, one of the most popular heroes in the novel, later even acquired the status of the guardian of early dynasty of Chosŏn Korea in Korean folk literature and popular religion.[3] In this regard, several adaptations of the novel in which Guan Yu plays the most important role have appeared in the late Chosŏn period. Such diverse adaptations of the original demonstrate that readers with different cultural and national backgrounds favored different heroes, and that in many cases, the biggest heroes in these adaptations were not necessarily those who played the most important roles in the original. Such shifts in terms of the narrative structure in rewritings of *Three Kingdoms* is worth noting in that they eventually result in myriad open endings, as seen in contemporary *Three Kingdoms*–based role-playing games.

To be more specific, the first full-scale rewriting of *Three Kingdoms* was initiated by Yoshikawa Eiji (吉川英治, 1892–1962), who serialized his rewriting of the work in a newspaper from 1939 to 1942, and his rewriting followed the narrative tradition of his samurai novels, such as *Taikō ki* and *Miyamoto Musashi*. Yoshikawa's *Three Kingdoms* literally influenced most subsequent Korean and Japanese translations, with each translator or rewriter highly conscious of that work's status and success. More importantly, in his rewriting of *Three Kingdoms*, Yoshikawa did not hesitate to change the plot while rendering a traditional Chinese novel into the style of a samurai novel. In his rewriting, Yoshikawa routinely follows the patterns and ideologies typical in samurai novels. One outstanding feature of samurai stories is that the relationship between the feudal lord (*shōgun* 將軍 or *daimyō* 大名) and his retainers functions as an underlying principle of the work. This feudal relationship has survived the downfall of the *bakufu* 幕府. Indeed, it has taken on new connotations regarding the relationship between corporate leaders and so-called *sararīman* ("salary man," i.e. male salaried employees), a social class in modern Japanese society. Since the Second World War, the social norm for the ordinary Japanese man involves becoming a *sararīman* at a big corporation and getting promoted step by step while owing loyalty to company life, thus ensuring a stable, middle-class lifestyle for himself and his family. Japanese men often compare themselves to a retainer and their boss to a shōgun or daimyō. By the same token, rivalry between factions in a company can be compared to a power struggle between smaller daimyōs, or subordinates under a bigger daimyō or shōgun.

In such circumstances, samurai stories that emphasize notions such as the relationship between feudal lord and retainer and related survival skills under such situations are recognized as having a value that goes beyond simple entertainment. In Yoshikawa's rewriting, such notions as the relationship between a lord and his subjects and choosing the right lord and paying loyalty to him are more emphasized than in the original work. This partly explains why the Yoshikawa-style revisions of *Three Kingdoms* have been more popular and influential in Japan and Korea than the translations based on the Mao edition.

In this respect, it is no coincidence that the *Romance of the Three Kingdoms* game series published by the Koei company resembles Koei's other historical role-playing games that deal with the power struggles for unification of Japan during the Sengoku (Warring States) period and feature many heroes who appeared during that period. Koei's *Romance of the Three Kingdoms* series remains the best-known and best-selling role-playing game series in terms of re-creating key events in Asian history and representing hundreds of historical personages of the later Han empire.

However, given the close relationship between the Japanese rewritings of *Three Kingdoms* based on the narrative features of samurai fiction, one realizes that it is not a coincidence that from the first installment of the *Romance of the Three Kingdoms* series up to the most recent twelfth installment, the relationship between the feudal lord and his retainers functions as an underlying principle of the work. Throughout the role-playing game series, the player is requested to adopt the role of a feudal lord in the *Three Kingdoms* period and recruit, control, and increase his retainers in order to conquer the Central Plain (*zhongyuan* 中原) and reunite the country to win the game. As is the case with Japanese and Korean rewritings of *Three Kingdoms*, many players of the *Romance of the Three Kingdoms* game series have taken the line that by playing the game series, they gain survival skills in a society characterized by constant power struggles, which has been offered as a reasonable excuse for Japanese adult males to play the game after work. The appearance of Japanese Warring States period heroes such as Oda Nobunaga in some expansions of *Romance of the Three Kingdoms* can be understood in the same context, albeit seemingly as an absurd anachronism.

The above-mentioned examples, which suggest that one can acquire survival skills by appreciating *Three Kingdoms*–related cultural products, demonstrate a key reason behind *Three Kingdoms'* enduring popularity, as reflected in contemporary east Asian popular culture and literature. The ever-increasing popularity of *Three Kingdoms* today can be attributed, in part, to the relentless modification and re-creation of its contents by famous authors. *Three Kingdoms* still remains a steady best seller in east Asia, and is also one of the most popular and steadily re-produced cultural products in the field of animation, manga, and computer games.

Progress of *Three Kingdoms* readership

Having elucidated the cultural politics that have made *Three Kingdoms* into a work with enduring popularity in east Asia, especially in Japan and Korea, I seek to examine the progress of *Three Kingdoms* readership, a key to comprehending the secret of its ever-increasing popularity. In fact, one cannot help but wonder why people, even after they have finished appreciating the work itself, become even more interested in purchasing and appreciating *Three Kingdoms*–related cultural products in different formats, which include computer games and manga. The answer is its growing fandom. There are numerous fans of *Three Kingdoms*–related cultural products, and they are eager to consume the latest versions of the work, whether these represent a mere tweak or a thorough reinterpretation of the original, whether they are new role-playing games or animations. In other words, one first develops his or her interest in the work by reading the novel, and his/her escalated interest in the work leads him/her to explore *Three Kingdoms* in other formats and in various other revisions, or vice versa.

It is virtually impossible for a modern Korean or Japanese to lead a life divorced from *Three Kingdoms*, whether one desires to or not. Even given that male readers tend to show a more apparent mania for the work in general, people of all backgrounds are nonetheless affected by *Three Kingdoms*, noticeably in terms of its cultural and sociopolitical authority in modern Korean or Japanese society.[4] Virtually everybody comes into contact with certain types of *Three Kingdoms* re-production at some point in their life. Those who develop a predilection for the work are expected to continue consuming *Three Kingdoms*–related cultural products. *Three Kingdoms* is an exceptional work in that a classical novel that first appeared some 400 years ago has developed into a continuously evolving creation based on collaborative work reflecting feedback from numerous readers and appreciators of the work. In other words, to its many fans it has evolved into a cultural product of enduring fame. It is notable that, among the numerous Korean and Japanese versions of *Three Kingdoms* available, many provide readers with opportunities to compare the historical facts with their fictitious manipulations in the novel.[5] After learning of the gap between the realities of the historical figures and the fictional characters in the novel, readers can become somewhat sympathetic to the figures whose historical images are deliberately distorted and stigmatized in the original novel. The increasing tendency of modern Japanese and Korean *Three Kingdoms* revisions to set Cao Cao as the real hero or the main protagonist instead of Liu Bei is a case in point.

Such tendencies often escalate to the point where the reader develops a preference for revisions that are based strictly on historical facts rather than on the traditional novel. Some readers deliberately favor revisions that portray characters in the work in reverse. That is, they enjoy reversing their character roles in terms of the dichotomy of good and evil, and want to see the positively depicted characters in the original work shown in a negative light, and vice versa.[6]

Many of these readers come to acquire near-expert or even expert knowledge of *Three Kingdoms*, which includes detailed knowledge of the discrepancies between historical facts about the *Three Kingdoms* period of China and the novel, the revisions made to major editions of the novel, and the way that historical figures and their deeds are reflected in the protagonists in the work. Such a high level of expertise is made possible by the emergence of numerous *Three Kingdoms* reference books, websites, and digital databases. The reader often attempts to accommodate new *Three Kingdoms* revisions enhanced with more liberated and imaginative interpretations and re-creations in terms of translations or adaptations of the novel, console games, Internet role-playing games, cartoons, and animations. At this stage, the reader's primary concern, in most cases, is not how characters are portrayed in the revised work, whether positively or negatively, but whether the revised work demonstrates a high level of achievement as an independent complete work. In fact, they are willing to accept uninhibited interpretations of the characters, such as altering the gender of the characters in the original work. This last tendency is more apparent in *Three Kingdoms*–based comics, animations, and computer games than in translations or other written adaptations of the novel. For example, Guan Yu, Zhang Fei, and Zhuge Liang have been portrayed as women in several revised works.[7]

As for the development of readership through various each stages, not all readers start from reading the book first, nor do they all end up acknowledging that creations and revisions of *Three Kingdoms*, a historical novel, are reflections of its contemporary context. Depending on each reader's specific background and circumstances when he or she first encounters the work, each person starts from a distinct stage and displays a distinct pace of progress. For example, a (Japanese) author of a *Three Kingdoms* reference book began his acquaintance with the work by playing a console game and ended up writing books on the historical background of the novel.[8] Some readers (male readers in many cases), even after going through numerous revisions and reference materials about the work, tend to stay at the basic level, which mainly involves comparing the level of martial arts prowess and intelligence of the characters in terms of numerical points. As a matter of fact, ranking of the characters based on a point system has been a fundamental feature of *Three Kingdoms*–related computer games (both online and console). For example, in terms of points for martial valor (*wuli* 武力), Lü Bu often acquires the full score (100), followed by ninety-nine points for Guan Yu. Accordingly, for intelligence, Zhuge Liang perennially scores the highest points (100), followed closely by Pang Tong's ninety-nine points.[9]

This rather unsophisticated ranking of *Three Kingdoms* characters can be observed not only among adolescent users of *Three Kingdoms* computer games, but also in serious academic research conducted by scholars. A team of six Korean literature scholars in the Center for Korean Studies at Inha University, upon performing a two-year research project on Korean translations of *Three Kingdoms*, announced their nominations for the Top Ten Warriors in Martial Valor (*muryŏk sipkŏl* 武力十傑) and Top Six Strategists (*mosa yukkŏl* 謀士六傑) in 2005.[10]

This example demonstrates that even researchers of the novel are highly likely to be devoted fans as well. Ardent fans of *Three Kingdoms* have a mania for the work that rivals that of fans of the *Star Wars* series. Numerous *Star Wars* fans seek out sequels after watching the initial installment and mostly end up watching all sequels, prequels, and "director's cut" special editions; they also end up purchasing *Star Wars*–related toys, souvenirs, animations, and games.[11] Likewise, ardent devotees of *Three Kingdoms* continue to consume *Three Kingdoms*–related products, which include various versions of *Three Kingdoms* revisions/re-creations, movies, drama series, comic books, animations, and computer games. *Three Kingdoms* is a textbook example of a "one-source multi-use" product with unlimited marketability. It should also be noted that numerous distinct kinds of re-creations of the work are being produced to satisfy consumers of the *Three Kingdoms* cultural entertainment industry so that each reader, player, or viewer can select the revision that suits his or her stage of preference best. Sometimes the emergence of distinct re-creations of the work leads the fans of *Three Kingdoms* into specific trends. By the same token, the erudition of the consumer urges the producers to create new versions of the work. In this context, "The reader is both the producer and the consumer of a text."[12]

Koei's *Romance of the Three Kingdoms* series: Failed aspirations realized virtually

As noted above, among the copious number of *Three Kingdoms*–based computer games, the *Romance of the Three Kingdoms* series by the Japanese video game publisher, Koei, has been the best known for the past two decades and counting. With its first installment published in Japan in 1985, twelve installments of the game have been published in Japan, Korea, China, Taiwan, and North America. It is a series of turn-based role-playing war games.

That said, many game players and critics point out that the *Romance of the Three Kingdoms* series, especially its first installment, was in fact based roughly on *Nobunaga's Ambition* (*Nobunaga no yabō* 信長の野望), the first strategy game produced by the same publisher in 1983. These two games have many things in common; they are both turn-based role-playing war games. The player strives to unite the warring kingdoms into a unified empire by playing one of the most famous heroes/generals in a time of political turmoil where many warlords played by the computer (artificial intelligence) also compete with each other to be the winner. In reality, *Nobunaga's Ambition* series has tended to be equally or more popular than the *Romance of the Three Kingdoms* series in the Japanese domestic market, reaching its thirteenth installment to date. However, in other Asian countries where *Three Kingdoms* has enjoyed enduring popularity, the *Romance of the Three Kingdoms* series has always trumped *Nobunaga's Ambition* series. As a matter of fact, many installments of *Nobunaga's Ambition* series were not even imported to the above Asian countries that had suffered frequent Japanese invasions, with the Second World War being the most recent one.[13]

Critics' descriptions of gameplay show how these two games resemble each other. Speaking about *Nobunaga's Ambition*, Evan Brooks of *Computer Gaming World* observes:

One may transfer soldiers between fiefs, go to war, increase taxes (which causes a decrease in peasant loyalty which may lead to rebellion), transfer rice or gold to another fief, raise the level of flood control (which decreases productivity), make a nonaggression pact or arrange a marriage, cultivate (which increases productivity, but decreases peasant loyalty), use a merchant (to buy/sell rice, borrow funds, or purchase weapons), recruit for the military (soldiers or ninja), train the army (which increases fighting efficiency), spy on a rival, expand a town (which increases taxes collected, but decreases peasant loyalty), give food/rice to peasants/soldiers (to raise morale), steal peasants from rival daimyos, allocate military strength, recuperate (even a daimyo can get sick), turn over a controlled fief to the computer for administration, or pass a turn (hint: when one has no idea of what to do, train the troops).[14]

Dave Arneson reviews the *Romance of the Three Kingdoms* as follows:

[It is] a great historical simulation and will keep players at their keyboards for many a night in order to win their empires. It has economics, intrigue, bribery, covert action, diplomacy, war, and more! There are many ways beyond simple conquest to accomplish one's goals.[15]

After all, what has been attracting game players most is that one can try to conquer the Central Plain (*zhongyuan* 中原, which is equivalent to the entire "civilized" world according to Confucian ideologies) and (re)unite the country to win the game. In other words, the player himself/herself can serve the historical justice that had never been realized in history.

During the Sengoku period in Japan, Oda Nobunaga, with his brilliant strategy and audacious nature, came quite close to subduing all of his rivals and uniting Japan, only to be betrayed by one of his closest subordinates and die in Honnōji, a temple in Kyoto. His unparalleled epic adventures and tragic death made him the most popular hero of the Sengoku period not only in history but also in many historical novels dealing with his and his rivals' aspirations for uniting Japan.[16]

In reality, it was the Sima clan who succeeded the State of Wei established by Cao Cao and reunited China. Additionally, in official history Cao Cao was commander of the Han forces and prime minister of the Han empire, and many historians such as Chen Shou, the author of *Chronicles of the Three Kingdoms*, acknowledged Cao Cao as the legitimate ruler of China in the *Three Kingdoms* period. However, in Chinese popular literature and oral tradition, Liu Bei and his sworn brothers have long been the real heroes while Cao Cao has been remembered as a cunning and evil villain. The Mao edition of *Three Kingdoms* deliberately favors Liu Bei as the only legitimate ruler in terms of Confucian ideology, although in reality he had controlled only one of China's eleven provinces (roughly, modern Sichuan province), while Cao Cao occupied many of the remaining provinces. Despite the pro-Liu bias, the novel itself cannot twist the very fact that Liu Bei was not a real victor in that he died a warlord and his son capitulated to his archenemies instead of reuniting China. As a matter of fact, after the main protagonists of the Kingdom of Shu all die out in the original work, readers' interest diminishes drastically.[17] In this sense, many translators of the novel cut and abbreviate the chapters following the death of Kongming, the one last hero of the Kingdom of Shu (in Chapter 104). This has been a perennial problem of *Three Kingdoms* since by the time Liu Bei and his sworn brothers all die out, it is likely that most readers' enthusiasm fades along with it. They feel too empty to finish the book and often end up just skimming through the remaining part. It marks the point where many readers come to dislike the fact that *Three Kingdoms* is essentially a historical novel, even if they appreciate the historical accuracy of the work.

The *Romance of the Three Kingdoms* series (and *Nobunaga's Ambition* series as well) helped to solve this dilemma. Game players, who used to be readers of the work and whose hands were tied in that they could not intervene in the plot, can now rewrite the historical "truth" in terms of re-creating key events in Asian history and re-living hundreds of historical personages of the later Han Empire. Game players can freely choose their own hero and try to unite the divided empire on their own; they can write alternative histories that they wished to be true and imagined prior to this game's arrival. They can intervene in history at various stages and levels; players can slightly alter minor details of history or totally rewrite it. In fact, earlier installments of *Romance of the Three Kingdoms* only allowed the game players to play warlords and major generals. However, with each passing installment, players acquire more freedom; even a minor character in the work, including a commoner, can win the game and reunite the empire, which demonstrates that Koei had to accommodate game players' aspirations, which could not see the light of the day for over a millennium. Of course, it needs far more strategic planning, time, resources, effort, and luck (most importantly) to win the game as a commoner. Yet it is not impossible.

In fact, there was an instance of a player who chose a commoner in the tenth installment of the *Romance of the Three Kingdoms*, defeated all warlords, and reunited China. He deliberately selected the weakest character in the game in terms of the numerical point system to measure the abilities of characters in the game. The commoner is given the lowest points for all five aspects of the point system; only one point is given for each aspect of his abilities for leadership, martial valor, intelligence, statesmanship, and attraction. He even has an extremely short lifespan; he has only five years to live when the player starts the game and frequently needs to acquire items to prolong his life.

Yet the commoner overcame all ordeals and finally reunited China. It is a case in point showing that *Romance of the Three Kingdoms* allows virtually limitless combinations of endings, accommodating requests from the players and fulfilling people's aspirations for *Three Kingdoms* the novel.

Conclusion

The appearance of various *Three Kingdoms*–related cultural products has contributed to the ever-increasing popularity of the work. However, we should never ignore *Three Kingdoms*' intrinsic greatness as a narrative and its entertainment value as the fundamental key for maintaining its popularity for over four centuries in Korea. As Robert Hegel points out, *Three Kingdoms*' achievement lies largely in "humanizing historical types, in drawing poignant parallels between winners and losers, and in lamenting human inability to establish any moral order."[18] The legacy of *Three Kingdoms* will continue as readers are attracted to its intrinsic greatness in addition to various collaborative modifications that fulfill their desires to witness the unrestrained evolution of the masterpiece. In other words, modern translators and producers of *Three Kingdoms*–related cultural works have revived one of the richest legacies in human history and have brought about the heyday of a work that first appeared some 400 years ago. There is no doubt that *Three Kingdoms* will continue to thrive in the years to come; how it will evolve depends solely on those who continue to cherish this masterpiece, be they those re-creating it or those appreciating it.

Notes

1 According to Moss Roberts, *Three Kingdoms*' popularity in these countries is due to the fact that "in the four nations of Asia directly influenced by Confucianism, history is the main concern of the respective cultures" (*Three Kingdoms*, abridged ed. Berkeley, CA: University of California Press, 1999), 410.

2 Roberts, inner front cover.

3 Hyuk-Chan Kwon, "How Guan Yu Became a National Hero of Korea," *Chungguk sosŏl nonch'ong* [*Journal of Chinese Novels*], 29 (2009): 41–56.

4 See the study by Yi Sŭngch'ae, "Taehaksaengdŭl ŭi panbok toksŏ kyŏnghŏm e kwanhan yŏn'gu" [A Study on Repeat Reading Practices of College Students], *Han'guk munhŏn chŏngbo hakhoeji*, 41, no. 2 (2007): 161–180.

5 For example, each chapter of Yi Munyŏl's version of *Three Kingdoms* ends with his appended critical notes, which often provide comparisons of specific occasions in the novel with historical accounts. In *Sōten Kōro* 蒼天航路 a Japanese manga by King Gonta and Yi Hagin based on *Three Kingdoms*, the storyline primarily uses the original historical account of the era, *Chronicles of the Three Kingdoms* by Chen Shou 陳壽 as a reference rather than the *Three Kingdoms* novel. Ri Tonghyŏk's recent translation of the novel compares differences between each major edition of *Three Kingdoms* and also compares them to historical accounts. In his book, he adds brackets in the translated text and appends critical notes to the end of each chapter.

6 *Sōten Kōro* is a case in point for its highly positive portrayal of its main character, Cao Cao, who is traditionally the antagonist in *Three Kingdoms* and in many of its revisions. By the same token, Liu Bei and Zhuge Liang, the traditional heroes of *Three Kingdoms,* take on relatively less important roles and are portrayed in a less positive light. As a matter of fact, in this manga revision, contrary to the original novel, Kongming is often defeated by Cao Cao in terms of military strategy and leadership and grows excessively jealous of him. Quite a few role-playing games based on *Three Kingdoms* also treat the heroes who received less attention in the original work— namely the heroes of the states of Wei and Wu—as equal to or sometimes even more important than the traditional heroes of the House of Shu-Han. By so doing they provide game players with opportunities to play as many heroes in the role of protagonist as possible, thereby enhancing the so-called multi-play function. This approach also appeals to devoted gamers, who tend

to have a more detailed and objective knowledge of historical accounts of the *Three Kingdoms* period. As is the case with the *Romance of the Three Kingdoms*, Koei's famous *Three Kingdoms*–based game series, these *Three Kingdoms*–related games often provide dictionary entries (embedded in the game) for all characters in the game plot as well as an illustrated history of the *Three Kingdoms* period. These are provided to help game players become acquainted with the game more easily and also culminates in enhancing game players' *Three Kingdoms*–relevant knowledge.

7 Zhang Fei, one of the most masculine characters in *Three Kingdoms*, is portrayed as a young female general in a *Three Kingdoms*–based Korean comic, *Samguk changgun chŏn* 三國將軍傳 [The Story of Three Kingdoms Generals] written by Pak Suyŏng (Seoul: Champ Comics, 1997–2008). *Koihime musō: Doki otomedarake no "Sangokushi engi"* 恋姫†無双 ～ド キッ☆乙女だらけの三国志演義, a Japanese animation and strategy game released in 2007 by BaseSon, portrays all main characters save Liu Bei as cute young girls.

8 This is a reference to Koide Fumiik'o, *Samgukchi inmul sajŏn* 三國志人物辭 典, translated by Kim Chunyŏng (Korean translation of *Sangokushi jinbutsu jiten* by Koide Fumihiko). Koide Fumihiko (born in 1967) says he began his acquaintance with the work by playing a console game as a teenager, then moved on to reading *Three Kingdoms* mangas, then to reading histories about the *Three Kingdoms* period and *Three Kingdoms* the novel, and finally ended up writing books on the historical background of the novel.

9 Among the copious number of *Three Kingdoms*–based computer games, the *Romance of the Three Kingdoms* series by the Japanese video game publisher, Koei, is the most well known; all such games tend to apply numerical point systems to measure the abilities of characters in the game.

10 This ranking was published in the following news article: Kim Hakchun, "*Samgukchi* changsu chung nuga kajang selkka" [Who Is the Mightiest among the *Three Kingdoms* Generals?], *Seoul Sinmun*, 2 April 2005.

11 *Star Wars* fans also resemble fans of *Three Kingdoms* in that they are also actively creating more liberated and imaginative interpretations and re-creations of the original work. Henry Jenkins notes this visibility of fan culture, saying "fans are the most active segment of the media audience, one that refuses to simply accept what they are given, but rather insists on the right to become full participants." See Henry Jenkins, *Convergence Culture*. New York and London: New York University Press, 2006, 131.

12 Jinhee Kim, "The Reception and Place of *Three Kingdoms* in South Korea," in Eds. Kimberly Besio and Constantine Tung, "*Three Kingdoms*" and Chinese *Culture*. New York: SUNY Press, 2008, 143–151: 149.

13 Toyotomi Hideyoshi, one of the major heroes in *Nobunaga's Ambition* series, invaded Chosŏn Korea in the 1590s. As an example of Japan's aspirations to become the dominant power in Asia, Palais mentions, "In a letter Hideyoshi sent to Korea before the invasion in 1592 he revealed his plan to conquer Ming China, install the Japanese emperor in the Chinese capital, and assign his adopted son to rule Korea, before subjugating other countries

like Ryūkyū, Taiwan, and the Philippines" (*Confucian Statecraft and Korean Institutions*. Seattle, WA: University of Washington Press, 1996, 78). It is not unusual that *Nobunaga's Ambition* was not welcomed in the Asian countries where the *Romance of the Three Kingdoms* series gained great popularity over two decades.

14 Evan Brooks, "Nobunaga's Ambition," *Computer Gaming World*, 51 (September 1988): 48.

15 Dave Arneson, "Romance of the Three Kingdoms," *Computer Gaming World*, 51 (September 1988): 12–13, 31.

16 *Tokugawa Ieyasu* 徳川家康, Yamaoka Sōhachi's (1907–1978) best-known historical novel, was first published in Korea in 1970, shortly after its serialization was completed in 1967 in Japan (serialized 1950–1967). In the 1970s both *Tokugawa Ieyasu* and various editions of *Three Kingdoms* were advertised as the same kind of story, satisfying the same purpose: teaching survival skills to readers. Publishers have often introduced *Tokugawa Ieyasu* as the "Japanese *Three Kingdoms*" and compared the three protagonists in *Tokugawa Ieyasu*—Oda Nobunaga, Toyotomi Hideyoshi, and Tokugawa Ieyasu—to the three protagonists in *Three Kingdoms*, Cao Cao, Sun Quan, and Liu Bei.

17 Among all the main characters of the novel, Kongming is the one whose entry into the novel is delayed the most. He does not appear until Chapter 38, which makes for a long-anticipated appearance when the narrative is more than one-third completed. He also outlives the other protagonists. In Chapter 78, Guan Yu dies. Cao Cao dies in Chapter 78, Zhang Fei dies in Chapter 81, and Liu Bei dies in Chapter 85.

18 Robert Hegel, "Review: *The Four Masterworks of the Ming Novel*," *Harvard Journal of Asiatic Studies*, 50, no. 1 (1990), 346–352.

Works cited

Arneson, Dave. "Romance of the Three Kingdoms," *Computer Gaming World*, 51 (September 1988): 12–13, 31.

Brooks, Evan. "Nobunaga's Ambition," *Computer Gaming World*, 51 (September 1988): 48.

Hegel, Robert. "Review for *The Four Masterworks of the Ming Novel*," *Harvard Journal of Asiatic Studies*, 50, no. 1 (1990): 346–352.

Humiik'o, Koide. *Samgukchi inmul sajŏn* 三國志人物辭典 *[Dictionary of Three Kingdoms characters]*. Trans. Kim Chunyŏng. Seoul: Tŭllyŏk, 2000. Korean translation of *Sangokushi jinbutsu jiten* by Koide Fumihiko.

Jenkins, Henry. *Convergence Culture*. New York and London: New York University Press, 2006.

Kim, Jinhee. "The Reception and Place of *Three Kingdoms* in South Korea," in Eds. Kimberly Besio and Constantine Tung, *"Three Kingdoms" and Chinese Culture*. New York: SUNY Press, 2008, 143–151.

Kwon, Hyuk-Chan. "How Guan-Yu(关羽) Became a National Hero of Korea,"
    Chungguk sosŏl nonch'ong [Journal of Chinese Novels], 29 (2009): 41–56.
Palais, James. *Confucian Statecraft and Korean Institutions*. Seattle, WA:
    University of Washington Press, 1996.
Roberts, Moss, trans. *Three Kingdoms*, abridged ed. Berkeley, CA: University of
    California Press, 1999.
Sŭngch'ae, Yi. "Taehaksaengdŭl ŭi panbok toksŏ kyŏnghŏm e kwanhan yŏn'gu"
    [A Study on Repeat Reading Practices of College Students], *Han'guk munhŏn
    chŏngbo hakhoeji*, 41, no. 2 (2007): 161–180.

Games cited

Nobunaga's Ambition (Nobunaga no yabō 信長の野望). Yokohama, Japan: Koei,
    1983.
Romance of the Three Kingdoms. Yokohama, Japan: Koei, 1985.

9

Falling in Love with History: Japanese Girls' *Otome* Sexuality and Queering Historical Imagination

Kazumi Hasegawa

Emory University

Introduction

Hakuōki, a PlayStation 2 digital game produced by Idea Factory in 2008, is based on the historical story of the Shinsengumi, a partisan force formed to protect the Tokugawa *bakufu* (the Shogunal government) in the 1860s. Their heroism had been reproduced in various Japanese media for over a century. This Japanese digital game offers players a way of "queering history," a project that challenges the particular historicism and constrained discourse of difference and identity.[1] And the primary players—80 percent—are young women and girls.[2]

This project of "queering history" is central not only to this particular game, but also to the genre of *otome* games. *Otome* games, a popular gaming genre in Japan designed specifically for girls and women, allow them to date a range of figures that are usually—but not exclusively—male, and in the case of *Hakuōki*, heroic Shinsengumi members. In those games, the protagonists are usually girls, and they explore romantic love with male figures.

What happens when girls fall in love with historical figures in digital games? Should we regard it simply as another kind of virtual dating in the same vein as online dating? How can we interpret the historical dimension of the figures and the inevitable time lag between female players and historical figures? In examining *Hakuōki*, then, this essay offers both an overview of that game and other similar ones, but it also offers a way to examine the ways in which Japanese culture allows an opportunity to explore *otome* pleasure, sexuality, and sensitivity. The surface narratives of *Hakuōki* are nationalistic and masculine. But while "heterosexual" romance does not seem subversive or explicitly "feminist" or "queer," I argue that by "falling in love" with historical figures, these Japanese girls embrace romance as a new way to interact with history, to imagine their space in the past, as well as to produce alternative narratives. The players' sexuality should be regarded as the act of "queering history," challenging the constrained discourse of difference and identity. Their *otome* pleasure, sexuality, and sensitivity should be examined positively, on the grounds that their *otome* and queer sexuality and pleasure open up a possibility of queering our way of knowing history.

Otome games

Otome games have been particularly popular among young girls and women since the early 1990s. *Otome* games are played in a range of formats on a variety of platforms, including Nintendo, PlayStation, and smart phones. The genre of *otome* games or *ren'ai* (love romance) games is now the fastest growing genre of applications in the mobile and smart phone business market. The major cell service provider NTT Docomo attributed much of its growth to the *ren'ai* game market.[3]

The game *Hakuōki—Shinsengumi Kitan* 薄桜鬼-新撰組奇譚 (*The Pale Cherry Blossom Demons: or, the Strange Ballad of Shinsengumi)*, was released by Idea Factory as a PlayStation 2 video game in 2008. Different versions have been produced for three different platforms including PlayStation 2, PlayStation Portable, and Nintendo DS.[4] This game is extremely popular and successful in the Japanese game market. For example in 2009, *Hakuōki Zuisōroku* (PS2) and *Hakuōki Portable* (PSP) won first place and third place, respectively, in the contest for Otome Game of the Year of 2009.[5]

There are several factors driving the popularity and success of *ren'ai* games. For instance, dating games were first created for boys and men to enjoy virtual heterosexual romance, which in turn laid the basis for *otome* games. What is worth mentioning is the active involvement of female game producers in *otome* production and marketing in the early 1990s. In 1992, Erikawa Keiko (a founder and Executive Director of the company called Tecmo Koei Holdings where she is currently an honorary chief) established a professional team of female game developers called the "Ruby Party." This team inaugurated several gaming projects *for women and by women*, addressing the absence of computer games with female audiences.[6] This female project team produced a popular series of *otome* games over the years, and this series in total became million sellers.[7]

What is *otome* anyway?

Otome is a nostalgic term that refers to a young girl or maiden because *shōjo* is commonly used in contemporary Japanese society. It is therefore retrospective in a literal sense but novel and queer in aesthetics, pleasure, and sexuality when it is used in popular culture, as I will discuss in this chapter. *Otome* culture seems to revive conventional ideas of femininity or girl-ness and heterosexual narratives. It could be considered a revival of traditional gender roles, which construct female agents as "mere girlfriends" of important male figures. However, these girls actively celebrate the positive energy of romance and fantasy as a way to interact with historical figures and narratives. These girls, because of their active and crystalized pleasure, tend to be regarded as deviant, queer, or *otaku*, and some of them are even called "*fujoshi* 腐女子" (rotten girls). Many young women embrace those negative and derogatory inclinations or even celebrate their queer natures while others completely hide their interests in *otome* culture.

Though many scholars of cultural studies and gender studies have examined Japanese girl culture since the 1980s, most focus on the culture of manga, particularly manga created for girls. This genre is called "*shōjo* manga," literally "girls' manga." While this research is valuable, the newer phenomenon of *otome* culture deserves more critical attention. The culture of *otome*, unlike the cases of *shōjo* or modern girls that appeared in the 1920s–1930s, does not produce visual images about these girls in themselves, but instead inscribes girls' straight but queer pleasure retrospectively, while incorporating novel aesthetics and sexuality. I will show that *otome* games play a definitive role in forming this *otome* aesthetic and sexuality in romance.

Continuities and discontinuities between *shōjo* and *otome*

Otome is not a neologism. It traditionally refers to an unmarried girl, and it invokes the ideal of her femininity and virginity. To the contemporary Japanese public, *otome* sounds classic and outdated. For example, Kitamura writes in his book about *otome*:

Are there any women who describe themselves as "*otome?*" Probably not. It's better to say that this word *otome* doesn't exist anymore. It just evokes nostalgia, or it exists as a ruin at the margins of society. An experienced actress may look back at her past and see her younger *otome* figure there. Or, perhaps those *otome* figures only exist in films and images. There are no women who want to dream *otome* figures. It might be only a territory of men's imagination. Is it then only men who seek *otome* images? Is there a gulf between men and women that never can be bridged? Women completely diverge from an image that men created.[8]

As this passage shows, *otome* is generally considered an outdated word, but in popular culture, it has been revived and is actively used by girls to describe their interest, sexuality, and aesthetic. Therefore, in this sense, the word *otome* is retrospective but novel.

Many scholars, including Honda Masuko, Kan Satoko, and Kawamura Kunihiko, point out that the word *shōjo* appeared in the process of Japanese modernity as a contrast to *shōnen* (boy) in the Meiji period.[9] The first boom of girl's culture occurred between the 1910s and the 1930s.[10] While *shōjo* is a modern act of naming (and it refers to the particular phase in a woman's life, the time of schooling and before marriage, therefore, adolescence and virginity), the word "*otome*" appeared as a reference to a young girl in Japanese literature as old as *Man'yōshū* ("the Collection of Ten Thousand Leaves"), which is the oldest existing Japanese poetry compiled after 759 AD.[11]

The creation of *otome* culture owes much to *shōjo*'s culture which developed from the 1970s. The works and cultures of *shōjo* manga have been a critical aspect of Japanese girls' or women's culture. Researchers unanimously claim that the act of reading,[12] writing, and sharing the works of *shōjo* manga among girls and women greatly contributed to create a progressive and/or experimental space where various boundaries of sexual desires and sexuality are either contested or reinscribed.[13] For example, in the early 1980s Honda Masuko classified *shōjo* culture as the culture of "*hirahira*," which describes an image "in motion" ("a free and gypsy-like sense, which doesn't rely on fixed footing") because "dreaming of fantasy and alternative worlds blurs the boundary between the 'daily reality' and the 'fantasy.' "[14] As early as the *ūman ribu* (women's liberation) movement of the 1960s, Japanese women organized their own alternative media, which was called *minikomi* ("small-scale, not-for-profit, printed matter including newsletters, zines, pamphlets, and bound journals, comprising a massive corpus of self-published feminist literature that circulated through women's networks").[15] In addition to exclusive and alternative forms of manga and publications by women, the emergence and establishment of a genre of "ladies' comics" marked a significant transformation of the *shōjo* manga culture.[16] The popularity of ladies' comics in the 1990s (*redeikomi*) showed a significant shift in the manga industry and an "evolution" of *shōjo* manga. Many of the ladies' comics include explicitly sexual, erotic, and sometimes violent contents and stories.[17] Shigemastu explains:

> Ladies' *eromanga* signaled at once a shift away from and an evolution of *shōjo* manga (comics for girls). On the one hand, ladies' comics broke away from conventional representation of female sexuality, shattering stereotypical depictions of the passivity or "tameness" of women's sexual capacities and drives. On the other hand, *redikomi* can be interpreted as a development of the exploratory forms of sexual representation that *shōjo* manga's creators gave birth to.[18]

While *shōjo* manga stories became more realistic and lost romantic elements, some girls have attempted to re-appreciate conventional romantic narratives with their own twists and moderations.[19] The emergence and popularity of Boys Love (BL) manga, focused on same-sex relations, along with *otome* game/culture, explain such a re-appreciation. In the stories of BL, Japanese girls have reconfigured heterosexual love stories as homosexual love or romance in their *shōjo* manga. Mark McLelland argues that romance between "beautiful boys" in manga is a form of Japanese girls' resistance against patriarchy, which constrains their sexuality only to a means of reproduction within heterosexual marriage. Japanese girls are able to transgress constrained or stigmatized female sexuality by finding an idealized figure that can freely fall in love with "beautiful" boys.[20]

Otome culture is frequently regarded as equivalent to BL romance; however, as various online groups on Japanese social network Mixi suggest, this is not entirely true. The BL fans are not exclusively constituents of *otome* culture. Kitsukawa Tomo, a self-identified *otome*, outlines the important difference between the fans of BL and *otome* culture. She claims that girls' preference for BL reveals their disappointment in boys who do not merit the same admiration as the male characters in manga stories. In BL, girls are not the object of boys' love. Unlike a BL story, in *otome* culture girls are the main protagonists, therefore they are "in" story. *Otome* culture, she argues, is the last place where "real" love romance is still imagined and desired.[21] Instead of the absence of girls in BL romance stories, *otome* romantic narratives in fact transcribe girls' sexuality, pleasure, and agency.

Hakuōki—Shinsengumi Kitan 薄桜鬼−新撰組奇譚 (The Pale Cherry Blossom Demons: or, the Strange Ballad of the Shinsengumi)

The main narrative of *Hakuōki* is a story of a young girl, Yukimura Chizuru, and her interactions with five Shinsengumi members and an *oni* or ogre, who is hired to work for the Satsuma domain. When a player starts up the game, she first experiences the introductory animation video that introduces a main protagonist, Yukimura Chizuru, and her five possible dates, the members of Shinsengumi. These figures are visually and aurally introduced through their voice actors called Character Voice (CV).[22] These character voices also contribute to shaping characteristics of the figures.

After this introduction, the player now prepares to enter a historic fantasy romance. She chooses a given name for the protagonist, Yukimura Chizuru. The family name Yukimura cannot be changed, but players can replace her given name Chizuru. This act of naming sets up the fantasy for a player, who becomes the protagonist Yukimura.

The Shinsengumi members are shown as romanticized, eroticized, and desirable through visual images and character voices. Visually, they are androgynous and handsome figures, which is a definitive element of girls' romance narratives and comics.[23] The personal characterization of the Shinsengumi members overlaps with the images from Shiba Ryōtarō's *Moeyo Ken* (*Blaze, My Sword*), a historical novel that originally appeared in serialized form from November 1962 to March 1964. That novel established an "archetypal" conception of the Shinsengumi as national heroes, as well as character traits for each member, a legacy followed by *Hakuōki*.[24] Similarly to Shiba's work, it positions Hijikata Toshizō, the vice-commander of the Shinsengumi, as the main protagonist who fights against the anti-*bakufu* radicals. Hijikata's character is depicted as strict, intrepid, and determined; for example, he issues strict rules on behavior enforced by capital punishment.[25] He is a determined fighter even in a period of political turmoil, and even when the political power of *bakufu* is apparently declining. It sheds light on the lives of Hijikata as well as Okita Sōji (the captain of the first unit) in the similar way that Shiba describes, instead of Kondō Isami, the head commander of the Shinsengumi. In *Hakuōki*, Kondō appears frequently in the games; however, he is an "off" character, a non-playable character that a player cannot "officially" date in the game.

The story progresses using texts and conversations between Yukimura and other characters, and by following choices that Yukimura makes. Scenes change by shifting different images and animations. The Introductory Chapter sets the context of the game: it is December 1863, the end of the Tokugawa shogunate, when the *bakufu* regime was declining and anti-*bakufu* forces were growing. Yukimura arrives in a residential area of Kyoto. She has travelled all the way from Edo, disguising her gender by wearing a *hakama* (Japanese men's trousers) so that people will not recognize her as a girl. She is looking for her father, who left Edo a month earlier and has disappeared. In Kyoto, she accidentally witnesses a sword fight between the Shinsengumi and master-less samurai (*rōnin*) and is shocked by the sight of monstrous Shinsengumi members covered with human blood. Because she saw what happened on the street, she was captured by the bloodied Shinsengumi members and taken to their residence to be interrogated and punished.

Yukimura's subsequent life with the Shinsengumi allows her to establish romantic relations with the six male characters. The goal is to make choices that lead her to "good" and happy conclusions with specific figures. The game provides twelve stories of "good" and "bad" endings with the male characters. The traditional grand completion of the game is to establish "good" relations with all six characters. Multiple-choice scenes let her decide which character she wants to go with—in other words, to date—as well as offering a range of possible actions, such as whether to leave for battles with a particular figure or instead run from dangerous situations. If her choices please her partner, an image of cherry blossom is displayed indicating that their relationship is going well.

Another romantic, erotic, and fantasy element added to the narrative of *Hakuōki* is found in the non-human features of the characters. Yukimura finds out that she is a descendent of—and in fact the only female survivor of—the Yukimura family, which is a dominant, powerful, and authentic *oni* (ogre) family in eastern Japan. An authentic *oni* has supernatural power and lives much longer than humans. The Shinsengumi was ordered by the *bakufu* to develop a special medicine called *ochimizu* (elixir of life) in order to create a physically strong military group. *Ochimizu* transforms humans to semi-ogres called *rasetsu*, but they are weaker and incompatible with authentic ogres. *Rasetsu* have some flaws; they are weak under the sun and have to suck human blood to sustain their lives. Shinsengumi members end up taking this *ochimizu* and transform themselves into *rasetsu*. When they are thirsty for blood, they take a special medicine that alleviates the thirst, or kill a human and suck one's blood, or else suck an authentic *oni*'s blood, which includes that of Yukimura. Having Yukimura's blood is the most efficient means to satisfy the hunger of the *rasetsu*. When Yukimura allows her dates to suck her blood, they are connected bodily through the exchanges of blood and life, which suggests intimate sexual relations. Such a sexually charged transfer of fluids goes further than the kissing scenes between Yukimura and the Shinsengumi. In an *otome* game like *Hakuōki*, as I have discussed before, romance is traditionally favored over explicit sex scenes, which are more characteristic of BL and lady's comics.

Textual inserts, which players read as they move between various scenes, offer context to the game narratives. On-screen text mainly describes Yukimura's subjective experience and provides descriptions of historical time, events, and landscape to help players understand the scene. Furthermore, it is an important medium because a player can read and understand Yukimura's experience such as what she thinks, feels, decides, and says to other figures. Where the conversations of other male characters are conducted both through texts and through voice actors, Yukimura's conversation is restricted to text without voice. The absence of character voice provides a certain freedom to substitute her voice with a girl player's own voice, fostering a sense of imaginary substitution. A player thus not only identifies with Yukimura but virtually assumes her position, allowing the two girls to overlap within the gaming experience. The voice actors contribute to establishing a certain aura of the figures as well as in producing romantic effects both within and outside the game. Their conversations and sweet whisperings are delivered with the voices of the professional voice actors, which helps to produce a romantic and eroticized effect through the game, which transcends the textual interchange. Their voices are symbolic and realistic representations of the Shinsengumi members, especially at fan meetings organized by Otomeito. These voice actors are invited to attend as main guests to perform the images of the Shinsengumi members that are created in the game. By listening to their voices, fans are able to re-experience their relationships with the Shinsengumi members in the non-virtual setting of a fan meeting.

Hakuōki as national and masculine narrative

Hakuōki reproduces the story of shinsengumi, which is symbolically masculine and national in Japanese imagination. Although not all were samurai, they set up strict samurai codes and manners and their core principle was to obey the orders from the Tokugawa government. Their strong and even fanatical devotion, along with the strict praxis of the codes of samurai, appeared to contradict the radical transformations that Japan was experiencing. Despite the fact that the historical record about them is very limited, the Japanese have re-created and reproduced their stories repeatedly with various moderations over the years, most especially in postwar Japan through an overwhelming number of novels, films, TV dramas, and video games, as Rosa Lee discusses in "Romanticising Shinsengumi."[26] Those imaginary works have established the national popularity of this very samurai-like and heroic war story of the Shinsengumi. The Japanese people have romanticized not only the shinsegumi figures but also the time of *bakumatsu*, as a key transforming historical phase which has lost the "old" values symbolized by the samurai's values and culture.

The members of Shinsengumi are iconic and romanticized figures because their stories illustrate the prototypical legends of Japanese tragic heroes; some of whom died in an attempt to hold on to the old (pre-modern) and "traditional" Japanese values represented in the codes of the samurai.[27] These legends about historical figures illustrate popular nostalgia for this particular period, *bakumatsu*, shifting from the "old" and feudal time to the modern time. People memorialize them by establishing their ideal figures of "authentic" samurai, unwaveringly loyal to the *bafuku* even until the last moment of its overthrow. The vanishing of old Japanese values overlaps with the overthrow of the Tokugawa government. In the crucial historical phase, the Shinsengumi members acted autonomously with their strong will as well as devotedly, attempting to stop and even reverse the modernizing forces with their swords, with samurai values.

Their masculine devotions to the *bakufu* are idealized intensively when it comes to the fact that they came from other societal classes. They were not technically "samurai" figures. Nonetheless, they attempted to become ones by their faithful praxis of the codes of samurai. They symbolically became the "authentic" samurai heroes especially through the imagination of later generations of the Japanese. Much as Benedict Anderson notes in his discussion of the "imagined communities" as the nation, through the shared imaginative community the members of Shinsengumi became national legendary heroes.[28] Japanese people have invented, popularized, and praised these figures.[29] The romanticized stories about the Shinsengumi contributed significantly to reproducing the romanticized Japanese past, particularly *bakumatsu* as a critical period of transformation in Japanese history.

Feminist and gender theorists who examine the relations between gender and nation have often argued that national identity is a masculine construction, and women and femininity are strategically used to supplement and reinforce the national legacy in the roles of a mother, wife, and daughter. Cynthia Enloe's succinct but well-informed statement, "nationalism typically has sprung from masculinized memory, masculinized humiliation and masculinized hope" reveals that gender has been a core mechanism in reproducing nationalistic narratives.[30] Julie Mostov discusses women's sexuality and agency in the context of former Yugoslavia and claims that

[I]magining herself as male or imagining the pleasure of male guardians/ warriors, a women's attachment to this national mythology is a denial of her sexuality and alienation of pleasure, or the sublimation of pleasure in the acts of reproducing and nurturing the nation's sons, tending to its wounded, remaining faithful to its protectors.[31]

These feminist analyses are applicable to *Hakuōki* because particularly Yukimura, a main character in the game, only plays a role of being a lover to the Shinsengumi members. Interestingly, she is only one remainder of the authentic *oni* line in the Eastern region. Therefore, she is depicted as an important "womb" and "mother" to reproduce the *oni* lineage and sustain the lives of the Shinsengumi members who were turned into *oni* because of their newly developed medicine that granted them supernatural powers.

It is indisputable that *Hakuōki* reproduces the traditional nationalistic and masculine story, and gender roles that were illustrated in the story may not be radically subversive. However, such an appeal to earlier gender roles does not necessarily represent a "denial of sexuality and alienation of pleasure, or sublimation of pleasure" as Mostov claims above. Romance, specifically "falling in love with" historical figures, both virtually and in reality, enables these girl players to express their own sexuality, pleasure, and their desire. Dismissing their agency because of academic feminist theories does not help us to discuss their own sexuality with their own words, which does not always have to be defined by the academic feminist discourse.

The issues surrounding girls' identification and performance are more complex. Who do they want to identify with and how do they fall in love with the figures? Like other products of popular culture, gaming experiences are theatrical and social rather than individual and private. The female fans connect both on- and offline to create communities based on mutual interests in *otome* games. Fan meetings provide them with opportunities to meet each other and work creatively and collaboratively with stories and images. Costume play is very popular in those spaces, particularly performing the male characters, in this case the Shinsengumi and other *oni* characters, even though there is a female protagonist, Yukimura. When observing these fan meetings, many girl fans choose to imitate the Shinsengumi members as their cosplay figures and to reenact various romantic stories with fellow cosplayers and fans. Through historical reenactment the girl fans perform the aura of national and historical masculinity, but by cross-dressing they transgress gender and sexuality boundaries. In these spaces, gender, sexuality, and historicity were all played and performed simultaneously. In other words, the girls' *otome* play and pleasure do not constrain their historical imagination to their "assigned" or socially "recognized" gender, sexuality, difference, and identity.

Rather than finding queers and alternative sexualities in the past, Goldberg and Menon's critical project of "queering history," particularly "queering Renaissance," challenges historicism, universalism, historical processes of alterity, and categories of difference and sameness or identity. Their critical project of "queering history" provides a direction to understand the Japanese women's *otome* play and interactions with Japanese history. These young girls look as though they are simply reproducing the national and masculine legacy of Japanese history; however, their *otome* sexuality enables them to interact with the past, as well as with their own sexuality and romance of "falling in love." Goldberg and Menon claim that "this [homohistory] would be invested in suspending determinate sexual and chronological differences while expanding the possibility of non-hetero, with all its connotation of sameness, similarity, proximity, and anachronism." *Otome*'s play and pleasure join in this project of "queering history."[32]

Notes

1   Jonathan Goldberg and Madhavi Menon, "Queering History," *PMLA*, 120, no. 5 (2005).

2   This figure is calculated based on the voters for the Otome Game of the Year 2007. http://trendy.nikkeibp.co.jp/article/column/20080623/1015877/?P=5

3   *Otome* games became popular as forms of cell phone and smart phone applications:

> After the genre of "ren'ai games" (romantic love games) was established in August 2007, the number of registered customers has increased, and it became more than 300,000 in November 2008. We only had 23 sites in August 2007, however, now [as of December 15, 2008], the number has become tripled to 64. In the market of cell phone business, the "ren'ai game" is the hottest and fastest growing genre. (interview with Takeyoshi Masanori, Department of DoCoMo Consumer Service appeared in "Futsū no on'nanoko ga moeru kētai ren'ai gēmu' te," *Nikkei Entertainment* published in February 2009)

> "Torendo: Degipedia: on'na ga muchūna kētai otome gāmu no sekai," *SPA* (15 December 2009): 104–105.

4   As PSP (PlayStation Portable) games, *Hakuōki Portable*, *Zuisōroku Portable*, *Hakuōki Yūgiroku*, and *Hakuōki reimeiroku* were released in 2009 and 2010. As Nintendo DS games, *Zuisōroku* and *Yūgiroku* were sold in 2011. As a PS 3 game, *Junsōroku* was released in 2010.

5   This contest was organized by the Freem, a research company of media and games. http://ogy.jp/history/2009/

6 "Ren'aigē ni muchūna joshi zokushutsu♥ danshi kinsei 'neoroma' no sekai toha?" *Saizō*, 74–75, July 2008.

7 "Ren'aigē ni muchūna joshi zokushutsu♥ danshi kinsei 'neoroma' no sekai toha?" 74–75. The industry of *otome* game expands its territory to various sectors (called media-mix), which includes the sales of related goods, plays, and fan events. The overall sales in the industry of *otome* games are now over ten billion yen.

8 Kunimitsu Kawamura, *Otome no yukue: Kindai josei imēji no tanjō*. Tokyo: Kinokuniya Shoten, 2003, 26.

9 Masuko Honda, "Ima shōjo wo kataru koto," in Ed. Kan Satoko, *Shōjo shōsetu wondārando (Girls Novels Wonderland)*. Tokyo: Meiji shoten, 2008, 26. Honda argues that the *shōjo* figure was produced in the process of Japanese modernity, in relation to the establishment of gender roles, the creation of the adolescence phase as life cycle, as well as the modern educational system. She claims that the image of *shōjo* was particularly shaped in Yoshiya Nobuko's *Hanamonogatari* which appeared in the magazine, *Shōjo gaho* published from 1916 to 1924.

10 Kunimitsu Kawamura, *Otome no inori: Kindai josei imēji no tanjō*. Tokyo: Kinokuniya Shoten, 1993, 12.

11 Kawamura, *Otome no inori*, 12.

12 Tomoko Aoyama and Barbara Hartley, *Girl Reading Girl in Japan*. New York: Routledge, 2010.

13 For example, Setsu Shigematsu's "Dimensions of Desire: Sex, Fantasy, and Fetish in Japanese Comics," in Ed. John A. Lent, *Themes and Issues in Asian Cartooning*. Bowling Green, OH: Bowling Green State University Popular Press, 1999, 127–164, analyzes the lady's comic (which consists of pornographic contents) and argues that it provided sexual liberation for the women.

14 Masuko Honda, *Ibunka to shiteno kodomo*. Tokyo: Kinokuniya Shoten, 1982, 165.

15 Masami Saito, Ph.D. Diss., *Feminism riron ni yoru hihanteki discōsu bunseki no tenkai*, Ochanomizu University, 2000 cited in Shigematsu, "Dimensions of Desire."

16 Shigematsu, "Dimensions of Desire."

17 Shigematsu, "Dimensions of Desire," 138–139.

18 Shigematsu, "Dimensions of Desire," 139.

19 Tomo Kitsukawa, "On'nanoko no 'kibō' toshiteno anime gēmu," *Yuriika*, 513, no. 1 (2005): 163–171: 163.

20 Mark McLelland, "The Love between 'Beautiful Boys' in Japanese Women's Comics," *Journal of Gender Studies*, 9, no. 1 (2000): 13–25.

21 Kitsukawa, "On'nanoko no 'kibō' toshiteno anime gēmu," 169. Here, Kitsukawa's argument is based on her assumption that "true" love romance is heterosexual.

22 These five Shinsengumi members are Hijikata Toshizō (CV: Miki Shinichirō), Okita Sōji (CV: Morikubo Shōtarō), Saitō Hajime (CV: Toriumi Kōsuke), Tōdō Heisuke (CV: Yoshino Hiroyuki), Harada Sanosuke (CV: Yusa Kōji). In addition, Kazama Chikage (CV: Tsuda Kenjirō), who works for the Satsuma domain in the game, is also introduced as an object of her possible love.

23 The graphic designer of these figures is Kazuki Yone, who became very popular through her previous *otome* games works such as *Hiirono kakera* (*Fragment of Scarlet Color*) first published by Idea Factory in 2006. Her "ferocious but elegant" designs were enthusiastically praised by her girl fans. She is now one of the established artists in *otome* games industry (http://www.cyzowoman.com/2012/01/post_4744.html).

24 For more on Japanese people's fascination with the Shinsengumi, see Rosa Lee's article, "Romanticising Shinsengumi," *New Voices*, 4 (2011): 168–187, accessed and downloaded on 18 April 2011.

25 Lee, "Romanticising Shinsengumi," 181.

26 Lee, "Romanticising Shinsengumi," 168.

27 For analysis of Japanese tragic heroes, see Ivan Morris, *The Nobility of Failure: Tragic Heroes in the History of Japan*. New York: Farrar, Straus and Giroux, 1988. As Lee points out in the note, the story of the Shinsengumi, particularly the story of Hijikata Toshizō can be aligned with the story of *Akō gishi*, who avenged their lord's death in the eighteenth century, "Romanticising Shinsengumi," 175.

28 Benedict Anderson, *Imagined Communities: Reflections on the Origins and Spread of Nationalism*. New York and London: Verso, 1991.

29 Eric Hobsbawm, "Introduction: Inventing Traditions," in Eds. Eric Hobsbawm and Terence Ranger, *The Invention of Tradition*. New York: Cambridge University Press, 2003, 1–14.

30 Cynthia Enloe, *Bananas, Beaches, and Bases: Making Feminist Sense of International Politics*. Berkeley, CA: University of California Press, 2000, 44.

31 Julie Mostov, "Sexing the Nation/Desexing the Body: Politics of National Identity in the Former Yugoslavia," in Ed. Tamar Mayer, *Gender Ironies of Nationalism: Sexing the Nation*. New York: Routledge, 2001, 89–110: 102.

32 Goldberg and Menon, "Queering History," 1609.

Works cited

Anderson, Benedict. *Imagined Communities: Reflections on the Origins and Spread of Nationalism*. New York and London: Verso, 1991.

Aoyama, Tomoko and Barbara Hartley. *Girl Reading Girl in Japan*. New York: Routledge, 2010.

Enloe, Cynthia. *Bananas, Beaches, and Bases: Making Feminist Sense of International Politics*. Berkeley, CA: University of California Press, 2000.

"Futsū no on'nanoko ga moeru kētai ren'ai gēmu'te" in *Nikkei Entertainment*, (February 2009): 64–67.

Goldberg, Jonathan and Madhavi Menon. "Queering History," *PMLA*, 120, no. 5 (2005): 1608–1617.

Hobsbawm, Eric. "Introduction: Inventing Traditions," in Eds. Eric Hobsbawm and Terence Ranger, *The Invention of Tradition*. New York: Cambridge University Press, 2003, 1–14.

Honda, Masuko. *Ibunka to shiteno kodomo*. Tokyo: Kinokuniya Shoten, 1982.

Honda, Masuko. "Ima shōjo wo kataru to iu koto," in Ed. Kan Satoko, *Shōjo shōsetsu wondārando: Meiji kara heisei made*. Tokyo: Meiji shoten, 2008, 24–35.

Kawamura, Kunimitsu. *Otome no inori: Kindai josei imēji no tanjō*. Tokyo: Kinokuniya Shoten, 1993.

Kawamura, Kunimitsu. *Otome no yukue: Kindai josei no hyōsō to tatakai*. Tokyo: Kinokuniya Shoten, 2003.

Kitsukawa, Tomo. "On'nanoko no 'kibō' toshiteno anime, gēmu," *Yuriika*, 513, no. 1 (2005): 163–171.

Lee, Rosa. "Romanticising Shinsengumi in Contemporary Japan," *New Voices*, 4 (2011): 168–187, http://www.jpf.org.au/newvoices, accessed and downloaded on 18 April 2011.

McLelland, Mark. "The Love between 'Beautiful Boys' in Japanese Women's Comics," *Journal of Gender Studies*, 9, no. 1 (2000): 13–25.

Morris, Ivan. *The Nobility of Failure: Tragic Heroes in the History of Japan*. New York: Farrar, Straus and Giroux, 1988.

Mostov, Julie. "Sexing the Nation/Desexing the Body: Politics of National Identity in the Former Yugoslavia," in Ed. Tamar Mayer, *Gender Ironies of Nationalism: Sexing the Nation*. New York: Routledge, 2001, 89–110.

"Otome gēmu ni hamaru joshi ga zōkachū: Janīzu teki bijinesu de shijōga kakudai," http://trendy.nikkeibp.co.jp/article/column/20080623/1015877/?P=5, accessed April 18, 2011.

"Otome game of the year 2009," http://ogy.jp/history/2009/, accessed April 17, 2011.

"Ren'aigē ni muchūna joshi zokushutsu♥ danshi kinsei 'neoroma' no sekai toha?" *Saizō* (July 2008): 74–75.

Saito, Masami. *Feminism riron ni yoru hihanteki discōsu bunseki no tenkai*, Ph.D. Diss., Ochanomizu University, 2000.

Shigematsu, Setsu. "Dimensions of Desire: Sex, Fantasy, and Fetish in Japanese Comics," in Ed. John A. Lent, *Themes and Issues in Asian Cartooning*. Bowling Green, OH: Bowling Green State University Popular Press, 1999, 127–164.

"Torendo: Degipedia: on'na ga muchūna kētai otome gēmu no sekai," *SPA* (15 December 2009): 104–105.

Games cited

Hakuōki Portable (PSP). Tokyo, Japan: Idea Factory/Design Factory, 2009.

Hakuōki Reimeiroku (PSP). Tokyo, Japan: Idea Factory/Design Factory, 2011.

Hakuōki Shinsengumi Kitan. Tokyo, Japan: Idea Factory/Design Factory, 2008.

Hakuōki Yūgiroku (PSP). Tokyo, Japan: Idea Factory/ Design Factory, 2010.

Hiirono Kakera (Fragment of Scarlet Color). Tokyo, Japan: Idea Factory/Design Factory, 2006.

Junsōroku (PS3 2010). Tokyo, Japan. Idea Factory/Design Factory, 2010.

Yūgiroku (Nintendo DS, 2011). Tokyo, Japan. Idea Factory/Design Factory, 2011.

Zuisōroku (Nintendo DS, 2011). Tokyo, Japan. Idea Factory/Design Factory, 2011.

Zuisōroku Portable (PSP). Tokyo, Japan: Idea Factory/Design Factory, 2010.

PART THREE

User-Generated History

Part Three turns to the question of simulation and realism in games' engagement with the past in order to examine the ways in which history can be remade by the player. This is, as discussed in the Introduction, one of the major differences between video games and films, in that the agency and freedom granted to the player to invent, explore, subvert, and question the past ultimately changes the ways in which games allow us to engage with history. This part thus engages with the ways in which the players themselves put history together.

Beginning by examining what they term "Brand WW2," Salvati and Bullinger explore the important difference between accuracy and authenticity in depicting the past to show that authenticity in fact depends not only on what was accurate, but on what players *think* is accurate, or *expect* to be there. This leads to Köstlbauer's essay on similar territory, but which he takes in a different direction to argue that the *kriegspiel* (war game), by allowing users to play with simulations based on real military engagements, ultimately blurs the line between simulation and reality. Thus, in the case of a Syrian tank, playing with the past sometimes leads to playing with the future. Apperley then moves on to the issue of "modding," allowing players to modify the source code of games, which can often expose decisions made by game designers in bringing the past to life—and which thus lay bare the process of simulation itself. This is continued by Crabtree who explores *Battlefield* as a case study, arguing that when fans are allowed agency they very often reveal a passion for adherence to facts discounted by many casual observers.

Recommended books to understand more about consumption of history and the concept of user-generated content:

Adair, Bill, Benjamin Filene, and Laura Koloski. *Letting Go?: Sharing Historical Authority in a User-Generated World*. Philadelphia, PA: The Pew Centre for Arts and Heritage, 2012.

Black, Jeremy. *Using History*. London: Hodder Arnold, 2005.

De Groot, Jerome. *Consuming History: Historians and Heritage in Contemporary Popular Culture*. London: Routledge, 2009.

Greengrass, Mark and Lorna M. Hughes. *The Virtual Representation of the Past*. Surrey, UK and Burlington, VT: Ashgate Publishing, Ltd., 2008.

Popek, Emily. *Understanding the World of User-Generated Content*. New York: The Rosen Publishing Group, 2010.

Rosenzweig, Roy and David Thelen. *The Presence of the Past: Popular Uses of History in American Life*. New York: Columbia University Press, 1998.

Whalen, Zach and Laurie N. Taylor, eds. *Playing the Past: History and Nostalgia in Video Games*. Nashville, TN: Vanderbilt University Press, 2008.

10

Selective Authenticity and the Playable Past

Andrew J. Salvati and Jonathan M. Bullinger
Rutgers University

Introduction

We purchase video games with the expectation of being entertained, yet games that engage historical subject matter are often criticized for superficial interpretations of past events. For example, in an article in *New York* magazine, economic historian Niall Ferguson appraised computer games like Electronic Arts' (EA) World War II shooter *Medal of Honor* as "profoundly unhistorical," emphasizing shoot-'em-up action at the expense of any realistic depiction of combat, or of critical, educational engagement with the past.[1] "At root," Ferguson contends, these games are essentially "*Space Invaders* ... with fancy graphics."[2]

Though asking the question "is the past *accurately* represented?" constitutes one type of conversation about what "really happened" in history, this chapter argues that simulation games like Activision's *Call of Duty*, and Electronic Arts' *Medal of Honor* series provide alternate schemes for apprehending the historically real (our perception of what actually happened in the past) that privileges story, genre, and details over critical analysis or the production of new historical knowledge. These alternative schemes are similar to Rosenstone's belief that historical filmmakers are historians whose milieu presents a different set of demands when engaging with the past.[3] These demands often include the invention of characters, dialogue, and incidents designed both to convey an overall sense of the past and to offer metaphoric truths to comment and challenge traditional historical discourse. We introduce the term *selective authenticity* to describe how game designers draw upon a chain of signifiers assembled from historical texts, artifacts, and popular representations of World War II—an ensemble that we have defined as *BrandWW2*.[4]

Whether pointing out the sins of commission or omission, charges of historical inaccuracy suggest a crisis in historical representation that privileges inquiry and explanation over dramatic storytelling. However, as discussed in the introduction, by empowering players to engage and "play" with the past as simulation, computer games offer the potential to destabilize linear narratives and received historical authority. While recognizing this potential of simulation, we argue that in the mass-market video games under examination, generic conventions and master narratives of World War II nevertheless configure gameplay.

Like cinematic blockbusters, graphic novels, or dramatic television series, *Medal of Honor* and *Call of Duty* are mass cultural forms, and so tend toward the epic melodrama, featuring the intense action, cinematic photography, soaring soundtrack and compelling characters that shape a successful World War II product. Cultural myths are likewise important. As the IGN fan blogger Bacchus451 has opined, game producers "should feel quite fortunate that there was such a historical event as World War 2. Never before in history has there been such a clear cut 'good vs. evil' scenario from which to draw inspiration to make entertaining, suspenseful and ... educational software" (para. 1).[5]

Selective authenticity may be understood as a form of narrative license, in which an interactive experience of the past blends historical representation with generic conventions and audience expectations, all within a reductive frame of *BrandWW2*. Though simulations rely on a complex and often subtle array of mechanisms to engineer an immersive sensory experience, we identify three categories of selective authenticity across the *Medal of Honor* and *Call of Duty* franchises. The first prioritizes the accuracy of weaponry representation (*technology fetishism*); second, the utilization of documentary-style and newsreel cutscenes (*cinematic conventions*); lastly the representation of documents, photographs, maps, and period-accurate information technologies (*documentary authority*). Together, these elements synthesize a historical realism—a *selective authenticity*—that situates immersive gameplay by satisfying audience expectations.

Simulation and poststructuralist history

There's not much gameplay associated with that [dropping of the atomic bombs] and that's something that we never tried to focus on. We are making a game, we're not making a political statement. What we try to do as we strive for authenticity is: well, that was part of the war. The Imperial Japanese were different than the current people who run the country, and to sanitize that situation, to actually not show that they had this honor and code that these soldiers fought with would have been a dishonor. We just tried to tell a story about a part of the war that actually happened.

TREYARCH STUDIO HEAD MARK LAMIA on *Call of Duty: World at War*[6]

In this interview, Lamia reveals a key tension underlying historical representation. Despite assurances that his studio's product is "just a game," Treyarch's unwillingness to depict the atomic bomb nevertheless grafts an ideological position onto the game narrative. Backing away from potentially controversial images that may have harmed sales, Treyarch's selectivity reproduced the unambiguous morality of a "Good War" narrative. Commenting on the reluctance, even refusal, of popular American representations to engage with the war's nuclear legacy for example, the journalist and historian Tom Englehardt explained, "for the victorious Americans ... the crucial thing was to pass from August 5 to August 7 [1945] as if nothing but the expected victory had occurred."[7] While Lamia insists it was important that game developers not "sanitize" Imperial Japanese tactics by explaining them away as "part of the war," sanitization evidently becomes acceptable when concerning sticky moral dilemmas involving the American protagonists. Furthermore, Lamia constructs a double-protection for his potential Japanese gaming audience by assuring that "the current people who run the country" are different from Imperial Japanese, and also by emphasizing that Japanese soldiers fought with an "honor and code"—a detail at once historically authentic, but safely distant in the past.

   This example foregrounds a poststructuralist critique of historical representation within game studies, which challenges the organizing assumptions of conventional historiography. The process of writing history, of shaping data about the past into narrative form, entails creative interpretation guided by the historian's selection of materials, her style, audience, and the language she employs. Though empirical evidence and objectivist accounts may give us a sense of a "real" past, the poststructuralist critique initiated by Hayden White and Dominick LaCapra, among others, understands historical writing as a literary form indelibly marked by subjectivities—the sensibilities of the author, by interpretation, context, aesthetics, and argument. As the theorist Keith Jenkins writes, histories "are never 'in and for themselves,'" as objective accounts of the past should like to claim, "but only always for 'someone'."[8]

Recent scholarship has drawn upon this discourse to frame the possibilities for historical engagement offered by computer simulations. Concurring with Uricchio, Harrison Gish has argued, "the interactive possibilities games provide have the potential to call into question fixed narrative histories that prescribe deterministic conceptions of the past."[9] According to this view, interactive historical *simulations* encourage a dynamic engagement with the past based on creation, imagination, and replayability, allowing players to reconfigure stable or totalizing *representations*. The distinction here is crucial. "Unlike representation, which tends to be fixed in nature," Uricchio explains, simulations are "capable of generating countless encounters that may subsequently be fixed as representations ... a simulation is a machine for producing speculative or conditional representations."[10] As Mir and Owens argue in Chapter 6, this type of speculative play finds one expression in simulations like *Sid Meier's Civilization* series, or the World War II strategy game *Making History: The Calm and the Storm*, in which players assume leadership of a belligerent nation.[11] These games encourage the player to devise "what if" scenarios, allowing for engagement with historical political economy, diplomacy, and military strategy.

In contrast, simulations based on the individual's perspective like the *Call of Duty* and *Medal of Honor* series do not generally foster the type of speculative play in which the course of history can be altered—the Allies invariably win the simulated war. Rather than historical play on the order of *Civilization*, *Call of Duty*, and *Medal of Honor* prioritize what narrative scholar Janet Murray has called *immersion*: "the sensation of being surrounded by a completely other reality, as different as water is from air that takes over all of our attention, or whole perceptual apparatus."[12] Immersion privileges the kinesthetic experience of shooting, running, jumping, and navigating through richly rendered landscapes populated by allies, enemy troops, and challenging objectives. Though this experience differs from other simulations where one might reenact the diplomatic tinderbox of 1938, or mobilize a national economy for war, the capacity to explore well-designed game environments is often cited by players as offering rewarding, authentic engagements with the past. Articulating the relationship between authenticity and immersion, one reviewer of the *Medal of Honor* series explained, "the attention to detail in all of them is outstanding, with city levels that look like they were taken straight from the pages of history."[13]

While immersion may be a source of "player pleasure" and orient the historical narrative to the first-person perspective, the possibilities of historical "play" in the *Call of Duty* and *Medal of Honor* simulations are nevertheless scaffolded by a set of familiar narratives and generic conventions.[14] As the historian Jerome De Groot has explained, First Person Shooter (FPS) players are "granted agency of some description within what is not narrative history but simulation—although simulation that mimics narrative history such as film and documentary."[15] This anchoring is often recognized by reviewers noting where game levels re-create scenes from popular World War II films, or alternately, when complaining of "an abundance of stereotypical war-era personalities."[16] The original *Call of Duty*'s (2003) emulation of the conventions of World War II blockbusters was promoted on the game's package, which invited players to "experience the cinematic intensity of World War II's epic battles."[17]

Selective authenticity

Commenting on the original *Call of Duty*, Infinity Ward cofounder Vince Zampella explained, "we put a lot of effort into creating an authentic environment for *Call of Duty*. This type of game really needs that kind of attention to accurately portray some of the more epic moments of WWII."[18] Paying special attention to specific events, objects, and environments in this way tends toward a relatively narrow, but richly detailed, set of representations that approximates the soldiers' experience on the battlefield. This negotiation between historical detail and the fictive elements of storytelling are at the heart of *selective authenticity*, which is concerned more with creating a "feel" and "experience" than with strict factual fidelity. It is not fact vs. fiction *per se*, but rather which elements are foregrounded as establishing authenticity, and which of those are absent.

Far from disqualifying *Medal of Honor* and *Call of Duty* as historiographical tripe however, their use of fictive elements calls attention to what the historian Hayden White has identified as the figurative and literary aspects of historical writing.[19] The primary job of the historian, White explains, is to familiarize readers with the past through narrative composition—a process that entails the creative arrangement of information, poiesis (the figurative use of language), and emplotment. For White, the historical work makes the past familiar "not only because the reader now has more *information* about the events, but also because he has been shown how the data conform to an *icon* of a comprehensible finished process, a plot structure with which he is familiar as part of his cultural endowment."[20] Selective authenticity examines what elements of this "cultural endowment"—what we have called *Brand WW2*—structure the simulated past.

Deploying a common aesthetic and narrative structure, *Brand WW2* is a stabilized set of representations employed by multiple cultural producers that inform, and are informed by, dominant ideologies. Since the 1990s, disparate memories, myths, genre conventions, discourses, and products have stabilized so as to constitute a metanarrative that must conform to the same rules followed by any recognized brand. While this branding began almost as soon as the United States entered the war, the process has crystallized since the fiftieth anniversary of World War II, and particularly with the release of *Saving Private Ryan* (1998). The myth of a good and just war has proven to be profitable—the audience's immaterial labor as social relation carries a shared or common meaning, from which the brand attains increased valorization.[21] This is partially explained because such a myth is very appealing to a generation curious about the particular historical period, their fathers and grandfathers who participated in it, and the audiences' expectations regarding their actions.[22]

Working within this brand and its focus upon "epic" historical events as interpreted by game designers, *Medal of Honor* and *Call of Duty* then are not purely creative machines in the hands of players, as the games tend to reinscribe fixed outcomes. The brand's value is partially derived as a historical product or "fact" and thus an air of authenticity is required to be present within it. The components that contribute to this atmosphere of authenticity include a technological fetishism, reliance upon cinematic conventions, and an authority derived from the documentary form.

Technological fetishism

Technological fetishism is constructed from a desire for vicariously experienced power—the awe that accompanies the destructive fruits of man's inventions that is augmented when represented as the tools of the "Greatest Generation," comprised of fathers or grandfathers. The resulting fetishism of "our father's tools" is situated within a transformative war narrative in which boys become men, and in which these tools are privileged as authentic in the retelling of the conflict. Prior to the release of *Call of Duty 2*, lead designer Zied Rieke explained designers' careful attention to weaponry for the sequel: "we've redone every single weapon to add more detail and take advantage of our new graphics technology, which allows us to make the wood look real and metal to shine—like real metal—as well as include the tiniest details ... all the way down to the serial number."[23]

This fetishism is rooted in part in the tradition of meaningful mythologized weaponry enjoying a starring role within media narratives and in a particular social construction of masculinity as one that is violent and militarized.[24] The medium of FPSs act as rich environments for this fetishism due to their focus on weapons as the primary tool for accomplishing objectives and the player's immediate perspective. The portion of the *Medal of Honor* and *Call of Duty* audiences who comprise the fanbase of historical conflicts arrive to the game with an expectation of highly accurate representations of weapons via name, sound, function, and appearance. The wider audience for FPSs may place more emphasis upon functionality of the tools/weapons available regardless of whether they pass as authentic.

Online reviews of the best FPS weapons (e.g. *Doom*'s BFG900, *Deux Ex*'s GEP gun) place an emphasis on those that allow obstacles to be overcome quickly (*Half Life 2*'s Gravity Gun) and objectives completed more efficiently (*Perfect Dark*'s FarSight).[25] Each of the *Medal of Honor* and *Call of Duty* releases offers a selection ranging from a minimum of a dozen to upward of over forty accurately re-created weapons. The only outlier is *Medal of Honor: Infiltrator* (2003) on the portable platform Game Boy Advance, which provides a selection of weapons identified only by type ("machine gun"), rather than specific model number (MP40) or brand (Thompson). One aspect comprising this fetishism includes an immersion in weapon statistics, similar in the level of detail and fanaticism to the amateur baseball fan statistician. Load screen representations (*Medal of Honor: Airborne*) depict schematics detailing a particular weapon's attributes.

Cinematic conventions

One of the strategies historians employ to familiarize their audiences with the past builds upon recognizable metaphors and story-types.[26] Whether they reenact scenes from acclaimed World War II movies (*Big Red One*, *Saving Private Ryan*), employ the same actors and consultants, or weave dramatic cutscenes into gameplay, the *Medal of Honor* and *Call of Duty* franchises adopt *cinematic conventions* that both provide a familiar narrative structure and perpetuate what the historian Studs Terkel (1984) canonized as the "Good War." For instance, *Medal of Honor*'s (1999) introductory film sequence summarizes the war as the rise of Hitler, the RAF victory in the Battle of Britain, and the United States ultimately turning the tide. Across other releases, World War II is overwhelmingly situated as a noble war (*Medal of Honor: Frontline*) that was fought by many (*Call of Duty*) working together that ultimately fostered a brotherhood between nations (*Call of Duty: Finest Hour*) and the soldiers themselves (*Call of Duty 2:Big Red One*).

Releases within both franchises often return to the representation of newsreel form within introductory game sequences and level sequences and assorted cutscenes. Though in decline by the start of World War II, the amount of newsreel footage devoted to the conflict was nonetheless substantial.[27] The newsreels' heyday was pre–World War II, but nevertheless the newsreel continues to be associated with the conflict as the dominant visual record of its various events.

Cutscenes often rely upon two forms to convey authenticity: first, an inclusion of 1940s black-and-white newsreel footage or still photographs, and second, an appropriation of cinematic styles from popular US war films. While cutscenes are often shot in the style of a Hollywood blockbuster, the FPS medium demands an almost documentary-style perspective as these scenes play out. The resulting aesthetic achieves authenticity by situating the player as an interactive participant inside a grand dramatic representation of stylized war. Early *Medal of Honor* releases relied more on documentary-style footage (*Medal of Honor, Medal of Honor: Frontline*) to establish an atmosphere of authenticity around gameplay missions. As game engines became more powerful, cutscenes increasingly came to incorporate game-style animation; first in a hybrid formation with documentary footage (*Medal of Honor: Rising Sun, Medal of Honor: European Assault*) and eventually as standalone introductions and cutscenes edited in the style of an action-based US war films (*Medal of Honor: Pacific Assault, Call of Duty 2*).

Documentary authority

Historical information systems are commonly chosen to represent an authenticity within these games moored within technology, providing a double utility. It first authenticates the representation by embodying period-specific physical information systems whose form also helps suspend the player's awareness of the contemporary technological simulation, resulting in a form of *documentary authority*. These documents come in the form of representations of typewriters (*Call of Duty 3*), manila folders (*Medal of Honor: Allied Assault, Medal of Honor: Heroes*), and printed photographs: file (*Call of Duty: Finest Hour*), surveillance (*Medal of Honor: Airborne, Medal of Honor: Heroes 2*), and personnel (*Call of Duty*). These information systems represent the other tools of war; a capacity to introduce strategy and order to the otherwise seemingly chaotic and irrational nature of war.

Another set of documents employed in an attempt to bring context and understanding to war is the use of quotations from famous personalities about war (*Medal of Honor, Call of Duty*). In *Call of Duty* (2003) there are quotations selected to appear for both death and victory scenarios from forty-two different personalities with the highest frequencies occurring from Winston Churchill (8), George S. Patton (7), Napoleon Bonaparte (6), Douglas MacArthur (5), Ernest Hemingway (4), Ralph Waldo Emerson (4), and Joseph Stalin (4). The quotations are from overwhelmingly male sources, with writer Barbara Kingsolver representing the lone female voice. The sources are also overwhelmingly white male Western figures from government, science, the military, literary canon, philosophy, and even film (John Wayne). The only salient aberrations are Emiliano Zapata (Western, but non-white) and Ali ibn-Abi-Talib. Since the quotes are from a variety of sources and indexed by scenario (death and victory) there is space created for questioning the rationality and morality of participation in war such as Bertrand Russell's "patriots always talk of dying for their country and never of killing for their country."

Maps are constructed representations for terrain that we agree to allow to stand-in for physical geography.[28] The ability to render complex three-dimensional physical environments to abstract or at least reductive two-dimensional representations is itself an expression of power.[29] These representations can affect how one understands her place within a particular territory, and her relation to other areas is placed front and center within this perspective. Representations of two-dimensional maps are ready props in *Call of Duty* and *Medal of Honor*, and act as objects of authoritative cartography—as artifacts through which players filter their understanding of complex terrain, cultures, motivations, and conflicts that ground the simulation. The reliance on period-specific two-dimensional maps is reinforced by the medium of the FPS—an environment in which success requires an understanding of level cartography. The combined effect is to habitually select these period maps as markers of objective authenticity regardless of the perspective embedded within their construction.[30]

Interacting with history

Given that game designers incorporate fixed elements (representations) to "familiarize" a simulated world, what opportunity, if any, remains for players to actively engage with history via simulations?[31]

The pasts depicted by *Call of Duty* and *Medal of Honor* have inspired some players to conduct their own research. In a post titled "An Academic Analysis of Historical Accuracy in *Call of Duty 2*" the IGN fan blogger Bacchus451 examines that particular game's depiction of the American assault on Pointe-du-Hoc on D-Day, noting the game's attention to details like weather and troop strength, concluding that "*Call of Duty 2* does an exemplary job of depicting this epic struggle."[32] While Bacchus451's efforts may be interpreted as merely reinforcing the already substantial interest in strategic statistics and variables—and through his bibliography, support for *BrandWW2* pillars such as Ambrose—this player is nonetheless engaging the medium as a historical text. Likewise, The Gaming Historian's blog praises the "realistic experience" of *Medal of Honor* (1999), and supplements the game narrative with his own history of the Office of Strategic Services, of which the game's protagonist is an agent. In this way, The Gaming Historian melds the long-standing tradition of vicarious war-participation imaginings with the ability to concretely and publicly narrativize via the Internet and fan communities.

Admittedly out of millions of players, these two blogger-historians are most likely outliers. Here, the tension between programmed representation and audience agency becomes significant. These games' selective representations of World War II sell millions of copies, but does this quantity alone mean it changes users' understanding of the historical event? Selective authenticity likewise aims to account for how players react to these narrative conventions. Fans and users, in the form of game reviewers, do note an awareness of repeated and overused elements, and at times yearn for relationship dynamics and community building that can be an outcome of battlefield experiences as a marker of an "authentic" experience.

Noting the use of stereotypical plots and generic conventions, these complaints may be because the game itself is unremarkable, but also surface when games revolve around obligatory D-Day levels, or around "shooting a lot of Nazis."[33] At other times, reviewers note where narrative does not feel authentic enough. In one review of *Call of Duty: Big Red One*, for example, the reviewer writes, "Treyarch should have worked to develop the real relationships between these soldiers, especially since, according even to their own behind the scenes footage, all of the soldiers fought for the guy next to them and nothing else. Why then is that not represented?"[34]

While the relationship dynamics are not re-programmable by the user, other more rudimentary game elements are in the form of modding. These modding communities can provide for alternative interpretations and re-imagining of history. While structured partially by the stock game platform, players nonetheless create additional tools to modify and add to the gameplay initiated by the producers. While much of this modding focuses on weapons (single shot to fully automatic, swapping a Garand for a Carbine, or simply adding a sci-fi-flavored "ray-gun"), or appearances (more obese Germans, female Banzai attackers, new uniforms), these interventions are more about enhancing the FPS experience rather than adding historical detail.

At times, modding is anticipated by some producers, as in the case of *Call of Duty: World at War*'s survival game mode in which Nazis are re-configured as zombies, resulting in a sort of *Night of the Living Dead*, World War II-style. The multiplayer mini-game *Nazi Zombies* marks a creative intervention on behalf of producers that underscores the capabilities of computer simulations to destabilize familiar narrative structures in a creative mash-up. In *Nazi Zombies*, the "Good War" narrative is taken to a hyperbolic extreme. This parody emphasizes what the theorist Roland Barthes understands as the core function of myth—the emptying of history from the signifier in favor of culturally produced meaning.[35] Twinned with zombies—a mainstay pop culture villain—evil (the signified) becomes the singular meaning ascribed to anybody in a period German uniform. This figure—the rank-and-file World War II German soldier—acts as a discrete example for tension inherent in the potentiality of game simulation as a site for active historical engagement on the part of the user. The soldier's symbolic essence is immutable—he is evil—for the narrative, our moral foundations, and for making sense out of history.

Conclusion

As the lines between history-as-knowledge and history-as-entertainment become increasingly blurred, it is important for historians and students to recognize not only how historically themed products situate the past factually, but also how certain depictions of the historically "real" resonate culturally. As Ferguson acknowledges, "the Game Boy generation is growing up. And, as they seek a deeper understanding of the world we live in, they may not turn first to the bookshelves."[36] While selective authenticity does not suggest that any and all interpretations of history are equally valid, we argue that the FPS draws attention to how we socially produce historical knowledge and derive meaning from the past. In the case of FPSs this is achieved not through factual fidelity but instead through a selective authenticity, relying heavily upon technological fetishism, cinematic conventions, and documentary authority; often viewed through the lens of *BrandWW2*. Today, the "*Call of Duty* or *Medal of Honor* generation" is interacting with World War II within this atmosphere; thinking about what elements are highlighted, and which are absent is significant—for in the past winners wrote history; now they are programming and selling it.

Notes

1 Niall Ferguson, "How to Win a War," *New York Magazine*, 23 October 2006.

2 Ferguson, "How to Win a War."

3 Robert A. Rosenstone, *History on Film/Film on History*. Harlow: Longman and Pearson, 2006.

4 Jonathan Bullinger and Andrew J. Salvati, "A Theory of BrandWW2," *Reconstruction: Studies in Contemporary Culture*, 11, no. 4 (2011).

5 Bacchus451, "An Academic Analysis of Historical Accuracy in Call of Duty 2—Blog by Bacchus451—IGN."

6 Kevin Kelly, "Joystiq Interviews Mark Lamia of Treyarch and Call of Duty the Fifth," *Joystiq*, 24 June 2008.

7 Tom Engelhardt, "The Victors and the Vanquished," in Eds. Edward Tabor Linenthal and Tom Engelhardt, *History Wars: The Enola Gay and Other Battles for the American Past*. Basingstoke: Macmillan, 1996.

8 Keith Jenkins, *At the Limits of History: Essays on Theory and Practice*. London and New York: Routledge, 2009, 7.

9 Harrison Gish, "Playing the Second World War: *Call of Duty* and the Telling of History," *Eludamos: Journal for Computer Game Culture*, 4, no. 2 (11 April 2010): 167–180; William Uricchio, "Simulation, History, and Computer Games," in Eds. Joost Raessens and Jeffrey H. Goldstein, *Handbook of Computer Game Studies*. Cambridge, MA: MIT Press, 2005, 168.

10 Uricchio, "Simulation, History, and Computer Games," 333.

11 *Sid Meier's Civilization, Making History: The Calm & The Storm.*

12 Janet Horowitz Murray, *Hamlet on the Holodeck: The Future of Narrative in Cyberspace*. Cambridge, MA: MIT Press, 1998, 98.

13 T. Rivers, "Medal of Honor Frontline Review," *Gamespot* (31 May 2002).

14 The expression "player pleasure" comes from Uricchio, "Simulation, History, and Computer Games," 327.

15 Jerome de Groot, *Consuming History: Historians and Heritage in Contemporary Popular Culture*. London: Taylor & Francis, 2009, 135.

16 Greg Kasavin, "Medal of Honor Pacific Assault Review," *Gamespot*; Jeremy Dunham, "Call of Duty 3 Review: The Most Persistent Sound Which Reverberates Through Men's History Is the Beating of War Drums," *IGN.com* (20 November 2006).

17 *Call of Duty*. Santa Monica, CA: Infinity Ward, Activision, 2003.

18 Staff, "Call of Duty Q&A," *Gamespot* (26 June 2003).

19 Hayden White, *Tropics of Discourse: Essays in Cultural Criticism*. Baltimore, MD: Johns Hopkins University Press, 1978.

20 White, *Tropics of Discourse*, 86.

21 Adam Arvidsson, "Brands," *Journal of Consumer Culture*, 5, no. 2 (1 July 2005): 235–258.

22 Richard Goldstein, "World War II Chic—Page 1—News—New York—Village Voice," 12 January 1999.

23 Vince Zampella and Zied Rieke, "Call of Duty 2 Q&A—Story, Characters, Weapons, Vehicles, AI," *Web* (3 May 2005).

24 Carl James Grindley, "The Hagiography of Steel: The Hero's Weapon and Its Place in Pop Culture," in Eds. Martha W. Driver and Sid Ray, *The Medieval Hero on Screen: Representations from Beowulf to Buffy.* Jefferson, NC: McFarland, 2004; Henri Myrttinen, "Disarming Masculinities," *Disarmament Forum,* no. 4 (2003): 37–46.

25 Brendan Palgn, "The Best FPS Guns of All Time," *PALGN* (6 February 2005); Andy Yates, "First Person Shooters—The Top 10 Weapons!" *PC Games and Reviews* (28 March 2009).

26 White, *Tropics of Discourse.*

27 Raymond Fielding, *The American Newsreel: A Complete History, 1911–1967.* Jefferson, NC: McFarland, 2011.

28 Eduard Imhof, *Cartographic Relief Presentation.* Redlands, CA: ESRI, Inc., 2007.

29 Denis E. Cosgrove, *Mappings.* London: Reaktion Books, 1999.

30 Wiebe E. Bijker, Thomas Parke Hughes, and Trevor J. Pinch, *The Social Construction of Technological Systems: New Directions in the Sociology and History of Technology.* Cambridge: MIT Press, 1987.

31 White, *Tropics of Discourse.*

32 Bacchus451, "An Academic Analysis of Historical Accuracy in Call of Duty 2."

33 Bob Colayco, "Call of Duty 2 Review," *Gamespot.*

34 Ivan Sulic, "Call of Duty: Big Red One a Controllable Action Movie," *IGN.com* (1 November 2005).

35 Roland Barthes, *Mythologies.* Basingstoke: Macmillan, 1972.

36 Ferguson, "How to Win a War," 132.

Works cited

Arvidsson, Adam. "Brands," *Journal of Consumer Culture,* 5, no. 2 (1 July 2005): 235–258.

Bacchus451. "An Academic Analysis of Historical Accuracy in Call of Duty 2—Blog by Bacchus451–IGN," *IGN,* http://www.ign.com/blogs/bacchus451/2011/03/15/an-academic-analysis-of-historical-accuracy-in-call-of-duty-2, accessed 25 September 2012.

Barthes, Roland. *Mythologies.* Basingstoke: Macmillan, 1972.

Bijker, Wiebe E., Thomas Parke Hughes and Trevor J. Pinch. *The Social Construction of Technological Systems: New Directions in the Sociology and History of Technology.* Cambridge, MA: MIT Press, 1987.

Bullinger, Jonathan and Andrew J. Salvati. "A Theory of BrandWW2," *Reconstruction: Studies in Contemporary Culture*, 11, no. 4 (2011), http://reconstruction.eserver.org/114/Salvati-Bullinger.shtml, accessed 24 May 2013.

Colayco, Bob. "Call of Duty 2 Review," *Gamespot*, http://l.gamespot.com/wO2SqW, accessed 25 September 2012.

Cosgrove, Denis E. *Mappings*. London: Reaktion Books, 1999.

de Groot, Jerome. *Consuming History: Historians and Heritage in Contemporary Popular Culture*. London: Taylor & Francis, 2009.

Dunham, Jeremy. "Call of Duty 3 Review: The Most Persistent Sound Which Reverberates through Men's History Is the Beating of War Drums," *IGN.com* (20 November 2006), http://www.ign.com/articles/2006/11/21/call-of-duty-3-review-3, accessed 24 May 2013.

Engelhardt, Tom. "The Victors and the Vanquished," in Eds. Edward Tabor Linenthal and Tom Engelhardt, *History Wars: The Enola Gay and Other Battles for the American Past*. Basingstoke: Macmillan, 1996, 210–250.

Ferguson, Niall. "How to Win a War," *New York Magazine* (23 October 2006).

Fielding, Raymond. *The American Newsreel: A Complete History, 1911–1967*. Jefferson, NC: McFarland, 2011, 42–132.

Gish, Harrison. "Playing the Second World War: Call of Duty and the Telling of History," *Eludamos: Journal for Computer Game Culture*, 4, no. 2 (11 April 2010): 167–180.

Goldstein, Richard. "World War II Chic—Page 1—News—New York—Village Voice," 12 January 1999, http://www.villagevoice.com/1999-01-12/news/world-war-ii-chic/, accessed 23 May 2013.

Grindley, Carl James. "The Hagiography of Steel: The Hero's Weapon and Its Place in Pop Culture," in Eds. Martha W. Driver and Sid Ray, *The Medieval Hero on Screen: Representations from Beowulf to Buffy*. Jefferson, NC: McFarland, 2004, 151–166.

Imhof, Eduard. *Cartographic Relief Presentation*. Redlands, CA: ESRI, Inc., 2007.

Jenkins, Keith. *At the Limits of History: Essays on Theory and Practice*. London and New York: Routledge, 2009.

Kasavin, Greg. "Medal of Honor Pacific Assault Review," *Gamespot*, http://l.gamespot.com/wlu5qr, accessed 25 September 2012.

Kelly, Kevin. "Joystiq Interviews Mark Lamia of Treyarch and Call of Duty the Fifth," *Joystiq* (24 June 2008), http://www.joystiq.com/2008/06/24/joystiq-interviews-mark-lamia-of-treyarch-and-call-of-duty-the-f/, accessed 25 May 2013.

Murray, Janet Horowitz. *Hamlet on the Holodeck: The Future of Narrative in Cyberspace*. Cambridge, MA: MIT Press, 1998.

Myrttinen, Henri. "Disarming Masculinities," *Disarmament Forum*, 5, no. 4 (2003): 37–46.

Palgn, Brendan. "The Best FPS Guns of All Time," *PALGN* (6 February 2005), http://palgn.com.au/1844/the-best-fps-guns-of-all-time/, accessed 24 May 2013.

Rivers, T. "Medal of Honor Frontline Review," *Gamespot* (31 May 2002), http://l.gamespot.com/yRVLAU, accessed 24 May 2013.

Rosenstone, Robert A. *History on Film/Film on History*. Harlow: Longman and Pearson, 2006.

Staff. "Call of Duty Q&A," *Gamespot* (26 June 2003), http://l.gamespot.com/AnyYEK, accessed 23 May 2013.

Sulic, Ivan. "Call of Duty: Big Red One: a Controllable Action Movie," *IGN.com* (1 November 2005), http://www.ign.com/articles/2005/11/02/call-of-duty-big-red-one, accessed 24 May 2013.

Uricchio, William. "Simulation, History, and Computer Games," in Eds. Joost Raessens and Jeffrey H. Goldstein, *Handbook of Computer Game Studies*. Cambridge, MA: MIT Press, 2005, 327–338.

White, Hayden. *Tropics of Discourse: Essays in Cultural Criticism*. Baltimore, MD: Johns Hopkins University Press, 1978.

Yates, Andy. "First Person Shooters—The Top 10 Weapons!" *PC Games and Reviews* (28 March 2009), http://www.pc-games-and-reviews.com/First-Person-Shooter-Weapons.html, accessed 25 May 2013.

Zampella, Vince and Zied Rieke. "Call of Duty 2 Q&A—Story, Characters, Weapons, Vehicles, AI," *Web* (3 May 2005), http://www.gamespot.com/forums/topic/20759562/new-info-of-call-of-duty-2-d, accessed 25 May 2013.

Games cited

Call of Duty. Santa Monica, CA: Infinity Ward, Activision, 2003.

Deus Ex. London, UK: Ion Storm, Eidos Interactive, 2000.

Doom. Richardson, TX: id Software, 1993.

Half Life 2. Kirkland, WA: Valve Corporation, Sierra Entertainment, 2004.

Making History: The Calm & The Storm. Newburyport, MA: Muzzy Lane, 2007.

Medal of Honor. Playstation. Redwood City, CA: Dreamworks Interactive, Electronic Arts, 1999.

Perfect Dark. Twycross, UK: Rare, 2000.

Sid Meier's Civilization. Alameda, CA: MicroProse, 1991.

11

The Strange Attraction of Simulation: Realism, Authenticity, Virtuality

Josef Köstlbauer

University of Vienna

It is not readily explicable why many people take so readily to complex simulation games, which are hard to master and offer little in the way of instant gratification to players. A simulation classic like *Microsoft Flight Simulator* allows players to fly from point A to point B, in which the sole excitement on offer are starting and landing maneuvers. Even in the case of a military flight sim geared toward realism like *Falcon 4*, the excitement of being allowed to fire a missile or drop a bomb is afforded only after mastering the drudgery of target acquisition and lining up the plane for the attack, all the while keeping an eye on navigational instruments and maintaining situational awareness. What do such games mean to players? What do they say about our culture and our world? To explore such questions, a broader cultural and historical context of simulations needs to be considered; it will not be enough to simply regard specific games as isolated phenomena, even though many scholarly studies treat electronic games that way.

The meaning of the term "simulation" in popular usage has become rather vague nowadays. It encompasses a heterogeneous range of games, from *The Sims* or *Sim City* to extremely realistic vehicle or battlefield simulations such as the *Digital Combat Simulator* or *Armed Assault 2* (*ArmA 2*). To study the way simulations deal with reality and their significance for conceptions of reality, a more specific definition is called for. Therefore, I define simulations as attempts to represent reality (or an aspect of reality) as faithfully as possibly.

Simulation games tend to offer not so much a set of rules or predefined goals and conditions, but instead a variety of possibilities and options to "play" within a re-created slice of reality. This creative aspect is reinforced by the inclusion of powerful editors to many commercial simulation games, giving gaming communities unprecedented creative possibilities.

Military-themed simulations provide a promising subject for a study of simulations. To begin with, a significant part—if not the majority—of simulation games have a distinctly military character. Second, simulation games and the military use of simulations for training and planning purposes are historically co-dependent, offering insights into how concepts of reality have influenced the formation of game types and vice versa. Third, military simulations far predate the computer, as do the shared characteristics and overlaps between apparently utilitarian military simulations and the distinctly non-utilitarian world of play.[1]

In order to get closer to understanding the attraction of simulations, we will take a closer look at some of the reasons why we play them before exploring the historical antecedents of the modern military simulation.

Why do we play? The challenge

First, it is worthwhile reiterating that if any satisfaction is derived from "playing" such simulations—and this very obviously is the case for many people—it seems to be a satisfaction derived primarily from mastering intricate and complex problems. It is the challenge that is sought, one of the basic motivations of play.[2]

Why do we play? Authenticity

Another reason why such games find an audience seems to lie in the single defining characteristic of simulation games, namely the claim of realism and authenticity. Whether it is the cockpit of an airplane, race-car, or fork-lift, whether it is the details of an urban landscape, the arms and armor of historical armies, the simulated physics of virtual worlds, or the prowess of artificial intelligence controlling the player's digital foes or allies: in all of these cases what is at stake is realism and authenticity. As Salvalti and Bullinger demonstrate in Chapter 10, demanding and often enthusiastic communities of gamers take apart each game, poring over photographs, maps, technical manuals, and historical accounts, ever ready to criticize and condemn a game that puts forward claims of authenticity as mere marketing ploys.

Even more astonishing is the creative energy set free by this hunger for realism. Many games are constantly and often decisively improved upon by enthusiastic and diligent fans who produce ever more refined add-ons and mods (see also Apperley, Chapter 12, and Crabtree, Chapter 13). Moddability has become a crucial factor, determining how long a game will stay in the market because mods and add-ons increase replay value, not only by extending gameplay or offering new iterations of the game, but also because the creative act of modding is a satisfying experience in itself. Both gamers and game designers increasingly seem to regard such games as open processes. Releases of demos, full versions, extensions, mods, etc. increasingly seem to be merely stages in an iterative process situated at the intersection of play, market, craftsmanship, and creative production.

A telling example is provided by the games of the Armed Assault series developed by Bohemia interactive, a Czech Company based in Prague. The first of these games was *Operation Flashpoint* (2001), set in a fictitious Cold War crisis involving a clash between renegade Soviet and US forces. The follow-up titles *Armed Assault* 1 and 2 were published in 2006 and 2009, respectively; since then several expansion packs have been produced.[3] At the heart of these tactical combat simulation games lies a powerful editor that makes it very easy to create new missions on the fly, but also to build intricate, narration-driven campaigns with cinematic cutscenes and complex scripting. This has engendered a plethora of community-created content ranging from weapons and vehicle add-ons to scripts, missions, and campaigns.[4] Recently a total conversion mod called *Day Z* turned the *ArmA 2* expansion *"ArmA 2: Operation Arrowhead"* into an open-world zombie survival game. According to the mod's developing team, more than 1.5 million players have downloaded the mod by January 2013[5] and already by May 2012 sales of the required original Best in Slot (BIS) game had increased almost fivefold![6]

Why do we play? Mimicry

Most of us will never pilot a Boeing 747 or an F16, not even a Cessna. In fact, it is highly probable that the vast majority of those who play flight simulators do not even aspire to getting a flying license—which is an achievable goal, after all. Therefore, it is logical to surmise that playing such games is not motivated by a craving for a kind of surrogate life. Instead a fascination with the real thing is transported into the confines of play; one enters a make-believe situation for its own sake—a simple cultural technique regarded by Johan Huizinga as a primordial characteristic of play.[7] Roger Caillois, who elaborated on Huizinga's famous assessment of the cultural significance of play, proposed a category of play that quite aptly fits what many seem to seek and find in simulation games.[8] He named it mimicry, because like animals who outwardly appear as another, more dangerous, or larger beast, there are games where players assume the roles of other, more interesting, spectacular, or simply fictional characters. It happens in children's play, acting, or during carnival. And the same is true for gamers playing simulation games. Like children, actors, or carnival-revelers, these persons, although absorbed into the sphere of play, where reality is suspended, are well aware of the fact that they are neither pilots nor generals.[9]

The ambivalence of simulation games

The pretension to realism expressed in digital simulation games has led to interesting imputations: one telling example is the popular claim that the perpetrators of the 9–11 attacks used Microsoft's *Flight Simulator* to plan and train for their operations.[10] No matter whether that is true or not, it demonstrates how palpably evident such a claim seemed at the beginning of the twenty-first century, and it highlights both the power and the astounding measure of realism that some, or many, people ascribe to readily available simulation games. From matters of blissful divertissement these games have turned into weapons that carry the promise of power over life and death. Microsoft itself swiftly reacted to these rumors and had the twin-towers as well as damage models for planes taken out of the game. No longer could the attack on the World Trade Center be replayed; suddenly such features were deemed too realistic.

Thus simulation games inhabit the spaces in between play and reality. That this is not readily understood or obvious can be ascribed to the way we distinguish between play and real life. This distinction also finds expression in a common bias against play as a flippant waste of time, something that is felt surprisingly strongly by gamers and researchers doing games studies.[11] One of the more popular contrarian arguments in this respect has come from Jane McGonigal, who with well-rehearsed if not slightly messianic enthusiasm tries to convince us that we should not play less but more, because playing games makes the world a better place.[12]

Historically, play and games have always been an esteemed part of social, spiritual, and cultural life. Play is an element of culture, or, indeed, an important part of the human condition, it is something all social animals do.[13] And throughout history games have been valued for their didactic qualities, which adds a utilitarian factor to the equation. This is plainly apparent in the case of simulations, which more often than not have been regarded as tools of teaching and training. Famous polymath Gottfried Wilhelm Leibniz (1646–1716) speculated on the potential uses of a war game (*neü erfundenes Kriegsspiel*) for the education of officers;[14] and in the German city of Ulm the patrician Christoph Weickhmann (1617–1681) published a "Game of Kings" (*Königgspiel*): a chess-based, highly idealized representation of the hierarchies and functions at a European court in the seventeenth century. Its author intended it for the education and refinement of future ministers and courtiers.[15]

Kriegsspiel

But far more influential proved to be a game that was invented in war-torn Prussia at the beginning of the nineteenth century. In 1806 Napoleon had shattered Prussia's military might at Auerstedt and Jena. This cataclysmic experience led to far-reaching reforms, which completely transformed the military and civil structures of the Prussian State. Progressive military thinkers like Gerhard von Scharnhorst, August Neidhardt von Gneisenau, and Carl von Clausewitz, and intellectuals like Wilhelm von Humboldt, despite being mistrusted by a conservative and autocratic court, nevertheless attained positions that enabled them to build a military force and state that could challenge (and beat) the French army in the field.[16]

The progressive vigor of the times transcended the institutions of administration, military, and science. Nothing exemplifies this better but the fact that in 1810 both the university at Berlin and the War School (*Kriegsschule*) were established. At the *Kriegsschule* cadets as well as serving officers were taught all those practical and theoretical subjects deemed necessary for the waging of war. One of the lecturers was Carl von Clausewitz himself, who served in this capacity until 1812, when he quit Prussian service to take a command in the Tsar's army and fight Napoleon.[17]

Right at the time when Clausewitz left Berlin for Russia, King Friedrich Wilhelm was presented with a game that intended to exemplify many of the characteristics of war expounded by Clausewitz. It was the *Taktische Kriegsspiel* (tactical war-game), devised by the *Kriegsrat* (war councillor) Georg Leopold von Reiswitz (1760–1828),[18] who is often referred to as father of the military simulation.[19] While that verdict may be contested, considering the political circumstances it is hardly surprising that Reiswitz and his son created and popularized this war game in Prussia at that time.

The *Kriegsspiel* presented to the King in 1812 consisted of a large wooden cabinet with a huge rectangular tabletop divided into a numerated quadratic field of fifteen by eighteen squares. With painted rectangular terrain pieces, varied terrains featuring rivers, woods, meadows, and hills could be created. Colored pieces represented military units of different types. This amazing wooden box can be regarded as a kind of analog computer allowing for a great variation of battlefield conditions and tactical moves.[20]

Many earlier war games of the eighteenth century had relied on a mechanical understanding of warfare and were heavily influenced by chess and its abstracted agonistic confrontation of black and white.[21] Their highly idealized representations were based on strictly geometrical dispositions, which reduced the outcome of every game session to a matter of mere calculation. Reiswitz's game left all that behind: now the outcome of engagements was determined by throwing dice against odds derived from the type and size of units, as well as various other conditions. For the first time, chance and unpredictability, the imponderables of war, entered into the game.

Later Reiswitz's son, then a promising officer in the Prussian army, successfully propagated his father's game as a training tool throughout the army and turned it into an a serious simulation of the work of a military staff on the battlefield: on each of the opposing sides a commander and several officers represented a rudimentary staff; the tabletop had been done away with, instead the game was played on topographic maps, which became available in increasing quantities and quality. The first holder of the newly created position of Chief of General Staff, General Karl von Müffling (1820–1829), vigorously promoted not only the *Kriegsspiel* but also the topographic survey of Prussia. As the lay of the land was quickly transferred into the symbolic sphere of cartographic abstraction, virtual battles and skirmishes could be played out in these two-dimensional representations of actual landscapes. Unit markers were not any longer moved across fields but across specific distances, and players did not act in turns but in time-sequences determined by distance and estimated unit speed. The game had become a simulation that enabled military professionals to fight possible conflicts instead of purely fictitious ones.[22]

The dispositions of the participants remained hidden to each other and were only revealed when forces came into contact. An umpire or referee, whom Reiswitz fittingly named "Vertrauter" (Confidante), decided which information became accessible to the players at the beginning and during the game and he formulated the "Situation," that is the mission and its conditions. In a further step toward scientification of the *Kriegsspiel*, Reiswitz and Scharnhorst systematically test-fired weapons fielded by contemporaneous European forces, and used the data to model the effects of fire and their variability in his game.[23]

As an Austrian officer explained in a war game study published in 1874, maneuvers were well suited to familiarize soldiers and officers with terrain and the conduct of drills, but they could hardly demonstrate "the effect of enemy fire, which is the actual destructive element [in battle], and its impact on morale."[24] The officer probably had in mind a situation akin to the fictitious Indian army maneuvers described by Rudyard Kipling, where the regiments "had been turned loose . . . to practice in peace what they would never attempt in war."[25]

The younger Reiswitz strove to capture the unknown and the openness, the contingency of every decision, every action on the field of battle. His game was an implementation of the fundamental tenet of Clausewitz, who repeatedly asserted that "in war all is undetermined, and the calculation has always to be made with varying quantities."[26]

Blurred distinctions

There is much to be said of the adoption of the Prussian war game as an all-important training and planning tool by all European armies throughout the nineteenth century, and the development of war games during the Second World War and the Cold War. But in all these increasingly sophisticated military simulations the interconnectedness of simulation and play is firmly established. The world had ceased to be ruled by providence and rules, and instead appeared to be a product of chance and complex relationships of cause and effect. Introducing contingency was the precondition for advanced applied mathematics, which calculated probabilities and turned the world into calculable and computable models.

At times the process of dissolving the material world into a system of symbols of and signs brought reality and play so close together as to blur the difference. German art historian and philosopher Claus Pias used a striking anecdote from 1944 to illustrate this effect. In November of that year, German Field-Marshal Model had assembled the staff of the fifth army for a war game. They were to test strategies for defending against expected US offensives. But as the game commenced, news of American operations began to arrive at headquarters. Instead of stopping, the reports were incorporated into the game, and for the next hours the symbolic sphere of play and the reality of a fighting staff blended into each other as more and more units of Fifth Army became involved in actual combat actions.[27]

The situation at the map table need not be different whether the players are staff officers playing a war game, staff officers conducting an operation, or civilians playing for entertainment. For a spectator not privy to the actual situation, it would have been impossible to decide whether the reports were based on actual or on fictitious events. The difference between play and not-play, fundamental as it may be, lies in the results on the actual battlefield far removed from the staff. In the case of digital military simulations, the software has assumed both the roles of Reiswitz's confidante and that of the opposing force. It simulates the events on the ground and translates them into messages and visual representations that form the player's/commander's perspective on the battle. As both military and gaming communities have become digitized, the difference between these two spheres has narrowed still.

In another instance illustrating the connection between simulation and reality, the simulation already had anticipated events: the 10 January 2012 edition of *Foreign Policy* contained an article by Michael Peck titled "The Syrian Invasion," which was headed by a picture showing a Leopard Main Battle Tank in Middle Eastern surrounding. This was not, however, a Photoshopped image, instead it was a screenshot of a commercial simulation game named *Combat Mission: Shock Force*.[28] This game was published in 2008 and it featured a large-scale conflict between Syria and NATO. The reasons for this—at that time rather odd—thematic decision by American developer and publisher Battlefront.com was quite simple: they wanted to simulate engagements across the whole spectrum of modern warfare, which cannot be done by Western forces combating lightly armed insurgents like those encountered in Iraq or Afghanistan, while the Syrian military is a large and formidable force.[29] But what in 2004 was a rather unrealistic event, by late 2012 has become a worrying possibility, as the United States, Saudi Arabia, or Britain clandestinely support Syrian rebel factions and an apprehensive Turkish government has deployed strong forces along the Syrian Border. Already players have begun to simulate possible future scenarios featuring rebel factions as well as the Turkish army.[30]

Such connections between simulation and reality suggest a potential to employ war games to anticipate and explore potential conflicts, and this has bled over into the sphere of commercial gaming. A counterfactual, what-if aspect is intrinsic to video games with historical narratives, and this is especially true for simulation games. Maybe this can be interpreted as an inheritance from traditional military history that understood battles and campaigns as "turning points" of history: refighting them means changing history's course. But there also is an earnest interest in historical research and historical fact that seems to motivate many simulation gamers. To them simulations seem to be a medium for approaching history (and historiography). Therefore, in community forums one can read long discussions on the consequences and causes and what might happen if a given battlefield variable is changed. An interesting source can be found in After Action Reports (itself a term borrowed from military parlance) on virtual engagements, in which hypotheses on the merits of specific tactics or weapon systems are tested. While the workings and the exploitation of game mechanics are also being debated, it is the aspect of historical accuracy and realism that very obviously seems most important to most community members. Literature as well as various primary sources are cited frequently and discussed thoroughly.[31]

Meanwhile there are also a number of simulation games that have been adopted by the military for its own means; well-publicized examples are the US Marine Corps adaption of *Doom 2* (*Marine Doom*, 1996) or the simulation *America's Army* developed and released by the US Army in 2002. The connections between the military and the video game industry always have been strong and may have further increased in recent years.[32] Mutual interest has led to private–public partnerships and cross-investments involving considerable amounts of public money, especially in the United States. But many, more mundane, connections slip off the public radar. For example, the Australian Department of Defence in 2004 purchased an enhanced version of *Combat Mission: Afrika Korps* (*CM:AK*) for use in teaching historical military tactics. *CM:AK* is a cheap but well-rounded tactical simulation, typically depicting short engagements on a small scale (frequently company level or below); game mechanics are easily learned, and it comes with a capable editor.[33]

Another example is the decision by the US Army Command and General Staff College to add the Civil War simulation *Scourge of War: Gettysburg* (published by NorbSoftDev) to its suite of training simulations. Similar to the Prussian *Kriegsspiel*, *Scourge of War* closely simulates the command and communication structures of nineteenth-century armies.[34]

Far more ambitious is the professional tactical combat simulation *Virtual Battlespace* (VBS 1 and 2). These highly modular simulations are based on the very same Virtual Reality Engine (sic!) as the *ArmA* series of games. It is intended for use by professional armed forces. The first major client was the US Marine Corps, though important buyers also included the Australian and British military, as well as numerous other Western armed forces. *VBS 2* was released in 2007.[35]

Apparently civilian gamers were interested too, since in 2004 a limited public version of VBS 1 (*VBS Lite*) was made available for free download. Bringing this development full circle, Britain's Ministry of Defense distributed a free *VBS 2* version for marketing and recruiting purposes.[36] Thus gamers' interest in this simulation game, produced for and with the cooperation of military institutions, led those military institutions to provide or sell stripped-down versions of these simulations as games back to civilians. To put it more drastically: now gamers are playing with military software. The sole difference that remains is one of different user rights and the question of control over different layers of realism and specific datasets. The real and the simulated have converged: games are making history, while war has become a matter of games.

On a final note, the growing interconnectedness of the commercial video game industry and the military complex can have unexpected consequences: Bohemia Interactive's upcoming game *ArmA 3* will be set in the future on a fictional Greek island; for its topography and flora sceneries from the real island Lemnos are going to be reproduced in detail. In a faint echo of the adoption of topographical maps for the Prussian *Kriegsspiel*, today only the most faithful digital representation of reality seems to suffice for simulation games—even if the terrain in question is to be found on an obscure Mediterranean island. But in an unexpected turn of events two employees of Bohemia Interactive visiting Lemnos on a fact finding mission in September 2012 were arrested by Greek authorities, apparently on spying charges.[37] Operating in the blurred borderlands between reality and virtuality, game designers have become part of war, like journalists, photographers, or radio amateurs before them.

Notes

1 The beginnings of military simulation may be dated back even further if one were to understand the term simulation to include the various forms of mock battle and combat in which all military cultures engage—to train for war as well as to promote martial prowess and social standing of the participants. Valid examples may be the far-ranging melees of twelfth-century tourneys colorfully described in the *histoire* of Guilleaume le Maréchal (Georges Duby, *William Marshal: The Flower of Chivalry*. New York: Knopf Doubleday Publishing, 1987, 133–141) or the "mimic battles" of Spartan youth bands mentioned by Plutarch (Plutarch, "Lycurgus and Numa," in Ed. Loeb Classical Library, *The Parallel Lifes*, vol. 1. Cambridge: Harvard University Press, 1914, Section 17.2).

2 Jane McGonigal, *Reality Is Broken: Why Games Make Us Better and How They Can Change the World*. New York: Penguin, 2011, 430–436.

3 "Bohemia Interactive Wiki."

4 A relatively complete collection can be found at a community website called "ArmaHolic", in the download section.

5 "dayzmod.com."

6 Luke Plunkett, "Back From the Dead. PC Zombie Darling Causes Sale Explosion, ArmA Devs Happy to Help," *Kotaku* (15 May 2012). The Day Z mod is based on the ArmA 2 expansion "Armed Assault 2: Operation Arrowhead."

7   Johan Huizinga, *Homo Ludens: A Study of the Play Element in Culture*. London: Routledge, 2008, 8.

8   Roger Caillois, *Man, Play, and Games*. Urbana, IL: University of Illinois Press, 2001, 19–23.

9   Caillois, *Man, Play, and Games*, 49.

10 There seems to be no evidence to support these allegations. Instead the 9–11 attackers attended official flight schools in the United States, acquired private and commercial pilot licenses and bought training time on various professional airplane simulators. The report of the 9–11 commission describes this in some detail and does not mention any of the flight simulator games available at that time. *9/11 Report: With reporting and analysis by the New York Times*. New York: St. Martin's Press, 2004, 323–328; The Daily Mail in 2005 pointed to the MSFS without naming sources: Kobina Amoakwa, "The Flight Software that 'Trains the Terrorists', " *Mail Online* (25 July 2005), accessed 10 October 2012.

11 Jesper Juul, *Casual Revolution: Reinventing Video Games and their Players*. Cambridge MA: MIT Press, 2010, 152; McGonigal, *Reality Is Broken*, pos. 137–143, 316, 343–346. On the related discussion of violence and video games, see Cheryl K. Olson, "Children's Motivations for Video Game Play," *Review of General Psychology*, 14 (2010): 180–187.

12 McGonigal, "Gaming Can Make a Better World," *TED Talk* (TED 2010), accessed 10 October 2012.

13 See Huizinga, *Homo Ludens*, 3. On current state of research, see G.M. Burghardt, "Play," in *Encyclopedia of Animal Behavior*. Westport CT: Greenwood, 2004, 740–744.

14 Philipp von Hilgers, *War Games: A History of War on Paper*. Cambridge, MA: MIT Press, 2012, 28.

15 Christoph Weickhmann, *New-erfundenes Grosses Königs-Spiel*. Ulm: 1664.

16 On military reforms, see, for example, Peter Paret, *The Cognitive Challenge of War: Prussia 1806*. Princeton, NJ: Princeton University Press, 2009, 55, 83–103.

17 Peter Paret, *Clausewitz and the State*. Princeton, NJ: Princeton University Press, 1987, 186–187.

18 There are several alternative versions of that name: Reißwitz, Reiswitz, Reisswitz.

19 See, for example, Ben Brown, "Simulation Games," MA Thesis, Naval Postgraduate School Monterey, 2010, 13.

20 von Hilgers, *War Games*, 43–48.

21 Examples are Johann Georg Ludwig Hellwig, *Versuch eines aufs Schachspiel gebaueten taktischen Spiels*. Leipzig: S.L. Crusius, 1780 and Georg Venturini, *Beschreibung und Regeln eines neuen Krieges-Spiels zum Nutzen und Vergnügen, besonders aber zum Gebrauch in Militair-Schulen*. Schleswig: J.G. Röhß, 1798.

22 von Hilgers, *War Games*, 51–53.

23 von Hilgers, *War Games*, 48–53.

24 Edmund Edler von Mayer, *Studie über das Kriegsspiel*. Vienna: Verlag des militärwissenschaftlichen Vereins, 1874, 6.

25 Rudyard Kipling, *The Courting of Dinah Shadd*, 1.

26 Carl von Clausewitz, *On War*, trans. Michael Howard. New Jersey: Princeton University Press, 2007, 99.

27 Claus Pias, *Computer Spiel Welten*. Munich: Sequenzia, 2002, 171. The primary source for this remarkable piece of history is a postwar report written by German General Rudolf Hofmann and translated by the US Army: Rudolf Hofmann, "War Games," U.S. Army Historical Document MS P-094.

28 Michael Peck, "The Syrian Invasion," *Foreign Policy* (10 January 2012), accessed 10 October 2012.

29 *Combat Mission: Shock Force—Field Manual v1.20*, 10–12.

30 See, for example, this discussion on a user-made scenario for CM Shock Force: "Syrian-Civil War—Baba Amr (DAR)."

31 An example is a discussion on fuses used in WWII and rounds used during WWII on the Battlefront Community Forum for Combat Mission: Barbarossa to Berlin: "BR350A and B HE fuse and Pzgn39 HE fuse."

32 The history and structure of this marriage between creative software industry and the United States Military has been aptly documented by Tim Lenoir in "All but War is Simulation: The Military-Entertainment Complex," *Configurations*, 8 (2000): 289–335.

33 "Afrika Korps licensed by the Australian Department of Defence," *Battlefront. com* (20 May 2004).

34 Norb Timpko, "US Army Trains with 1863 US Army," *Norbsoftdev* (29 December 2011).

35 *VBS1* (2001); *VBS2* (2007). A list of customers can be found at the website of Bohemia Interactive Simulations: "Customers."

36 "JCOVE Lite."

37 "Official statement by CEO of Bohemia Interactive Studios."

Works cited

The 9/11 Report: With Reporting and Analysis by the New York Times. New York: St. Martin's Press. 2004.

"Afrika Korps licensed by the Australian Department of Defence," *Battlefront. com*, May 20, 2004, http://www.battlefront.com/index.php?option=com_content&task=view&id=250&Itemid=81, accessed 10 October 2012.

Amoakwa, Kobina. "The Flight Software that 'Trains the Terrorists', " *Mail Online* (25 July 2005), http://www.dailymail.co.uk/news/article-357006/The-flight-software-trains-terrorists.html, accessed 10 October 2012.

"ArmaHolic. Covering the ArmA Series," http://www.armaholic.com/list.
php?c=files, accessed 10 October.

Brown, Ben. "Simulation Games," MA Thesis, Naval Postgraduate School
Monterey, 2010.

"Bohemia Interactive Wiki," Main Page, http://community.bistudio.com/wiki/
Main_Page, accessed 10 October 2012.

"BR350A and B HE fuse and Pzgn39 HE fuse," August 22–December 10, 2012,
Battlefront.com Community Forums, http://www.battlefront.com/community/
showthread.php?t=106028, accessed 10 October 2012.

Burghardt, G.M. "Play," in Ed. Marc Bekoff, *Encyclopedia of Animal Behavior*,
vol. 2. Westport CT: Greenwood, 2004, 740–744.

Butts, Steve. "Arma II Review. Proving that a Game Can Be Both Brilliant
and Awful at the Same Time," *IGN* (2 July 2009), http://www.ign.com/
articles/2009/07/02/arma-ii-review, accessed 10 December 2012.

Caillois, Roger. *Man, Play, and Games*. Urbana, IL: University of Illinois Press,
2001.

Combat Mission: Shock Force–Field Manual v1.20, PDF (2009) 10–12.

"Customers," Bohemia Interactive Simulations, http://products.bisimulations.
com/customers, accessed 10 October 2012.

Duby, Georges. *William Marshal: The Flower of Chivalry*. New York: Knopf
Doubleday Publishing, 1987.

Hellwig, Johann Georg Ludwig. *Versuch eines aufs Schachspiel gebaueten
taktischen Spiels: Von zwey oder mehern Personen zu spielen*. Leipzig: S.L.
Crusius, 1780.

Hofmann, Rudolf. "War Games," U.S. Army Historical Document MS P–094.

Huizinga, Johan. *Homo Ludens: A Study of the Play Element in Culture*. London:
Routledge, 2008.

"JCOVE Lite," Bohemia Interactive Simulations, http://products.bisimulations.
com/jcove-lite, accessed 10 October 2012.

Juul, Jesper. *Casual Revolution: Reinventing Video Games and their Players*.
Cambridge MA: MIT Press, 2010.

Kipling, Rudyard. "Dinah Shadd," in *The Courting of Dinah Shadd*. New York:
Cosimo, 2005, 1–38.

Lenoir, Tim. "All But War Is Simulation: The Military-Entertainment Complex,"
Configurations, 8 (2000): 289–335.

McGonigal, Jane. *Reality Is Broken: Why Games Make Us Better and How They
Can Change the World*, Kindle ed. New York: Penguin, 2011.

McGonigal, Jane. "Gaming Can Make a Better World," *TED Talk* (TED 2010),
http://www.ted.com/talks/jane_mcgonigal_gaming_can_make_a_better_world.
html, accessed 10 October 2012.

"Official statement by CEO of Bohemia Interactive," Bohemia Interactive, http://
www.bistudio.com/english/home/news/company/330-update-lemnos-arrests,
accessed 10 October 2012.

Olson, Cheryl K. "Children's Motivations for Video Game Play," *Review of General
Psychology*, 14 (2010): 180–187.

Paret, Peter. *Clausewitz and the State*, 2nd ed. Princeton, NJ: Princeton
University Press, 1987.

Paret, Peter. *The Cognitive Challenge of War: Prussia 1806.* Princeton, NJ: Princeton University Press, 2009.

Peck, Michael. "The Syrian Invasion," *Foreign Policy* (10 January 2012), http://www.foreignpolicy.com/articles/2012/01/10/the_syrian_invasion, accessed 10 October 2012.

Pias, Claus. *Computer Spiel Welten.* Munich: Sequenzia, 2002, 171–183.

Plunkett, Luke. "Back From the Dead. PC Zombie Darling Causes Sale Explosion, ArmA Devs Happy to Help," *Kotaku* (15 May 2012), http://kotaku.com/5910279/pc-zombie-darling-causes-sale-explosion-arma-devs-happy-to-help, accessed 10 October 2012.

Plutarch, "Lycurgus and Numa," in Ed. Loeb Classical Library, *The Parallel Lifes*, vol. 1. Cambridge: Harvard University Press, 1914, 50.

Timpko, Norb. "US Army Trains with 1863 US Army," *Norbsoftdev* (29 December 2011), http://www.norbsoftdev.net/articles-mainmenu-59/news-mainmenu-2/latest-news-mainmenu-57/161-2011-us-army-trains-with-1863-us-army, accessed 10 December 2012.

"Syrian-Civil War–Baba Amr (DAR)," October 16–December 20, 2012, *Battlefront Community Forums,* http://www.battlefront.com/community/showthread.php?t=106751, accessed 20 December 2012.

Venturini, Georg. *Beschreibung und Regeln eines neuen Krieges-Spiels zum Nutzen und Vergnügen, besonders aber zum Gebrauch in Militair-Schulen.* Schleswig: J.G. Röhß, 1798.

von Clausewitz, Carl. *On War,* trans. Michael Howard. Princeton, NJ: Princeton University Press, 2007.

von Hilgers, Philipp. *War Games: A History of War on Paper.* Cambridge, MA: MIT Press, 2012.

von Mayer, Edmund Edler. *Studie über das Kriegsspiel.* Vienna: Verlag des militärwissenschaftlichen Vereins, 1874.

Weickhmann, Christoph. *New-erfundenes Grosses Königs-Spiel.* Ulm: Balthasar Kühn, 1664.

Games cited

America's Army. United States Army, 2002.

ArmA: Armed Assault. Prague: Bohemia Interactive, 2006.

ArmA II: Armed Assault 2. Prague: Bohemia Interactive, 2009.

Arma II OA: Operation Arrowhead. Prague: Bohemia Interactive, 2010.

Arma III: Armed Assault 3. Prague: Bohemia Interactive, announced for, 2013.

Combat Mission: Afrika Korps. Battlefront.com, 2003.

Combat Mission: Barbarossa to Berlin. Battlefront.com, 2002.

Combat Mission: Shock Force. Battlefront.com, 2007.

DayZ. Dean "Rocket" Hall, Bohemia Interactive, 2012. (Mod to *Arma II*).

Digital Combat Simulator. Moscow: Eagle Dynamics, The Fighter Collection, 2008.

Doom 2: Hell on Earth. Richardson, TX: Id Software, GT interactive, 1994.

Falcon 4. Alameda, CA: Microprose, 1998.

Microsoft Flight Simulator X. Redmond, WA: Microsoft Game Studios, 2006.

Operation Flashpoint: Cold War Crisis. Prague: Bohemia Interactive, 2001.

Scourge of War: Gettysburg. Epsom, UK: NorbSoftDev, Matrix Games/Slitherine, 2012.

Sim City Societies. Redwood City, CA: Tilted Mill Enterntainment, Electronic Arts, 2007.

The Sims 3. Redwood City, CA: The Sims Studio, Electronic Arts, 2009.

Virtual Battlespace 1 (VBS 1). Bohemia Interactive, Bohemia Interactive Australia, Coalescent Technologies, 2001.

Virtual Battlespace 2 (VBS 2). Bohemia Interactive, Bohemia Interactive Australia, 2007.

12

Modding the Historians' Code: Historical Verisimilitude and the Counterfactual Imagination

Tom Apperley
The University of New South Wales

These suppositions are theoretically conceivable; and one can always play a parlour game with the might-have-beens of history. But they have nothing to do with ... history.

E.H. CARR[1]

The genre of alternative history became widely known during the twentieth century as a mainstay of popular culture. Enduring tropes emerged: What if the Nazi's had won World War II? What if the South had won the Civil War? While most of the popular texts were decidedly pulp-ish, a few literary works of alternative history were eventually acknowledged for their artistic merit, and respected authors—such as Michael Chabon, and Phillip Roth—dabbled in the genre, giving it an air of literary respectability. The genre was also given a degree of academic respectability through the collection *Virtual History*, edited by Niall Fergusson. Tropes from alternative history are commonly adapted to other popular formats like cinema and digital games. Ubisoft's blockbuster *Assassin's Creed* series exemplifies how digital games have utilized the genre. *Assassin's Creed II*, set against the backdrop of the feuding Italian city-states of the Renaissance, intricately involves the player in subplots involving Rodrigo Borgia, Niccolò Machiavelli, and Leonardo de Vinci. This theme is revisited more explicitly in "The tyranny of King Washington"— three downloadable content episodes for *Assassin's Creed III* that tell " ... an alternate history of the American Revolution. In this new timeline, George Washington decides to become king of the American colonies instead of establishing a democracy."[2] Is this anything more than simple entertainment?

In the era in which parlor games have given way to digital games as the *de rigueur* after-dinner form of entertainment in many households, can Carr's absolute dismissal of alternative history still stand?[3] He asserts that while alternative history is enjoyable, it is ultimately a meaningless, bourgeois intellectual diversion. This chapter argues, contra to Carr, that far from being meaningless, the emerging popular genres of alternative history offer a substantial way of critically engaging with history. Digital games, particularly strategy games—exemplified by *Europa Universalis II*—offer a mode of engagement with an alternative historical text that provides an opportunity for the player to consider critical and reflective interpretations of historical events.

Europa Universalis II spans the era of 1420–1820; the main focus of the game is the expansion of the European powers to dominate trade and create colonies around the globe. Important strategic concerns in the game include: developing technology, trade, diplomacy, and military; well-managed colonial expansion is also crucial. The player is invited to select the country they will play; the initial choices are Austria, England, France, the Ottoman Empire, Poland, Portugal, Russia, Spain, and Sweden. However, a key innovation of the game is that ultimately the player may select any country. While it is impossible for many nations to win, another innovation of this game is the remarkable flexibility in terms of goal setting. Appropriate goals can be discussed and shared through dedicated online communities hosted by Paradox Interactive (the designers of *Europa Universalis II*).

This chapter will argue that what players do with *Europa Universalis II* provides them an opportunity to reflect critically on historical events. A critical level of engagement with the game is encouraged by two drives in the online community: the desire for historical verisimilitude leads players to discuss styles of play aimed at making the historical events depicted more realistic; and the desire to explore counterfactual imaginings of history, where players discuss how to establish and explore fantastic alternative histories with the game. Through the materials shared by the online community, both of these apparently contradictory drives are able to provide an accessible segue from expert play and deep knowledge of the game, to a more technical understanding of its operations and design. First, it is important to contextualize this discussion of *Europa Universalis II* against other key scholarly works on the representation of history in digital games, particularly in order to highlight how digital games differ from other representational media, in that they are designed as algorithmic processes. Second, the chapter will argue that the game provides a great deal of scope for players to explore counterfactual imaginations that bring official versions of history into question. The final section of the chapter demonstrates the different ways that the counterfactual imagination emerges in online communities, especially among those players who understand the game as code.

Gaming, ideology, and code

Scholarly analysis of how digital games represent history has paid relatively little attention to *Europa Universalis II* in favor of the less obscure, easy-to-use, and popular *Sid Meier's Civilization* series. This series is often collectively referred to as "Civilization" or just "Civ." While the series does depict history—or historical processes—these depictions are almost entirely abstract, they completely lack the historical verisimilitude of *Europa Universalis II*. However, criticism and analysis of "Civ" is relevant to this discussion, in particular the crucial distinction that Galloway makes between: *ideological* critique, which focuses on the ideological biases in how digital games represent history; and, *informatic* critique, which argues digital games are merely the visual output of complex algorithms, which in themselves have very little to do with history.[4] The core of Galloway's argument is that the particular ideologies of "Civ" become less relevant concerns than "the transcoding of history into specific mathematical models."[5] The modeling of historical processes through algorithms means that each ideological factor becomes simply a variable or input within an overarching informatic system.

Past research on "Civ" has focused on ideological critiques, in particular the problems associated with representing history abstractly. This position is outlined eloquently by Friedman, who argues that *Civilization II* obscures the violence of "exploration, colonization, and development."[6] Further criticisms in this vein include: that "Civ" focuses on Western-style development, misrepresents indigenous cultures, and overemphasizes the role of the military.[7] The concern is that while playing "Civ," the player adheres to the structuring logic of the game's rules and thus uncritically accepts its ideologies.[8] Other discussions of the ideological layer are more sympathetic. Stephenson maintains that *Civilization II* supports the development of a "skeptical, critical attitude."[9] Understanding its rules and parameters not only allows one to play within that arbitrary framework, but importantly, also allows one to play *with* the ideologies that those frameworks represent.[10] A thorough knowledge and acceptance of the rules of the game cannot, then, be simply equated with accepting their ideology.

Europa Universalis II allows for play that varies across a spectrum, from attempting to complete the game with a total historical accuracy, to an exploration of alternative history. Digital games allow players to stage a wide "range of interrogations,"[11] however, in the case of *Europa Universalis II* these are interrogations of history. These interrogations take place across both the ideological and informatic critiques outlined by Galloway as players both recognize the ideological underpinnings of the game, and unpack and modify its coding. Conceptualizing the relationship between these two layers during play is crucial to the argument outlined below. The players' drive to produce certain outcomes is not limited by their prowess, since they also have the opportunity to mod the code of the game.

Playing counterfactuals

As discussed in the introduction to this book, in Europe, the discipline of history has traditionally been dominated by a teleological paradigm.[12] This notion, that history makes purposeful progress toward a particular end reached its apex in the philosophical paradigms of Hegel, Marx, and Smith. This was further entrenched when the scientific discoveries of Darwin were incorporated into the social sciences, serving to justify the hegemonic view of the European Empires.[13] However, in the twentieth century, the teleological view of history began increasingly to be regarded with skepticism.[14] A more empirical approach was demanded, as increasingly historians considered their role to be one of reconstructing the past through surviving sources. In the last quarter of the century this approach also came to be questioned. Critics pointed out that despite its empirical claims, the history it produced was highly subjective; in particular, criticism was directed at how this approach to historical scholarship involved imposing a normative and coherent order upon past events.[15] This position suggests that writing history is an interpretive act; historians are not discoverers of the truth about the past, they are participants in the making of historical "truth." By accepting the historians' subjective and interpretive role, history becomes not a discussion of the truth, but a dialogue where competing discourses can emerge and exist.

One of the key problems with establishing a coherent narrative over historical events is that it imposes a notion of teleological inevitability that fails to acknowledge past contingencies. In *The Landscape of History*, John Gaddis writes:

> it would make no sense, for example, to begin an account of the Japanese attack on Pearl Harbor with the launching of the planes from their carriers: you'd want to know how the carriers came to be within range of Hawaii, which requires explaining why the government in Tokyo chose to risk war with the United States. But you can't do that without discussing the American oil embargo against Japan, which in turn was a response to the Japanese takeover of French Indochina. Which of course resulted from the opportunity provided by France's defeat at the hands of Nazi Germany, together with the frustrations Japan had encountered in trying to conquer China.[16]

Gaddis's point is that each historical factor is contingent; the importance of the factor is only established when they are "discovered" to contribute to a significant event. *What was contingent in the present seems inevitable in hindsight.* In the past the future was a field of plural possibilities to the subject present in that past. Teleology legitimizes the present as the only possible (thus inevitable) result of the cumulative events that constitute history. While the future is open to speculation and the consideration of plural possibilities, the past is homogenized; by focusing on the chain of events, a single path is forged that ignores branches of possibilities.

Counterfactual history is a notion that challenges the tendency of the multiple contingencies of the past being homogenized into a singularity in hindsight. Unlike the literary genre of alternative history, it provides a legitimate historical approach to the speculation on how events might have otherwise occurred. This notion permits a plural approach to the past, each past is still an interpretation, but they are no longer necessarily hegemonic.[17] Thus, counterfactual history becomes a powerful tool for examining both the past and present. Counterfactual history examines "the ways in which multiple potential temporal and spatial trajectories of change exist simultaneously at different conjunctures."[18] This approach opens up the past to heterogeneous and multiple possibilities.

The vastness of this multiplicity, however, threatens to undermine the scholarly use of the counterfactual. Carr's rather negative appraisal of counterfactual history in the epigraph of this chapter frames the discussion of counterfactuals in a strict "all or nothing" fashion. But it is simply not the case that the only choice is between accepting teleological interpretations of history, and *declaring nothing to be feasible apart from actual historic events*; or *accepting that history is meaningless*, that literally anything is possible. Warf suggests this dilemma is resolved by rethinking the arbitrary boundary between the "real" and the "possible." He states:

If, however, the "real" is not simply equated with the observed we broaden the definition of "reality" to include not only what is, but what might have been, then the lines between the real and the might-have-been become blurred in productive and imaginative ways.[19]

Even the more orthodox Ferguson is able to accommodate the counterfactual into his historical methods by strictly limiting his inquiry to those scenarios that are both plausible and articulated in historical evidence.[20] Rather than rejecting counterfactual history as unhistorical both Ferguson and Warf embrace productive positions that acknowledge its usefulness. The strict limits imposed by Ferguson indicate how the counterfactual can be used as a starting point for historical knowledge when it is used to interrogate history. Counterfactuals encourage reflection on what is considered as valid historical evidence, and an evaluation of plausibility. By evoking the imaginative dimension of counterfactuals, Warf suggests a broader basis of its interpretive function. Counterfactuals allow people to imagine a different world where strange and unfamiliar mappings and trajectories of time and space have been produced. This allows the "what if" to challenge deeply held certainties, and opens the historical dynamics of power to question.

Europa Universalis II provides scope for players to articulate and explore their counterfactual imaginary. It does this in two key ways. First, by encouraging reflection on historical rigor by providing a platform for dialogue around plausibility; and second, by encouraging imaginative approaches to history by permitting and encouraging gameplay that is divergent from strict historical events. It encourages counterfactual play and reflection because it deals specifically with the representation of history.

The core play of *Europa Universalis II* revolves around a dynamic, real-time map that displays the movement of troops, development of infrastructure in towns and provinces, the establishment of trading posts and colonies, and the changing market forces at play. On this map the players deploy their troops and other commands, producing through conflict and expansion numerous variable counterfactual mappings, while also dealing with the demands of the "real" historic events for the country that they have chosen to play. Engaging in counterfactual mappings through play creates the opportunity to reimagine the actual event, as it involves considering how that event may have otherwise occurred, or indeed what the world would be like had it not.

Through play—and modding—players may change and transform the paradigm provided by the "official" version of history. In this respect the game works to deconstruct teleological paradigms that declare events to be inevitable. More specifically, counterfactuals can undermine the sense of fate that dominant groups adopt to justify their hegemony. Warf argues that

Counterfactual histories point to alternative schemas for categorizing the world, demonstrating that received categories of structuring space are no more "real" or proper than are the arbitrary lenses that we use to make sense of the past.[21]

By offering plural possibilities for representing the past, *Europa Universalis II* contributes to understanding the arbitrary dimensions of "official" history. The game opens up the past to the possibility of being scrutinized by the player—but this does not mean that all players will approach the game in a counterfactual way.

Modding the historians' code

Europa Universalis II certainly can be played in a counterfactual manner. In this case the player uses the game as a tool to create a vision of the world that suits them. In some cases this vision will be difficult to achieve because of the difficulties posed by the interventions of rival factions controlled by AI (Artificial Intelligence) or other human players. Players may explore their counterfactual imaginings through mastering the game; the more expert the player, the more likely that they will be able to achieve their desired outcomes based on skill alone. As players become more involved in expert play, and in discussion of expert play, they develop an understanding of the algorithm of the game, and what variables to change in order to produce the outcomes that they desire from that algorithm.[22]

The relationship between the available variables and the algorithm is contextualized through the play—and replay—of the game. However, this contextualization is also supported by involvement in the gaming community through the use of chat rooms, bulletin boards, gaming blogs and journalism, etc. Collectively these forums may be described as "paratexts." Paratexts are "communications and artifacts" pertaining to digital games that are derived both from official and from unofficial sources.[23] Paradox Interactive has extensive forums on their official site, which include player-authored strategy guides, and player-created wikis that aim to break down and examine every aspect of playing—and modding—the game. A subgenre of paratexts that is particularly important for illustrating the role of the counterfactual imagination in the play of *Europa Universalis II* has also emerged in the official game forums, that of the after-action report (also known as AAR—see Köstlbauer, Chapter 11). The after-action report focuses on reporting sessions of play, often in episodes as it is played, with an emphasis on the counterfactual imaginary. The report may be made in a purely instrumental manner, in the style of a walkthrough; however, it is more common that they are recounted in the form of an elaborate fiction, which may include occasional references to the practicalities of play.

In the following example from the Civilization Fanatics forum, a player, using the pseudonym "Dell19," writes an after-action report on a game played as Venice.

> With our old alliance members either having been destroyed or annexed it was time to find a new alliance and that was found with France and Genoa. Forming an alliance would last for a number of years and at one point form an alliance [sic] that owned provinces from Coventry to Constantinople. With Albania becoming a core province it was time to fight the Ottomans again.
>
> The navy would win the war for Venice by effectively blocking any crossing that the Ottomans tried to make from Asia whilst their provinces were besieged on the European side. Ironically the poor performance of the French, by throwing away troops against the Ottomans in Asia saw only Albania added to the Venetian empire. To worsen the matters we would lose Albanian culture the day before we took the province making the war largely a waste. Things were not too bad though as the Venetians were technologically advanced and we were progressing.
>
> The alliance would ensure some major benefits with regular military successes. A war against Austria would see Steiermark added and weaken the Austrian empire, which were struggling after Hungary had diplomatically annexed Bohemia instead.[24]

The after-action report acts as a dual display of game and writing prowess; in some cases the posts are illustrated with maps and portraits of the historic figures being discussed. The AAR may also be used to share the tactics that the writer adopted to succeed in their goals (in Dell19's case it was to unify Italy under Venice). After-action reports often show a remarkable counterfactual imagination, although many illustrate the tension between counterfactual imagination and the desire to adhere to historical verisimilitude by using the AAR as a forum to discuss and justify the plausibility of the scenario that they postulate. Other reports, however, discuss the pitfalls and difficulties of using the game to re-create historical events accurately.

In the paratexts found on the official online forums maintained by Paradox Interactive, the relationship between the variable inputs and the algorithm itself is discussed in a number of ways. In particular, a great deal of effort goes into discussing—and evaluating—in an elaborate fashion the various strategies and tactics for the many playable factions. But the discussion continues past the formal limits of the game, expanding into the area of modding the game code.

Some users of these forums turn to the algorithmic layers of *Europa Universalis II*, in order to have better control over the ideological layer; their desire to explore their counterfactual imaginary in a way that reflects their predilections leads them to explore the coding of the game itself. Participants in the official online discussion boards often articulate their concerns with both the play and modding of *Europa Universalis II* in relation to a notion of historical verisimilitude, often wanting to create more realistic play experiences, or conversely perceiving realism as an undesirable, inhibiting factor. Nuanced discussions emerge on topics such as how to alter the game code to allow the historical "losers" to win (Can the Aztec repel the Spanish?), without the fight seeming one-sided or unrealistic. The online forums negotiate the conflicting concerns of those players who wish official history to be strictly observed because they desire play to be "authentic" and those players who regard exploring the historical possibilities presented in the game as fun. Players from both camps will discuss and share tactics of play and modding, in order to produce the play experience they desire.

An exemplary online discussion is "Rise of the Condor," a thread reporting on a game where the Incas successfully repelled Spain from South America.[25] In the standard version of *Europa Universalis II* it is possible to play as the Incas—or a number of other historically important civilizations—but the game is coded in such a way that it is improbable they will be able to win the game (or even survive the onslaught of European expansion into the New World). Even a highly skilled expert player, playing as the Incas would eventually be defeated because of the sheer inequality of resources and infrastructure between them and the typical European sea-faring power. When the coded rules and values of *Europa Universalis II* strongly suggest that despite being more flexible than many other historical strategy games it still should be played in particular ways, modding becomes a crucial intervention. "Rise of the Condor" commences with a discussion of how to mod the game to make the Incas "playable." This is done by modifying certain easily editable text files to change key variables that represent the Incan Empire. The AAR discusses increasing the size of both the Incan armies, and its economic infrastructure, importantly it also illustrate how these changes were made. In this case the counterfactual imaginary is tempered by the desire to be as historically accurate as possible, whilst still providing reasonable scope for the player of the Inca faction to consolidate their power and repel the Spanish within the, albeit modified, rules of the game.

Historical verisimilitude is also a major concern on both the official and unofficial forums. Much discussion is devoted to elaborate and controversial evaluations of how authentically *Europa Universalis II* represents events in the past. Participants may draw upon their own historical expertise in order to contribute to the discussion. For example, one fan forum, Vojska.net, based in Croatia, has advocated serious changes to the existing map of the Balkans.[26] They argue that the current version does not have provincial boundaries drawn in a historically authentic manner. The Vojska.net community produced their version of map, which they distributed as a mod. This allows other players to play *Europa Universalis II* using an arguably more historically realistic geography of the region.

In both the examples of "Rise of the Condor" and Vojska.net, the boundaries between talking about the game, playing the game, and making modifications to the game are being blurred. The easy segue between playing, writing an AAR, and modding the game is supported by the relative simplicity of the process, and the wealth of easily accessible community-created guides that describe it step by step. Guides cover all aspects of modifying *Europa Universalis II* and are made by both individuals and collectives. One collective, "The Alternate Grand Campaign and Event Exchange Project," was formed through the merging of two separate projects.[27] The focus of the project is to develop mods that introduce more historic events into the game. As the game was originally designed, particular events were typically connected to a certain country, and only the countries that were originally intended as the main playable factions have large numbers of events designed for them. The project has two strategies for increasing historical verisimilitude. First, by modifying the events already embedded in the game in order that they simulate actual historic events more realistically; and second through generating new events for the game that are based on events that occurred historically in individual nations that are not one of the main playable factions.

Conclusion

On both the ideological and algorithmic layer, *Europa Universalis II* presents an official history. The game does not question the dominant portrayal of the past, rather, it attempts to simulate it. Through play, often in encounter with the online community, this simulation can form amusing, unusual, and challenging depictions of history. While seeking to both conform to and challenge official versions of history on the ideological layer, players must understand the algorithmic layer. This layer reduces all ideological representations to numerical—and text editable—values within a larger algorithm. Though playing by the rules, players are not forced uncritically to accept the official version of history that is portrayed. Rather, there are opportunities within the game, in the gaming community, and through customizing the game that provide key moments of opportunity for critical reflection.

The core critical element of counterfactual play is the focus on feasibility and the possibilities provided by imagining things "differently." Desire for historical verisimilitude drives a constant evaluation of feasibility and redesign of the variables built into the game. This push to produce an authentic ideology—while naïve—leads to an engagement with the algorithmic layer. The counterfactual imaginary stimulates a similar impulse; led by the designed counterfactual possibilities, players begin to explore more fantastic scenarios. However, because this takes place within the framework of a game, counterfactuals must also be playable—in order to remain a game there must still be some sense of challenge and balance.

Through modding the game, players challenge its authority as a text that represents the official version of history. By producing a version of history that is a dialogue between the official history of the game, their own understanding of feasibility and verisimilitude, or their counterfactual imagination, players contribute to an understanding to the past as plural and contingent. In this sense, *Europa Universalis II* encourages players to mod the historian's code by challenging the authority of the hegemonic and linear official history.

Notes

1 Edward Hallett Carr, *What Is History?* Harmondsworth: Penguin Books, 1964, 97.

2 Pete Haas, "*Assassin's Creed 3 The Tyranny of King Washington* is single-player DLC Campaign," *Gaming Blend*, 3 October 2012.

3 Stephen E. Siwek, *Video games in the 21st Century: A 2010 Report.* Entertainment Software Association, 2010, 1.

4 Alexander Galloway, *Gaming: Essays on Algorithmic Culture.* Minneapolis, MN: University of Minnesota Press, 2006, 95–103.

5 Galloway, *Gaming*, 103.

6 Ted Friedman, "*Civilization* and its Discontents: Simulation, Subjectivity and Space," in Ed. Greg M. Smith, *On a Silver Platter: CD-ROMS and the Promise of a New Technology.* New York: New York University Press, 1999, 145.

7 Nick Caldwell, "Theoretical Frameworks for Analyzing Turn-based Computer Games," *Media International Australia*, 110 (2004): 50; Christopher Douglas, "'You have Unleashed a Horde of Barbarians': Fighting Indians, Playing Games, Forming Disciplines," *Postmodern Culture*, 13, no. 1 (2002): 27;

Patrick Crogan, "Gametime: History, Narrative and Temporality in *Combat Flight Simulator 2*," in Eds. Mark J.P. Wolf and Bernard Perron, *The Video Game Theory Reader*. New York: Routledge, 2003, 279.

8   Douglas, "You have Unleashed a Horde of Barbarians," 24.

9   William Stephenson, "The Microserfs Are Revolting: *Sid Meier's Civilization II*," *Bad Subjects*, 45 (1999): 4.

10 Anna Everett, "Serious Play: Playing with Race in Contemporary Gaming Culture," in Eds. Joost Raessens and Jeffrey Goldstein, *The Handbook of Computer Game Studies*. Cambridge: The MIT Press, 2005, 318–319.

11 William Uricchio, "Simulation, History, and Digital Games," in Eds. Joost Raessens and Jeffery Goldstein, *The Handbook of Computer Game Studies*. Cambridge: The MIT Press, 2005, 330.

12 Niall Ferguson, "Introduction: Towards a 'Chaotic' Theory of the Past," in Ed. Niall Ferguson, *Virtual History: Alternative and Counterfactuals*. London: Picador, 1998, 26–43.

13 Ferguson, "Introduction: Towards a 'Chaotic' Theory," 41–42.

14 Ferguson, "Introduction: Towards a 'Chaotic' Theory," 44–52.

15 Ferguson, "Introduction: Towards a 'Chaotic' Theory," 64.

16 John Lewis Gaddis, *The Landscape of History: How Historians Map the Past*. Oxford: Oxford University Press, 2002, 95.

17 Barney Warf, "The Way It Wasn't: Alternative Histories, Contingent Geographies," in Eds. Rob Kitchin and James Kneale, *Lost in Space: Geographies of Science Fiction*. London: Continuum, 2002, 31.

18 Warf, "The Way It Wasn't," 21.

19 Warf, "The Way It Wasn't," 30–31 (Emphasis in the original).

20 Ferguson, "Introduction: Towards a 'Chaotic' Theory," 34.

21 Warf, "The Way it Wasn't," 34.

22 David Myers, *The Nature of Video Games: Play as Semiosis*. New York: Peter Lang, 2003, 44.

23 Mia Consalvo, *Cheating: Gaining Advantage in Video games*. Cambridge: MIT Press, 2007, 8–9.

24 Dell19, date (7 November 2005) thread title EU2 AAR: Venice a great power? website: Civilization Fanatics Forum, http://forums.civfanatics.com/showthread.php?t=138618, accessed 22 December 2012.

25 Mike von Bek, date (14 July 2003) thread title Inca: Rise of the condor' website: Paradox Interactive: Forums, http://forum.paradoxplaza.com/forum/showthread.php?95387-Inca-Rise-of-the-Condor, accessed 22 December 2012.

26 "*Europa Universalis II*. Stockholm: Strategy First, Paradox Development Studios, 2001."

27 author/date unknown, page name "introduction" website AGCEEP, http://www.agceep.net/introduction.htm, accessed 1 September 2012.

Works cited

Caldwell, Nick. "Theoretical Frameworks for Analysing Turn-based Computer Strategy Games," *Media International Australia*, 110 (2004): 42–51.

Carr, Edward Hallett. *What is History?* Harmondsworth: Penguin Books, 1964.

Consalvo, Mia. *Cheating: Gaining Advantage in Video games*. Cambridge: MIT Press, 2007.

Crogan, Patrick. "Gametime: History, Narrative and Temporality in *Combat Flight Simulator 2*," in Eds. Mark J. P. Wolf and Bernard Perron, *The Video Game Theory Reader*. New York: Routledge, 2003, 275–301.

Douglas, Christopher. "'You Have Unleashed a Horde of Barbarians': Fighting Indians, Playing Games, Forming Disciplines," *Postmodern Culture*, 13, no. 1 (2002), http://muse.jhu.edu/journals/pmc/v013/13.1douglas.html, accessed 26 January 2013.

"EU2 AAR: Venice, a Great Power?" *Civilization Fanatics Centre*, http://forums.civfanatics.com/showthread.php?t=138618, accessed 25 October 2012.

"Europa Universalis 2." *Vojska.net*, http://www.vojska.net/eng/games/europa-universalis-2/, accessed 25 October 2012.

Everett, Anna. "Serious Play: Playing with Race in Contemporary Gaming Culture," in Eds. Joost Raessens and Jeffrey Goldstein, *The Handbook of Computer Game Studies*. Cambridge: The MIT Press, 2005, 311–327.

Ferguson, Niall. "Introduction: Towards a 'Chaotic' Theory of the Past," in Ed. Niall Ferguson, *Virtual history: Alternative and counterfactuals*. London: Picador, 1997, 1–89.

Frasca, Gonzalo. "Digital Games of the Oppressed: Critical Thinking, Education, Tolerance, and Other Trivial Issues," in Eds. Noah Wardrip-Fruin and Patrick Harrigan, *First Person: New Media as Story, Performance, and Game*. Cambridge and London: The MIT Press, 2004, 85–94.

Friedman, Ted. "*Civilization* and its Discontents: Simulation, Subjectivity, and Space," in Ed. Greg M. Smith, *On a Silver Platter: CD-ROMs and The Promise of a New Technology*. New York: New York University Press, 1999, 132–150.

Gaddis, John Lewis. *The Landscape of History: How Historians Map the Past*. Oxford: Oxford University Press, 2002.

Galloway, Alexander. *Gaming: Essays on Algorithmic Culture*. Minneapolis, MN: University of Minnesota Press, 2006.

Haas, Pete. "*Assassin's Creed 3* The Tyranny of King Washington is Single-Player DLC Campaign," *Gaming Blend*, 3 October 2012, http://www.cinemablend.com/games/Assassin-Creed-3-Tyranny-King-Washington-Single-Player-DLC-Campaign-47708.html, accessed 25 October 2012.

"Inca: Rise of the Condor." *Paradox Interactive*, http://forum.paradoxplaza.com/forum/showthread.php?95387-Inca-Rise-of-the-Condor, accessed 25 October 2012.

"Introduction." *ACPEEP*, http://agceep.net/introduction.htm, accessed 25 October 2012.

Myers, David. *The Nature of Video Games: Play as Semiosis*. New York: Peter Lang, 2003.

Siwek, Stephen E. *Video games in the 21st Century: A 2010 Report.* Entertainment Software Association, 2010, http://www.theesa.com/facts/pdfs/video games21stcentury_2010.pdf.

Stephenson, William. "The Microserfs are Revolting: *Sid Meier's Civilization II,*" *Bad Subjects,* 45 (1999), http://bad.eserver.org/issues/1999/45/stephenson.html.

Uricchio, William. "Simulation, History, and Digital Games," in Eds. Joost Raessens and Jeffrey Goldstein, *The Handbook of Computer Game Studies.* Cambridge: The MIT Press, 2005, 327–338.

Warf, Barney. "The Way it Wasn't: Alternative Histories, Contingent Geographies," in Eds. Robert Kitchin and James Kneale, *Lost in Space: Geographies of Science Fiction.* London: Continuum, 2002, 17–38.

Games cited

Assassin's Creed II. Montreal, Quebec: Ubisoft Montreal, 2009.

Assassin's Creed III. Montreal, Quebec: Ubisoft Montreal, 2012.

Europa Universalis II. Stockholm: Strategy First, Paradox Development Studios, 2001.

Sid Meier's Civilization II. Alameda, CA: MicroProse, 1996.

13

Modding as Digital Reenactment: A Case Study of the *Battlefield* Series

Gareth Crabtree
Independent Scholar

Introduction

This book approaches an important issue, that the mechanisms and methods of the expression of computer game history need to be more firmly theorized and understood. Such an analysis has become increasingly important as contemporary video games consistently seek to act as commemorative texts, claiming the authority to offer a celebration of the efforts of real soldiers and recognize their personal sacrifice. This chapter aims to demonstrate how games contribute to what the historian Jay Winter, borrowing from Pierre Nora, describes as the "Theater of Memory"; that is how they shape public understanding of past wars through their visual tropes, rules, and provision of community.[1]

The historical experience of digital games is investigated through the active form of consumption and production known as modding. A useful and concise definition of a mod is provided by Alexander Galloway, who states that, "a mod is a video game that has been modified or otherwise hacked by a user or group of users."[2] Modding, a play on "modifying," is an integral part of game culture. As one of the most involved forms of war play, mod practitioners reinterpret game structures and in a demonstration of considerable technical skill spend many hours of personal effort rewriting the code of commercial games to fashion a new play experience.

Modding is investigated through three main strands of inquiry. First, mods are placed fully in their context as both an element of video game culture and as a collaborative media practice. Second, discussion focuses upon the range of motivations for creating historical mods. Individuals are driven both by creative desire and a need to provide a more "realistic" experience of war. Modding communities are thus presented by their participants as being an online form of digital reenactment groups who are using the latest technologies to bridge the physical distance between group members whilst creating what they view to be authentic artifacts. Third, the mechanics of this representation is further analyzed in an effort to chart the historical narratives that have been produced for a number of mods that reinterpret elements of the Second World War.

To provide a sense of coherence, all examples adduced here of modding communities have created additional content for Digital Illusions Creative Entertainment's (DICE's) award-winning and bestselling *Battlefield* series of games.[3] Within the series players direct squads of soldiers and military vehicles from a third-person perspective in a range of historical and near-future scenarios. This chapter draws on game contents; interviews with members of the modding communities Battlegroup 42, Experience WW2, WWII Reality, and Forgotten Hope 2; and a reading of related materials (websites and discussion groups).[4]

A brief history of, and theoretical approaches to, modding

To fully contextualize and situate the creation of historical mods as an element of video game culture, it is useful to provide a brief history of modding as well as academic approaches to its practice. Player involvement through the creative altering of game code has long been a feature of computing. Indeed one of the first recognizable digital games, *Spacewar!* (1961), was produced as an experiment in hacking for the PDP-1 computer in the spare time of the MIT students, Steve Russell, Martin Graetz, and Wayne Wiitanen.[5] The first large-scale modification of a commercially released computer game, known as a "total conversion," is generally considered to have taken place in 1983 with a reworking of the Second World War themed *Castle Wolfenstein*.[6] Demonstrative of the creative and subversive forms that modding can take, the art style of the game, which originally featured an American operative attempting to infiltrate an *SS*-guarded castle, was replaced by characters from the popular television series *The Smurfs*.[7] What modding allows is an alteration of the game's original narrative, and it is that alteration that allows the gaming activity to be expanded in ways that the original producers may never have considered.

Facilitated by the growth of the Internet as a domestic technology and the opportunities for communication this allowed, community-based modding began to emerge in the early 1990s.[8] A major catalyst for the early modding scene was the release of id software's iconic game *Doom*.[9] In a move often repeated since, id built a specific brand of consumer loyalty by allowing players to incorporate their own individually designed characters, levels, art, and music with players collaborating on projects by utilizing newsgroups, websites, and IRC (Internet Relay Chat).[10] Modification culture continued to develop and diversify throughout the 1990s and 2000s as players were granted access by games companies to increasingly complex production tools. Once again id software was at the center of developments, with strong support for the community surrounding their *Quake* series. In 1999, the vast economic potential of modding for the game industry was made evident by the efforts of the two amateur developers Minh Le and Jess Cliffe. Their mod *Counterstrike* and its subsequent sequels altered Valve's *Half Life* (1998) from a rich science-fiction world to one where teams of terrorists and antiterrorist forces battle it out within urban environments.[11] In an unusual move for a fan-produced mod, *Counterstrike* was purchased by Valve and released commercially, selling 1.5 million copies globally by 2003. Games companies duly took full note of *Counterstrike's* success, and the appetite for players to be able to shape their own games. Modding is now widely accepted by the game industry, and the majority of PC games incorporate some element of functionality for players to create their own material.

The majority of academic literature has so far focused on how modding facilitates a fascinating dynamic between producer and consumer. For scholars such as Sarah Coleman and Nick Dyer-Witheford, modding is an example of a distinct alteration within this relationship, one driven by the "new tools and technologies which enable consumers to archive, annotate and appropriate and recirculate media content." This development is promoted as enabling the flourishing of a subculture that promotes Do-It-Yourself (DIY) media arising from within a "fan culture that regards games not as fixed properties," but rather as a "raw material for continuous collective authorship whose products, even if they eventually pass back into commodity, enjoy sustained and often indefinite, free circulation."[12] Modding is presented here as an entirely new form of connection between the production and consumption of digital media, one that allows an audience to have a fully active involvement in shaping their play.

Modding explicitly alters the economic dynamic between producer and consumer by extending the shelf life of games through the provision of extra content at no cost to the developer. Players are in effect helping to increase the commercial appeal of a product by making their favorite games better and last longer. Games scholar David Nieborg has gone as far as to argue that the influence of modding teams is so great that by supplying a free workforce for the commercial game development industry they are able to "directly influence the game development on all levels, ranging from technological influence to (future) game design." This relationship is positioned by Nieborg as a "symbiotic relationship," one full of "mutual respect and dependency."[13] Nieborg's assessment is hard to dispute as there are currently scores of active war-game modding groups producing thousands of different game objects and scenarios for players to utilize.

The considerable amount of work needed to successfully complete a mod has led to attempts to analyze the hobby in terms of labor theory. Olli Sotamaa has argued, in his original study of modding communities, that this level of commitment indicates an activity that at times is far removed from that of a pure leisure hobby. Instead of the pursuit of simple consumption and immediate pleasures, modding should be seen to be a volunteer activity, "which captivates its participants with its complexity and many challenges."[14] As the head of the modding project *Forgotten Hope 2* details during one interview, over the period of a couple of months he would regularly spend five to six hours a day creating his new gamic vision of the Second World War.[15] As Tiziana Terranova has observed, "free labor" is a major source of value creation in the new networked economy. Terranova argues that economic capital has learned to "digitally tap outside all boundaries of work-time or place," in what has been termed a "diffuse" or "collective intelligence."[16] Modding is the most prescient example of this as thousands of man hours are utilized to produce a product that is then willingly distributed for free.[17]

The pleasures and production of mods

Interviews with members of modding communities highlight the range of motivations and pleasures that make all this work worthwhile for its participants. For many the main inspiration is to see other players play with their work, transforming their historical artifact into something pliable, attractive, and fun.[18] One clear element that was expressed by all interviewees is that they enjoy the opportunity to demonstrate their technical skills within a highly collaborative environment. As one member of the *Forgotten Hope 2* mod team states, "my main motivation is collaborating with creative minds in creating something fun, and playing a good game with like-minded people."[19] As an example of the possibility of rich and varied friendships that can be built within the largest modding groups, the community that created the Vietnam War themed mod *Eve of Destruction* has a core team of 14 people with another 105 participating from countries including the United States, the United Kingdom, Germany, and Denmark at some stage of development.[20]

Within these networks individuals play a range of roles that have to be designated and carried out successfully. The efforts of level designers, coders, artists, musicians, game testers, and historical researchers all have to be tightly coordinated by a central management team.[21] In a division of labor process, individuals often pool their resources together and work on a single item such as a tank or military uniform. For example, when an artist completes their design of a Sherman Tank, this is then passed on to a coder who programs the model with the necessary mathematical properties to be able to operate correctly within the game world. The coder then places the object onto a map and tests its properties correcting any inconsistencies such as movement speed or the wrong elevation angle of the tank barrel.[22]

Guiding the community is an effective management structure that pulls together the team's efforts combining the completed pieces together to make sure a finished and successful product is delivered.[23] Project management has to constantly deliver feedback, and at times criticism, to its team of the work they have produced. Without this communication and honesty a mod will often fail to be delivered on time or at all. Within some modding groups individual politics dominate prolonging the production process as a range of senior team members insist on auditing completed work. Many groups often add a further level of inspection as for any game artifact to make it into the final mod it has to be voted on and accepted by the wider community to see if it is historically accurate enough to be included.

Technical and social capital is won by surviving the peer review process and succeeding in getting an item included in the final version of a mod. Rigorous scrutiny leads to many modding members and teams attempting to outdo each other with boasts regarding the amount of historical research that they have carried out, presenting themselves as amateur historians who are attempting to create what they perceive to be a "professional" standard of history. Websites feature details of research visits that have been carried out and breakdowns of the blueprints, pictures, technical data, and other materials that have been consulted in the design process. For one member of the *Forgotten Hope 2* team, extra personal significance was to be found in producing a mod with a strong historical validity. For him his countless trips to museums and hours spent in libraries was not caused solely by the desire to win the respect of his peers. Instead he was driven by the strong belief that his work has more value than the simple provision of entertainment for his audience. The interview participant recounted that "by adhering to historical accuracy we can educate others (and ourselves!) about the less popular aspects of World War 2." He had spent his time involved in the project in the strong belief that by "keeping the memory of WWII alive we can prevent history from repeating itself."[24] His creative efforts were born out of a desire in whatever way possible to provide a personal warning against the repetition of one of the darkest periods of human history.

Defined by constant claims to authenticity, and through efforts to elevate the hobby beyond the level of mere leisure, modding reinterprets many of the values held by traditional real-world reenactment. Both share characteristics of being centered on communities drawn together from different strata of society and professional disciplines by a shared passion for military history, and both consume popular and academic representations to form their own visions and narratives of events. As the historian Vanessa Agnew argues, the value of reenactment to its participants is that they consider it to be a serious form of historical expression, one in which they measure the success of their contribution by the extent to which they are able to adhere to period minutiae, and a fidelity to the authentic. Similarly, for Stephen Gapps reenactment is a ritual of "performance that is conceived by invoking a supposedly closer simulation of past realities than other forms can offer." History is "done over and over again whilst each time purporting to be closer to the real thing."[25]

Reenactment, its participants claim, is the expression of a "living history," an exercise predicated on the notion that reliving the past is the best way to learn about it.[26] As the English scholar Jerome De Groot has argued, "reinscribing the past through a particularized set of bodily actions—a reperformance or reanimation" is becoming increasingly widespread throughout Western culture. For reenactors, "historicized performance is a keynote to contemporary society's obsession with 'authenticity.' Reenactment in its many forms is so powerful, because it blends the experience of historical artifacts such as the experience of museums with individual revelation."[27] Removed from any need for physical engagement, I would argue that modding offers one of the strongest conduits for personal revelation possible. Battlefields and the course of history can be analyzed, debated, and modified all from the comfort of the bedroom. Technological literacy affords an incredibly strong investment in presenting a shared historical vision.

Reenacting military histories

The final section of this chapter discusses the general characteristics of historical mods that are based upon the Second World War. Though the practice of modding should be viewed as a significant potential opportunity for players to act in a creative and fertile space for the imagining of war, the creation of historically themed mods is defined by a strong degree of conservatism. Economic, cultural, and technical factors combine to act as gatekeepers to the range of narratives that are produced. Modding does not exist within a vacuum, and though games companies constantly are impressed by the imagination and technical skill of their audience, they are also keen to guide the communities related to their games in the topics of the mods that they produce. As John Dovey and Helen Kennedy have persuasively argued, the relationship between games companies and modders "is not a precondition for a utopian democratization, mods still exist within the prevailing economic nexus."[28] For example, a commercial company would be highly unlikely to support a team through the provision of extra access to production tools and design documentation if it was planning on creating a Holocaust simulator as the risk of negative media coverage would be too high.

Cultural elements also act to severely limit whose history is being told within mods. Reflecting the largely male-centered world of modding, and war gaming in general, the Second World War hero is delineated along strictly defined gender parameters, with women largely denied the role of protagonists in combat. For most of its history the computer game industry has largely dismissed the needs of its female players, failing to provide a large number of positive female characters. When they do appear, female characters often fulfill the role of trophy in a number of forms. Female characters are largely presented as an object that must be rescued from some misfortune by the player if the game is to be completed. Heroic protagonists such as Lara Croft from the *Tomb Raider* series are steeped in explicit sexuality, often having been molded into the perfect male fantasy, displaying anatomically impossibly proportioned limbs, waists, and breasts.[29]

Furthermore, the distinct lack of opportunity to embody female combatants reflects national traditions of limiting the discussion of the roles of women combatants, or perceiving women as active agents in war. Throughout the conflicts of the twentieth century, gender constructs have been built primarily around attempts to maintain the values of heroic masculinity (see also Hasegawa, Chapter 9). The contributions of the male warrior have largely been presented in binary opposition to female contributions made within the domestic sphere.[30] As Paul Higate and John Hopton amongst others have observed, the link between militarism and male warriors has often been conceived in terms of an ideology of an "idealized masculinity that valorize[s] the notion of strong active males collectively risking their personal safety for the greater good of the wider community."[31] Using Britain as an example, in conflicts as diverse as the total war of the First and Second World Wars, and through limited conflicts such as the Falklands and the First Gulf Wars, female contributions to military campaigns have been undermined and underplayed within British national consciousness. Instead female military involvement has been presented as being a disruptive force, destabilizing and diluting an imagined masculine heroic warrior ideal.

Instead of attempting to craft rich and nuanced social and cultural histories, it is the case as with the vast majority of commercially released computer games that the historical vision that is being produced is very much a projection of military strategy and technology. It is fascinating that many modding groups build the justification for their work in relation to what they see as the failure of games companies to provide an experience that is "real" enough. It is through the incorporation of greater detail in regard to military technology that modders claim to have elevated the historicity of their play to another level. Through this detail, mod teams make claims to ownership of their own play and historical representation. The Experience World War Two team state that through their work, they aim to

> Give the player a much more realistic play experience by using actual history as our guideline. So, not only is realism our goal but also from a historical viewpoint our additional aim is to immerse the player into World War II.[32]

Typically, like a lot of mod teams, The Experience World War Two team pride themselves solely on the authenticity of the digital simulation of weapons. To incorporate the necessary details this mod community believed to be necessary, a considerable amount of research was conducted. To gain a personal insight into combat, detailed interviews were carried out with family members of veterans who served in the conflict. This insight is used to make sure that within the mod the correct equipment and military technology feature in the accurate chronological sequence of how it was developed.[33] The oral histories of combat experience are reduced and used solely to make sure that the technologies of killing are modeled accurately.

This is far from the creation of a humane vision; instead it is very much a history of the bullet and the mechanics of combat. This is military fetishism brought to life. This is not a criticism; I am an avid player of war games and immensely enjoy the hours spent behind the virtual scope of a gun as I lead my forces onto the beaches of Omaha and fight as a British SAS officer in the North African Desert. It is also not my intention to belittle the difficulties that mod communities face as their artistic medium necessitates the constant negotiation of the delicate balance between accuracy and creating an entertaining experience. The very essence of a computer game is provision of a fun environment. Modding teams must constantly balance the conflicting desires to create a historically accurate, but enjoyable, scenario.[34] For the moment the balance is firmly in favor of providing narrow military spectacle.

Within the wider historical modding community, there is some evidence that certain groups are making an effort to educate their audience on conflicts that are not traditionally represented in other entertainment mediums. *Battlefield Korea* (2008) is an American-produced mod designed to inform players on aspects of the Korean War (1950–1953).[35] The primary aim of the mod is to allow players to experience "The Forgotten War," and correct a perceived feeling amongst players that to a Western audience the Korean conflict would be typified as "a small and unimportant conflict."[36] Play here is used as a device to inform on a conflict that is perceived to be slipping out of popular memory. Similarly, the mod *Eve of Destruction* (2004) allows the playing through of all of the battles of the Indochina Vietnam conflict (1946–1973), and focuses on a colonial aspect of the war that does not traditionally feature in film and other media.[37] The most interesting and complete attempt to highlight an aspect of a war not usually present in pleasure cultures is the mod *Finn Wars* (2003). Created by an all Finnish team, *Finn Wars* is designed to offer an interactive lesson on Finnish involvement during the Second World War. Players embody the Finnish army in war fought against the Soviet Union in 1939–1944, and the War of Lapland fought against Germany in 1944–1945.[38] *Finn Wars* operates as an active community where players can gather to discuss aspects of Finnish military history and plan the future construction of mods relating to other underrepresented conflicts within popular memory.

Conclusion

Within this chapter, I have argued that modding communities are a new form of digital reenactment group, facilitated by communication technologies. Modding has a long history within computer game culture and its practice facilitates a strong sense of community within its participants. Like traditional reenactment groups, modding is facilitated through rich networks guided by a strong sense of creative spirit, personal achievement, authorship, and at times an obsessive desire for the authentic. Games such as the *Battlefield* series inspire individuals to put many hours of work to fashion their own experience of play. Their activities can be read as both a celebration and a critique of commercial war games. A critique is offered that their play is not "real" enough, and through their own labor modding communities can manufacture a more authentic historical document. For the most part, authenticity in this sense is defined by the incorporation of a larger portfolio of weapons and the inclusion of more technical details. A number of modders are attempting to inform the general public of conflicts that are not traditionally featured in other media. It will be fascinating to view the historical narratives that are developed by armies of committed hobbyists as both the practice of modding and the medium of the video game mature.

Notes

1 Jay Winter, *Remembering War: The Great War between Memory and History in the Twentieth Century.* Yale: Yale University Press, 2006, 2.

2 Alexander Galloway, *Gaming: Essays on Algorithmic Culture.* Minnesota: University of Minnesota Press, 2006, 107–108.

3 Major games within the *Battlefield* series include DICE, *Battlefield 1942,* Electronic Arts, PC (2002); DICE Canada, *Battlefield Vietnam,* Electronic Arts, PC (2004); DICE, *Battlefield 2,* EA Games, PC (2005), DICE, *Battlefield 2,* EA Games, PC (2005); DICE, *Battlefield 1943,* Electronic Arts, Xbox 360 (2009).

4 *Battlegroup 42* Community Page, http://www.battle group42.de, accessed 27 July 2010; *Experience WW2* Community Page, http://www.moddb.com/mods/exprience-ww2, accessed 27 July 2010; *WWII Reality* Community Page, http://www.moddb.com/mods/wwii-reality, accessed 27 July 2010; *Forgotten Hope 2* Community Page, http://forgottenhope.warumdarum.de, accessed 27 July 2010.

5 Steve Russell, Martin Graetz, and Wayne Wiitanen, *Spacewar!,* PDP-1 (1961).

6 Muse Software, *Castle Wolfenstein,* Commodore 64 (1981).

7 James Au Wagner, "*Triumph of the Mod,*" http://dir.salon.com/story/tech/feature /2002/04/16/modding/index.html, accessed 1 October 2010.

8 For the emergence and spread of hacking culture in the 1980s and early 1990s, see Amanda Chandler, "The Changing Definition and Image of Hackers in Popular Discourse," *International Journal of the Sociology of Law,* 24 (1996): 229–251; Rena Upitis, "From Hackers to Luddites, Game Players to Game Creators: Profiles of Adolescent Students Using Technology," *Journal of Curriculum Studies,* 30, no. 3 (1998): 293–318; Graeme Kirkpatrick, *Critical Technology: A Social Theory of Personal Computing.* Aldershot: Ashgate Publishing, 2004, 26–32; Tim Jordan and Paul Taylor, "A Sociology of Hackers," *Sociological Review,* 46, no. 4 (2008): 757–780.

9 id software, *DOOM,* PC (1993).

10 For a detailed discussion of *DOOM* as a sociocultural phenomenon, see David Kushner, *Masters of Doom—How Two Guys Created An Empire And Transformed Pop Culture*. London: Random House Inc., 2004, 140–176.

11 Valve Software, *Half-Life,* Sierra Studios, PC (1998); *Counterstrike,* Vivendi Universal, PC (1999).

12 Sarah Coleman and Nick Dyer-Witheford, "Playing on the Digital Commons: Collectivities, Capital and Contestation in Video game Culture," *Media, Culture & Society*, 29 (2007): 943.

13 David Nieborg, *Am I Mod or Not?—An Analysis of First Person Shooter Modification Culture*, Paper presented at the creative games seminar Exploring Participatory Culture, University of Tampere, 11–12 January 2005.

14 Olli Sotamaa, "On Modder Labour, Commodification of Play, and Mod Competitions," *First Monday*, 12, no. 9 (2007), http://firstmonday.org/issues/issue 12_9/sotamaa/index.htm, accessed 7 August 2009.

15 Interview with member of the *Forgotten Hope 2* team.

16 Greig de Peuter and Nick Dyer-Witheford, "FCJ-024 A Playful Multitude? Mobilising and Counter-Mobilising Immaterial Game Labour," *The Fibreculture Journal*, 5 (2005), http://five.fibreculturejournal.org/fcj-024-a-playful-multitude-mobilising-and-counter-mobilising-immaterial-game-labour, accessed 8 August 2009.

17 Hector Postigo, "From Pong to Planet Quake: Post-Industrial Transitions from Leisure to Work, Communication & Society," *Communication & Society*, 6, no. 4 (2003): 602.

18 Interview with member of the *Forgotten Hope 2* team.

19 Interview with member of the *Forgotten Hope 2* team.

20 Interview with member of the *Eve of Destruction* team.

21 Interview with member of the *Battlegroup 42* team.

22 Interview with member of the *Battlegroup 42* team.

23 Interview with member of the *Battlegroup 42* team.

24 Interview with member of the *Forgotten Hope 2* team.

25 Stephen Gapps, *Performing the Past: A Cultural History of Historical Reenactments*, Ph.D. Diss., University of Technology, Sydney, 2002: 3.

26 Dennis Hall, "Civil War Reenactors and the Postmodern Sense of History," *Journal of American Culture*, 17, no. 3 (1994): 8.

27 Jerome de Groot, *Consuming History: Historians and Heritage in Contemporary Culture*. Abingdon: Routledge, 2008, 103.

28 John Dovey and Helen Kennedy, *Game Cultures: Computer Games as New Media*. Berkshire: Open University Press, 2006, 134.

29 Core Design, *Tomb Raider,* Eidos Interactive, Playstation (1996).

30 See Margaret Higonnet and Patrice Higonnet, "The Double Helix," in Eds. Margaret Higonnet, et al., *Behind the Lines Gender and the Two World Wars*. Yale: Yale University Press, 1987, 31–50.

31 Paul Higate and John Hopton, "War, Militarism and Masculinities," in Eds. Jeff Hearn and Robert Connell, *Handbook of Studies of Men & Masculinities*. London: SAGE, 2005, 43.

32 Email interview with member of the *Experience World War Two* team.

33 Email interview with member of the *Experience World War Two* team.

34 Andrew Moshirnia, "The Educational Potential of Modified Video Games," *Issues in Informing Science and Information Technology*, 4 (2007): 513.

35 *Battlefield Korea* Website, http://www.bf-korea.de/eng/infos.php, accessed 28 July 2010.

36 *Battlefield Korea* Website.

37 *Eve of Destruction* Website, http://www.eodmod.org, accessed 29 July 2010.

38 *Finn Wars* Website, http://www.iceflakestudios.com/ finnwars.html, accessed 29 July 2010.

Works cited

Battlefield Korea Website, http://www.bfkorea.de/eng/infos.php, accessed 28 July 2010.

Battlegroup 42 Community Page, http://www.battle group42.de, accessed 27 July 2010.

Chandler, Amanda. "The Changing Definition and Image of Hackers in Popular Discourse," *International Journal of the Sociology of Law*, 24 (1996): 229–251.

Coleman, Sarah and Nick Dyer-Witheford. "Playing on the Digital Commons: Collectivities, Capital and Contestation in Video game Culture," *Media, Culture & Society*, 29 (2007): 934–953.

de Groot, Jerome. *Consuming History: Historians and Heritage in Contemporary Culture*. Abingdon: Routledge, 2008.

de Peuter, Greig and Nick Dyer-Witheford. "FCJ-024 A Playful Multitude? Mobilising and Counter-Mobilising Immaterial Game Labour," *The Fibreculture Journal*, 5 (2005), http://five.fibreculturejournal.org/fcj-024-a-playful-multitude-mobilising-and-counter-mobilising-immaterial-game-labour, accessed 8 August 2009.

Dovey, John and Helen Kennedy. *Game Cultures: Computer Games as New Media*. Berkshire: Open University Press, 2006.

Eve of Destruction Website, http://www.eodmod.org, accessed 29 July 2010.

Experience WW2 Community Page, http://www.moddb.com/mods/exprience-ww2, accessed 27 July 2010.

Finn Wars Website, http://www.iceflakestudios.com/ finnwars.html, accessed 29 July 2010.

Forgotten Hope 2 Community Page, http://forgottenhope.warumdarum.de, accessed 27 July 2010.

Galloway, Alexander. *Gaming: Essays on Algorithmic Culture*. Minnesota: University of Minnesota Press, 2006.

Gapps, Stephen, *Performing the Past: A Cultural History of Historical Reenactments*, Ph.D. Diss., University of Technology, Sydney, 2002.

Hall, Dennis. "Civil War Reenactors and the Postmodern Sense of History," *Journal of American Culture*, 17, no. 3 (1994): 7–11.

Higate, Paul and John Hopton. "War, Militarism and Masculinities," in Eds. Jeff Hearn and Robert Connell, *Handbook of Studies of Men & Masculinities*. London: SAGE, 2005, 432–448.

Higonnet, Margaret and Patrice Higonnet. "The Double Helix," in Eds. Margaret Higonnet, Jane Jenson, Sonya Michel and Margaret Collins Weitz., *Behind the Lines Gender and the Two World Wars*. Yale: Yale University Press, 1987, 31–50.

Jordan, Tim and Paul Taylor. "A Sociology of Hackers," *Sociological Review*, 46, no. 4 (2008): 757–780.

Kirkpatrick, Graeme. *Critical Technology: A Social Theory of Personal Computing*. Aldershot: Ashgate Publishing, 2004.

Kushner, David. *Masters of Doom—How Two Guys Created an Empire and Transformed Pop Culture*. London: Random House Inc, 2004.

Moshirnia, Andrew. "The Educational Potential of Modified Video Games," *Issues in Informing Science and Information Technology*, 4 (2007): 511–521.

Nieborg, David. *Am I Mod or Not?—An Analysis of First Person Shooter Modification Culture*, Paper presented at the creative games seminar Exploring Participatory Culture, University of Tampere, 11–12 January 2005.

Postigo, Hector. "From Pong to Planet Quake: Post-Industrial Transitions from Leisure to Work, Communication & Society," *Communication & Society*, 6, no. 4 (2003): 593–607.

Sotamaa, Olli. "On Modder Labour, Commodification of Play, and Mod Competitions," *First Monday*, 12, no. 9 (2007), http://firstmonday.org/issues/issue12_9/sotamaa/index.htm, a ccessed 7 August 2009.

Upitis, Rena. "From Hackers to Luddites, Game Players to Game Creators: Profiles of Adolescent Students Using Technology," *Journal of Curriculum Studies*, 30, no. 3 (1998): 293–318.

Wagner, James Au. *Triumph of the Mod*, http://dir.salon.com/story/tech/feature/2002/04/16/modding/index.html, accessed 1 October 2010.

Winter, Jay. *Remembering War: The Great War between Memory and History in the Twentieth Century*. Yale: Yale University Press, 2006.

WWII Reality mod-a *Battlefield 1942* mod, mod.db.com, http://www.moddb.com/mods/wwii-reality, accessed 27 July 2010.

Games cited

Battlefield 1942. Redwood City, CA: DICE, Electronic Arts, PC, 2002.

Battlefield 1943. Redwood City, CA: DICE, Electronic Arts, 2009.

Battlefield 2. Redwood City, CA: DICE, EA Games, PC, 2005.

Battlefield Vietnam. Redwood City, CA: DICE, Electronic Arts, PC, 2004.
Castle Wolfenstein. Baltimore, MD: Muse Software, Commodore 64, 1981.
Counterstrike. Kirkland, WA: Valve Software, Vivendi Universal, PC, 1999.
Doom. Richardson, TX: id Software, 1993.
Half-Life. Kirkland, WA: Valve Software, Sierra Studios, PC, 1998.
Spacewar! Russell, Steve, Martin Graetz and Wayne Wiitanen, PDP-1, 1961.
Tomb Raider. Wimbledon, UK: Core Design, Eidos Interactive, Playstation, 1996.

PART FOUR

The Politics of Representation

The fourth part of this book exposes another significant problem with historical engagement when based on selection, namely the question of what is selected, who selects it and for what reasons. This has long been a central concern for historians but is of significance for games too, since, as we saw in the preceding part, it underpins what we understand by the concept of authenticity.

In the first essay, Dow recognizes that a lack of accuracy in some cases actually *enhances* authenticity in those instances where players expect to see something historical. This is what he terms a historical "veneer," which in the case of *Assassin's Creed II*'s Florence literally can be found in the façades of certain buildings; such a veneer helps viewers to engage with history but reveals a degree of conscious selection at the level of the game design. Likewise, Wackerfuss examines WWI flight simulations to show that narrative possibilities of depictions of the past are limited by the computer technology available to power them; as a result he suggests that the proliferation of flight sims distorts our subsequent impressions of the role of aerial combat in WWI. The final two essays of this section take on the question of politics more explicitly by looking at representations of Cold War politics. Reisner examines *Call of Duty: Black Ops* to argue that as a new generation of players engage with the Cold War through video games, this culture of remembrance is dependent on *which* facts are selected to remember (or memorialize) as well as *who* is selecting them. Schulzke continues this idea following what he calls "speculative history" in which the replayable, memorialized Cold War shapes and prefigures our imagination of future politics as well as, perhaps more dangerously, our current understanding of international relations. Thus, the selection inherent in historical inquiry can be seen to have important political consequences.

Recommended books to understand more about the politics of representation:

Barraclough, Geoffrey. *History in a Changing World*. Oxford: Blackwell, 1955.

Benson, Susan Porter, Stephen Brier, and Roy Rosenzweig. *Presenting the Past: Essays on History and the Public*. Philadelphia, PA: Temple University Press, 1986.

Ferro, Marc. *The Use and Abuse of History, or, How the Past Is Taught to Children*. London: Routledge, 2003.

Kramer, Lloyd S. and Donald Reid. *Learning History in America: Schools, Cultures, and Politics*. Minneapolis, MN: University of Minnesota Press, 1994.

Walsh, Kevin. *The Representation of the Past: Museums and Heritage in the Post-Modern World*. London: Routledge, 2002.

14

Historical Veneers: Anachronism, Simulation, and Art History in *Assassin's Creed II*

Douglas N.Dow
Kansas State University

It is a crucial fact for art history of the second half of the twentieth century that the majority of people spend much of their spare time staring entranced by myriads of multiple registers of representations that flicker before them on small screens in their homes and which increasingly blur the distinctions between what is real and what is staged, what takes place and what is only simulated.

MICHAEL CAMILLE[1]

Reality has passed completely into the game of reality.

JEAN BAUDRILLARD[2]

Assassin's Creed II, a third-person action adventure game set in Renaissance Italy, has an open-world format that encourages its player to roam freely through elaborate re-creations of historical locations that include Florence, Venice, and the Tuscan countryside. The gamer's avatar, Ezio Auditore da Firenze, learns early on that his family belongs to a secret society known as the Assassins, a group that has been locked in a power struggle with the Knights Templar for centuries. Ezio's objective is to acquire the skills, weapons, fighting techniques, and general knowledge that he needs to redress the wrongs inflicted upon his family by the customary villains of Renaissance Florence, the Pazzi. Along the way Ezio assists the Assassins as they thwart world domination by the Templars. As the player works through the game's narrative, which Seth Schiesel compared to "an interactive Dan Brown or James Clavell novel," he or she also explores virtual re-creations of Renaissance Italy.[3] Schiesel also noted that "over the next few semesters some teachers of Italian history will be surprised … as some of their students confess that they have already explored fifteenth-century Florence and Venice in a video game," suggesting that students' interactions with the game might color their understanding of Renaissance Italy.[4] My recent teaching experiences buttress this assertion. Students have emailed links to videos of *Assassin's Creed II* gameplay and have approached me after lectures to discuss the game. The immensely popular game franchise has sold over forty million units worldwide since 2007.[5] In light of its global success, the historical aspects of the game's narrative, and its compelling and detailed environments, it is worth exploring what effects playing the game might have on an individual's perceptions of the historical locations represented in *Assassin's Creed II*. This chapter uses the writings on simulation and hyper-reality by the French sociologist and philosopher Jean Baudrillard to examine how the inclusion of anachronistic monuments in the cityscape of the game's Florence influences the player's understanding of the built environment of the city as it exists today. It also demonstrates how the imaginative interaction with historical monuments in the game resembles the idiosyncratic way people of Renaissance Florence interpreted their own historical past.

The fifteenth-century Florence of *Assassin's Creed II* contains many recognizable landmarks, including the Palazzo Vecchio, the cathedral, the church of Santa Maria Novella, and the church of Santa Croce (Figure 14.1). These striking replicas are not simply scenography, however, for the player must navigate them to accomplish the objectives of the game. Indeed, the cityscape was designed to accommodate the free-running mechanics of the avatar, who jumps and climbs like an acrobat. Using the ledges, cornices, crenellations, rustications, tie-rod ends, and putlog holes that proliferate in the Florentine built environment, Ezio hoists himself up the facades of churches and palaces in order to run and jump across the tiled rooftops (Figures 14.2 and 14.3). The experience of controlling Ezio's movement in, on, and through the built environment immerses the player in a detailed re-creations of Renaissance Florence. For Baudrillard, this type of immersive simulation signaled the "end of perspectival and panoptic space … and … the *very*

FIGURE 14.1 *Game version of Santa Croce*

FIGURE 14.2 *The current "reality" of Santa Croce*

abolition of the spectacular."[6] Although he was responding to an early form of reality television, Baudrillard's comments are relevant to games like *Assassin's Creed II* that further erase the boundary between the viewer and the viewed. During gameplay, the gamer is not an alienated witness to a spectacle like the member of the audience at a film; instead, the player manipulates and controls

FIGURE 14.3 *Architecture within the game* Assassin's Creed

the spectacle, interacting with the simulation, which, in turn, responds to the gamer's actions.[7] This characteristic of the video game marks a distinction between representation and simulation, since a moviegoer can only observe a representation, whereas the gamer can manipulate the game simulation.[8] For example, in the film *Hannibal*, one can only watch as Hannibal Lecter dispenses with Inspector Pazzi by hanging him from the Palazzo Vecchio. In *Assassin's Creed II*, however, the player decides whether to push a guard off the ramparts or to sneak past him to enter the palace. In sum, the interactive environment of the game (the simulation) is more responsive to the gamer than the cinematic spectacle (the representation) is to the moviegoer. Admittedly, both bear the imprint of their writers, directors, designers, and editors, but the game environment is predicated upon interactivity as a basic component of play. According to Baudrillard's logic, this immersion in and control of the representation effaces the boundary between the medium and the real, or, in his words, "There is no longer a medium in the literal sense: it is now intangible, diffused and diffracted in the real . . . ."[9] In an essay published in 1976, Baudrillard speculated about the future of immersive simulations, and his description prefigures the interactive space of games like *Assassin's Creed II*: "No more scenes, no more cuts, no more 'gaze', the end of the spectacle and the spectacular, towards the total, fusional, tactile and aesthesic (and no longer the aesthetic) etc., environment."[10] From Baudrillard's perspective, guiding Ezio through the Florence of *Assassin's Creed II* immerses the player in a simulation of the city and blurs the distinction the representation and the real.

Upon a closer inspection, however, the Florence of *Assassin's Creed II* turns out to be not an exact re-creation of the fifteenth-century city, and must be seen instead as a simulacrum, a version of the city that purports to be a true representation of Florence, but that presents a false likeness instead. According to Michael Camille, a simulacrum "calls into question the ability to distinguish between what is real and what is represented."[11] In this sense, the game's Florence, which modifies the street plan and lacks major landmarks (the Baptistery is the most glaring omission), is a simulacrum of Florence, "a deviation and perversion of imitation itself—a false likeness."[12] The inclusion of monuments that had not been built during the time in which the game is set represents another deviation in the Florence of *Assassin's Creed II*. The Ponte Vecchio, for example, carries a section of Vasari's corridor—a passageway erected in 1565—while the profile of the church of San Lorenzo is dominated in the game (and in today's Florence) by the dome of the Cappella dei Principi, a feature added to the cityscape in the seventeenth century.

Because the presence of these later monuments in the fifteenth-century Florence of the game suggests that they existed at a point in time before they had been built, they must be understood as anachronisms.[13] The game's version of the church of Santa Croce, for example, is decorated with a façade that closely resembles the one that adorns the actual church (Figure 14.1). This façade, however, was not constructed until 1863 (Figure 14.4), although

FIGURE 14.4 *Real-world version of existing architecture*

its presence in the game suggests it is much older. The inclusion of the nineteenth-century façade in the fifteenth-century environment of *Assassin's Creed II* is further problematized by the neo-Gothic revival style of the actual façade. Designed to resemble thirteenth-century architecture, the nineteenth-century façade blends into the game's fifteenth-century environment and appears to be a medieval monument rather than an anachronistic insertion. In other words, even before its anachronistic placement in the game's fifteenth century, the façade of Santa Croce was already a historical simulacrum—a nineteenth-century structure designed to resemble thirteenth-century architecture—and, in a sense, the revival style of the neo-Gothic façade has been de-anachronized (or, perhaps, re-synchronized) by its appearance in the fifteenth-century Florence of *Assassin's Creed II*. Seen in this light, the façade in the game's Florence is what Annette Barnes and Jonathan Barnes called a "nonobvious anachronism, the anachronism that has been skillfully blended in," and they proposed that "unobtrusive anachronisms are potentially vicious, for their subtle blend of fiction and fact can render observers unable to distinguish between falsity and truth."[14] In other words, the nonobvious anachronism confuses the spectator and leaves the historical accuracy of what is seen in question.

Randy Schroeder suggested that when immersive media "collapse distinctions between different kinds of space," it is the game that changes the perception of the real, and that "in a world of immersive simulation the real doesn't leak into the playworld; the playworld leaks into the real."[15] The inclusion of the nonobvious anachronism of the nineteenth-century façade in the fifteenth-century Florentine cityscape of *Assassin's Creed II* encourages a visitor to contemporary Florence to overlook the anachronism of the actual façade because the game presents a fictitious history for the structure that makes it seem older than it is. The notion that the immersive environment of *Assassin's Creed II* creates alternative histories for some of the city's monuments is reinforced by an examination of another façade in the game. As Ezio enters the piazza and the cathedral comes into view, it becomes apparent that the stonework on the cathedral's façade is incomplete (Figure 14.5). Although this reflects the unfinished state of the cathedral in the Renaissance, the façade under construction in *Assassin's Creed II* does not resemble the partial façade that was on the cathedral in the fifteenth century. Instead, it recalls the nineteenth-century structure that millions of tourists see when they visit Florence today (Figure 14.6).[16] In this instance, the fictitious point of origin is enhanced by the fact that the gamer witnesses the façade being built in the fifteenth century of the game. Unless otherwise informed, a player would interpret the construction project represented in the game as a

FIGURE 14.5 *The game version of the cathedral in Florence*

FIGURE 14.6 *That cathedral as it stands in Florence today*

reflection of the actual history of the façade, and accept that the façade was built during the fifteenth rather than the nineteenth century.

Not every church that lacked a façade in the Renaissance has been given one in the game's fifteenth-century Florence. Further exploration of the city leads to the church of San Lorenzo with its face left rough and unadorned (Figure 14.7). The unfinished façade on San Lorenzo in the game, however, reflects the appearance of the church today (Figure 14.8). In this respect, the omission of a façade on San Lorenzo in the game—as well as the anachronistic inclusion of other monuments not built during the time period in which the game is set—guarantees that a person who first experienced the major landmarks of Florence in the simulated version of the city in *Assassin's Creed II* would recognize them upon visiting the actual city. Thus, the exploration of the immersive virtual Florence inevitably colors how the gamer experiences the actual monuments of the city. Indeed, it is likely that the first glimpse of a prominent structure like Santa Croce would spark a sense of recognition, and cause the player to recall guiding Ezio as he scaled its marble face in an attempt to flee pursuing enemies. The visitor's response to the façade of Santa Croce—just one of many landmarks with which Ezio interacts—is therefore refracted through the gamer's experience of the monument within the Florence of *Assassin's Creed II*.

The tendency of representations to influence how people experience actual architecture has been noted at least since the eighteenth century, when travelers to Italy found their reactions to the country's monuments at odds with the perceptions they had formed from viewing printed reproductions of them. When German writer Johann Wolfgang von Goethe visited the temples at Paestum, he struggled to reconcile his experience of the structures with the idea of them he had generated from seeing reproductions, and explained that

FIGURE 14.7 *The Church of San Lorenzo in the game*

FIGURE 14.8 *The church of San Lorenzo as it appears today*

"they seem more elegant in architectonic projections, cruder in perspective drawings, than they are."[17] The eighteenth-century artist John Flaxman told a contemporary that he found Rome disappointing, and that "when he came among the ruins of ancient buildings he found them on a smaller scale, and less striking, than he had been accustomed to suppose them after having seen the prints of Piranesi."[18] In a similar vein, D. Medina Lasansky argued that nineteenth-century photographs of Florence produced by firms such as Fratelli Alinari "provided a series of scrims that mediated the experience of architecture" and that these images shaped the way people viewed the city and "created a way of looking" that was informed by the visual language of photography itself.[19] As reproductions become more sophisticated and interactive, experiences are more likely to be mediated through reproductions and simulations. Indeed, even simulated worlds can bleed into each other, leading a young man who had played a game based on a film to imagine himself as a participant in the movie's narrative.[20] Although this type of reaction might be more common after exploring an immersive video game environment, the disappointment of the eighteenth- and nineteenth-century Europeans over the cities and monuments of Italy is evidence that reproductive media have long affected perceptions of the actual environment.

Baudrillard embraced the idea that simulations influence perceptions of and reactions to the real, and there would have been little question for him that the exploration of the Florence of *Assassin's Creed II* would color the player's experience of the real Florence. Once experienced in the game, an authentic experience of the city is inaccessible to the gamer who will always see it refracted through the gaming environment. In this respect, the game environment (the simulation) alters the player's experience of Florence's built environment (the real). But even this assertion that the simulation troubles and colors the experience of the real requires qualification, since "Baudrillard's aim ... is to show that no adequate analysis of systems of representation can, simply, refer to the 'real' world ... as if this was unproblematic."[21] Baudrillard mapped this interaction in a famous example that analyzed the relationship between Disneyland (the simulation) and Los Angeles (the real). "Disneyland is presented as imaginary in order to make us believe that the rest is real, whereas all of Los Angeles and the America that surrounds it are no longer real, but belong to the hyperreal order and to the order of simulation."[22] The "play of illusions and phantasms" that characterizes the simulation that is Disneyland "rejuvenate[s] the fiction of the real" and encourages one to overlook the extent to which Los Angeles is itself a hyper-real simulation.[23] For Baudrillard, there can be no authentic experience. The issue is not that Disneyland alters how one views the real, but rather that what is perceived as real—in this case, Los Angeles—is no longer real in any meaningful sense.[24]

Baudrillard's theory can also be applied to the relationship between the simulated and the real presented by video games like *Assassin's Creed II*. For a player who has navigated the Florence of the game, the experience of walking through the city of Florence would resemble that of the tourist who leaves Disneyland's parking lot and merges with the traffic of Los Angeles. The experience of the simulation—Disneyland or *Assassin's Creed II*—encourages the belief that the real—Los Angeles or Florence—actually exists and is not merely another simulation. Baudrillard's description of Los Angeles, a young American city that developed the art of fictional and spectacular entertainment as its main industry, as a place that "belong[s] to the hyperreal order and to the order of simulation" is especially apt.[25] Within Baudrillard's theoretical framework, however, the city of Florence should also be seen as a simulation that belongs to the order of the hyper-real. When tourists arrive in the city, they are confronted by a dizzying array of artifacts and monuments. Not all of these are authentic. Some of the most important on public display are replicas. Michelangelo's *David*, which stands enshrined in a museum, has a double that occupies the site of the original. The *Gates of Paradise* are a simulation of Ghiberti's monumental doors, yet they frequently attract more attention than Ghiberti's earlier set of doors visible on the Baptistery's north side.[26] The façades on some of the largest and most ancient churches in the city assume a deceptive antiquity, even without the fictitious histories generated by their appearance in *Assassin's Creed II*. In short, Florence replicates its monuments and stands partly in the hyper-real, a simulation of itself. In this respect, the immersive simulation of the game's Florence acts as a Baudrillardian Disneyland for the actual Florence, disguising the simulated aspects of the city. Thus, someone who has played *Assassin's Creed II* visits the real Florence already primed to accept the city, with its neo-Gothic façades and sculptural replicas, as authentic and not as a simulation. From Baudrillard's perspective, the gamer is isolated from authentic experience but the simulation of the game acts as a veneer that masks the hyper-reality of Florence and makes the city seem real.

The "apocalyptic tones" and "millennial fervor" of Baudrillard's writings on simulation have been criticized as a "nightmarish vision of art [that] offers no constructive alternatives to our image culture."[27] The bleak pessimism of Baudrillard's theory can be ameliorated, however, by observing that *Assassin's Creed II*'s imaginative use of historical monuments resembles how people of the Renaissance interpreted and understood their own history. Even artists, architects, and their patrons, all of whom were especially attentive to historical artifacts, frequently saw works of art through thickets of misidentifications, misrepresentations, and modifications, and the myths that had grown up around them. For example, during his visit to Rome in 1450, Giovanni Rucellai, the Florentine merchant and art patron, drew on a medieval legend when he described the Basilica Nova, built during the fourth century CE, as "the Templum Pacis, which one says was a temple of idols and which, the Romans said, would last until a virgin gave birth, and it fell in and was ruined on the very night that our saviour Jesus Christ was born."[28] In this description, Rucellai misdated the monument by a wide margin (a basilica not built until the fourth century could have hardly fallen into ruin in the first century CE), and misidentified its building type (Rucellai called it a temple, ascribing a religious function to a basilica used for secular purposes). Leonardo da Vinci's admiration for the *Regisole*, an ancient equestrian statue in Pavia, provides another example of the difficulties Renaissance people faced when they interpreted ancient works. When Leonardo praised the statue in 1490, he was responding to a sculpture that had been destroyed in 1315 and reassembled from fragments in 1335. During its restoration, the sculpture was modified. Because the work is no longer extant, it is impossible to know how much of it was ancient, "but it is clear that Leonardo's words of appreciation addressed a significantly remanaged late antique work, hardly a classical antiquity."[29] Alexander Nagel and Christopher Wood argue that this type of confusion is not surprising. The fifteenth century had no "modern art-historical libraries stocked with comparative material" that would have allowed for the precise identification of which aspects of a sculpture or a building were truly ancient and which were later interventions.[30] When the historical interpretations of Renaissance artists and patrons are compared to those of modern historians, they seem imprecise and imaginative because "modern scholars have a more acute sense of historical distance than Renaissance humanists, and as a result the humanists may appear to them to lack any sense of distance."[31] This acute sense of historical distance of modern people is especially sensitive to anachronism and historical inaccuracy, so much so that historical plays are staged in modern dress in order "to shock audiences whose 'horizon of expectations' now includes the absence of anachronism."[32] Indeed, it was a contemporary sensitivity to anachronism that gave rise to this analysis of incongruous additions to the fifteenth-century Florence of *Assassin's Creed II*.

Instead of decrying what are to modern eyes glaring inaccuracies in the game's Renaissance Florence, it would be better to imagine how people of the fifteenth century might see these monuments. The previous examples demonstrated that when Renaissance observers interpreted historical monuments they did not do so in the same fashion or with the same goals as modern historians. The Florentine Baptistery, an eleventh-century building that during the fifteenth century was repeatedly described as an ancient structure, provides a well-documented example of how Renaissance Florentines interpreted their past. The notion that the Baptistery was an ancient Roman building had a long tradition. The fifteenth-century Codex Rustici, for example, asserted that the building was "made in the time of the emperor Octavian" and even in the middle of the sixteenth century, Giorgio Vasari referred to the Baptistery as a "most ancient temple."[33] When Filippo Brunelleschi and Leon Battista Alberti recast the forms of Tuscan Romanesque architecture in their own buildings, repurposing the design elements of the Baptistery, they made no "distinction between 'late antique' and 'Romanesque' buildings, between Santa Costanza and the Florentine Baptistery, a distinction crucial to all modern models of European art history, [because it] was simply not meaningful in the fifteenth century."[34] For these Renaissance architects, the Baptistery was seen as an ancient structure because the "identity of a building was its *meaning*, not its physical being" and these men were able "to *look through* the eleventh- and twelfth-century buildings of Florence to the true meaning hiding behind them, namely the normativity of the ancient Roman building manner."[35]

The more imaginative and subjective approach to monuments of the past taken by Brunelleschi and Alberti contrasts with the precise and carefully dated stylistic periodization that has characterized the modern discipline of art history, but the emphasis on meaning rather than form that Nagel and Wood described closely resembles the interpretive approach put forward by Camille in his prescription for "a history, not of art but of simulacra."[36] This hermeneutic model would be "based upon the premise that images do not so much replicate the real or substitute for it but are encounters with another order of reality entirely, it would be a history of art that could not claim to be about objects at all but about strategies of their simulation."[37] In this respect, Camille's version of a history of simulacra shares several features with Nagel and Wood's description of the Renaissance approach to the past. When someone in the fifteenth century "looked through" the Baptistery and discerned its origin in ancient Roman architectural tradition, they were less interested in the Baptistery as an "object" and more interested in how it resembled earlier structures, what Camille called a "strategy of simulation." This strategy of simulation resembles Nagel and Wood's "hypothesis of substitutability," which allowed fifteenth-century Florentines to see the "true meaning hiding behind" the Baptistery, or, in Camille's formulation, "another order of reality entirely."[38] Although their terms differ, both approaches suggest that the status of an object as authentic or simulated is less important than the meanings that it embodies and evokes. For the purposes of this argument, Camille's suggestion of how the history of art might employ different interpretive strategies to better analyze simulations and Nagel and Wood's description of how fifteenth-century people configured history both overlap within the confines of *Assassin's Creed II*. The intersection of these two hermeneutic methods not only provides an escape from Baudrillard's closed system, what Schroeder called a "feedback loop" that results in "a loss of the real," but also suggests how one aspect of the gameplay in *Assassin's Creed II* encourages a certain kind of historical interpretation.[39] Rather than criticize the anachronistic elements in the game for their lack of historical accuracy, one might follow the models of fifteenth-century Florentines (or the suggestions of Camille) and engage the game's environment in an imaginative way that, although it might not meet exacting historical standards, allows the player to better understand how fifteenth-century Florentines interpreted history. In other words, once authenticity or historical accuracy cease to be overriding concerns, it is possible to see how *Assassin's Creed II* presents a view of Florence that emphasizes "its meaning, not its physical being," and in doing so the game conforms closely to Nagel and Wood's description of fifteenth-century habits of historical interpretation.[40]

Finally, it should be noted that the narrative format of *Assassin's Creed II* encourages its player to interact with its environments in an imaginative and interpretive way. Structured as a game within a game, the events taking place in Renaissance Italy are themselves a virtual reality constructed in the mind of a man named Desmond who lives in the early-twenty-first century and who has been drafted by the contemporary Assassins as they struggle with the modern Templars to control the past and the present. A distant relative of Ezio Auditore, Desmond is perfectly suited to enter a virtual reality constructed from the memories of his long dead ancestor. The player's true avatar, therefore, is Desmond, who, within the game's narrative, is also a gamer who uses the virtual reality device to control Ezio as he navigates through the Renaissance. This framing mechanism sets the stage for an imaginative interaction with the game's Florence by placing the player at another remove from the simulation. In fact, the game emphasizes the status of its Florence as a simulation every time Desmond enters the virtual reality machine, at which point an animation shows the city being built up as a three-dimensional environment from a computer matrix. That the game's Florence is a simulation is therefore an inescapable component of the story of *Assassin's Creed II*. In order to stop the Templars and to avenge the deaths of his ancestors, Desmond must use Ezio to explore historical sites, to become acquainted with historical figures, and to make sense of the environment, all of which encourages the player to engage the simulation in an imaginative way. In this respect, the objectives of the gamer begin to resemble those of fifteenth-century Florentines who also struggled to decipher the past, not only to better understand their history, but also—through an act of imaginative interpretation—to make sense of their present.

Notes

1 Michael Camille, "Simulacrum," in Eds. Robert S. Nelson and Richard Shiff, *Critical Terms for Art History*. Chicago, IL: University of Chicago Press, 2003, 35–48: 43.

2 Jean Baudrillard, "The Order of Simulacra," in trans. Iain Hamilton Grant, *Symbolic Exchange and Death*. London: Sage, 1993, 50–86: 74.

3 Seth Schiesel, "On the Scenic Trail of Intrigue: Adventures in 15th-Century Italy," *New York Times*, New York edition, 8 December 2009.

4 Schiesel, "On the Scenic Trail of Intrigue."

5 Ubisoft Group, "About Ubisoft: Facts and Figures."

6 Emphasis original. Jean Baudrillard, "The Precession of Simulacra," in trans. Sheila Faria Glaser, *Simulacra and Simulation*. Ann Arbor, MI: University of Michigan Press, 1994, 1–42: 30.

7 Randy Schroeder, "Playspace Invaders: Huizinga, Baudrillard and Video Game Violence," *Journal of Popular Culture*, 30, no. 3 (1996): 143–153: 144; Mark J.P. Wolf, "Introduction," in Ed. Mark J.P. Wolf, *The Medium of the Video Game*. Austin, TX: University of Texas Press, 2001, 1–9: 3.

8 Gonzalo Frasca, "Simulation versus Narrative: Introduction to Ludology," in Eds. Mark J.P. Wolf and Bernard Perron, *The Video Game Theory Reader*. New York: Routledge, 2003, 221–235: 223–224.

9 Baudrillard, "Precession," 30.

10 Baudrillard, "Order," 71. Schroeder, "Playspace Invaders," 144 suggested that unlike television and film, "immersive media begin to collapse the distinction

between real and imaginary, as they completely engage the participant in realistic simulation."

11 Camille, "Simulacrum," 35.

12 Camille, "Simulacrum," 36.

13 Annette Barnes and Jonathan Barnes, "Time Out of Joint: Some Reflections on Anachronism," *Journal of Aesthetics and Art Criticism*, 47, no. 3 (1989): 253–261: 258.

14 Barnes and Barnes, "Time Out of Joint," 259.

15 Schroeder, "Playspace Invaders," 148; Kate Cox, "Virtual Tourism Has Never Felt More Real," *Kotaku* (blog), 9 November 2012.

16 Terry Kirk, *The Architecture of Modern Italy. Volume I: The Challenge of Tradition, 1750–1900*. New York: Princeton Architectural Press, 2005, 204–212.

17 Johann Wolfgang von Goethe, Eds. Thomas P. Saine and Jeffrey L. Sammons, trans. Robert R. Heitner, *Italian Journey*. New York: Suhrkamp Publishers, 1989, 179.

18 Joseph Farington, Ed. James Grieg, *The Farington Diary*, vol. 1. London: Hutchinson & Co., 1923, 123.

19 Medina D. Lasansky, *The Renaissance Perfected: Architecture, Spectacle, and Tourism in Fascist Italy*. University Park, PA: Pennsylvania State University Press, 2004, 52–53.

20 After playing *Rebel Assault*, a game centered on the activities of a soldier in *Star Wars'* Rebel Alliance who experiences the events depicted in *The Empire Strikes Back* from his own point of view, Janet H. Murray's thirteen-year-old son watched the movie again. "After mastering the complex video game, he jumped up and down with excitement when he recognized the parallel sequence. 'I was there!' he cried out. 'I stayed on the planet after Han leaves. It was even more dangerous for me!' "; Janet H. Murray, *Hamlet on the Holodeck: The Future of Narrative in Cyberspace*. New York: Free Press, 1997, 265.

21 Mike Gane, *Baudrillard's Bestiary: Baudrillard and Culture*. New York: Routledge, 1991, 95.

22 Baudrillard, "Precession," 12.

23 Baudrillard, "Precession," 12–13.

24 Baudrillard, "Precession," 12–13.

25 Baudrillard, "Precession," 12.

26 Lasansky, *The Renaissance Perfected*, xxii.

27 Camille, "Simulacrum," 40, 43.

28 Robert Tavernor, *On Alberti and the Art of Building*. New Haven, CT: Yale University Press, 1998, 17.

29 Alexander S. Nagel and Christopher Wood, *Anachronic Renaissance*. New York: Zone Books, 2010, 137.

30 Nagel and Wood, *Anachronic Renaissance*, 136.

31 Peter Burke, "The Renaissance Sense of Anachronism," in Ed. Enno Rudolph, *Die Renaissance und ihr Bild in der Geschichte. Die Renaissance als erste Aufklärung III.* Tübingen: Mohr Siebeck, 1998, 17–35: 21.

32 Burke, "The Renaissance Sense of Anachronism," 34.

33 Nagel and Wood, *Anachronic Renaissance*, 135.

34 Nagel and Wood, *Anachronic Renaissance*, 140.

35 Emphasis original. Nagel and Wood, *Anachronic Renaissance*, 136, 142.

36 Camille, "Simulacrum," 44.

37 Camille, "Simulacrum," 44.

38 Camille, "Simulacrum," 44; Nagel and Wood, *Anachronic Renaissance*, 136.

39 Schroeder, "Playspace Invaders," 149.

40 Nagel and Wood, *Anachronic Renaissance*, 142.

Works cited

Barnes, Annette and Jonathan Barnes. "Time Out of Joint: Some Reflections on Anachronism," *Journal of Aesthetics and Art Criticism*, 47, no. 3 (1989): 253–261.

Baudrillard, Jean. "The Order of Simulacra," in trans. Iain Hamilton Grant, *Symbolic Exchange and Death*. London: Sage, 1993, 50–86.

Baudrillard, Jean. "The Precession of Simulacra," in trans. Sheila Faria Glaser, *Simulacra and Simulation*. Ann Arbor, MI: University of Michigan Press, 1994, 1–42.

Burke, Peter. "The Renaissance Sense of Anachronism," in Ed. Enno Rudolph, *Die Renaissance und ihr Bild in der Geschichte. Die Renaissance als erste Aufklärung III.* Tübingen: Mohr Siebeck, 1998, 17–35.

Camille, Michael. "Simulacrum," in Eds. Robert S. Nelson and Richard Shiff, *Critical Terms for Art History*. Chicago, IL: University of Chicago Press, 2003, 35–48.

Cox, Kate. "Virtual Tourism Has Never Felt More Real," *Kotaku* (blog), 9 November 2012, http://kotaku.com/5959328/virtual-tourism-has-never-felt-more-real, assecced 14 November 2012.

Farington, Joseph. *The Farington Diary*, 8 vols. London: Hutchinson & Co, 1923.

Frasca, Gonzalo. "Simulation versus Narrative: Introduction to Ludology," in Eds. Mark J.P. Wolf and Bernard Perron, *The Video Game Theory Reader*. New York: Routledge, 2003, 221–235.

Gane, Mike. *Baudrillard's Bestiary: Baudrillard and Culture*. New York: Routledge, 1991.

Goethe, Johann Wolfgang von. "Naples," Eds. Thomas P. Saine and Jeffrey L. Sammons, trans. Robert R. Heitner, *Italian Journey*. New York: Suhrkamp Publishers, 1989, 179.

Hannibal. Directed by Ridley Scott. Beverly Hills: Metro-Goldwyn-Mayer, 2001.

Kirk, Terry. *The Architecture of Modern Italy. Volume I: The Challenge of Tradition, 1750–1900*. New York: Princeton Architectural Press, 2005.

Lasansky, Medina D. *The Renaissance Perfected: Architecture, Spectacle, and Tourism in Fascist Italy*. University Park, PA: Pennsylvania State University Press, 2004.

Murray, Janet H. *Hamlet on the Holodeck: The Future of Narrative in Cyberspace*. New York: Free Press, 1997.

Nagel, Alexander S. and Christopher Wood. *Anachronic Renaissance*. New York: Zone Books, 2010.

Schiesel, Seth. "On the Scenic Trail of Intrigue: Adventures in 15th-Century Italy," *New York Times*, New York edition, 8 December 2009.

Schroeder, Randy. "Playspace Invaders: Huizinga, Baudrillard and Video Game Violence," *Journal of Popular Culture*, 30, no. 3 (1996): 143–153.

Tavernor, Robert. *On Alberti and the Art of Building*. New Haven, CT: Yale University Press, 1998.

Ubisoft Group. "About Ubisoft: Facts and Figures," https://www.ubisoftgroup.com/en-US/about_ubisoft/facts_and_figures.aspx, accessed 14 November 2012.

Wolf, Mark J.P. "Introduction," in Ed. Mark J.P. Wolf, *The Medium of the Video Game*. Austin, TX: University of Texas Press, 2001, 1–9.

Games cited

Assassin's Creed II. Montreal: Ubisoft, 2009.

15

"This Game of Sudden Death": Simulating Air Combat of the First World War

Andrew Wackerfuss

United States Air Force Office
of Historical Studies, The Pentagon

Options for WWI wargaming are surprisingly limited. Any gamer knows the vast array for WWII: from *Call of Duty* to *Medal of Honor* and *Battlefield 1943*, many have won acclaim not only as wargames, but also as some of the most successful and top-selling titles of any genre. But there is no *Battlefield 1916*. EA Games has not published a *Medal of Honor: Western Front*, although over 100 men received the Medal of Honor for their WWI heroism. Despite the upcoming 100-year anniversary of the war's outbreak, no massively multiplayer game exists to allow us to re-live the experience of the trenches, the epic conflict in the expanses of the east, or the critical naval struggles of the high seas. But we can do one thing: we can fly.

Ever since the earliest video games began appearing for the nascent home computer and console markets of the early 1980s, WWI air combat simulations have formed a popular and influential part of the wargaming catalogue. Some feature child-friendly and cartoonish combat, such as the early examples of *Blue Max* and *Sky Kid*, as well as the more recent record-breaking Xbox live game *Snoopy Flying Ace*. Most of the most prominent titles since 1990, however, followed in *Microsoft Flight Simulator*'s heritage of rigorously difficult experiences that promise to give players an experience as close as possible to reality. Games like *Red Baron*, *Rise of Flight: The First Great Air War*, or *Over Flanders Fields* faithfully reproduce weather conditions, period maps, the effect of battle damage on flight, and the specific quirks of historical aircraft. They provide equal measures of frustration and reward for expert virtual pilots, and at their best they offer players the chance to live an entire combat career spanning thousands of hours of flying and fighting. The quality and influence of WWI air combat simulators, however, comes at the price of being nearly the only type of game portraying the Great War. While the task of numbering video games, especially in their early years, is a difficult one that can never be considered fully authoritative, of 42 WWI games I have been able to identify, the following genre divisions emerge (Table 15.1):

If the contest between genres was itself a war, air combat games would have already won a total victory. They are the earliest WWI games, the most popular recent titles, the most casual, and the most hardcore. They far outnumber any other genre, and indeed equal the output of all other genres combined. But in dominating the catalogue, they risk imparting a warped view of the war to those gamers who play them, who could conclude that the most important part of the war was the struggle in the air. This, however, was not the case. In fact, the air war was an exciting but militarily marginal aspect of the conflict.

For most of the war, air power was of primary use in reconnaissance and artillery observation. Though all sides experimented with air attacks, these were only damaging on a small scale such as when passing planes would strafe or drop small bombs. Later efforts led by American airpower pioneer Billy Mitchell began to organize larger formations of bombers to make greater strategic impacts, but this development took place only in the final phase of a war whose tipping point had already been reached.[1] Although military aviation

TABLE 15.1 World War I video games by genre

24	Air combat simulation
5	Science fiction or supernatural combat
4	Grand strategy / turn-based strategy
4	Naval combat simulation
3	Real-time strategy
2	Tower defense
0	Ground combat / FPS

captivated people at the time, air power did not emerge as in itself a decisive element of war until World War II, when strategic bombing crushed Germany and incinerated Japan.

Why, then, do air combat simulations prove to be the most popular and enduring forms of World War I video gaming? What does their popularity have to teach us about the war itself, and the historical memory surrounding it? This chapter will consider these issues from two sides. On the one hand, the primacy of the air war in video games reflects and re-creates the ways in which this earliest generation of military aviators captured the public imagination of the time. This alone can account for the games' enduring popularity, through fidelity to the historical memory of the war. Authenticity is rarely the goal of video games, but in this case a combination of technical and design influences have encouraged a type of authenticity that further privileges air combat simulators. Combined, the historical and design elements not only explain why air combat remains the defining way to game World War I, it also serves to freshen our insight into the original experience of the war itself.

Technical realism as a measure of WWI combat simulator accuracy

Like all games of their era, the earliest WWI flight simulators were crude suggestions rather than detailed simulations. Games of the early 1980s like *Blue Max*, *Sopwith*, and *Sky Kid* featured basic controls, limited flight paths, and simple weapons. Players moved back and forth along a scrolling terrain and destroyed enemies to rack up points, starting over when killed until they exhausted their number of lives. The games presented few or no narrative elements, nor did they attempt to pose as either realistic or informative. But alongside such simple games, a different type of game emerged that promised to re-create cockpit conditions and depict what it was really like to fly in WWI. Technological limitations of the era made this promise more of a utopian ambition than a goal that could be practically reached at the time. But the first game to aspire to achieve this holy grail, *Microsoft Flight Simulator*, proved so popular that it validated the quest as an enduring feature of future aviation wargames.

Flight Simulator began life as an engineering thesis by programmer Bruce Artwick, who eventually developed it as software for the various warhorses of early home computing. The program's 1982 shift to Microsoft and IBM-PCs made its biggest splash by including better graphics, more sensitive and detailed controls, maps based closely on the real world, and simulated weather. It also included a "British Ace" mode in which the pilot could fly Sopwith Camel against a small number of German opponents. This dogfight mode transformed what had been a formal experiment in computer graphics and physics engines into an attempt to simulate military operations. It helped make the program a massive hit, to the point where *Microsoft Flight Simulator* is often credited with both catering to and creating a market for desktop computer games as a whole, as it became a baseline program that all true aficionados used to measure the performance of their home machines.[2] The success of its dogfight mode set the tone for future air combat simulators, and wargames generally, by establishing simulated authenticity as among wargames' highest goals.

In 1990, three games suddenly appeared that for the first time seemed to deliver on this promise. Dynamix's *Red Baron*, MicroProse's *Knights of the Sky*, and Cinemaware's *Wings*—all built on the *Flight Simulator* formula by styling themselves as a faithful reproduction of WWI aviation. While all three succeeded both critically and commercially, *Red Baron's* receipt of Computer Gaming World's 1991 award for Simulation of the Year marked it as particularly influential in setting the tone for future air combat simulators. *Red Baron's* manual promised the game to be "a historically accurate and detailed recreation of flight during the era that launched aerial combat."[3] Players would be responsible for controlling ailerons, elevators, rudders, and throttles, all the while monitoring altimeters, fuel and airspeed indicators, and an array of other instruments. They had to manually shift their point of view to keep situational awareness of the battlefield, a mindset that then and now counts among the most important skills and instincts a military aviator can possess. Once in combat, the game simulated battle damage, gun jams, pilot wounds, a chance of blackout, and an array of other challenges that added to the all-important sense of authenticity.

However, in the game's first nod toward playability over authenticity, the designers included three realism settings through which players could determine how much of a piloting challenge they wished to face. On the easiest, aircraft were immune to their natural tendency to lose altitudes in turns and were generally easier to fly in all respects. The standard setting reintroduced various real-world necessities such as a need to pull back on controls in order to keep a plane's nose above the horizon, while the highest realism setting caused aircraft to behave according to exact laws of physics, as well as according to the specific quirks of the aircraft flown. (A Sopwith Camel, for instance, had trouble with turns because its engine produced gyroscopic effects.) Players could manually toggle each of the realism settings to customize the balance of authenticity and playability they sought. According to commentary by lead designer Damon Slye, the team "strove for as much historical accuracy as possible," but sometimes "had a choice to make between realism and playability. Wherever possible, we left this choice to the player by making it a preference on the Realism Panel."[4] Such an approach continues to be the standard for air combat simulators, as seen in one of the most recent contenders for best of genre, *Rise of Flight*, which allows players to turn off wind and turbulence, eliminate misfires and collisions, and provide for automatic controls of rudders, radiators, engine speed, and other mechanical elements so that they may fly at whatever level of realistic difficulty they choose.[5]

One of the areas in which designers most often deviate from historical accuracy concerns the number of aircraft involved in combat and the size of the battlefield, which for *Red Baron* remained limited by 1990's processing power. "Perhaps in ten years," wrote Slye, "Red Baron 4.0 will include dogfights with eighty planes instead of eight."[6] As it turned out, Slye was largely correct in his assessment. *Red Baron*, *Knights of the Sky*, and *Wings* all presaged wargame developments since the 1990, when games steadily expanded the realism and scale of their simulations with continually improved graphics, better physics engines, larger and more historically accurate maps, and other such technical developments. Wargamers began to assume that a game's technical fidelity, simulation of real-world physics, and reproduction of historical armaments were of highest importance to creating accurate experiences of warfare. Games would thus base their narrative plausibility and claim to historical authenticity on having demonstrated a high degree of technical-historical accuracy.

Simulating human behavior and the historical memory of WWI

In addition to technical and mechanical realism, wargames also promise players an authentic experience of fighting in a historical war. This element of game design places behavioral and psychological authenticity alongside technical simulation as the requirement for a successful game, and games that violate known rules for how historical combatants behaved can therefore come under criticism. A 1996 game, *Flying Corps*, encountered this difficulty when programmers inserted events that some players interpreted as pranks against them. Wingmen might turn back in the middle of a mission, or the battlefield could suddenly be covered in a mysterious red mist. Such interventions can enrage gamers, a notoriously prickly audience given to emotional outbursts when their expectations are violated. As one offended party complained, these elements of *Flying Corps* turned the game into "a complete travesty (an insult to the pilots of WWI, in fact), and in particular a waste of the great work that was put in to the aesthetics and accuracy of the game by the artists."[7] This player's complaint highlights the challenges designers face when meeting the demands of an audience hungry for accuracy-based authenticity.

Red Baron and its comrades approached this element of the authenticity trap by conducting extensive research into the historical background and human behavior of WWI-era pilots. Indeed, *Red Baron*'s manual functioned as a veritable flight manual that brimmed with historical context, technical specifications for all major aircraft, and instructions for how and when to perform various named maneuvers. It included historical training materials such as "Boelcke's Dicta," a set of eight principles for air combat laid out by one the German air force's most prominent early aces. It gave descriptions of famous missions, background on the various medals (a section sure to be read by players eager to win some for themselves), as well as biographies for many of the major aces. Simulating pilot behavior was a major obstacle for *Red Baron*'s designers, according to Slye, whose team exerted great effort into "getting the computer controlled pilots to choose the proper tactics at the right times."[8] The question was not just a matter of choosing the right maneuvers, but also of ensuring that famous pilots behaved in historically appropriate ways. "You will never see," said Slye, "Manfred von Richtofen do a loop in this product. He believed loops had no place in combat."[9]

The manual's pedagogical tone transformed it into a work of history in its own right, one based on three pages of bibliographic references. In their research, Slye and his fellow designers seem to have absorbed a critical element of historical memory concerning WWI: the contrast between the dirty, deadly, and futile combat of the trenches with the bright, heroic, and valorous combat of the skies. Indeed, the manual's historical narrative described the muddy and disease-ridden environment that ground soldiers lived in, their growing hopelessness as "generals ordered pointless charges across open ground into withering machine gun and artillery fire," and the continual piling up of corpses until the battlefields became "monuments to carnage and futility."[10] This context of misery on the ground was not the main subject, however, but rather a way to further brighten the prospect of heroic combat in the skies. The manual thus taught players about the context of their adventures and primed them to take to the skies as elite, heroic combatants of an otherwise unglamorous war.

Tellingly, the manual began with the illustration of a knight and the opening statement:

The aces of World War I were heirs to a valiant tradition. Like the lance-wielding warriors who roamed Europe in medieval times, the aviators of the Great War often did battle alone, one man against another. Mounted on magnificent, temperamental steeds, they did the bidding of kings and emperors, fighting for their honor with a spirit that recalled the knights of old.[11]

This approach may seem pandering to a gamer's desire for simulated heroism. It was, however, entirely faithful to the ways that both contemporary and later sources immortalized the war experience. Though Paul Fussel's *The Great War and Modern Memory* was not referenced in *Red Baron's* bibliography, his famous work analyzed how young men's beliefs and expectations about warfare clashed with the reality they experienced after 1914. Literary reactions to WWI at first employed a prewar "system of high diction" that glamorized warfare as a heroic enterprise, but which was itself one of "the ultimate casualties of the war."[12] In this language, for example, a horse (or an airplane) is a steed, the enemy is the foe, and to die is to perish. But this remnant of nineteenth-century mentality died in the trenches, as seen in the works of Siegfried Sassoon and other prominent veteran-poets. Sassoon's "The Poet as Hero" used the language of shattered heroism to depict a boy who once "sought the Grail" through service in the British army, but whose views on heroism could not recover from their encounter with actual warfare:

But now I've said good-bye to Galahad,
And am no more the knight of dreams and show:
For lust and senseless hatred make me glad,
And my killed friends are with me where I go.

For Sassoon, the only heroic potential left in the aftermath of the First World War was to become a proselytizer against war. But for many others at the time, there remained one realm where they could preserve their conception of warfare as a contest between skilled and heroic individuals, without having to accept that industrialization threatened to make this impossible. Thus, technological innovations in aviation combined with psychological need to prompt would-be warriors to look to the skies and see knights in the clouds. The dynamic can be seen in American beliefs about the air power's heroic and transcendent role in modern warfare.[13] One proponent of American air power in WWI declared that while "mere numbers of men count little in this great struggle," the unbarred path of the air would allow smaller numbers of empowered individuals the ability to strike directly at the enemy and achieve a breakthrough. "The eagle," he declared, "must end this war."[14]

These eagles, more than any other type of combatant in the First World War, retained the language and attitude of heroism that others saw shattered.

Where history books on ground warfare receive such titles as *Eye-Deep in Hell* or *To Conquer Hell*, books on air warfare are called *Heroes of the Sunlit Sky*, *The Years of the Sky Kings*, or *The Wonder of War in the Air*. World War I aviators retained a sense of warfare as a great game, much like the games of rugby, soccer, or football that they had practiced in schools before the war. Capt. Roy Brown, a Canadian credited with shooting down the Red Baron himself, lauded a comrade as possessing the quality that "makes champions in any game of combat": a combination of passion and detachment, of the type displayed by the best hunters and athletes.[15] Brown relied on sporting and gaming imagery throughout his description of his paragon comrade, who according to Brown "made no secret of the fact that he was out to pile up a score."[16] Brown wrote in a letter home that the war was "great sport. ... I never enjoyed myself so much in my life."[17] These men analogized air warfare to shooting clay pigeons, to sinking putts, and other sporting accomplishments that demanded focus, concentration, and calm skill. With practice, a pilot could become "superb in his mastery of this game of sudden death."[18]

The association of war and games is in fact an ancient relationship, testified to in some of the oldest written sources. Though ancient sources disagreed on whether sports were complementary or conflictive with a warlike education, the Victorians and other contemporary westerners prized team games as vital to building proper warlike characters.[19] In addition to the nineteenth century's physical contests, games played on maps using toy soldiers or tokens became popular in both Europe and America. The Prussian Army's famous "Kriegspiel" (literally, wargame: see Köstlbauer, Chapter 11) provided direct links to preparation for war, while H. G. Wells in 1913 created a formal rulebook for toy soldier games that he called *Little Wars*.[20] It is therefore no surprise that in this atmosphere, men spoke of war using the language of the game, at least until the reality of war made this obscene. While wargames largely lost their popularity after 1918, they reappeared in the 1960s once the realities of industrialized warfare had grown romantically distant.[21] These games grew increasingly complex through the 1980s, when the growth of computing power liberated them from physical constraints and freed players from the burden of enacting the simulation's rules. Simulation scholars have described the dynamic as "minimizing the trade-off between detail and playability" by pushing all mechanics into an invisible virtual realm.[22] By the 1990s, a computer could perform a simulation's mechanical tasks at a level so detailed as to allow the possibility of immersive experience, which now became the prime goal.

The present situation thus returns us to this chapter's starting point, with the question of why air combat simulators dominate WWI gaming, while ground combat simulators do not exist. The answer is simple: the constraint of producing wargames as simulated authentic experiences negates the possibility of a trench warfare simulation. Such a simulation would be boring and tedious, since soldiers often sat hunkered down for days under artillery fire. Most flight simulators, however, share this problem, which they overcome with time-lapse modes that allow the player to autopilot and fast-forward long stretches of uneventful flight until they arrive at the scene of a dogfight. The true difference between air and ground games therefore would come when combat begins: in the air, a contest of skill and chivalric valor, but on the ground a meaningless death unavoidable by any display of skill. It is this element—the lack of skill and control—that makes trench warfare such an unsuitable subject for games prizing simulated first person reality. According to Fussel, "Every war is ironic because every war is worse than expected."[23] Video games following the grail of authenticity, however, reject irony and instead promise gamers that they can experience war in precisely the way they hope to do so: by fighting in an honorable contest in which one's skill and valor bring victory. Indeed, we can observe both the original and the virtual WWI combatants as displaying the same thought process of taking psychological flight and looking to the skies as a refuge from the trenches' brutality. Both soldiers and gamers shared the same expectations about what makes for a satisfying and honorable conflict. Both expected that warfare be fought according to certain rules, foremost among them that victory could be earned through skill, training, valor, and honor. The failure of these qualities to influence industrialized ground warfare offended and horrified the generation of 1914, and today shapes the market for video games about 1914. Of course, any game about war must at times be horrific.

Alternative approaches: Abandoning simulation for narrative fidelity

Historians who analyze films often take the approach that it is useless to criticize entertainment industry products for their fidelity or divergence from historical accuracy.[24] Scholars must instead accept that entertainers will change historical details to streamline narratives, create engaging characters, and manipulate emotions rather than intellect. Given this reality, historians should not seek to criticize inaccuracy, but rather to analyze whether the inevitable changes lead viewers toward or away from historical authenticity. The tension between realism and historicism exists just as profoundly in the newer medium of video games, though here the same logic of entertainment that creates inaccuracy in film tends to promote accuracy in games. But in video games about war, surface-level accuracy paradoxically introduces inauthenticity regarding narrative or psychological truths about war. Therefore, in addition to other genre distinctions we can make, we must also divide wargames into those that adhere to problematic concept of simulated accuracy, and those that do not. Games that free themselves from slavery to technical accuracy may become able to portray the mythical and cultural importance of WWI in a way that those constrained by reality do not. In this sense, some WWI games have achieved meta-historical fidelity through three techniques: by using gameplay to organically promote lessons on the high mortality rate of the war; by introducing supernatural elements into the structured narrative; and by choosing genres whose mechanics convey messages of futility and repeated destruction.

Red Baron, *Rise of Flight*, and other WWI air combat games that prize accurate flight simulation each present a reality of air combat that goes beyond the mechanics of flight. By being so difficult and unforgiving, they teach players about aviators' high mortality rates without needing to spell out the lesson. Using ludonarrative—a storyline that emerges organically as players play the game—rather than scripted story or conversation, they remind players that flying in WWI was a high-risk profession that even the best pilots did not survive. Many players who pick up one of these games without previous familiarity with flight simulators will die within seconds of their first takeoffs. Some may never get off the ground without initially turning down the realism settings. Games may decide to enhance these ludonarrative elements by consciously divorcing a player's success or failure from any larger impact on the war. While some games connect players' victories and defeats in individual scenarios to their side's progress or setbacks in the overall conflict, the WWI front changed little, and without any connection to the actions of any individual. *Red Baron* therefore divorced players altogether from the larger war, which thus becomes all but meaningless to the pilot. The true conflict, in the game and in history, was over the degree of skill and honor the aviator could demonstrate through the course of play.

A second way that WWI games can sacrifice accuracy of detail for accuracy of narrative can be seen in the handful of titles that do portray an individual experience of war on the ground. Tellingly, the only first-person shooters set in World War I—*Darkest of Days*, *NecroVisioN*, and its prequel *NecroVisioN: Lost Company*—use obviously supernatural or satirical elements in order to foreground messages of horror or dark comedic futility. They thus remain authentic to the meta-narrative of the First World War even as they transgress against even loose adherence to historical accuracy. In *Darkest of Days*, 8Monkey Labs' time-traveling first-person shooter from 2009, sci-fi elements contrasted with an otherwise-realistic style by giving players abilities and weaponry far above that of any historical combatant. During the climax of one WWI mission, the players' handler provides an automatic missile launcher for use in defense of a trench against massed assault. Using this gadget, the player can smite wave upon wave of enemy soldiers with ease, thus enacting in a hyperstylized way an archetypical WWI trench battle. Indeed, the deployment of advanced technology mirrors that era's dream of developing technological solutions to deadlocked warfare: the same mentality that promoted the inventions of military aviation, tanks, landmines, and chemical weapons. *NecroVisioN*, a 2009 title by Polish developer The Farm 51, used supernatural elements to convey the pervasive sense of horror that haunted the battlefields of WWI, where here the dead themselves rise from the trenches, and players descend into a literal hell. Clearly, both *NecroVisioN* and *Darkest of Days* do not seek accurate depictions of what really happened in the First World War. They do, however, use their inaccuracies in order to work with, not against, the prevailing historical memory of that war, and thus secure a kind of authenticity.

A final way to appropriately convey WWI's historical lessons is to choose genres whose mechanics themselves promote fidelity to that war's themes of depersonalized, industrial slaughter. The creation of turn-based and later real-time strategy games has made this possible by allowing players to take the role not of an individual soldier, but rather of a distant commander who must take into account both the positioning and requisitioning of forces. *HistoryLine: 1914–1918*, a 1992 game developed by the German company Blue Byte Software, took an explicitly didactic approach to the genre, mixing game text drawn from historical documents with a conscious rejection of violence. The new genre of tower defense games is equally suited to match its mechanics with the WWI narrative: commanders in both defended fixed positions from waves of enemies. One example, *World War I Medic*, rejects graphical realism for a crude retro style in which the player pursues an often fruitless task of keeping comrades alive through a hail of 8-bit fire. The game therefore conveys historical experience through ludonarrative mechanics rather than by devotion to a problematic concept of simulated authenticity. A more traditional tower defense game, *Toy Soldiers* by Signal Studios, has been among the genre's most successful, with more than half a million units sold and nominations for numerous awards for its depiction of trench warfare fought by toys. The setting constantly reminds players that they are not playing soldiers, but rather playing *with* soldiers. The game's honest inauthenticity therefore never seduces players into the authenticity trap. It is therefore perhaps the most accurate simulation yet made of how boys of the era played at war, just as H. G. Wells enshrined in 1913.

Wargaming about WWI has therefore come full circle. Although companies are sure in the future to continue the attempt toward authenticity, and some may perhaps even one day try such a game for the ground war, the current environment of experimentation, stylization, and genre-crossing will likely continue to encourage games that pursue narrative and thematic fidelity over problematic authenticity.

Notes

1 Warren A. Trest, *Air Force Roles and Missions: A History*. Washington, D.C.: Air Force History and Museums Program, 1998, 10–19.

2 Jos Grupping, "Flight Simulator History," 1 January 2013, http://fshistory. simflight.com/fsh/versions.htm

3 *Red Baron* manual, (1990), C-2.

4 *Red Baron* manual, X-2.

5 *Rise of Flight* manual, (2012), 22–23.

6 *Red Baron* manual, X-2.

7 "Talk page for Flying Corps," 1 January 2013, http://en.wikipedia.org/wiki/Talk:Flying_Corps

8 *Red Baron* manual, X-1.

9 *Red Baron* manual, X-1.

10 *Red Baron* manual, 1–7.

11 *Red Baron* manual, 1–2.

12 Paul Fussel, *The Great War and Modern Memory*. Oxford and New York: Oxford University Press, 1975, 22–23.

13 Mark Clodfelter, *Beneficial Bombing: The Progressive Foundations of American Air Power, 1917–1945*. Lincoln, NE: University of Nebraska Press, 2010, 3–5.

14 Quoted in Linda R. Robertson, *The Dream of Civilized Warfare: World War I Flying Aces and the American Imagination*. Minneapolis, MN: University of Minnesota Press, 2005, 30.

15 Frank C. Platt, Ed. *Great Battles of World War I in the Air*. New York: Weathervane Books, 1966, 9.

16 Platt, *Great Battles*, 11.

17 Platt, *Great Battles*, 19.

18 Platt, *Great Battles*, 21.

19 Tim J. Cornell, "On War and Games in the Ancient World," in Eds. Tim J. Cornell and Thomas B. Allen, *War and Games, Studies in the Nature of War*, vol. 3. San Marino, CA: The Boydell Press, 2002, 38–40.

20 H.G. Wells and J.R. Sinclair, *Little Wars*. London: F. Palmer, 1913.

21 Philip Saban, "Playing at War: The Modern Hobby of Wargaming," in Eds. Cornell and Allen, *War and Games*. Suffolk: Boydell Press, 2002, 200–201.

22 Philip Saban, *Simulating War: Studying Conflict through Simulation Games*. New York: Continuum, 2012, 22.

23 Fussel, *The Great War and Modern Memory*, 7.

24 Robert Rosenstone, *Visions of the Past*. Cambridge, MA: Harvard University Press, 1995.

Works cited

Clodfelter, Mark. *Beneficial Bombing: The Progressive Foundations of American Air Power, 1917–1945*. Lincoln, NE: University of Nebraska Press, 2010.

Cornell, Tim J. and Thomas B. Allen, Eds. *War and Games*. Suffolk: Boydell Press, 2002.

Grupping, Jos. "Flight Simulator History," 1 January 2013, http://fshistory. simflight.com/fsh/versions.htm, accessed 23 May 2013. *Medal of Honor*. Electronic Arts. 1999.

Platt, Frank C. Ed. *Great Battles of World War I in the Air*. New York: Weathervane Books, 1966.

Robertson, Linda R. *The Dream of Civilized Warfare: World War I Flying Aces and the American Imagination*. Minneapolis, MN: University of Minnesota Press, 2005.

Rosenstone, Robert. *Visions of the Past*. Cambridge, MA: Harvard University Press, 1995.

Saban, Philip. *Simulating War: Studying Conflict Through Simulation Games*. New York: Continuum, 2012.

"Talk page for Flying Corps." 1 January 2013. http://en.wikipedia.org/wiki/ Talk:Flying_Corps

Trest, Warren A. *Air Force Roles and Missions: A History*. Washington, D.C.: Air Force History and Museums Program, 1998.

Wells, H.G. and J.R Sinclair. *Little Wars*. London: F. Palmer, 1913.

Games cited

Battlefield 1943. Stockholm: EA Digital Illusions Creative Entertainment, 2009.

Blue Max. Richmond, CA: Synapse Software, 1983.

Call of Duty. Encino, CA: Infinity Ward, Activision, 2003.

Darkest of Days. Cedar Falls, IA: 8Monkey Labs, Phantom EFX, 2009.

Flying Corps. Runcorn, UK: Rowan Software, Empire Interactive, 1996.

HistoryLine: 1914–1918. Düsseldorf: Blue Byte Software, Strategic Simulations, Inc, 1996.

Knights of the Sky. Alameda, CA: MicroProse, 1990.

Microsoft Flight Simulator. Redmond, WA: Microsoft, 1982.

NecroVisioN. Gliwice: The Farm 51, 505 Games, 2009.

NecroVisioN: Lost Company. Gliwice: The Farm 51, 505 Games, 2010.

Over Flanders Fields: Between Heaven and Hell. OBD Software, 2009.
Red Baron. Oakhurst, CA: Dynamix, Sierra Entertainment, 1990.
Rise of Flight: The First Great Air War. Moscow: Neoqb, 777 Studios, 2009.
Sky Kid. Tokyo: Namco, 1985.
Snoopy Flying Ace. Redmond, WA: Smart Bomb Interactive, Microsoft Game
    Studios, 2010.
Sopwith. BMB Compuscience, 1984.
Toy Soldiers. Salt Lake City, UT: Signal Studios, Microsoft Game Studios, 2010.
Wings. Burlingame, CA: Cinemaware, 1990.
World War I Medic. Silverdale, WA: Bay12 Games, 2004.

16

"The Reality Behind It All Is Very True": *Call of Duty: Black Ops* and the Remembrance of the Cold War

Clemens Reisner
University of Vienna

Video games and the Cold War have a fairly strong interconnection. As Claus Pias and Patrick Crogan have demonstrated, the genealogy of the medium is firmly rooted in the advancements in Cold War military technology.[1] Also, their timelines correlate in a specific way. The period of the elevation of computer games to the status of mass media during the 1980s coincided with the final act and eventually the dissolution of the Cold War deadlock.

Another aspect of this relation is the recurrence of the Cold War as a topic in computer games. A quick search in Wikipedia and the popular game-database website Mobygames alone delivers over 160 titles that in one way or another address the Cold War period. Wikipedia has even devoted one of its numerous subject lists to this particular topic.[2] Based on these circumstances, it is safe to say that computer games participate in the popular remembrance of the Cold War. Thus, computer games appear to actively partake in shaping the public view of the Cold War as a historic period.

Within this wealth of games dealing with the Cold War one can also find the seventh installment of one of the best-selling computer game franchises of all time: *Call of Duty: Black Ops*. As of 20 September 2012, according to the website vgchartz.com, the game has sold twenty-eight million units.[3] Thus, *Call of Duty: Black Ops* in particular, as well as the whole series in general, comes close to what is generally known as a blockbuster for the movie industry. The games of the series are equally applauded for their high-quality production and criticized for their reliance on linear gameplay.

By taking a closer look at the interaction between gameplay and audiovisual elements, this chapter aims to explore how *Call of Duty: Black Ops* remembers the Cold War. The history of the Cold War, as it appears in *Call of Duty: Black Ops*, is interpreted as a form of simulation that includes authenticating elements and places the player in a specific way within a historically charged space. The ensuing logic turns out to resemble that of a theme park ride.

History as a simulation

History depends on representation. Be it in a scientific or a popular context, our understanding of the past as history is shaped by a procession of mediation—that is, by its representation and retransmission to new audiences. This processing of the past has been described as a "culture of history," "a dynamic factor with its own historiography of shifts and changes that frequently occur in the wake of social events and turning points."[4]

Consequently, the possibilities and limitations of the media involved in representing history are receiving a great deal of attention. The set of elements that constitute the singularity of a specific medium have been labeled with the term "mediality". In this conception, the media produce meaning by drawing on a set of codes and signs (audiovisual conventions, tropes, etc.) that they quote and process via their specific mediality. This reservoir of representational conventions has been described as a "cultural archive".[5]

In order to understand how computer games process the past, I propose to proceed in two steps.

First, the specific mediality of computer games and their governing mode of representation have to be addressed.[6] I assume simulation to be the governing mode of representation in computer games. Hereby I am drawing on two complementary definitions: Gonzalo Frasca states that to simulate means, "to model a source system through a different system which maintains for somebody some of the behaviors of the original system."[7] Ian Bogost builds on Frasca's definition and specifies simulation as, "a representation of a source system via a less complex system that informs the user's understanding of the source system in a subjective way."[8]

Taking the Cold War, or more precisely the system of knowledge about the Cold War, as the source system, *Call of Duty: Black Ops* is understood as processing this historic period via a less complex system. This is established by the game designer's subjective choice from the prevailing cultural archive and thus informs the player's conception of the Cold War.

Second, the specific strategies employed by the designers of a particular game during the process of simulating history are of interest. A key term in understanding this process is "authenticity." As Salvati and Bullinger argue in Chapter 10, in popular representations of history, the concept of authenticity proves to be an important benchmark as these representations are measured, by specialists and laymen alike, by the degree of historical accuracy they achieve. The idea of what constitutes an authentic representation, however, is subject to the culture of history in a certain period, i.e. a set of conventions that have been socially agreed upon as being historically accurate.[9]

This set of conventions leads back to the concept of a "cultural archive" introduced above and, as the focal point is on sociocultural potency, is not limited to conventions from the historic sciences but includes products of popular culture as well.

Built into the marketing concept of a game like *Call of Duty: Black Ops*, however, is the claim for both delivering a believable, authentic representation of a historic period and providing an entertaining experience (see Wackerfuss, Chapter 15). *Call of Duty: Black Ops*'s producer Dan Bunting gives an example for this dual aspiration during an interview for the online gaming-magazine *joystiq*. Asked about the political implications of a game built around covert operations during a historical period that has also seen heightened criticism for US imperialism, Bunting replied:

> At the end of the day it's an entertainment product and we're creating an entertainment experience…. So, we're not trying to make any political messages or give any history lessons. It is about experiencing this game within the context of that war.[10]

When the interviewer proceeded to ask whether this circumstance provided the producers with more freedom in designing the game as opposed to previous installments of the *CoD*-franchise that dealt with non-classified content such as the Second World War, Bunting replied:

I don't think we changed a lot about our process. We still do the research, we still have our military advisers who come in. (...) So the authenticity that motivates the creativity in the game is still very much part of what we do.[11]

The aim of serving the dual claim of historical authenticity and entertainment value is clearly filtering through these statements. In order to fulfill these aspirations, the game designers draw on at least two strategies whilst simulating history.

On the one hand, these consist of a subjectively chosen set of audiovisual and textual conventions from the cultural archive that the game designers use to lend authenticity to the games.

On the other hand, the limitations the game designers impose on the players in terms of freedom and the range of performable actions by the implementation of rules and spatial structures, are of interest. The term "gameplay" encompasses these elements, which, apart from enhancing the entertainment value, also allow for an understanding of the "designers'" presuppositions, in this case their view of the Cold War.[12]

Hence *Call of Duty: Black Ops*'s specific embodiment of the Cold War has to be interpreted as being intertwined with a wider culture of history/cultural archive of the Cold War from which the quotations derive and to which it contributes its own interpretation. Staying with Frasca and Bogost's definition of simulation, my main interest lies in understanding how *Call of Duty: Black Ops* manages to reduce the complexity of the system of knowledge about the Cold War, whilst still maintaining a level of authenticity that enables the player to recognize the historic period in question. The main questions in analyzing this process concern those areas of the culture of history of the Cold War from which the mediated elements derive, the limitations and freedom the gameplay imposes, and finally the overall interpretation of the Cold War the game delivers by creating an authentic space with ludic limitations.

A witness in an authentic space

How then is *Call of Duty: Black Ops*'s internal structure designed in order to fulfill the dual claim of delivering an entertaining yet authentic experience?[13] I suggest that for this purpose the game aims at placing the player in the position of a witness and immersing him/her in an authentic space.

This arrangement first needs a set of authenticating elements that connect to the cultural archive of the Cold War. *Call of Duty: Black Ops* finds these elements in several sources. This is achieved, for example, by resorting to archival aesthetics, as throughout the game a vast amount of archival film footage, showing significant historical persons and war scenes mainly from the Vietnam War, is presented in numerous cutscenes, that is sections of the game where the player is supposed to watch as the story unfolds rather than to interact with the game. The film footage shown is reminiscent of historical TV-news and especially calls to mind the Vietnam War as a televised war. Furthermore, the spread (of communism) is touched upon rather directly by the depiction of animated, gradually reddening maps. The overall graphical layout of the cutscenes with its visual emphasis on classified documents, papers, and files hints at the authority and authenticity of what is considered to be *sine qua non* primary source for historiography. This archival aesthetic reaches into the actual levels as they are introduced and contextualized by a short portion of text that is gradually blackened out as if containing classified information before the game hands over the controls to the player.

Another means by which *Call of Duty: Black Ops* achieves authenticity is by digitally remodeling significant historical actors, actual locations and weapon types. John F. Kennedy, Fidel Castro, and Robert McNamara, among others, make an appearance as computer-generated characters. The Pentagon War Room, the Vorkuta Gulag, the battlefields of Vietnam and Laos, as well as the Bay of Pigs can be roamed by the player, armed with hand weapons or operating heavier military equipment such as boats, helicopters and notably, at one point, even an U2 surveillance aircraft.

An interesting further variant of digital remodeling is the appearance of computer-generated TV screens. Television is often considered as the paradigmatic medium of the Cold War. Without delving too deep into his remarks, a point worth stressing at this juncture is Lorenz Engell's discussion of immediacy as one of television's characteristic properties. Connecting to the notion of the Cold War as a kind of permanent interim period, the medium's immediacy establishes a close connection to reality.[14] Jay David Bolter and Richard Grusin also acknowledge this property of television when they state that "just as it remediates film or other media, television remediates the real."[15] *Call of Duty: Black Ops* identifies and uses this correlation. The introduction of virtual TV-screen models thus can be interpreted as a form of remediation, lending authority and authenticity to the images appearing on these screens and thereby also serving to establish an authentic space.

Call of Duty: Black Ops also relies on tropes, sequences, narrative structures, and some visual markers from movies. Especially the levels taking place in Vietnam and Laos establish several connections with feature films, the most obvious example being the Russian roulette scene from the film *The Deer Hunter*. Other references include *Apocalypse Now* and *Platoon*.[16] The actual quotations, however, are quite loose and seek only to display just enough elements to make their reference recognizable by evoking an atmosphere akin to the film in question. In any case, these films are themselves part of a range of discussions and controversies surrounding authenticity in their own depictions of the Cold War. The complexity and diversity of the discourses surrounding the representation of the Vietnam War make it difficult to assess exactly the position *Call of Duty: Black Ops* is taking.[17] Nevertheless, I would like to suggest that the quotation of elements from films primarily concerned with the fate of single soldiers adds to the player's immersion and serves to strengthen the subjective viewpoint of the game. This leads to the question of how *Call of Duty: Black Ops*'s gameplay is designed in general and how it achieves the desired immersive effect in particular.

Considering the spatial design, *Call of Duty: Black Ops*, as a prime example of the first person shooter genre, organizes the line of sight as an extension of the player's gaze into the screen through the eyes of the avatar. The main objective of the game is to gain territory by advancing into virtual space. This goes hand in hand with the elimination of enemies, who constitute a barrier against the player's advance. Hence the ensuing dynamic is one of "stop and go," fighting and advancing. The main gameplay mechanic, to state the obvious, consists of shooting. However, it is also shooting with little to no alternative, as *Call of Duty: Black Ops* is widely lacking alternative routes or possibilities to circumvent the enemy. The player's path seems to be largely predetermined (see Reynolds, Chapter 3). As a result, the gameplay breaks the progression of time, the plot, and ultimately history down to the decision between shooting and not-shooting, with the latter being synonymous to stagnation, i.e. death. Well-timed decision making as well as speed serve to create the flow of the game.

The frequent use of scripted events, in which certain actions of the play trigger predetermined gameplay events that in turn lead to other actions, furthermore adds to emphasizing flow as a gameplay element. This also includes quick-time events in some parts of the game during which the player is meant to press a certain sequence of buttons within a specified amount of time. At these points the players' advancement into virtual space progresses in the form of a chain of events, whereby the immersion deepens as the player attempts to keep the gameplay uninterrupted.

Overall, *Call of Duty: Black Ops* explicitly aims at deepening immersion and making the players' experience as intense as possible.[18] This approach becomes apparent right at the start of the game where the player, by means of an introduction, is initially confronted with an overwhelming amount of rapidly cut documentary footage, followed by a setup that shows Mason, the protagonist, in an interrogation room. Surrounded by TV-screens and only allowed to move his head, i.e. the camera, as if being constrained, and thus only able to look around in a small radius, the main character finds himself being questioned about the military campaigns he took part in by a bodiless, distorted voice urging him to remember. At the same time, the TV-screens present the player with the image of the protagonist, a mysterious number code and, at later points (as the interrogation room setup serves as a bridge between the levels), even more documentary footage.

The fact that it is on these virtual models of TV-screens that the player is shown the avatar's face for the first time firmly establishes a connection between film footage and computer-modeled characters. Both are marked as belonging to the same authentic space. As the protagonist searches his memory, the actual levels are loaded while, similarly to the introduction, cutscenes displaying a vast array of rapidly cut film footage, animated maps, graphical interfaces mimicking disclosed archival files and computer-generated characters fill the screen. These images are designed to introduce the levels and illustrate the interrogation dialogue by contextualizing the flashbacks from the protagonists' memory.

This framing cascade of intermedial quotations in the cutscenes is counterbalanced by the possibility of moving the camera in the interrogation room setup. Arguably, this dynamic is one of the main features of how the game structures the gaming experience.

Audiovisual elements and gameplay elements can be situated within a spectrum, with on- and offline sequences as its opposing poles. The classification "online" denotes a high level of player involvement as it can be found in playable sections, whereas "offline" refers to sections of no direct player involvement, such as cutscenes.[19] In the overall experience, however, the player rarely engages with the game in a state of either pure on- or offline reception. James Newman has coined the term "ergodic continuum" in order to describe sections in the game where the player is experiencing a state between being on- or offline, i.e. between direct involvement and mere observation.[20]

In the case of *Call of Duty: Black Ops*, the game aims to keep the player at the center of the ergodic continuum, to the effect that he/she becomes a witness of a series of authenticating devices. At the point of entering the first actually playable sections, the combination of on- and offline elements has established an authentic space in which the player is henceforth meant to move and immerse him-/herself. From the moment of establishing an authentic space in the interrogation room setup onwards, the strategy to make the player a witness by shifting his/her position in the ergodic continuum becomes a recurrent phenomenon.

It is encountered already in the first level, set in the Bay of Pigs, where the players' squad at one point near the end enters Fidel Castro's bedroom, however, only, as it later turns out, managing to assassinate the Cuban leader's body double. The moment of the assassination is presented in slow motion, a tool regularly employed during the game. In this case it shifts the player's position in the ergodic continuum from a tilt to the online side toward the offline pole, as missing the shot becomes virtually impossible and observing becomes imperative. This serves to assure that the player recognizes and witnesses that he/she actually is shooting Castro.[21]

Another example is the entire third level that takes place in the Pentagon War Room and solely consists of witnessing the location and the appearance of the political personae. Similarly to the interrogation room setup, the player's range of action in this level is limited to moving the camera as Mason is guided through the Pentagon War room to meet and talk to virtual models of Secretary of Defense McNamara and President Kennedy.

Whenever *Call of Duty: Black Ops* quotes elements from films, the game follows the same strategy of presenting visual contents from other media in the form of computer graphics. Clearly, the aim here is to enable the player to feel as if he/she is actually taking part in a film scene, which serves as another form of the witness mechanism.

As a conclusion deriving from these observations, *Call of Duty: Black Ops*'s gameplay can be said to follow the logic of a theme park ride. The game enables the player to witness authentic attractions from a subjective viewpoint, whilst during some passages even forcing him/her to look around. By handing some of the controls to the player even during the narrative sequences, however, he/she is held in the ergodic continuum. Thereby the game tries to immerse the player as a witness in a historically authentic space that aims at aligning photographic and computer-generated images.

In a way, the freeze-frame that is presented at the end of the game and shows the protagonist in Dallas on the day of John F. Kennedys' assassination is symptomatic not only for the game's aim to intertwine photographic and computer-generated images but also for the game's strategy of immersing the player into history and making him/her a witness.[22] *Call of Duty: Black Ops*'s narrative, as well as its gameplay mechanic, culminates in this picture with which the player is rewarded after completing the game. For a brief moment, *Call of Duty: Black Ops*, in a final, hypermedial move of authentication, suggests to be displaying proof that the player has actually "been there" and thus closes the authentic space.

Call of Duty: Black Ops and the remembrance of the Cold War

Returning to the main question of how *Call of Duty: Black Ops* remembers the Cold War, we can now turn to examine its dual aim of achieving historical authenticity as well as an entertainment experience and then, with consideration to the strategies outlined above, relate it to a broader perspective.

In an interview for the online edition of the British newspaper the *Telegraph*, *Call of Duty: Black Ops*'s lead writer Craig Houston, in reply to a question addressing the challenge of reconciling historical accuracy with the demands of the action game format, claimed that:

> The whole idea of wars taking place in other countries that were supported by the Russians and the Americans is something that more people should know about (…) a lot of the battles which took place in the Cold War aren't known about. It's not known by the general public. They may never be known. In a way, we had the luxury to make things up because no one can say that things like what we represent didn't ever happen. The reality behind it all is very true. It's all very firmly rooted in reality.[23]

Regarding the issue of how *Call of Duty: Black Ops* remembers the Cold War, Houston's statement is interesting in several respects. To start with, it points out that the game's designers purposefully aimed at engaging with and contributing to the culture of history of the Cold War, even to the extent of pursuing an educational ambition.

But Houston's comment also suggests an interplay between entertainment and authentication elements when he juxtaposes "the luxury to make things up" with "the very true reality behind it all." To begin with the first category, it can be assumed that the players cannot compare the range of actions and movements afforded by the rules of the game with actual historical events.[24] Thus, the degree of military accuracy concerning the range of actions can be considered as being indiscernible to laymen. The same is true for the possibility to determine to which degree this aspect is fictitious or not.[25]

Of further concern for this category is the overarching narrative. Parallel to the game's general theme of covert operations, the plot tells a tale filled with conspiracy, deceit, and Nazis. At first sight, the highly speculative narrative clearly suggests the game's plot to be of a purely fictional nature. Still, it engages with a concept the literary scholar Eva Horn has analyzed under the term "political secret." According to Horn, fiction allows for enough latitude to speak or speculate about political configurations that cannot be discussed in the political sphere proper.[26] By following films that take a similar stance, such as *The Manchurian Candidate*, *Call of Duty: Black Ops*'s narrative clearly aims at entering the realm of the political secret. This is combined with a triumphalist view[27] of the history of the Cold War, as in terms of warfare and military operations America ultimately prevails (including flying colors at the end of the last level).

Both of these fictional elements are geared toward the entertainment experience. The range of actions the player is allowed to perform is meant to establish a flow, the conspiracy-filled plot is meant to stimulate the player's imagination by evoking "what if" questions. In order to not only make this constellation work but also to add suspense and impact the strategy of authentication is imperative. It is only when the speculative and the arcane are happening within an authentic space that they are able to work at all. In this way "the luxury to make things up" corresponds to "the very true reality behind it all."

The gameplay mechanics also encourage all of these elements to converge at the vanishing point of subjectivity. Immersion and warfare are the main principles, the single soldier as a universal war machine is the perspective.[28] In *Call of Duty: Black Ops* the history of the Cold War is processed as the patterning of facts and authentic set pieces, as the grasp of higher forces for the individual. It is experienced from the perspective of the witness. The progression of historical time is proportional to the advancement of the soldier in the battlefield, whereby the paths are largely predefined.

With this emphasis on the soldierly experience, *Call of Duty: Black Ops* can be ranked among those games that are part of the so-called military–entertainment complex.[29] Thus, the remarkable feature of how *Call of Duty: Black Ops* remembers the Cold War lies less in the triumphalist picture the games' narrative creates. It is rather the fact that the game presents the Cold War as an actual war. In *Call of Duty: Black Ops* a historic period is recharged with military potential that in its popular reception gained exceptional status for being a conflict that never actually took place on a large scale. The strategy by which the game achieves this effect relies on the establishment of an ergodic continuum ensuing from the interplay between cascading authentication and immersion techniques. Referring to Frasca's and Bogost's definition of simulation, it can be said that *Call of Duty: Black Ops* simulates the complex system of knowledge about the Cold War via the less complex system of warfare from the perspective of a foot soldier. In the case of *Call of Duty: Black Ops* historical authenticity serves as a strategy to foster entertainment. The elements that denote authenticity play the role of set pieces, of attractions rushing by during a theme park ride.

While this chapter has aimed at tracing and analyzing the game designers' decisions and strategies in representing the Cold War, as a last point I would like to mention that ultimately computer games, as any other medium, are also about the meaning the recipients derive from the offer that is made to them by the producers. The analysis of this aspect certainly is a promising additional task in analyzing how computer games simulate history.

Notes

1 Patrick Crogan, *Gameplay Mode: War, Simulation and Technoculture*. Minneapolis, MN and London: University of Minnesota Press, 2011, 1–18; Claus Pias, *Computer Spiel Welten*. Zürich: Diaphanes, 2010, especially 244–306.

2 "Category: Cold War Video Games," http://en.wikipedia.org/wiki/Category:Cold_War_video_games, accessed 5 September 2012.

3 "Game Database. Global sales (in millions of units) per game," *VGChartz*, http://www.vgchartz.com/gamedb/?name=call+of+duty%3A+black+ops &publisher=&platform=&genre=&minSales=0&results=200, accessed 20 September 2012.

4 Thomas E. Fischer, *Geschichte der Geschichtskultur. Über den öffentlichen Gebrauch von Vergangenheit von den antiken Hochkulturen bis zur Gegenwart*. Köln: Verlag Wissenschaft und Politik, 2000, 11–13.

5 Sybille Krämer, "Was haben 'Performativität' und 'Medialität' miteinander zu tun? Plädoyer für eine in der 'Aisthetisierung' gründende Konzeption des Performativen," in Ed. Sybille Krämer, *Performativität und Medialität*. München: Fink, 2004, 13–32.

6 Dieter Mersch, "Medialität und Undarstellbarkeit. Einleitung in eine 'negative' Medientheorie," in Ed. Sybille Krämer, *Performativität und Medialität*. München: Wilhelm Fink Verlag, 2004, 85.

7 Gonzalo Frasca, "Simulation vs. Narrative. Introduction to Ludology," in Eds. Mark J.P. Wolf and Bernard Perron, *The Video Game Theory Reader*. New York: Routledge, 2003, 223.

8 Ian Bogost, *Unit Operations: An Approach to Video game Criticism*. Cambridge, London: MIT Press, 2008, 98.

9 Kevin Williams, "Flattened Visions from Timeless Machines. History in the Mass Media," in Eds. Siân Nicholas, Tom O'Malley and Kevin Williams, *Reconstructing the Past. History in the Mass Media 1890–2005*. Abingdon and New York: Routledge, 2008, 17–20.

10 Christopher Grant, "Interview: Call of Duty: Black Ops producer Dan Bunting," *joystiq*, 28 May 2010, http://www.joystiq.com/2010/05/28/interview-call-of-duty-black-ops-producer-dan-bunting, accessed 20 September 2012.

11 Grant, "Interview."

12 Frasca, "Simulation vs. Narrative," 232.

13 All following observations are based on *CoDBo*'s single player campaign mode. While the multiplayer mode is certainly a worthy object of study in its own right, the constraints of this chapter lead to leaving this task for another essay.

14 Lorenz Engell, "Zeit und Zeichen, Welt und Wahl. Das amerikanische Fernsehen und der Kalte Krieg," *Archiv für Mediengeschichte*, 4 (2004): 222–224.

15 Jay David Bolter and Richard Grusin, *Remediation: Understanding New Media*. Cambridge, London: MIT Press, 2000, 194.

16 In the case of *Platoon* it is the soldiers' outfit that is "quoted." Concerning *Apocalypse Now* the quotation is of an even vaguer nature and touches on the depiction of the boat ride.

17 These range from the interpretation of the Vietnam War as a futile endeavor at the various attempts to revalue it in the context of the 1980s. For a discussion by the example of "the Vietnam War veteran" in movies and literature, see Mark Taylor, *The Vietnam War in History, Literature and Film*. Edinburgh: Edinburgh University Press, 2003, 131–145.

18 Also resulting from this is the rather lenient nature of the game. A source for caustic remarks on the part of "true gamers," which nonetheless makes *CoDBo* accessible to a large audience not trained in playing first person shooters, including hopeless cases like me.

19 James Newman, "The Myth of the Ergodic Video game. Some Thoughts on Player-character Relationships in Video games," *Game Studies 2* (2002), http://www.gamestudies.org/0102/newman/, accessed 20 September 2012.

20 Newman, "The Myth of the Ergodic Video game."

21 Considering the reaction of the Cuban government, this strategy has obviously proven to be highly effective. See, for example, Adam Gabbatt, "Call of Duty: Black Ops upsets Cuba with Castro Mission," *The Guardian*, 11 November 2010, http://www.guardian.co.uk/technology/2010/nov/11/call-of-duty-black-ops-cuba-castro, accessed 20 September 2012.

22 The design suggests this to be a still from an amateur film. This may count as a hint at the Zapruder footage in any case it constitutes a strong marker for authenticity and witnessing.

23 Nick Cowen, "Call Of Duty: Black Ops writer Interview: Craig Houston," *The Telegraph*, 25 November 2010, http://www.telegraph.co.uk/technology/video-games/8155075/Call-Of-Duty-Black-Ops-writer-interview-Craig-Houston.html, accessed 20 September 2012.

24 Unless a contemporary witness with military experience would happen to play the game. As it happens, such military advisors can be found among *CoDBo*s' staff and surely serve the purpose of ensuring the audience of the games' military accuracy.

25 For a discussion of the question of how combat is best to be represented (if that is possible at all), see Taylor, *The Vietnam War*, 13–18.

26 Eva Horn, *Der geheime Krieg. Verrat, Spionage und moderne Fiktion.*
    Frankfurt am Main: Fischer, 2007, 32–36.

27 For an overview and critical analysis of triumphalist takes on Cold War
    history, see Ellen Schrecker, Ed. *Cold War Triumphalism. The Misuse of
    History after the Fall of Communism.* New York: The New Press, 2004.

28 The game continuously switches perspective between Mason and other
    characters. The character of the soviet soldier Reznov suggests the flattening
    of ideological differences in the face of the universalism of the soldierly
    profession and fate.

29 For an explication of this term, see Nina B. Huntemann and Matthew
    Thomas Payne, "Introduction," in Eds. Nina B. Huntemann and Matthew
    Thomas Payne, *Joystick Soldiers. The Politics of Play in Military Video
    Games.* New York: Routledge, 2010, especially 3–6.

Works cited

Bogost, Ian. *Unit Operations. An Approach to Video game Criticism.* Cambridge,
    London: MIT Press, 2008.
Bolter, Jay David and Richard Grusin. *Remediation. Understanding New Media.*
    Cambridge, London: MIT Press, 2000.
Cowen, Nick. "Call Of Duty: Black Ops writer Interview: Craig Houston," *The
    Telegraph*, 25 November 2010, http://www.telegraph.co.uk/technology/video-
    games/8155075/Call-Of-Duty-Black-Ops-writer-interview-Craig-Houston.html,
    accessed 20 September 2012.
Crogan, Patrick. *Gameplay Mode. War, Simulation and Technoculture.*
    Minneapolis, MN and London: University of Minnesota Press, 2011.
Engell, Lorenz. "Zeit und Zeichen, Welt und Wahl. Das amerikanische Fernsehen
    und der Kalte Krieg," *Archiv für Mediengeschichte*, 4 (2004): 219–231.
Fischer, Thomas E. *Geschichte der Geschichtskultur. Über den öffentlichen
    Gebrauch von Vergangenheit von den antiken Hochkulturen bis zur
    Gegenwart.* Köln: Verlag Wissenschaft und Politik, 2000.
Frasca, Gonzalo. "Simulation vs. Narrative. Introduction to Ludology," in Eds.
    Mark J.P. Wolf and Bernard Perron, *The Video Game Theory Reader.* New York:
    Routledge, 2003, 221–235.
Grant, Christopher. "Interview: Call of Duty: Black Ops producer Dan Bunting,"
    joystiq, 28 May 2010, http://www.joystiq.com/2010/05/28/interview-call-of-
    duty-black-ops-producer-dan-bunting/, accessed 20 September 2012.
Horn, Eva. *Der geheime Krieg. Verrat, Spionage und moderne Fiktion.* Frankfurt
    am Main: Fischer, 2007.
Huntemann, Nina B. and Matthew Thomas Payne. "Introduction," in Eds. Nina
    B. Huntemann and Matthew Thomas Payne, *Joystick Soldiers. The Politics of
    Play in Military Video Games.* New York: Routledge, 2010, 1–18.
Krämer, Sybille. "Was haben Performativität und Medialität miteinander zu
    tun? Plädoyer für eine in der Aisthetisierung gründende Konzeption des
    Performativen," in Ed. Sybille Krämer, *Performativität und Medialität.*
    München: Wilhelm Fink Verlag, 2004, 13–33.

Mersch, Dieter. "Medialität und Undarstellbarkeit. Einleitung in eine 'negative' Medientheorie," in Ed. Sybille Krämer, *Performativität und Medialität*. München: Wilhelm Fink Verlag, 2004, 75–97.

Newman, James. "The Myth of the Ergodic Video game. Some Thoughts on Player-character Relationships in Video games," *Game Studies 2* (2002), http://www.gamestudies.org/0102/newman/, accessed 20 September 2012.

Pias, Claus. *Computer Spiel Welten*. Zürich: Diaphanes, 2010.

Schrecker, Ellen, Ed. *Cold War Triumphalism. The Misuse of History after the Fall of Communism*. New York: The New Press, 2004.

Taylor, Mark. *The Vietnam War in History, Literature and Film*. Edinburgh: Edinburgh University Press, 2003.

Williams, Kevin. "Flattened Visions from Timeless Machines: History in the Mass Media," in Eds. Siân Nicholas, Tom O'Malley and Kevin Williams, *Reconstructing the Past. History in the Mass Media 1890–2005*. Abingdon and New York: Routledge, 2008, 7–28.

Games cited

Call of Duty: Black Ops. Santa Monica, CA: Infinity Ward, Activision, 2010.

17

Refighting the Cold War: Video Games and Speculative History

Marcus Schulzke
University of Albany

The Cold War was one of the longest and most significant conflicts of the twentieth century, lasting from the end of the Second World War in 1945 until the collapse of the Soviet Union in 1991. The conflict played a decisive role in shaping the foreign policy of countries around the world, and it continues to have such a profound influence on domestic and international politics that this is often described as the post–Cold War era.[1] The Cold War was also a major cultural event. It was defined by persistent threats of total war and nuclear destruction that were never realized, but which were continually explored in popular media.[2] Although the Cold War is officially over, it continues to live on in popular culture. The events of the era and the threat of a catastrophic war are a recurring subject of popular media and have been especially prominent in recent video games.

This chapter will discuss three different ways in which the Cold War is depicted in video games. First, there are historical simulations, which re-create real events and locations. These similar to works of historical fiction in that they immerse players in fictional narratives that are closely modeled on historical facts and that accurately reproduce many of the elements of real events. Second, post-apocalyptic games, such as the games of the *Fallout* series, reimagine the Cold War in terms of the consequences of the nuclear war that might have happened. This type of game simulates the worst fears about nuclear war, the hope of fleeing the destruction by retreating underground, and what life in the present might have been like had the Cold War gone differently. Finally, Third World War games simulate the Cold War as the large-scale conventional war that NATO and Warsaw Pact countries were constantly preparing to fight. *World in Conflict* (2007), *Modern Warfare 2* (2009), and *Modern Warfare 3* (2011) follow narratives involving a Russian invasion of Western Europe and the United States. These games are especially interesting when they link the Cold War threat of invasion with the current fear of terrorism. In doing so, they attempt to make sense of the threats presented by the ongoing War on Terror by reframing them in terms of the more familiar Cold War threats. Each of these three types of games provides a different perspective on the Cold War, each with its own historiographical strengths and weaknesses.

Cold War video games also offer several contributions to our understanding of that period of history. First, they capture the subjective dimensions of the conflict. Briley reports that one of the greatest pedagogical challenges when teaching about the Cold War is giving students a sense of how the people who lived through the conflict experienced it.[3] Conveying a sense of the historical context is always important in the study of history, but it is especially important when dealing with the Cold War because the conflict was largely defined by subjective feelings, especially fear and a sense of uncertainty.[4] These experiences are difficult to reproduce through traditional historical narratives, but video games have the advantages of allowing players to explore the era as participants, rather than viewers.

Second, video games are a way of exploring counterfactuals about historical events. They can present the world as it might have been had different decisions been made at key junctures. This is especially advantageous when it comes to games about the Cold War, as the conflict was largely defined by threats that were never realized or that were only partially realized. Finally, Cold War games can have a normative function. They serve as a reminder of the potential costs of war, especially nuclear war—threats that continue to persist after the Cold War has ended. Games help to convey the lessons the era can teach about conflict resolution and therefore facilitate the appropriation of history for normative purposes.

Historical simulations

The first type of video game about the Cold War, historical simulation, involves the reenactment of real events and exploration of real locations in the context of fictional narratives. These games are much like pieces of historical fiction in film or literature. Although they involve fictional narratives and characters, they can be fairly accurate in re-creating the context and representing key events. This type of Cold War game is especially common among first person shooters. Because these games are set in a first person perspective, they are ideally suited for immersing players in a historical context and allowing them to exercise some control over events without fundamentally altering the nature of the conflict or changing the course of history. Such games show history from the perspective of a single person living during a different time period. Games set in the Vietnam War, such as *Vietcong* (2003), *Vietcong 2* (2005), *Battlefield Vietnam* (2004), and *Call of Duty: Black Ops* (2010) are examples of this type. They illustrate the characteristics of historical simulations, as well as their historiographical strengths and weaknesses.

Vietcong takes players through the jungle fighting against Vietcong (VC) insurgents that characterized much of the American war in Vietnam. Players participate in many of the activities a typical infantry soldier might have experienced. They go on patrols through the jungle, search for cave complexes, explore the networks of caves, search for hidden supplies in Vietnamese villages, and defend remote outposts from attack.[5] The Vietcong guerrillas emulate the tactics used by the real VC. They set traps, ambush the American patrols, fire from spider holes, and attempt to isolate and overrun small outposts. This makes them a much different type of enemy from the conventional soldiers usually encountered in first person shooters. The sequel, *Vietcong 2*, deviates from the popular image of jungle combat, as most of the game involves urban fighting, but shows the main locations and events of a real battle. During famous 1968 Tet Offensive, VC and North Vietnamese Army (NVA) soldiers surprised the American and Army of the Republic of Vietnam (ARVN) forces in Hue and took control of large parts of the city. Recapturing the city took over a month of intense urban fighting.[6] In *Vietcong 2* players take the role of a soldier in MACV (Military Assistance Command, Vietnam) who is caught up in the failed attempts to repel the attack on the city and then in the battle to retake it. Players fight house to house through Hue in a way that mirrors the actual battle. They are even involved in some of the major events of the battle, such as the defense of the MACV Compound that was one of the communists' central objectives, the fighting along the Truoi River, and the assault on the city's ancient citadel.

Battlefield Vietnam is a multiplayer game that depicts combat between US forces and their NVA and VC opponents in an array of jungle and urban settings. Because the game involves multiplayer combat, it tends to deviate more from historical accuracy than a scripted single player game. Nevertheless, *Battlefield Vietnam* still retains some degree of realism. The game is relatively accurate with respect to the weapons and fighting styles used by those on both sides.[7] In earlier games in the series, which were set during the Second World War, sides were relatively evenly matched. Each used comparable weapons and occupying interchangeable defensive structures. This symmetry is abandoned in *Battlefield Vietnam*, as US forces can rely on much more powerful weapons including air and ground support, just as they would have had during the actual conflict. To make up for this, the communist forces may employ some of the classic weapons of guerrilla warfare. Players choosing to take the role of VC or NVA soldiers may plant traps and create respawn points that allow players to enter the battle at unexpected locations on the map. The respawn points simulate tunnel exits and can be used to launch surprise incursions into American positions.

Finally, the missions of *Call of Duty: Black Ops* are partly set in the Vietnam War and partly consist in fictional covert operations in the Soviet Union, Cuba, and China (see also Reisner, Chapter 16). The overarching story is more removed from historical fact than the events of the *Vietcong* series, as it follows a fictional narrative about the development of biological weapons and mind control. However, most of the game's missions are based on historical events or re-create real locations. Among the many real events that are re-created for the game are a Central Intelligence Agency (CIA) operation to assassinate Castro, the Studies and Observation Group's (SOG) search for evidence of Soviet involvement in the Vietnam War, the Battle of Hue, and the Siege of Khe Sanh. By introducing players to each of these operations the game provides a broad overview of the many covert operations carried out by the American government during the 1960s.[8] Even the game's fictional events take place in real locations: the Soviet biological weapons development site on Vozrozhdeniya Island, the rocket launch facility at Baikonur Cosmodrome, a nuclear command bunker at Mount Yamantau, the Kowloon Walled City in Hong Kong, and the Vorkuta Gulag. Moreover, each of the environments was modeled on the real locations.[9]

Historical simulations' greatest strengths from a historiographical perspective are their ability to immerse players in convincing environments that allow players to reenact history. Players can imaginatively become part of a different historical context while playing these games. As these examples show, games have been especially strong in terms of re-creating some of the personal experiences of wars. This fits with a shift in contemporary military historiography. Many military historians have attempted to refocus research on wars from the great generals and campaigns to the experience of the common soldiers and of fighting.[10] However, the extent to which traditional historical narratives can re-create this experience is limited when it can only be conveyed in writing. Historical simulation video games are perfectly suited for capturing history as a lived experience; they immerse players in detailed, complex worlds that players can personally explore and interact with. Games cannot reproduce the intense emotions of the battlefield, but they can give players some sense of how historical conflicts have been fought. This is why war video games have been used extensively in military training (see Köstlbauer, Chapter 11 and Wackerfuss, Chapter 15).[11]

Combat in each of these games is stylized in a manner typical of the first person shooter genre. Enemies are relatively simplistic caricatures, players are able to withstand far more damage than ordinary people, and allies are often invulnerable. Nevertheless, the setting, activities, and the depictions of war are fairly realistic. They coincide with the experiences recounted by many historians and veterans who have written about the Vietnam War and the CIA's covert operations.[12] Moreover, these games capture many of the subjective challenges of the war: the difficulty of locating and fighting guerrillas, the constant danger of stumbling into a tripwire, or stepping into a punji pit, and the challenges of fighting at night or in tunnels. This reflects the developers' attention to historical accuracy when developing these games. Treyarch, the company that developed *Black Ops*, conducted extensive research on the weapons and battles of the Vietnam War, interviewed veterans of the war, including former members of SOG, and examined real locations.[13] The developers of *Battlefield Vietnam* attempted to accurately reproduce Vietnam's landscape and designed maps that would force players to fight at around twenty meters—the average range of gunfights during the war.[14]

Perhaps the most serious limitation of these games from a historiographical perspective is that they tend to overlook many unpleasant realities of war. One rarely sees noncombatants in these games and they almost always avoid any of the moral ambiguities of war. Players do not have to build relations with the locals, nor do they have to help the South Vietnamese develop infrastructure or political institutions. Instead, the games represent the Vietnam War and American covert operations as being solely military affairs with little reference to the political context in which the Cold War was fought. This reinforces the ideal of the depoliticized soldier that is a core value of the American military.[15] It also leads the games to make the same mistake as many politicians and military commanders of the time—the mistake of interpreting the Vietnam War and other foreign military operations as though they were solely military affairs with no political or economic dimension.[16] This is a critical oversight. In focusing on Cold War military conflicts, historical simulations refrain from making any deeper points about Vietnam or the Cold War. These issues are addressed more directly in the other two types of Cold War games.

Post-apocalyptic games

Games set in speculative timelines in which the world has been devastated by a catastrophic nuclear war or by a conventional world war between major powers do not represent real events, yet they can offer deeper insight into the Cold War mentality (see Schulzke, Chapter 17, and Knoblauch, Chapter 18). They capture the intense fear and paranoia of the Cold War era—the persistent threat of small events escalating into major conflicts, of foreign agents entering the United States, and of nuclear annihilation. The games of the *Fallout* franchise are prime examples of the post-apocalyptic type of Cold War games (see November, Chapter 19, and Cutterham, Chapter 20). These role-playing games take place in an imagined future in which much of the world has been destroyed by a nuclear war. Although the story of the apocalyptic war only emerges gradually over the course of the games and is never fully explained, it is described as a war over depleted natural resources which escalated into a nuclear war. Each of the games, *Fallout* (1997), *Fallout 2* (1998), *Fallout: Tactics* (2001), *Fallout 3* (2008), and *Fallout: New Vegas* (2010), as well as the many expansion packs available for these games are set in different areas of the United States in the postwar future. Throughout the games, players explore various regions of the post-apocalyptic wastes, learn about how nuclear war changed the country, and attempt to repair some of the damage.[17]

The image of the postwar world is based on the pervasive Cold War era fears about the prospects of nuclear annihilation. The games show the potential effects of the doctrine of Mutual Assured Destruction (MAD), which was the American doctrine of nuclear response during much of the Cold War.[18] Moreover, they do so in a way that challenges propaganda narratives of the period. The *Fallout* games are known for their cynical humor, which usually consists of seeing the terrible post-apocalyptic wasteland through the lens of Cold War propaganda that litters the wasteland. The prewar artifacts that embody the naïve optimism of 1950s popular culture, such as cartoons advising players to take cover under a desk to protect themselves against nuclear bombs, are juxtaposed against the harsh realities of a world devastated by war.

The games' settings and narratives are replete with the misconceptions and stereotypes that dominated American popular culture during the Cold War. For example, the United States wages its nuclear war against the Soviet Union and China, who are depicted as being each other's allies. An alliance between these countries was one of American strategists' greatest fears during the era.[19] However, this alliance was largely illusory; the countries' different strategic goals led them to be more often in conflict than in cooperation.[20] The games continually invoke the fear of the hidden enemy that is subverting the country from within. Throughout the games players find evidence of prewar spies operating with the United States, of invasion plans, and of enemy reconnaissance vehicles. There are also signs of the American government's secret responses: massive underground fallout shelters, advanced weapons facilities, and laboratories to test new weapons on unwilling human subjects. The paranoia of hidden enemies leads *Fallout* to mirror entertainment produced during the Cold War. Whitfield says of entertainment during this time that "Literature, movies, art, and the media—particularly the then-new form, television—consistently hammered the theme of an enemy from within, working to subvert the American Way of Life."[21] However, *Fallout* addresses these topics from a critical distance; its derisive, cynical humor persistently challenges these fears and makes them seem unbelievable.

Much like the historical simulation games discussed in the previous section, post-apocalyptic games can help players understand the subjective experiences of the Cold War. However, unlike the historical simulation games, which attempt to re-create real experiences, the experiences presented by apocalyptic games are the ineffable fears and dreams of a different time. The fear of nuclear annihilation is difficult to convey using traditional narrative techniques but it can be made more concrete when they are embodied in a simulation. This is especially important when dealing with the Cold War because it was largely defined by subjective feelings. As Fields argues, "the very real threat of nuclear war during this age led to a profound sense of anxiety: the fear that all national boundaries could be obliterated."[22] By exploring the fears of nuclear war while also referencing the Cold War culture and the propaganda that attempted to downplay the threat of nuclear weapons, the *Fallout* series invokes the anxieties of the era while also critiquing the political decisions that created the Cold War and the attempts to influence perceptions of the conflict.

Apocalyptic games can also serve a normative function. History is often described as being a source of wisdom or lessons, suggesting that the successes and failures of the past can be read as a guide to follow in the future.[23] Each of the important junctures in the Cold War that might have initiated a nuclear war, including USSR's first atomic bomb test, the Korean War, the Cuban Missile Crisis, the Vietnam War, the Soviet-Afghan War, and the successive advances in nuclear weapons and delivery systems by those on both sides of the conflict, offers lessons about the mistakes that led to the crises and the successes in resolving them.[24] *Fallout* reinforces these lessons by showing the dystopian world that might have existed if different decisions were made at these important junctures. The importance of avoiding conflict that could escalate into crisis is especially clear because the crisis that triggered the *Fallout* universe's nuclear war is a shortage of natural resources—a threat that persists after the Cold War and that seems likely to become an increasingly serious concern in the future. By connecting a historical security dilemma to a potential future security dilemma, *Fallout* encourages players to apply the lessons of the past.

World War III

The final type of Cold War game involves the simulation of a large-scale conventional war between the Soviet Union and the United States, which we might label the Third World War typology. Aside from possibility of a nuclear war, the most serious Cold War threat was that the Soviet Union would launch a massive conventional attack against Western Europe or North America. The most likely scenario was a Soviet invasion of Western Europe, which would probably have been made through the Fulda gap in central Germany.[25] An aggressive attack might have overwhelmed NATO forces in the region before the United States or Britain could mobilize the bulk of their forces and move these into position. Another possibility that appears in Cold War era entertainment but that is more fantasy than reality, was an invasion of North America. These two possibilities for conventional conflicts between the countries of NATO and the Soviet Union have been represented in many video games, including the *Modern Warfare* series and *World in Conflict*. These games combine both Third World War scenarios, as their narratives show simultaneous invasions of Western Europe and North America.

In *World in Conflict* and its expansion pack, *Soviet Assault* (2009), the USSR launches a surprise attack against NATO forces in Europe and manages to seize control of Berlin. Although *World in Conflict* follows American forces after the war has begun, the expansion pack allows players to take part in the early moments of the war by commanding Soviet forces as they knock down the Berlin wall and overrun the defenders of West Berlin. After taking over Germany, the USSR takes control of Germany and launches an amphibious attack on Marseilles to enter Southern France. However, these attacks are only diversions. As soon as American forces are deployed to Europe, the USSR launches its main attack on the United States by taking control of Seattle and invading Washington. Players are left to command the weak American forces against the invaders and can do little more than slow the Soviet advance eastward. Ultimately, the overwhelmed American defenders are forced to use a nuclear bomb to halt the Soviet invasion. They must then counterattack the

Soviets and force them out of Washington before Chinese reinforcements can join the invasion.

The games of the *Modern Warfare* series take place in a post–Cold War world with Russia, not the USSR, carrying out the invasions of Western Europe and the United States. The first game in the series is distinctly post–Cold War. It follows two story-arcs: an American invasion of an unnamed country in the Middle East and British special operatives' attempt to prevent Russian terrorists from launching a nuclear missile at the United States. However, the series' second and third games focus on a major war between the United States and Russia and make extensive use of Cold War themes. The central event of these games is a Soviet invasion of Maryland, Virginia, and New York. In *Modern Warfare 3*, the Russian attack on the United States continues and, despite suffering heavy losses, Russia launches a massive attack on Western Europe.

The invasion of the United States in both games is reminiscent of the 1984 film *Red Dawn*, in which the USSR and its Central American allies launch an attack on the American Southwest. *Modern Warfare* 2 even references the movie, as one of the missions defending an American neighborhood is called "Wolverines"—the name of the resistance group in the movie. Scholars generally view *Red Dawn* as a propaganda film that expressed neoconservative fears about the spread of communism.[26] Ryan and Kellner call the movie "Perhaps the most audacious anticommunist film of the era."[27] They argue that *Red Dawn*'s underlying message is that American authoritarianism is the world's only hope for defense against Soviet communism and that patriots must do whatever is necessary to win, even if this means renouncing liberal democratic values.

To some extent, the underlying message of *World in Conflict* and *Modern Warfare* seems to be the same as that which Ryan and Kellner find in *Red Dawn*. The games depict the Soviet Union and Russia as serious threats with the power to wage war against all of the major western powers simultaneously and on multiple fronts. Moreover, in both games players must detonate nuclear weapons in the United States to stall the Russian advance. This implies that even the destruction of nuclear war is preferable to being conquered. However, the game narratives are more complex than that of *Red Dawn*. They reflect a post–Cold War perspective, as the Cold War enemy is blended with a new terrorist enemy. In *World in Conflict* the Soviet forces begin to fragment as the younger soldiers resort to terrorist attacks against civilians, against the wishes of the older, more traditional soldiers. In *Modern Warfare*, the attack on the West is carried out by regular Russian military and Russian terrorists.

The Third World Wars presented in *World in Conflict* and *Modern Warfare* are at the same time representations of the imagined climax of the Cold

War and indications of shifting threat perceptions. The old enemy of the Cold War is used as a model for representing a new terrorist enemy that is still poorly understood. The games explore a historical counterfactual and its possible consequences while also appropriating that counterfactual as a way of making sense of the ongoing war on terror (see Apperley, Chapter 12). From a historiographical perspective these games are similar to the post-apocalyptic genre. They depict a fictional world based on real fears and simulate an alternate reality based on different decisions made at key junctures in the Cold War. However, they go beyond simply representing these fears by significantly transforming them in light of contemporary challenges. This makes Third World War games partly simulations of historical counterfactuals and partly attempts to mobilize history as a way of understanding the present.

Conclusion

The Cold War continues to have profound influence on the world even decades after the Soviet Union has ceased to exist. Many contemporary international political tensions, such as the influence of American hegemony and the strained relations between Russia and the NATO countries, are the result of actions taken during the conflict. Moreover, the conflict shaped the identities of the people whose countries seemed destined to destroy each other. Kackman observes that "The Cold War was not simply an external conflict that was the province of official politics; instead, it was a persistent presence that shaped immediate questions of national identity, civic responsibility, and the limits of cultural expression."[28] The number of video games that reflect on the Cold War are evidence of its lasting influence and the ongoing struggle to understand the conflict and its potential long-term consequences.

The games discussed in this chapter show both the strengths and the weaknesses of understanding history through video games. They have the advantages of capturing the subjective dimensions of the Cold War. They help players see the world from the perspective of the soldiers who fought in Vietnam and/or to glimpse the future imagined by those who faced the threat of nuclear war. They also help to explore counterfactuals about the conflict. These strengths are especially important when representing the Cold War because the conflict was largely defined by possibilities of world war and nuclear annihilation that were never realized. However, it is important to be aware of these games' potential for distorting history. The games tend to portray events of the Cold War through the lens of perceived modern threats.

This is especially clear in the connections the *Modern Warfare* series makes between the Russian military and terrorism. They also have the limitations of stylizing the events of the Cold War so that they fit with fictional narratives. Nevertheless, even these faults, which arise when reality and fantasy are blurred, are understandable when games represent a conflict that was partly caused by the challenge of distinguishing reality from fantasy.

Notes

1 David S. Painter, *The Cold War: An International History.* New York: Routledge, 1999.

2 Stephen J. Whitfield, *The Culture of the Cold War.* Baltimore, MA: Johns Hopkins University Press, 1996; Richard Alan Schwartz, *Cold War Culture: Media and the Arts, 1945–1990.* New York: Checkmark Books, 2000; Tom Engelhardt, *Cold War America and the Disillusioning of a Generation.* Amherst, MA: University of Massachusetts Press, 2007.

3 Ronald Briley, "Reel History and the Cold War," *OAH Magazine of History*, 8, no. 2 (1994): 19–22.

4 Whitfield, *The Culture of the Cold War;* Robert L. Scott, "Cold War and Rhetoric: Conceptually and Critically," in Eds. Martin J. Medhurst, Robert L. Ivie, Philip Wander and Robert L. Scott, *Cold War Rhetoric: Strategy, Metaphor, and Ideology.* East Lansing, MI: Michigan State University Press, 1990, 1–18.

5 Kyle Longley, *Grunts: The American Combat Soldier in Vietnam.* Armonk, NY: M.E. Sharpe, 2008.

6 For a detailed outline of the conflict, see George W. Smith, *The Siege of Hue.* Boulder, CO: Lynne Rienner, 1999.

7 Gordan Rottman, *The US Army in the Vietnam War 1965–1973.* New York: Osprey, 2006.

8 Robert M. Gillespie, *Black Ops, Vietnam: The Operational History of Macvsog.* Annapolis, MD: Naval Institue Press, 2011.

9 Video Games Daily, *Call of Duty: Black Ops—the Ultimate Interview*, 2 June 2010.

10 John Keegan, *The Face of Battle.* New York: Penguin, 1994a; *A History of Warfare.* New York: Vintage, 1994b; Martin van Creveld, *The Culture of War.* New York: Presidio Press, 2008; Juliet Barker, *Agincourt: Henry V and the Battle that Made England.* New York: Little, Brown, and Company, 2005.

11 Ed Halter, *From Sun Tzu to XBox: War and Video Games.* New York: Thunder's Mouth Press, 2006.

12 Gillespie, *Black Ops, Vietnam.*

13 Video Games Daily, *The Ultimate Interview.*

14 Planet Battlefield. Battlefield: Vietnam Interview, http://planetbattlefield. gamespy.com/View.php?view=Interviews.Detail&id=13.

15 Samuel P. Huntington, *The Soldier and the State: The Theory and Politics of Civil-Military Relations*. Cambridge, MA: Harvard University Press, 1959; "Reforming Civil-Military Relations," in Eds. Larry Diamond and Marc F. Plattner, *Civil Military Relations and Democracy*. Baltimore, MA: Johns Hopkins University Press, 1996.

16 Lewis Sorley, *A Better War: The Unexamined Victories and Final Tragedy of America's Last Years in Vietnam*. New York: Harcourt Brace & Company, 1999.

17 Marcus Schulzke, "Moral Decision Making in Fallout," *Game Studies*, 9, no. 2 (2009), http://gamestudies.org/0902/articles/schulzke.

18 Herman Kahn, *On Thermonuclear War*. Princeton, NJ: Princeton University Press, 1960.

19 Matthew J. Ouimet, *The Rise and Fall of the Brezhnev Doctrine in Soviet Foreign Policy*. Chapel Hill, NC: The University of North Carolina Press, 2003, 17.

20 Adam B. Ulam, *The Communists: The Story of Power and Lost Illusions 1948–1991*. New York: Charles Scribner's Sons, 1992.

21 Whitfield, *The Culture of the Cold War*, vii.

22 Douglas Field, "Introduction," in Ed. Douglas Field, *American Cold War Culture*. Edinburgh: Edinburgh University Press, 2005, 7.

23 Michael Howard, *The Lessons of History*. New Haven, CT: Yale University Press, 1991; Will Durant and Ariel Durant, *The Lessons of History*. New York: Simon & Schuster, 2010.

24 Thomas C. Reed and Danny B. Stillman, *The Nuclear Express: A Political History of the Bomb and Its Proliferation*. Minneapolis, MN: Zenith Press, 2009.

25 Richard Felix Staar, *Foreign Policies of the Soviet Union*. Stanford, CA: Hoover Press, 1991; William P. Mako, *U.S. Ground Forces and the Defense of Central Europe*. Washington, D.C: The Brookings Institution, 1983.

26 Ben Dickenson, *Hollywood's New Radicalism: War, Globalisation, and the Movies from Reagan to George W. Bush*. London: I.B. Taurus & Co. Ltd, 2006; Harvey Roy Greenberg, "Dangerous Recuperations: Red Dawn, Rambo, and the New Decaturism," *Journal of Popular Film & Television*, 15, no. 2 (1987): 60–70; *Screen Memories: Hollywood Cinema on the Psychoanalytic Couch*. New York: Columbia University Press, 1994; Eric Lichtenfeld, *Action Speaks Louder: Violence, Spectacle, and the American Action Movie*. Middletown, CT: Wesleyan University Press, 2007.

27 Michael Ryan and Douglas Kellner, *Camera politica: The Politics and Ideology of Contemporary Hollywood Film*. Bloomington, IN: Indiana University Press, 1988, 213.

28 Michael Kackman, *Citizen Spy: Television, Espionage, and Cold War Culture*. Minneapolis, MN: University of Minnesota Press, 2005, xxvii.

Works cited

Barker, Juliet. *Agincourt: Henry V and the Battle that Made England*. New York: Little, Brown, and Company, 2005.

Briley, Ronald. "Reel History and the Cold War," *OAH Magazine of History*, 8, no. 2 (1994): 19–22.

Creveld, Martin van. *The Culture of War*. New York: Presidio Press, 2008.

Daly, Gregory. *Cannae: The Experience of Battle in the Second Punic War*. New York: Routledge, 2002.

Dickenson, Ben. *Hollywood's New Radicalism: War, Globalisation, and the Movies from Reagan to George W. Bush*. London: I.B. Taurus & Co, 2006.

Durant, Will and Ariel Durant. *The Lessons of History*. New York: Simon & Schuster, 2010.

Engelhardt, Tom. *Cold War America and the Disillusioning of a Generation*. Amherst, MA: University of Massachusetts Press, 2007.

Ferguson, Niall. "Introduction," in Ed. Niall Ferguson, *Virtual History: Alternatives and Counterfactuals*. New York: Basic Books, 1997, 1–90.

Field, Douglas. "Introduction," in Ed. Douglas Field, *American Cold War Culture*. Edinburgh: Edinburgh University Press, 2005.

Gillespie, Robert M. *Black Ops, Vietnam: The Operational History of Macvsog*. Annapolis, MD: Naval Institue Press, 2011.

Greenberg, Harvey Roy. "Dangerous Recuperations: Red Dawn, Rambo, and the New Decaturism," *Journal of Popular Film & Television*, 15, no. 2 (1987): 60–70.

Greenberg, Harvey Roy. *Screen Memories: Hollywood Cinema on the Psychoanalytic Couch*. New York: Columbia University Press, 1994.

Halter, Ed. *From Sun Tzu to XBox: War and Video Games*. New York: Thunder's Mouth Press, 2006.

Howard, Michael. *The Lessons of History*. New Haven, CT: Yale University Press, 1991.

Huntington, Samuel P. *The Soldier and the State: The Theory and Politics of Civil-Military Relations*. Cambridge, MA: Harvard University Press, 1959.

Huntington, Samuel P. "Reforming Civil-Military Relations," in Eds. Larry Diamond and Marc F. Plattner, *Civil Military Relations and Democracy*. Baltimore, MA: Johns Hopkins University Press, 1996, 9–17.

Kackman, Michael. *Citizen Spy: Television, Espionage, and Cold War Culture*. Minneapolis, MN: University of Minnesota Press, 2005.

Kahn, Herman. *On Thermonuclear War*. Princeton, NJ: Princeton University Press, 1960.

Keegan, John. *The Face of Battle*. New York: Penguin, 1994a.

Keegan, John. *A History of Warfare*. New York: Vintage, 1994b.

Lichtenfeld, Eric. *Action Speaks Louder: Violence, Spectacle, and the American Action Movie*. Middletown, CT: Wesleyan University Press, 2007.

Longley, Kyle. *Grunts: The American Combat Soldier in Vietnam*. Armonk, NY: M.E. Sharpe, 2008.

Mako, William P. *U.S. Ground Forces and the Defense of Central Europe*. Washington, D.C.: The Brookings Institution, 1983.

Ouimet, Matthew J. *The Rise and Fall of the Brezhnev Doctrine in Soviet Foreign Policy*. Chapel Hill, NC: The University of North Carolina Press, 2003.

Painter, David S. *The Cold War: An International History*. New York: Routledge, 1999.

Planet Battlefield. "Battlefield: Vietnam Interview," http://planetbattlefield. gamespy.com/View.php?view=Interviews.Detail&id=13, accessed 1 January 2013.

Reed, Thomas C. and Danny B. Stillman. *The Nuclear Express: A Political History of the Bomb and Its Proliferation*. Minneapolis, MN: Zenith Press, 2009.

Reeve, John and David Stevens. *The Face of Naval Battle: The Human Experience of Modern War at Sea*. Crows Nest, NSW: Allen & Unwin, 2003.

Ryan, Michael and Douglas Kellner. *Camera Politica: The Politics and Ideology of Contemporary Hollywood Film*. Bloomington, IN: Indiana University Press, 1988.

Schulzke, Marcus. "Moral Decision Making in Fallout," *Game Studies*, 9, no. 2 (2009), http://gamestudies.org/0902/articles/schulzke, accessed 14 August 2012.

Schwartz, Richard Alan. *Cold War Culture: Media and the Arts, 1945–1990*. New York: Checkmark Books, 2000.

Scott, Robert L. "Cold War and Rhetoric: Conceptually and Critically," in Eds. Martin J. Medhurst, Robert L. Ivie, Philip Wander, and Robert L. Scott, *Cold War Rhetoric: Strategy, Metaphor, and Ideology*. East Lansing, MI: Michigan State University Press, 1990, 1–18.

Smith, George W. *The Siege of Hue*. Boulder, CO: Lynne Rienner, 1999.

Sorley, Lewis. *A Better War: The Unexamined Victories and Final Tragedy of America's Last Years in Vietnam*. New York: Harcourt Brace & Company, 1999.

Staar, Richard Felix. *Foreign Policies of the Soviet Union*. Stanford, CA: Hoover Press, 1991.

Ulam, Adam B. *The Communists: The Story of Power and Lost Illusions, 1948–1991*. New York: Charles Scribner's Sons, 1992.

Video Games Daily. *Call of Duty: Black Ops—the Ultimate Interview*, 2 June 2010, http://video gamesdaily.com/interviews/201006/call-of-duty-black-ops-the-ultimate-interview/2/, accessed 2 August 2012.

Weber, Max. "Objective Possibility and Adequate Causation in Historical Explanation," in Eds. Edward Shils and Henry Finch, *The Methodology of the Social Sciences*. Glencoe, IL: Free Press, 1949, 164–188.

Whitfield, Stephen J. *The Culture of the Cold War*. Baltimore, MA: Johns Hopkins University Press, 1996.

Games cited

Battlefield Vietnam. Redwood City, CA: DICE, Electronic Arts, PC, 2004.

Call of Duty: Black Ops. Santa Monica, CA: Infinity Ward, Activision, 2010.

Call of Duty: Modern Warfare 2. Santa Monica, CA: Infinity Ward, Activision, 2009.

Call of Duty: Modern Warfare 3. Santa Monica, CA: Infinity Ward, Activision, 2011.

Fallout. Beverley Hills, CA: Interplay Entertainment, 1997.

Fallout 2. Beverley Hills, CA: Interplay Entertainment, 1998.

Fallout 3. Rockville, MD. Bethesda Softworks, 2008.

Fallout: New Vegas. Rockville, MD: Bethesda Softworks, 2010.

Fallout Tactics. Rockville, MD: Bethesda Softworks, 2001.

Vietcong. Texas: Pterodon, Gathering of Developers, 2003.

Vietcong 2. Novato, CA: Pterodon, 2K Games, 2005.

World in Conflict. Montreal: Massive Entertainment, Ubisoft, 2007.

PART FIVE

Looking Back on the End of the World

This last part examines what may well seem on the surface to be an unusual way of looking at history—by analyzing predictions of the future. However, as the following essays demonstrate, depictions of the future are very often based on a particular understanding of the past, which means that for our purposes such predictions, or future histories, are not substantially very different from the counterfactual histories discussed throughout other chapters of this book. They not only reveal historical reasoning, thus exposing an understanding of history as a process, but they can also tell us much about how ideas of the past affect our imagination of the future.

Beginning with Knoblauch's study of representations of Nuclear War in video games, the section opens by looking at imaginations of "the end" through nuclear annihilation, and reflects on games as a way of engaging with the past to imagine a counterfactual future. This emphasis on counterfactuals is continued by November, who discusses the counterfactual world of *Fallout*'s hypothetical dystopian future; arguing that the world of *Fallout* contains within it important lessons about our own past. Likewise, Cutterham explores *Fallout 3*'s continuation of the two earlier games, reading into this future, postnuclear world the postwar optimism of 1950s America. As he sifts through the charred remains of 2077, he finds an ironic reflection of 1950s America lurking beneath the surface. Finally, looking at Armageddon in its Biblical sense, Evans argues that the future technology of *Xenosaga* turns full circle from the end to the beginning, embracing ideas drawn from ancient religion in its imagination of the future. Overall, then, the essays in this section suggest that the counterfactual imagination does not concern itself only with parallel or potential worlds, but future ones too, and when it does so, the imagined world is always an expression of the logic and historical consciousness of our own time.

Recommended books to understand more about counterfactual/ virtual history:

Blight, James G., Janet M Lang, and David A Welch. *Virtual JFK: Vietnam If Kennedy Had Lived.* Lanham, MD: Rowan & Littlefield, 2010.

Ferguson, Niall, Ed. *Virtual History: Alternatives and Counterfactuals.* London: Picador, 1997.

Hawthorn, Geoffrey. *Plausible Worlds: Possibility and Understanding in History and the Social Sciences.* Cambridge: Cambridge University Press, 1993.

Roberts, Andrew, Ed. *What Might Have Been? Leading Historians on Twelve "What Ifs" of History.* London: Orion, 2005.

Staley, David J. *History and Future: Using Historical Thinking to Imagine the Future.* Plymouth: Lexington Books, 2007.

Tetlock, Philip Eyrikson and Geoffrey Parker, Eds. *Unmaking the West: What-If? Scenarios That Rewrite World History.* Ann Arbor, MI: University of Michigan Press, 2006.

18

Strategic Digital Defense: Video Games and Reagan's "Star Wars" Program, 1980–1987

William M. Knoblauch
Finlandia University

Introduction

In early 1983, US President Ronald Reagan's reelection was uncertain. In addition to an ongoing economic recession, Reagan's nuclear arms buildup proved unpopular, and triggered the largest antinuclear protests in American history. By January 1983 the President's approval ratings had plummeted to only 35 percent. On March 8, Reagan accused the Soviet Union of being the "focus of evil in the modern world," and this "Evil Empire" speech further alarmed those concerned about nuclear war. What Reagan needed was a game changer: something to halt the antinuclear movement's momentum, co-opt its peaceful message, and transform his image from a hardliner to a peacekeeper. On 23 March 1983, Reagan accomplished all three goals when, in a televised address, he announced his dream of space-based nuclear defense. He called upon the "scientific community ... those that gave us nuclear weapons," to build systems to render such weapons "impotent and obsolete." This logic contradicted the Cold War nuclear strategy of deterrence—the idea that comparable levels of American and Soviet nuclear weapons would deter a nuclear war. Put simply, Reagan's plan might actually destabilize deterrence, and his advisors cautioned against the plan. Undeterred, Reagan launched what became known as the Strategic Defense Initiative (SDI).[1]

What would SDI look like? Reagan offered no real specifics, but others dreamt big. The most futuristic ideas came from General Daniel O. Graham's High Frontier Inc., a non-government organization that, since the 1970s, had been promoting Anti-Ballistic Missile (ABM) systems and Ballistic Missile Defense (BMD) research and development. High Frontier argued that SDI could utilize atomic-powered lasers, space satellites, and kinetic energy beams to intercept Intercontinental Ballistic Missiles (ICBMs). American scientists, the very group Reagan called upon to make nuclear weapons "impotent and obsolete," scoffed at these suggestions. When they argued that such SDI visions resembled George Lucas' 1977 sci-fi film *Star Wars,* the pejorative name stuck. Many scientists rejected "Star Wars" because its very development would fuel the arms race, and almost immediately SDI became a contested political issue.[2]

SDI remained an uncertain proposition, but this lasers-in-space premise was ideal for 1980s video games. Video games and SDI shared similarities. Both were products of the Cold War, and both had their earliest prototypes built in US laboratories.[3] Many late Cold War video games were militaristic in nature, such as *Space Invaders*, *Defender*, *Battlezone*, and *Combat*. By the time of Reagan's SDI announcement, the American public had been imbibing video games featuring SDI-like weaponry for years. By the early 1980s, even president Reagan saw video games as a gateway to new, real technological innovations that might make America's military stronger. Consider Reagan's speech at Disney's EPCOT center, delivered on the same day of his famed "Evil Empire" speech, just two weeks before his SDI announcement:

> I recently learned something quite interesting about video games. Many young people have developed incredible hand, eye, and brain coordination in playing these games. [Just] watch a 12-year old take evasive action and score multiple hits while playing Space Invaders, and you will appreciate the skills of tomorrow's pilot. What I'm saying is that right now you're being prepared for tomorrow in many ways, and in ways that many of us who are older cannot fully comprehend.[4]

Reagan may not have fully comprehended how video games might influence future military technologies, but like his hopes for SDI, he remained optimistic that if Americans could dream of futuristic technologies, they could also realize them.

My thesis is simple: 1980s video games helped Americans envision what SDI might look like, and in the process made otherwise futuristic notions about SDI and space-based missile defense more plausible. These games distilled the arcane terminology of Cold War nuclear weaponry—such as Intercontinental Ballistic Missiles, Smart Bombs, and BMD systems—and helped SDI take hold in the public's imagination. By simulating how SDI might look and operate, video games allowed Americans to play missile defense and demystified the complexities of an otherwise highly technical proposal. By 1987, the pro-SDI organization High Frontier Inc. recognized video games' appeal, and helped to create *High Frontier*, a game that simulated SDI funding, research, development, and deployment. By the late 1980s, SDI proponents were using video games as propaganda tools.

To show the curious relationship between SDI and video games, this essay is organized into four sections. The first section begins with a brief recap of ABMs up until 1980 and shows how the arcade game *Missile Command* appropriated a ground-based ABM system to shoot down Cold War nuclear weapons. The second section examines *Wargames*, a game released shortly after Reagan's announcement, and which incorporated SDI-like technologies. The third section examines games based specifically on SDI, such as the appropriately titled *Strategic Defense Initiative*. The final section focuses on the game *High Frontier*. Part playable simulation, part propaganda piece, *High Frontier* was part of a media campaign to raise public support for Reagan's program. By the late 1980s, public support for SDI waned, but the decade's video games are cultural reminders of SDI initial promise for space-based missile defense.

Cold War missile defense and *Missile Command*

Like previous military innovations, people dreamt of SDI well before its realization. In *The Rise of American Airpower*, historian Michael Sherry argues that for centuries, from the Greek mythological figure of Icarus, to Leonardo da Vinci's Renaissance-era sketches, to Victor Hugo's 1864 speculations of aerial warfare, people dreamed of flight. In 1908, the Wright Brothers turned those dreams into a reality, and military applications almost immediately followed. Atomic weapon development followed a similar trajectory. Manhattan Project scientists built the first atomic bombs in 1945, but writer H. G. Wells imagined such weapons decades earlier. Best known for his 1898 alien invasion tale *War of the Worlds*, Wells suggested in his 1914 sci-fi story "The World Set Free" that atomic weapons and their threat of global extinction could lead to world peace.[5] The Cold War proved that such predictions were overly optimistic, and in the 1950s space-based super-weapons became popular in pop culture. Magazines like *Astounding Science Fiction* thrilled young readers with stories of space warfare and atomic attacks, while comic books popularized radioactivity's supposed mutative powers through atomic-heroes such as *The Amazing Spiderman, The Incredible Hulk,* and *X-Men.* In the 1960s, *Star Trek* brought space weapons to American television, and in the 1970s sci-fi films, especially George Lucas' *Star Wars* (1977), proved to be a profitable film genre. Yet it was a 1940s film that first depicted SDI technologies. In *Murder in the Air* a young Hollywood actor named Ronald Reagan starred as "Brass Bancroft," a secret agent seeking the "Inertia Projector," an energy beam that could defend against airborne attacks and become an instrument of peace. Forty years later, Reagan became president, and implemented a similar sounding program to protect Americans from nuclear weapons.[6]

Despite these fictional imaginings, ABM was more than mere fantasy. The first ABMs, which were ground-based missiles that would intercept incoming enemy missiles, emerged during the Eisenhower administration (1953–1961). In the 1960s, President Lyndon B. Johnson (1963–1969) approved studies on laser technologies, as well as the "Sentinel" research program for BMD. Richard M. Nixon (1969–1974) renamed the program "Safeguard," and despite technological improvements, bargained it away during his Strategic Arms Limitation Talks (SALT) with the Soviets. Nixon's agreement to limit ABM deployment and development enraged many hardliners in Washington DC who remained convinced that the Soviets were secretly developing ABMs and seeking global domination. These fears took on a new urgency when, in December of 1979, the Soviet Union invaded Afghanistan. This military action shocked the world and helped propel Ronald Reagan into the presidency. Reagan had campaigned on promises to stand strong against communism and renew ABM research and development, and as president he made good on such promises.[7]

It was in the wake of these events that Atari manager Steve Calfee tasked programmer Dave Theurer to create a missile defense game. The result was 1980's *Missile Command*, a fast-paced, fun, and accurate representation of ABM systems and Cold War weaponry. Initially, the game challenged players to operate an ABM system to defend six California coastal cities—including Los Angeles, San Francisco, Santa Barbara, San Luis Obispo, San Diego, and Eureka—against a nuclear attack. Fearing too much controversy, Theurer abandoned the use of actual cities; he also toned down the game's first, far more provocative title suggestions, including "Ground Zero," "The End," and "Armageddon."[8] In addition to these alterations, Theurer broke convention again when he abandoned the ubiquitous joystick for a track ball controller, which allowed for quicker cursor movement on the screen. Appropriately for the game's militaristic tone, the trackball resembled interfaces common in military aircraft intercept interfaces. According to one recruiter, scouting in a video game arcade nonetheless, the "multi-directional locater ball on the *Missile Command* game is pretty close to the system I use for air defense ... enemy aircraft [are] defined on the screen by radar. You have your sight as an electronic cursor directed by the ball. You push a button, the missiles fire, and 'poof' no more aircraft."[9]

In addition to realistic hardware, *Missile Command* incorporated Cold War nuclear weapons. The game's incoming ICBMs provide the most common threat, and when a missile reaches its target, the explosion produces a visible mushroom cloud, the symbol of atomic destruction. Atomic bombs are another constant threat, and in later levels satellites drop "smart bombs" that evade an ABM system's fire. *Missile Command* even included Multiple Independent Reentry Vehicles, or MIRVs. First introduced in the early 1960s, MIRVs are multiple warheads placed on a single missile, like a nuclear shotgun blast. In *Missile Command's* later levels, seemingly single ICBMs split mid-screen into multiple (MIRVed) warheads.[10] Theurer envisioned even more nuclear weapons that never made the game's final cut, such as nuclear submarines that would "pop up and shoot missiles" and "railroads haul[ing] missiles between the cities and the bases," both ideas with real Cold War roots. Submarine Launched Ballistic Missiles (SLBMs) had been a reality since the Eisenhower administration, and Theurer's rail-transported nukes recalled late 1970s plans to transport new and controversial "MX" (i.e. Missile Experimental) nuclear missiles on underground rail tracks. Indeed, the MX was a major public relations issue near the end of the Carter presidency (1977–1981). Despite technological constraints of the early 1980s, *Missile Command* remains a fairly accurate representation of the period's nuclear arsenal.[11]

Missile Command's ominous end-screen reflected late Cold War nuclear fears. In the 1980s, arcade gamers became well acquainted with the inevitable "Game Over" screen, but *Missile Command's* ending was different. When players finally succumb to this nuclear onslaught, instead of a "Game Over" sign, they encounter an ominous, flashing "The End" message that fills the screen. The choice of terms, remembers Theurer, was conscious: "The final lesson [of *Missile Command* was] that nobody wins a nuclear war, and that's why we have 'THE END' explode to fill the screen, after all the cities are gone." Such pessimism reflected a widespread belief that any nuclear exchange might escalate to full-blown Armageddon. *Missile Command* hit arcades just as the Nuclear Freeze campaign, the largest antinuclear movement in American history, was gaining momentum. Such fears made Reagan's SDI proposal—with its promise to protect Americans against a nuclear attack—all the more appealing. It did not take long for video games to build on *Missile Command's* ground-based ABM gameplay and incorporate SDI-like systems and defend against a nuclear attack from space.[12]

Wargames

Released less than three months after Reagan's SDI announcement, the 1983 motion picture *Wargames* achieved box office success because of its timely combination of atomic anxiety and video game tech. The film featured Matthew Broderick and Ally Sheedy, two teens who download a computer game entitled "Global Thermonuclear War." The film resonated with 1980s teens' fascination with emerging computer and video game tech, but also plagued by nuclear fears.[13] In *Wargames*, Broderick's character uses a phone line to "hack" into a game developer's network to download "Global Thermonuclear War"—a curious practice in a film that predated any workable public internet infrastructure—but discovers that the "game" is actually a realistic military wargame simulation that threatens to trigger an actual nuclear war. *Wargames'* finale was especially memorable. Set in the North American Aerospace Defense Command (NORAD) center, it showed how America's "Defense Readiness Condition" (i.e. DEFCON) elevates from five (relative peace) to one (global warfare) as the nuclear threat increases. The finale features flashing radar screens showing the United States being repeatedly obliterated in nuclear simulations as actors watch in awe. The film's concluding message, delivered from a computer named "Joshua," is that the "only way to win" a global thermonuclear war is "not to play"—a politically pacifist message during a tense atomic period.[14]

Wargames earned box office and critical success just as space-based missile defense proponents were becoming more vocal. Daniel O. Graham's High Frontier Inc. offered the most futuristic vision of space-based BMD. Two books, *A Defense That Defends: Blocking Nuclear Attack* and *High Frontier* (both published in 1983), explained how a "true defense" based in space might include a "manned space station in low Earth orbit" and some "development work on reliable, high-capacity energy systems in space." In short, in the early 1980s, High Frontier Inc. re-conceptualized how a space-based BMD program might look and function. Ground-based ABMs were a thing of the past; now, space-based BMD, like those planned for Reagan's SDI program, held the promise of future nuclear salvation.[15]

Produced for the Colecovision and Atari 800 home consoles, and based on the film of the same name, *Wargames* (1984) was the first game to incorporate SDI as a gameplay element. *Wargames* is not the most accurate conversion, as it abandons any antiwar message, but it does keep the film's giant NORAD screens, which split the United States into six different playable sections. Each map sector has a corresponding DEFCON meter, signifying the threat level of attack (five being low, and one high). Gamers must read these DEFCON meters and respond to enemy attacks. *Wargames* plays much like *Missile Command*, but incorporates SDI-like elements. In *Missile Command*, players only operate a ground-based ABM system; in *Wargames*, players have multiple countermeasures to stop different attacks: Jetfighters can scramble and destroy enemy planes; ground-based ABMs intercept incoming ICBMs; submarines engage with approaching enemy subs (which, if left unchecked, launch SLBMs); and finally, satellites with lasers. *Missile Command* had satellites, but they only dropped bombs. In *Wargames*, satellites are high-powered, laser-shooting super-weapons that can destroy any enemy threat. *Wargames* suggests that by 1984, ideas about ABM systems had evolved. Just as ABM systems appeared in *Missile Command*, *Wargames*' satellite weapon showed that after High Frontier's propaganda and Reagan's SDI announcement, space-based missile defense was becoming a popularly accepted idea.

Wargames may play like *Missile Command*, but the two games vary drastically in how they end. In *Missile Command*, gamers are ultimately overwhelmed by incoming ICBMs and meet Theurer's "THE END" message. *Wargames* is different. If any section of the United States is overwhelmed by enemy forces, and its threat level remains at DEFCON 1 for too long, the United States engages in a nuclear counterattack, and the game ends; but players who assuage the incoming attack long enough can avoid an American nuclear launch and win the game. The implied message, then, is that in the right hands, an effective SDI system can prevent nuclear war. In reality, the notion that a workable SDI system would perfectly defend against a nuclear launch was highly questionable. Still, Reagan's "peace shield" found an early representation in *Wargames*, and would continue to appear, in more complex forms, in later video games.

Strategic Defense Initiative
and *Missile Defense 3-D*

By 1987, thanks to organizations like High Frontier and the official government Strategic Defense Initiative Organization (SDIO), public perceptions of what a workable SDI program became more complex and technical. "Star Wars" might include "kinetic energy" vehicles, atomic lasers, and perhaps a "manned space station" in low Earth orbit. Any viable system would defend Americans in a three-tier defensive schema: an initial "boost phase," to shoot down vulnerable low-flying ICBMs; a middle "midcourse intercept phase," to intercept missiles in space; and a final "reentry phase." High Frontier Inc. first visually illustrated a three-tier plan in their 1984 television documentary *A Defense that Defends*. The documentary featured actor Lorne Greene— who played "Commander Adama" in the late 1970s sci-fi series *Battlestar Galactica*—and included computer-generated graphic depictions of this "three tier" system, complete with ground-based ABM guns, space-based lasers, and high-tech satellites.[16] These computer-generated graphics did not depict reality, and the White House continually refused to confirm High Frontier's optimistic predictions; instead, the SDIO chose to publicize SDI's moderate technological advances. For example, the successful laboratory test of a "railgun" prototype, a compact cannon that shot metal projectiles along a rail with enough force to pierce a sheet of metal, was a far cry from kinetic energy beams. Still, with SDI skepticism remaining high, the government needed to tout progress, however elementary. As government support for futuristic SDI proposals waned, video games retained both SDI's multi-tiered schema and most futuristic promises of space-based weaponry.[17]

In 1987, Sega released two SDI-themed games that reflected these SDI elements. The first, *Strategic Defense Initiative*, was a coin-op in which players defended against ICBMs in a multi-tiered SDI system. In the first "Offensive" stage, gamers guided a satellite through space debris to shoot down ICBMs and other obstacles. To navigate levels, gamers used a trackball and a joystick—the trackball targeting missiles, and the joystick navigating the satellite. If players miss any missiles, they play a "defensive" stage in which dozens of missiles descend onto Earth. Players must frantically fire particle beams to destroy these ICBMs and protect the planet. Unlike the ground-based ABM system of *Missile Command*, or the multi-weapon defensive arsenal of *Wargames*, *Strategic Defense Initiative* remains firmly grounded in 1980s SDI imagery. It uses satellite laser beams exclusively, and mimicked SDI proposals for phases of missile defense.

In another 1987 SDI-themed Sega release, *Missile Defense 3-D*, players control a satellite that must intercept Intermediate Range Ballistic Missiles (IRBMs, aka Cruise Missiles) and ICBMs. *Missile Defense 3-D's* interface abandons the trackball for a light gun to shoot down missiles. Still, the game maintains the three-tier schema of missile defense. Players first face "Cruise Missiles," a real class of IRBMs that in the mid-1980s were stationed throughout Western Europe, and which were central to Reagan and Gorbachev's 1987 Intermediate Range Nuclear Forces (INF) talks. IRBMs not intercepted in the "boost phase" can still be shot down in the next phase, categorized in *Missile Defense 3-D* as "the pole," (i.e. the North Pole). During the Cold War, the US Strategic Air Command (SAC) deployed atomic bombers to fly patterns outside of Soviet airspace in the Arctic Circle. In the missile age, ICBMs were plotted to fly over the arctic pole, the shortest distance to their targets. Appropriately, *Missile Defense 3-D's* "Pole" level features low-flying missiles over polar crevasses. Remaining missiles must be shot down in the third "re-entry phase," simplified in *Missile Defense 3-D* to the "just before" phase. In later levels, ICBMs replace IRBMs, and players' perspectives shift into outer space; gamers now see the "Pole" from "Space." Gamers adept enough to destroy all missiles are rewarded with a special "laser," signifying another "life," or another play. Players lose a life if ICBMs turn toward the screen and "hit" you, the satellite weapon. Lose all your satellites, and game ends with the message "Your space lasers have been destroyed." If only a single missile hits your city, the screen shakes and fades to red, and a final screen reminds players that when it comes to nuclear warfare, "one is all it takes."[18]

High Frontier

By 1987, it was becoming clear that SDI technologies might take a lot longer to create than anticipated. Scientists, especially Union of Concerned Scientists (UCS) members like Carl Sagan, successfully discredited SDI in newspaper op-ed pieces, university speaking tours, televised documentaries, and in Congressional testimonies. Sagan believed that the Soviets could defeat any SDI program by simply sending missile decoys to overwhelm the system. These insights had merit. Reagan's science advisor George Keyworth may have publicly supported SDI, but privately even he doubted that "solar-powered satellites" or "kinetic energy" proposals were realistic.[19] By late 1987, the Strategic Defense Initiative Organization (SDIO), the government organization Reagan tasked with creating SDI, scaled back the program's promises; instead of a peace shield, SDI would only enhance deterrence and protect US satellites.

Even though the SDIO scaled back SDI promises, High Frontier continued their campaign to boost public SDI support. When Reagan first announced SDI, High Frontier Inc. had already raised over a quarter of a million dollars for space-based BMD promotion. By 1985, at the peak of their publicity campaign, High Frontier had published books, created commercials, produced television documentaries, all to shape visions of SDI reflected in 1980s video games. With threats of reduced interest and government funding, the organization engaged in increasingly strange stunts, such as the "Star Spangled Sweepstakes." A ploy to increase public support for SDI, High Frontier's sweepstakes offered "over 135 chances to win valuable prizes" including $5,000 in gold coins, a Mercury Lynx Hatchback, an RCA Home Entertainment Center, a Polaroid Auto-focus Instant Camera, a General Electric Countertop Oven, a Smokeless Indoor Grill, a Re-Dial Telephone, or a Regal "Polly-Pop" Corn Popper, "all in the name of SDI."[20] The sweepstakes' effectiveness remains questionable, but the move suggested High Frontier's attempts to shape public opinion with consumer goods. The organization continued to push this strategy in the one medium that successfully represented what their vision of what a workable missile defense system might look like: in an SDI video game.

Released in 1987 for the Commodore 64 home console, *High Frontier: An SDI Wargame* was more than a missile shoot-em-up. The game simulated the government's struggle to turn SDI from a dream into a reality. Players engaged in the "construction and use of the proposed American Strategic Defence [sic] Initiative (SDI)—the 'Star Wars' system."[21] *High Frontier's* promotional materials in video game magazines promoted SDI's promise:

4,000 Soviet Nuclear Warheads are targeted at the North American Mainland. The only hope in a nuclear conflict would be the *High Frontier*. The most controversial defence [sic] policy this decade ... in HIGH FRONTIER, *you* are the project leader committing staff and funds to make SDI a reality. *You* deploy the satellite defence [sic] system as the world teeters on the brink of nuclear oblivion, and *you* must make the decisions that could save the American mainland ... or devastate it.[22]

In *High Frontier*, players can choose to be either the Americans or the Soviets; they can also choose to be an aggressive foreign policy "hawk" or a pacifistic "dove." Gamers play as an organization's director—presumably of High Frontier Inc.—and must assess departmental activities such as allocating funds for SDI research and development, engaging in espionage to monitor your enemies' own SDI programs, and, if necessary, conversing with the president via a hotline. Action intensifies when the enemy attacks, at which point gamers have hopefully developed a deployable SDI system. *High Frontier* then shifts from simulation to shooter, and players intercept incoming ICBMs with a defensive arsenal including elements from High Frontier's proposals and real SDIO experiments: players can use "high-energy pulse laser fitted to the Laser system and the Space Plane system," "Rail Gun" weapons, or an X-Ray Laser "with a nuclear bomb as its power source." *High Frontier* also included Sagan's warnings of a Soviet missile decoy threat. On the game's "easy level," incoming ICBMs are always real, but in higher difficulty levels "decoys" diminish SDI's effectiveness.[23] Overall, *High Frontier* plays less as a shooter and more as a simulation, or, as one game reviewer wrote, a "business management game for participants in the arms race."[24]

It may not have been a huge commercial success, but *High Frontier* was one of the first games to blur the lines between playable video game and political propaganda. The game's manual is extensive, and covers not only gameplay mechanics, but also political arguments for SDI. For example, Section 25, "SDI Explained," explains Cold War strategic defense, terminology (i.e. ICBMs, MIRVs, and ABMs), and the importance of SDI in providing a "layered defense." The manual assures readers that SDI could work, even if imperfectly: "Each layer does not have to be 100 per cent effective." The "First Layer" of defense intercepts missiles at the boost phase; the second scours the earth's atmosphere; and the "Third Layer" intercepts missiles reentering the atmosphere. *High Frontier*'s political agenda became more clear at the manual's conclusion, which features a bibliography on SDI literature such as *An Illustrated Guide to Space Warfare, Star Wars*, and, of course, *High Frontier*.[25]

Some game reviewers remarked on this pedantic video game instruction manual, one "which comprehensively explains the principles behind Star Wars and the type of weapons it would be effective against." Others pondered the political message of the text, suggesting that young players might play *High Frontier* and "absorb cultural assumptions without realizing it." Furthermore, "a game which focuses the mind of a young teenager so sharply on defending the world against the Big Bad Russians can't be a very peace-provoking thing." Others criticized *High Frontier's* premise, and especially the game's point system: "Creating an efficient SDI system will decide how much of America has survived [as well as] your final score. A very dubious assumption [as] the idea of anyone thinking conflict is acceptable is pretty frightening."[26] In short, *High Frontier* had politicized missile defense even in video games. As one reviewer summarized, "*High Frontier* attempts topicality at the cost of making two large and decidedly dubious assumptions about the real world: that it is possible to develop one or even several workable SDI systems, and that a Soviet Missile attack is imminent and inevitable." Not surprisingly, these were two premises that High Frontier took as givens, and that, ultimately, Reagan rejected in his rapprochement with Soviet leader Mikhail Gorbachev. Their 1987 INF treaty, limiting medium-range nukes in Europe, was arguably the first step toward the end of the Cold War, and with it, the appeal of nuclear-themed video games.[27]

Conclusion

In 1864, Victor Hugo wrote that in the future, flying machines might make armies "vanish, and with them the whole business of war." In the decades that followed, innovations including dynamite, machine guns, Hugo's flying machines, and atomic weapons, prompted equally hopeful, but premature, hopes for world peace. In 1983, Ronald Reagan proposed the latest hope for world peace, a space-based shield to protect Americans against a nuclear attack. As of 2012, surface-to-air BMD systems have grown more effective—as evidenced in the first Persian Gulf war, and, more recently, in missile attacks on Israel—but still no SDI program exists. Regardless, history suggests that if SDI ever becomes a reality, it would not lead to peace, and could not provide a 100 percent defense. As early as 1980, video games reinforced this reality. SDI-themed video games including *Missile Command, Wargames, 3-D Missile Defense, Strategic Defense Initiative,* and *High Frontier* digitally simulated SDI and revealed missile defense's fallibility. In 1983, Reagan expressed hopes that the video game generation was learning skills that would improve a technologically advanced military. It only takes a cursory look at America's unmanned flying drone program to validate Reagan's prediction. Yet no technology is perfect, and if determined gamers could not "win" these relatively simple games, it is doubtful that any SDI system could provide an infallible defense.

With the exception of *High Frontier*, video games did not set out to convince Americans of SDI's feasibility. Still, even if their message was not explicit, 1980s games reinforced concepts that, only a few years before, remained rooted in the realm of science fiction. Reagan's 1983 SDI announcement concerned his closest advisors who believed such a program to be unrealistic. Yet, since the 1970s, commercial video games represented space warfare in appealing ways. In the 1980s, numerous games used missile defense as a playable scenario; in the process, they made Reagan's dream of space-based missile defense seem all the more plausible. They may have been more effective than High Frontier, or even the SDIO, in making such dreams seem achievable. Video games were able to perform an important function in normalizing ideas about a yet-realized military program, and they could do so because SDI was still just a dream. According to SDI historian Edward Linenthal, Americans "easily forget ... that there is no 'it'; there is only the 'I' in SDI." With Star Wars, Reagan provided either "an *appealing* vision of a world made secure through missile defense or an *appalling* vision of a world nearer nuclear catastrophe because of missile defense." Video games reflected both these visions. The 1980 *Missile Command*'s vision was appalling, but also fun and addictive. The 1987 *High Frontier*'s vision was both appealing and politically charged. These games, and the SDI-themed games created between them, were arguably the closest the public ever came to assessing, firsthand and for themselves, SDI.[28]

Notes

1 SDI, or "Star Wars," remains a contested issue. Some Reagan supporters see SDI as a calculated move of economic warfare with the Soviets. Critics contend that SDI was nothing more than a political move to sway public opinion away from the antinuclear movement. For interpretations varying from laudatory to critical, see Peter Schweitzer, *Reagan's War: The Epic Story of His Forty-Year Struggle and Final Triumph over Communism*. New York: Random House, 2002; Paul Lettow, *Ronald Reagan and his Quest to Abolish Nuclear Weapons*. New York: Random House, 2005; Frances FitzGerald, *Way Out There in the Blue: Reagan, Star Wars, and the End of the Cold War*. New York: Simon and Schuster, 2000; Richard Rhodes, *Arsenals of Folly: The Making of the Nuclear Arms Race*. New York: Alfred A. Knopf, 2007; Reagan's SDI speech archived online: "Address to the Nation on National Security, 23 March 1983." *The Public Papers of President Ronald Reagan*. Ronald Reagan Presidential Library, http://www.reagan.utexas.edu/archives/speeches/1983/32383d.htm, accessed 16 May 2011.

2 Sanford Lakoff and Herbert F. York, *A Shield in Space? Technology, Politics, and the Strategic Defense Initiative*. Berkeley, CA: University of California Press, 1989, 9–10; FitzGerald, *Way Out There in the Blue*, 125–135, 380; on SDI debates and the array of editorial cartoons about "Star Wars", see Edward Linenthal's excellent *Symbolic Defense: The Cultural Significance of the Strategic Defense Initiative*. Urbana, IL: University of Illinois Press, 1989.

3 On 1980s antinuclear popular culture, see William Knoblauch, *Selling the Second Cold War: Antinuclear Cultural Activism and Reagan Era Foreign Policy*, Diss., Ohio University, 2012.

4 Ed Halter, *From Sun Tzu to Xbox: War and Video Games*. New York: Thunder's Mouth Press, 2006, 117–118; David Sirota, *Back to Our Future*. New York: Ballantine Books, 2011, 153–154.

5 H.G. Wells, *The World Set Free*. Sandy UT: Quiet Visions Publishing, 2000; on H. G. Wells and other imaginings of futuristic military applications, see Michael E. Sherry, *The Rise of American Airpower*. New Haven, CT: Yale University Press, 1989; Paul Boyer, *By the Bomb's Early Light*. New York: Pantheon Books, 1985, 75, 352–368.

6 *Star Wars: A New Hope*, directed by George Lucas, (1977; 20th Century Fox, 2004), DVD; for more on *Star Wars*, *Star Trek*, and comic book atomic pop culture, see Boyer, *By the Bomb's Early Light*, 14, 115, 257; Scott Zeman and Michael A. Amundson, Eds. *Atomic Culture: Or How We Learned to Stop Worrying and Love the Bomb*. Denver, CO: University of Colorado

Press, 2004; for more on Reagan, *Murder in the Air*, and SDI's origins, see FitzGerald, *Way Out There in the Blue*, 22–25; Linenthal, *Symbolic Defense*, 6–7.

7   The earliest U.S. Ballistic Missile Boost Intercept program was codenamed BAMBI. See FitzGerald, *Way Out There in the Blue*, 120–123; Paul Boyer, "Selling Star Wars," in Eds. Kenneth Osgood and Andrew K. Frank, *Selling War in a Media Age*. Gainesville, FL: University Press of Florida, 2011, 202–204; Daniel Wirls, *Buildup: The Politics of Defense in the Reagan Era*. Ithaca, NY: Cornell University Press, 1992, 22–23, 138–140.

8   "Coin-Op Capers: #10 Missile Command," *Retro Gamer* (Issue 88): 26–27; Theurer interview from "The Making of Missile Command," *Retro Gamer* (Issue 88): 62–65.

9   Halter also contends that *Missile Command*'s controls "resembled the Army's forward-area alerting radar (FAAR) system, or the warning set for low-altitude air-defense systems." See Gregory Byrnes, "Enlisting Tactics: Where the Young Go, the Marines Follow," *Philadelphia Inquirer*, 1 February 1982, B01; Halter's *From Sun-Tzu to Xbox*, 139, 143; Sirota, *Back to Our Future*, 155.

10 Rhodes, *Arsenals of Folly*, 69–101; FitzGerald, *Way Out There in the Blue*, 117–119.

11 Lawrence Freedman, *The Evolution of Nuclear Strategy*. New York: Palgrave, 2003, 215–216; 329, 374; FitzGerald, *Way Out There in the Blue*, 85–86; Fred Kaplan, *The Wizards of Armageddon*. Stanford, CA: Stanford University Press, 1983, 343–385.

12 Theurer, "The Making of Missile Command," *Retro Gamer* (Issue 88): 62–65.

13 On teenage fears of nuclear war in the 1980s, see Robert T. Schatz and Susan T. Fiske, "International Reactions to the Threat of Nuclear War: The Rise and Fall of Concern in the Eighties," *Political Psychology*, 13, no. 1 (March 1992): 1–29.

14 Wargames was released on 3 June 1983. See the Internet Movie Database at: http://www.imdb.com/title/tt0086567/, accessed 30 October 2012.

15 Daniel O. Graham and Gregory A. Fossedal, *A Defense that Defends: Blocking Nuclear Attack*. Old Greenwich, CT: Devin-Adair, 1983; Daniel O. Graham, *High Frontier: A Strategy for National Survival*. New York: Tom Doherty Associates, 1983, 43.

16 In 1984, James C. Fletcher, Chairman of the Defensive Technologies Study Team, provided a Congressional report arguing that for a workable SDI program must have three phases. See *The Reagan Strategic Defense Initiative: A Technical, Political, and Arms Control Assessment*. Cambridge, MA: Ballinger Publishing Company, 1985, 39–63; see also, Daniel O. Graham, *A Defense that Defends*, 1984, video recording, 27 minutes.

17 *War and Peace in the Nuclear Age: Part 12, Reagan's Shield*, 1988, 60 minutes (ABC); On SDI coverage in network news, see Robert Karl Manoff, "Modes of War and Modes of Social Address: The Text of SDI," *Journal of Communication*, 39, no. 1 (Winter 1989): 60; There is another "SDI" game released for the Amiga home computer in 1986. The Amiga game, however,

only uses a space-based missile defense shield for its plotline; otherwise, the game is a linear, hero-based narrative, not a simulation of actual missile defense.

18 Credits found at http://www.allgame.com/game.php?id=12139&tab=screen; for a play through online, see https://www.youtube.com/watch?v=3Uu6w UetgwU, accessed 30 October 2012.

19 Rhodes, *Arsenals of Folly*, 261–263; FitzGerald, *Way Out There in the Blue*, 198–199; on Weinberger's appraisal of High Frontier see Boyer, "Selling Star Wars", 5–7; Keyworth's remarks cited in Wirls, *Buildup*, 144.

20 Daniel Graham's letter included in the "Star Spangled Sweepstakes", ID#: 337322, PR014-09, WHORM: Subject File, Ronald Reagan Library; FitzGerald, *Way Out There in the Blue*, 125–137, 142; Lakoff and York, *Weapons in Space*, 10–11; Wirls, *Buildup*, 146.

21 Box art and captions for *High Frontier* came from the European release, hence the spelling of "defence" vs. "defense." The British spelling is maintained in quotes.

22 *Sinclair User* (Issue 65): 11; also, *Computers & Video Games* (Issue 70): 23; both referenced online at: http://www.worldofspectrum.org/infoseekid. cgi?id=0002313, accessed 30 October 2012; *High Frontier*'s developers Ian Bird and Alan Steel, had previously worked on *Theatre Europe* and *Guadal Canal,* which respectively simulated contemporary and past military escalations.

23 *High Frontier* game manual archived online at: http://www.digitalpress.com/ library/manuals/c64/highfrontier.txt, accessed 6 November 2012.

24 *Sinclair User* (Issue 68): 107, archived online at http://www.worldofspectrum. org/showmag.cgi?mag=SinclairUser/Issue068/Pages/SinclairUser06800107. jpg, accessed 10 November 2012; In an astute insight, the anonymous game reviewer of *High Frontier* noted that while "The Strategic Defence Initiative is basically a good idea ... it doesn't really exist at the moment and seems to be more of a bargaining tool at disarmament conferences than anything else." See "High Frontier," *ZZAP! 64* (1987): 123, http://www.gb64.com/ oldsite/gameofweek/31/gotw_highfrontier.htm, accessed 12 November 2012.

25 *Sinclair User* (Issue 64), 1987: 20, archived online at the *World of Spectrum* website: http://www.worldofspectrum.org/infoseekid.cgi?id=0002313, accessed 30 October 2012.

26 Game Magazine reviews from 1987 include *Popular Computing Weekly* (Issue 8.87): 142; *Your Sinclair* (Issue 8): 73; *Sinclair User* (Issue 11): 107; all can be accessed online at: http://www.worldofspectrum.org/infoseekid. cgi?id=0002313, accessed 11 November 2012.

27 In a fascinating and arguably astute insight, even the anonymous game reviewer of *High Frontier* noted that while "The Strategic Defence Initiative is basically a good idea ... it doesn't really exist at the moment and seems to be more of a bargaining tool at disarmament conferences than anything else." See "High Frontier," *ZZAP! 64* (1987): 123.

28 Linenthal, *Symbolic Defense*, xiii (italics in original quote); second quote from Burt Hoffman, a Washington D.C. PR man, in Stengel, "The Great Star Wars P.R. War." H. Bruce Franklin, *War Stars: The Superweapon and the American Imagination*. New York: Oxford University Press, 1988; for a variety of editorial cartoons can be found throughout Linenthal's *Symbolic Defense*; FitzGerald, *Way Out There in the Blue*, 147–209.

Works cited

Boyer, Paul. *By the Bomb's Early Light: American Thought and Culture at the Dawn of the Atomic Age*. New York: Pantheon, 1985.

Boyer, Paul. "Selling Star Wars," in Eds. Kenneth Osgood and Andrew K. Frank, *Selling War in a Media Age*. Gainesville, FL: University Press of Florida, 2011, 196–223.

"Coin-Op Capers: #10 Missile Command." *Retro Gamer*, 88 (2012): 26–30.

Demaria, Rusel and Johnny L. Wilson. *High Score!: The Illustrated History of Video Games*. Berkeley, CA: McGraw Hill-Osborne, 2002.

FitzGerald, Frances. *Way Out There in the Blue: Reagan, Star Wars, and the End of the Cold War*. New York: Simon and Schuster, 2000.

Franklin, Bruce H. *War Stars: The Superweapon and the American Imagination*. New York: Oxford University Press, 1988.

Freedman, Lawrence. *The Evolution of Nuclear Strategy*, 3rd ed. New York: Palgrave, 2003.

Goldberg, Harold. *All Your Base Are Belong to Us: How Fifty Years of Video games Conquered Pop Culture*. New York: Three Rivers Press, 2011.

Graham, Daniel O. "Star Spangled Sweepstakes," ID#: 337322, PR014-09, WHORM: Subject File, Ronald Reagan Library.

Halter, Ed. *From Sun Tzu to Xbox: War and Video games*. New York: Thunder Mouth's Press, 2006.

Lakoff, Sanford and Herbert F. York. *A Shield in Space? Technology, Politics, and the Strategic Defense Initiative*. Berkeley, CA: University of California Press, 1989.

Lettow, Paul. *Ronald Reagan and his Quest to Abolish Nuclear Weapons*. New York: Random House, 2005.

Linenthal, Edward. *Symbolic Defense: The Cultural Significance of the Strategic Defense Initiative*. Urbana, IL: University of Illinois Press, 1989.

Retro Gamer. Issue 88.

Rhodes, Richard. *Arsenals of Folly: The Making of the Nuclear Arms Race*. New York: Alfred A. Knopf, 2007.

Schatz, Robert T. and Susan T. Fiske. "International Reactions to the Threat of Nuclear War: The Rise and Fall of Concern in the Eighties," *Political Psychology*, 13, no. 1 (March 1992): 1–29.

Schweitzer, Peter. *Reagan's War: The Epic Story of His Forty-Year Struggle and Final Triumph Over Communism*. New York: Random House, 2002.

Sherry, Michael E. *The Rise of American Airpower*. New Haven, CT: Yale University Press, 1989.

Sirota, David. *Back to our Future*. New York: Ballantine Books, 2012.
Weart, Spencer R. *The Rise of Nuclear Fear*. Cambridge, MA: Harvard University Press, 2012.
Wells, H.G. *The World Set Free*. Sandy, UT: Quiet Vision Publishing, 2000.
Winkler, Alan M. *Life Under a Cloud: American Anxiety about the Atom*. Urbana, IL: University of Illinois Press, 1993.
Wirls, Daniel. *Buildup: The Politics of Defense in the Reagan Era*. Ithaca, NY: Cornell University Press, 1992.
Zeman, Scott C. and Michael A. Amundson, Eds. *Atomic Culture: How We Learned to Stop Worrying and Love the Bomb*. Denver, CO: University of Colorado Press, 2004.

Online

Allgame Database: www.allgame.com, accessed 2 August 2012.
Game Demos Viewed on www.youtube.com, accessed 2 August 2012.
Internet Move Database: www.imdb.com, accessed 2 August 2012.
Public Papers of President Ronald Reagan. Ronald Reagan Presidential Library, http://www.reagan.utexas.edu/archives/speeches/1983/32383d.htm
World of Spectrum http://www.worldofspectrum.org/, accessed 2 August 2012.

Multimedia

A Defense that Defends, 1983. Video Recording provided to the author by Edward Linenthal.
War and Peace in the Nuclear Age: Part 12, Reagan's Shield, 1988, Videocassette. ABC.

Games cited

High Frontier. Mountain View, CA: Allan Steel, programmer, Activison, 1987.
Missile Command. Sunnyvale, CA: Dave Theurer, programmer, Atari, 1980.
Missile Defense 3-D. Mountain View, CA: Sega, Activision, 1987.
SDI/Strategic Defense Initiative. Los Angeles: Cinemaware, 1987.
Theatre Europe. Coventry, UK: PSS, 1985.
Wargames. Manalapan, NJ: Coleco, 1984.

19

Fallout and Yesterday's Impossible Tomorrow

Joseph A. November
University of South Carolina

Introduction

The *Fallout* series of computer role playing games (RPGs) has introduced millions of players to the future as envisioned by American popular media between the late 1930s and the early 1960s.[1] The series received international acclaim for its painstakingly rendered and deeply satirical depiction of a post-apocalyptic wasteland littered with the detritus of an Atomic Age civilization that, unlike our own, realized the techno-utopian visions of the future introduced to mid-twentieth-century Americans by popular science fiction and futurist public exhibitions. Navigating the ruins of places like Washington DC and Las Vegas, the player encounters remnants of a destroyed world where the "American High," to borrow William L. O'Neill's term for the consensus among postwar Americans that their society was essentially good and that given enough effort anything could be accomplished by it, persisted not just until the mid-1960s but until 2077, when it was destroyed in a nuclear war against the Communists (see Shulzke, Chapter 17).[2]

In the world depicted in *Fallout*, many of the technologies so sanguinely predicted during the mid-twentieth century have been developed. Laser guns, talking robots, fission engines, and cybernetic medical devices abound. The landscape is strewn with hulking wrecks of nuclear-powered; tail-finned automobiles; devastated art-deco buildings; and an enormous variety of

1950s-style pop art advertising posters, clothing, furnishings, and food products. Missing, however, are the miniaturized electronic devices that have so thoroughly populated our own world. In *Fallout*'s future, there are no cellphones at all, and computers have not been miniaturized, let alone been embedded in other devices such as TVs and radios.

The rich and counterfactual world of *Fallout* is a tremendous resource for accessing and communicating complex ideas about the mid-twentieth-century United States. The game's heavy use of irony and satire are particularly effective in showing the ways in which Americans struggled to reconcile their desire to create new possibilities through the development of new technologies and their concern that the process of pursuing such technologies would erode civil liberties and indeed American values. With that in mind, this chapter aims to provide the tools to historicize one of the most important questions raised by the experience of playing *Fallout*: why did American society not continue along the trajectory depicted in mid-century works of futurism? I will make the case that many otherwise obscure dimensions of this question—and even some answers to it—become clear when one immerses oneself in the world of *Fallout*.

By putting players in situations where they guide characters to decide whether to preserve or destroy what little remains of American society and/or the technologies it produced, *Fallout* provides a unique opportunity meaningfully to explore the tensions between American liberal-democratic values and the political and the often-totalitarian social requirements of building the technological utopia so many Americans had envisioned. To help readers make the most of that exploration, this chapter will compare the timeline presented by *Fallout* to our own, focusing especially on the mid-to-late 1940s, the point at which the two histories diverged. In so doing, the chapter shows how *Fallout* engages with the priorities and consequences of actual mid-twentieth-century American visions of the future, particularly those visions that grew out of US federal government science and technology planning.

The point of departure

At some point in the late 1940s, our world and the world portrayed in *Fallout* each began to go in its own direction. Before "The Divergence," as it is called in *Fallout* fan lore, the histories of these worlds had been the same, and during the immediate post-Divergence decade of the 1950s there seems to have been little historical difference between the two worlds.[3] Looking back at the real 1950s, David Halberstam wrote, "In that era of general good will and expanding affluence few Americans doubted the essential goodness of their society."[4] During that time, many Americans had indeed experienced a tremendous improvement in the quality of living; Americans who had endured the Great Depression and World War II suddenly owned their own cars and houses, traveled the world in jet aircraft, and unlike their parents, did not live in fear of many infections (thanks to the new "wonder drug" penicillin) or what was arguably the nation's most dreaded disease, polio (which could be prevented by a simple injection of the vaccine Jonas Salk introduced in 1955). Looking to the future, these Americans observed the changes in their own lives and projected those changes ahead. In many ways, *Fallout* captures that projection—the game's future is in line with 1950s norms and expectations rather than our own.

By the late 1960s very noticeable differences begin to appear between *Fallout's* world and our own. The counter-culture and indeed the broader society's questioning of the 1950s consensus, which made our 1960s and 1970s so tumultuous, never arose in *Fallout's* world. Instead of dissipating in the haze of Sputnik, the Civil Rights movement, and anti-war demonstrations, *Fallout's* "American High" lasted for more than a century. In *Fallout*, the United States won the race to put a man in space, emerged victorious in Vietnam, and saw no social upheaval in the late twentieth century. In *Fallout*, the Cold War lasted into the twenty-first century, the Soviet Union did not break up in 1991, and the People's Republic of China remained ideologically Communist and hostile to the United States. This state of affairs persisted until 2077, when the world's nuclear powers destroyed each other (and presumably most everything else, too) in a two-hour nuclear exchange called "The Great War."[5]

The American society that was destroyed in The Great War was very different from our own. Culturally, this society seems to have never moved past our 1950s—practically every ruined building has some scrap of sincerely wholesome-sounding and forward-looking product advertisements. Technologically, meanwhile, *Fallout's* twenty-first-century America has realized many of the visions expressed in our world's popular futurism of the late 1930s to the early 1960s. The promises of a techno-utopia made in the World's Fair exhibitions "The World of Tomorrow" and "Futurama" and Disney's "Tomorrowland," which all seem so far-fetched in our world, have been fulfilled in *Fallout*. Before the bombs fell, Americans living in *Fallout's* technocracy had access to nuclear-powered cars and homes, cybernetic medical technology, talking and walking robots, and a staggering variety of death-ray-like weapons.

In keeping with *Fallout's* 2077 being a projection from the mid-twentieth century, missing from the game's world are many of our everyday technologies that were not foreseen during that time. Electronic devices such as televisions and radios seem not to have been transistorized or to have had computers embedded into them, while general-purpose computers remain as bulky as they did in the 1960s. Indeed a state-of-the-art computer terminal in *Fallout's* 2077, with its command-line interface and monochrome display would be unremarkable by the standards of our own 1977.[6] These computers could be used for e-mail, but it appears that the World Wide Web was never developed in *Fallout's* world. Cellphones, let alone smartphones, seem to be completely absent from *Fallout's* twenty-first century. The home of the alternate 2077, meanwhile, seems reminiscent of 1950s America; sorting through the ruins of one, the player finds all-metal household appliances, food tins, 1950s-style apparel, and flash-bulb cameras that still use celluloid film.

In creating this paradoxical world in which the future is very much mired in our past, *Fallout's* developers made every effort to create an uninterruptedly immersive environment. Most noticeably in *Fallout 3*, the necessity of using a personal computer (an impossibility in *Fallout's* world) to interact with one's character, i.e. to access and organize in-game and gameplay-related information, is transformed into a virtue by the Pip-Boy (Figure 19.1). Worn on the player character's wrist, the Pip-Boy serves as an in-game vital signs monitor, PDA (Personal Data Assistant), and the means to navigate game menus. Consistent with the course of technological development in Fallout's world, the Pip-Boy does not display information on something like an LCD

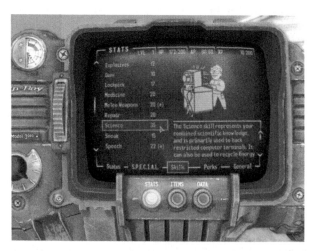

FIGURE 19.1 *Pip-Boy 3000 in action. Mounted on the player character's wrist, the Pip-Boy allows the player to monitor the protagonist's health, change weapons and clothing, track quests, and navigate game menus. The aesthetic of the Pip-Boy is derived from late 1970s computer terminals.*

or OLED screen (as these do not exist there); rather, monochrome text and primitive-looking 1-bit graphics are shown on a bulky CRT display housed in a cumbersome metal—rather than plastic—case. During gameplay, the Pip-Boy flickers and crackles just like a real time-worn CRT, and its green glow dimly illuminates surrounding objects when it is used in the dark. *Fallout*'s developers explain that in designing the Pip-Boy "inspiration came from both commercial product design and military industrial design of the 1950s to early 1960s.... As with all of *Fallout 3*'s industrial design, a careful balance of realism, future-retro-style and practicality was sought in the final product."[7] Working along these lines, they justified the Pip-Boy's primitive-looking display and user interface: "There were a host of restrictions placed on the UI because of the unique nature of the hardware as imagined. We looked at old computers from the '70s to early '80s, when operating systems were text-based, interfaces were not-so-graphical, displays were low-res, and color was a luxury many systems did not have."[8]

Exploring the past's future

Central to the player experience in *Fallout* is the paradoxical sense that the game is set both in the future and in the past. Fittingly, in terms of using the future to explore the past, many of the games' plots revolve around "vaults," self-contained underground habitats designed to survive a nuclear war. These strongly resemble scaled-up versions of Paul László's 1950 "Atomville USA," a subterranean shelter designed to allow inhabitants to continue a "relatively normal existence," complete with all the comforts of a typical American home, long after civilization on the surface is destroyed.[9] It is in such a vault that *Fallout 3*, the series' most popular installment, which is set in 2,277 (200 years after the apocalypse), begins. In that game, the player assumes the role of The Lone Wanderer, a teenaged vault-dweller who leaves the safety of Vault 101 to search for his/her father in the Capital Wasteland, the ruins of the Washington DC area. In contrast to life in Vault 101, where many of the social norms and technological artifacts of 2077 are intact, the Capital Wasteland is an anarchic place where basic survival depends on avoiding or overpowering marauding "mutants" and bandits, and on one's ability to scavenge bombed-out buildings for sustenance and for scraps with which to trade or improvise weapons. Amid the ruins, still-functioning radios blare in the background to provide a steady stream of patriotic speeches about liberty and freedom as well as hit songs by pre–rock-and-roll greats like Billie Holiday, Cole Porter, Bob Crosby, and Sid Phillips. In encounters with the many groups eking out their existence in the wasteland, The Lone Wanderer must face tough decisions about which personal values to uphold, which scientific knowledge and technologies to share, and ultimately whether or not to perpetuate the kind of society that existed before the Great War.

Whichever path one takes, whether one becomes a champion of liberal democracy, a slave-trading autocrat, an antisocial thief, or a psychopath who kills everyone in sight, or some combination of all of these, wandering the wastelands immerses the player into a world saturated by reminders of many of the now popularly rejected aspirations of post–World War II America. Scavenging in the wasteland, one finds the remnants of a society that enthusiastically embraced the unfettered growth of what President Dwight Eisenhower warningly called in 1961 the "military-industrial complex," an alliance in which large industrial corporations (with the help of research universities) developed and produced new high-technology weapons systems for a federal government deeply influenced by those corporations' visions of the future.

It is fitting that the products of defense manufacturers have proliferated so thoroughly in *Fallout*'s world, for they were among the most aggressive promoters of technological visions of the future in our own world. Pointing to these companies' prominent role in predicting the future in the 1950s, historians of futurism Joseph Corn and Brian Horrigan have argued in their book *Yesterday's Tomorrow: Past Visions of the American Future* that "defense contractors ... had good reason to foster rapid technological change and weapons obsolescence. Just as automobile makers depended on consumer dissatisfaction with present vehicles ... defense firms sought to keep the military constantly hungry for new and improved weapons."[10] *Fallout*'s 130-year Cold War (which occasionally turned hot), saw American defense companies, thus unchecked by the lack of an existential security threat, produce tools of war only imagined in our world's mid-twentieth century. Tactical nuclear weapons, the subject of so much tension between American military and civilian leaders in the 1950s and later decades (as discussed by Knoblauch in Chapter 18), were perfected in the world of *Fallout*.[11] There, the shoulder-mounted Fat Man gun seems to be a standard-issue military weapon; it is capable of firing a football-sized "mini-nuke" several hundred yards, to devastating effect. The world of *Fallout* is also awash with the death-rays imagined by mid-twentieth-century science fiction writers; along with traditional projectile guns like the AK-47, the player is spoilt for choice of laser pistols, plasma rifles, and nuclear-powered armor capable of mitigating damage from those weapons.Most prominent among the dozens of defense contractors featured in *Fallout*, RobCo Industries is depicted as having applied robotics research to warfare to produce combat-capable Securitron robots, the personal cybernetic system Pip-Boy, and (in cooperation with General Atomics International) the colossal Liberty Prime robot, which was to be America's secret weapon in land battles against the Communists. Another *Fallout* contractor, Big MT, pushed the envelope of biomedical research—often violating our society's medical ethics standards in the process—to develop automated robotic field surgeons, coyote–snake hybrid guard animals called Night Stalkers, and a wide variety of weaponry that could be wielded by humans or animals.[12]

As was the case in the pre-apocalypse American society portrayed by *Fallout,* where nuclear energy was embraced rather than becoming a focus of widespread anxiety, our own 1940s and early 1950s were a time when Americans generally saw nuclear energy as positive and promising. When construction began on America's first commercial nuclear power plant in Shippingport, Pennsylvania, in 1954, it was publically hailed as a triumph for Eisenhower's Atoms for Peace program.[13] Just days after overseeing the Shippingport groundbreaking, Lewis L. Strauss, then head of the US Atomic Energy Commission, famously predicted: "It is not too much to expect that our children will enjoy in their homes electrical energy too cheap to meter."[14] Around this time, a demonstration of a small working research reactor at the United Nations headquarters in New York City, far from generating an outcry about safety, was popularly received as a sign of American robustness and potential in this area.[15]

In *Fallout,* the visions of a nuclear-powered utopia—promoted, for instance, in Disney's *Our Friend the Atom* (1956)—have become real. While the 1958 Ford Nucleon, a fission-powered car, never made it past the concept stage in our world, in *Fallout* something very much like the Nucleon was mass-produced and the still-radioactive wrecks of these vehicles are strewn all over the landscape (Figure 19.2).[16] Fission batteries, too, litter the wasteland,

FIGURE 19.2 Ford Nucleon and *Fallout* counterpart.

Left: A concept drawing of the 1958 Ford Nucleon, a nuclear-powered car. This car was never produced, but Ford's vision was realized in *Fallout.* Right: A *Fallout 3* gameplay screenshot showing a burned-out nuclear-powered car and (in the background) a Red Rocket nuclear fueling station.

and their placement suggests they powered everything from household appliances to robots to weapons. Finally, the wasteland's ubiquitous (and sometimes still sealed) bottles of Nuka Cola, the leading soft drink of 2077 America, point to a society that was so comfortable with nuclear power that consumers would not wince at the thought of drinking something with a name that suggested radioactivity. That Nuka Cola comes in tall glass bottles reminiscent of the 1950s rather than plastic bottles or aluminum cans points to a connection the game designers saw between a certain time and a certain way of thinking.

Planning for tomorrow, yesterday

The exploration during *Fallout* gameplay of the connections between a society's values and the artifacts it produced raises many of the questions that real-world American policymakers grappled with in the years following World War II, that is, around the time of The Divergence. In the late 1940s and early 1950s, the most prominent technologies in *Fallout's* 2077, namely nuclear energy and computers, were new and were understood by Americans to have been products of the war. Indeed, wartime research and development had brought stunning changes, in the form of nuclear weapons, penicillin, jet aircraft, plastics, and computers. The war was also immensely disruptive. Factories, universities, even whole cities were radically reorganized for the purpose of developing and producing material to support the war. In the case of the Manhattan Project, an entirely new infrastructure, including the 75,000-person "secret city" of Oak Ridge, Tennessee, was built up in a few short years.[17]

For Vannevar Bush (1890–1974), who as director of the Office of Scientific Research and Development (OSRD), had overseen US research and development efforts during the war, the war had demonstrated that given enough institutional and political support American scientists and engineers could achieve hitherto unimaginable breakthroughs. During the war, the OSRD had reaped the fruits of massive popular support for the war effort; the agency had an enormous discretionary budget and the latitude to make sweeping changes to research and production—the "can-do" rhetoric that permeates the world of *Fallout* could be found in abundance in wartime America. In the top-secret Manhattan Project, which the OSRD oversaw, thousands of scientists and technological experts crossed their traditional disciplinary lines to harness national resources to build a world-changing weapon. In parallel to the OSRD's effort, the US Army took a "try anything" approach to research and development, leading to high-risk ventures such as building incendiary bombs filled with bats and the development of a replacement for human computers, the Electronic Numerical Integrator And Computer (ENIAC), an electronic calculating machine—and arguably the first electronic general-purpose digital computer—that was popularly hailed as a "giant electronic brain" when its existence was made public after the war.[18]

In 1945, as the war was drawing to a close, Bush sought to sustain the momentum the war had brought to the production of new ideas and devices.[19] In *Fallout*, that momentum certainly was sustained, though the exact mechanism of *how* is never made explicit. Back in our world, with victory looming, Bush feared that scientists, engineers, and the American public would return to their old ways, and thereby make progress of the sort achieved during the war impossible. In *Science, The Endless Frontier*, Bush's July 1945 report to President Truman, he contended that, "basic research is the pacemaker of technological progress" and proposed that the US federal government make permanent its wartime role of directing research and development on a national scale. Arguing that American industry depended heavily on new scientific ideas in order to manufacture high-technology products, Bush maintained that "if the colleges, universities, and research institutes are to meet the rapidly increasing demands of industry and Government for new scientific knowledge, their basic research should be strengthened by use of public funds." Such a heavy investment in research would be a radical departure from prewar norms in which the federal government left most educational and research funding decisions to the discretion to local communities. If the United States were to return to this laissez-faire approach to research funding, if there would be no "national policy for science," Bush insisted, then "a nation which depends upon others for its new basic scientific knowledge will be slow in its industrial progress and weak in its competitive position in world trade, regardless of its mechanical skill."[20] Thus, to maintain the pace achieved during the war, Bush proposed the establishment of the National Research Foundation, an agency answerable to (but not controlled by) the president and Congress that would use federal funds to coordinate and steer American research.

To sell his vision to the president and the American public, and to counter the reflexive libertarianism of many Americans, Bush cast science as a new, endless frontier for Americans to explore. Harkening back to Frederick Jackson Turner's 1893 "Frontier Thesis," which held that the basis of America's innovative, egalitarian spirit was the pioneer experience of expanding the American frontier, and which held that with the settlement of the West that spirit would vanish, Bush proclaimed: "New frontiers of the mind are before us, and if they are pioneered with the same vision, boldness, and drive with which we have waged this war we can create a fuller and more fruitful employment and a fuller and more fruitful life."[21] He added that, "We shall have rapid or slow advance on any scientific frontier depending on the number of highly qualified and trained scientists exploring it."[22] Thus, if Americans were to continue along the scientific and technological trails they had blazed during the war, the ones that were often the basis for the visions of the future realized in *Fallout*, then they would, according to Bush, need to keep giving the government a free hand in research.

To Bush's great disappointment, various US legislative bills that attempted to establish something like the National Research Foundation as a permanent, peacetime replacement for the OSRD, failed to pass in the mid-to-late 1940s. Resistance to his plans came from Congressmen and Senators wary of writing what amounted to a blank check for research and from university-based researchers concerned that a perpetual OSRD would erode their autonomy—in *Fallout's* late 1940s Americans seemed not to share this concern. In a departure from the trajectory, which Bush sought to follow and which *Fallout's* Americans seem to have enthusiastically pursued, when Truman finally passed legislation establishing the National Science Foundation (NSF) in 1950, much of the OSRD's power and freedom from oversight had been stripped away.[23] Without something like the OSRD in place then it would be impossible to support the many of the interdisciplinary collaborations and institutional restructurings that had made possible the development of the atomic bomb or the initial mass-production of penicillin.

Like the visions of popular futurists on whose work the technological accomplishments of *Fallout's* 2077 America is based, Bush's projection of wartime momentum into the future depended on American society's will to continue giving scientists and engineers the latitude and resources to work in hitherto unexplored areas. Were ENIAC, itself a high-risk research venture, to be developed into the "electronic brain" capable of endowing a robot with the ability to, as in the case of a *Fallout* Securitron, patrol a building in the same manner as a human security guard, then a massive amount of interdisciplinary work would have had to be done. Getting from a Divergence-era computer like ENIAC to a Securitron would require coordinating the expertise of electronic engineers, neuroscientists, mechanical engineers, computer programmers, and many others. While the OSRD-directed Manhattan Project was able to foster this kind of interdisciplinary collaboration at a time of national emergency, a long-term project involving many leaps of capability would require massive long-term federal support for the researchers and manufacturers involved. In an environment such as our own, where most manufacturers are beholden to shareholders seeking profits, high-risk projects unlikely to generate much near-term income do not tend to fare well.

A path not taken

Maintaining the momentum of the war effort, and thereby realizing the mid-century visions of the future that are featured in *Fallout* would have required both massive investment and intense management on the part of the US federal government. Since the early 1950s, annual US government R&D (research and development) expenditures have increased dramatically—they rose from under $50 billion to over $350 billion (both figures in 2005 dollars). During that same period, however, the ratio of R&D expenditures to the GDP (gross domestic product—i.e. the market value of all goods and services produced in this country) has trended downwards. At its peak funding, the wartime Manhattan Project alone consumed 0.4 percent of the GDP,[24] whereas the *total* federal investment into R&D in 2009 amounted to only 0.9 percent.[25] In short, while Americans continue to invest heavily in R&D, they have generally been less willing to give the federal government the resources and institutional power necessary to stay on the pace set during World War II.

In exploring the world of *Fallout*, it becomes clear that in the alternate postwar America visionaries like Bush ultimately got their way in the game's narrative. As the game so brilliantly demonstrates, the society that empowered its government to propel R&D further along the trajectory established during the war was a society that ultimately turned out to be very different from our own. In *Fallout*, Americans' technological hopes for the future were translated into their support for expensive programs to achieve those hopes. In the real 1950s, by contrast, an embattled Harry Truman's "50-year plan for the United States" was assailed because his rosy picture of a future filled with wondrous atom-powered technologies and prosperous, healthy Americans did not include any discussion of how to reduce the national debt—one critic pointed out that to achieve Truman's vision for 2000 AD, the national debt would exceed $1,000,000,000 by that time.[26] In the real 1950s, Lewis Strauss, who had promised "energy too cheap to meter," which effectively exists in *Fallout*, was marginalized for his insistence that the United States should go it alone to develop nuclear power, and that Americans should make a massive initial investment to ensure long-term exclusive control over technology. 1950s Americans, unlike their counterparts in *Fallout*'s universe, were not willing to make that investment, and were further alienated from such plans by the witch-hunt Strauss orchestrated against the left-leaning J. Robert Oppenheimer, who had been the scientific director of the Manhattan Project and who had argued that the development of nuclear energy would need to be internationalized to achieve success.[27] In the real 1950s, Vannevar

Bush retreated to the private sector, his dreams of establishing a peacetime OSRD unfulfilled—only the 1960s' Apollo Program came close to what he had envisioned.

It is telling that in our world the 1950s' visions of the future in which *Fallout* is grounded were all but abandoned two decades later. By the late 1960s, explains W. Patrick McCray in *The Visioneers*, his history of 1970s and 1980s futurism,

> many Americans had started to loudly and sometimes violently question technology's ability to resolve society's problems. Fears of environmental catastrophe and nuclear war coupled with anxieties about resource depletion and overpopulation had strained their optimism to the breaking point. By the time Nixon's presidency was embroiled in scandal, a new sense of the future, one constrained by limits and scarcity, had emerged.[28]

To challenge the perceived limits of a world that was by the 1970s characterized more by stagflation and austerity than technology-fuelled growth and opportunity, a new generation of American futurists moved away from Bush's call to treat science and technology themselves as a frontier. Instead, visionaries like physicist Gerard K. O'Neill promoted outer space as humanity's new frontier, leading to projected futures in popular magazines like *Omni* in which nineteenth-century American pioneers' railroads, axes, and log cabins would be replaced in the twenty-first century by space colonists blazing trails with "the rocket, the mass driver, and the rotating cylinder ... what resulted was an imagining of endless abundance and personal freedom coupled with laissez-faire thinking." Reflecting the more inclusive, environmentally aware sensibilities of the 1970s, the settlement of space was also depicted as a way to rekindle the American expansionistic spirit "without shooting any Indians" while also serving as the "moral inverse of genocide" by putting "mankind beyond accidental destruction or final collapse."[29] O'Neill's protégé Eric Drexler built on his mentor's vision to popularize another new frontier during the 1980s, this one based on the then-prevailing trends of the miniaturization of electronics and the increasingly effective manipulation of macromolecules such as proteins, where pioneers could use individual atoms as building blocks.[30] While rocketships and even extra-terrestrials are present in *Fallout*, the focus of 2077s' America is life on Earth, not in the stars—in keeping with the postwar vision of the future from which 2077s' America was projected, the miniaturization of electronics, let alone Drexler's nanotechnology vision and its ramifications, is absent from that world.

Conclusion

So, what would America really have had to be like if it were to achieve the visions realized in *Fallout*? Even a glance at futurism from the mid-twentieth century reveals that the society Americans foresaw as harnessing the atom and building intelligent robots was also a society of planned megalopolises full of uniform-looking dwellings and of rationally managed economies where the course of one's life would be determined by automated aptitude tests, ones very much akin to the Generalized Occupational Aptitude Test (GOAT) all new players of *Fallout 3* must take before their adventures begin.[31] In a word, it was a *totalitarian* future. As one roams the wastelands in the *Fallout* games, and particularly as one delves into the vaults, each of which preserved the values of 2077 and which often contained a miniature society ruled by an autocratic Overseer, the player is given many opportunities to explore the dimensions and consequences of the still very real tension between American liberal, democratic ideals and Americans' aspirations to develop the technologies of their dreams.

Notes

1 *Fallout 1* and *2* were created by Black Isle Studios (then part of Interplay). After Interplay closed Black Isle Studios, Bethesda Softworks acquired the rights to produce Fallout games. Bethesda developed *Fallout 3* and licensed the development of *Fallout: New Vegas* to Obsidian Entertainment.

2 William L. O'Neill, *American High: The Years of Confidence*, 1945–1960. New York: Free Press, 1986.

3 "Divergence" entry in *Nukapedia—The Fallout Wiki*, http://fallout.wikia.com/wiki/Divergence. The information in this entry was gathered from the content of the games *Fallout*, *Fallout 2*, *Fallout Tactics*, *Fallout Brotherhood of Steel*, *Fallout 3* (and expansions), and *Fallout: New Vegas* (and expansions), and from the *Fallout Bible*, a collection of documents assembled by Chris Avellone, designer of several *Fallout* titles.

4 David Halberstam, *The Fifties*. New York: Villard Books, 1993, x.

5 "Timeline" entry in *Nukapedia—The Fallout Wiki*, http://fallout.wikia.com/wiki/Timeline. The sources for this entry are the same as the "Divergence" entry.

6 *Fallout*'s Unified Operating System provides a user experience strongly reminiscent of the operating systems DEC developed for the VAX minicomputer in the late 1970s.

7 Istvan Pely, "Design and Development of the Pip-Boy Model 3000," *Fallout 3 Developer Diaries*, 24 October 2007, http://fallout.bethsoft.com/eng/vault/diaries_diary2-10.24.07.php, Pely was the Lead Artist for *Fallout 3*.

8 Pely, "Design and Development of the Pip-Boy Model 3000."

9 Joseph J. Corn and Brian Horrigan, *Yesterday's Tomorrow: Past Visions of the American Future*. Baltimore, MD: Johns Hopkins University Press, 1984, 84, 118.

10 Corn and Horrigan, *Yesterday's Tomorrow*, 120.

11 Amy F. Woolf, *Nonstrategic Nuclear Weapons*, Congressional Research Service (Library of Congress), Report for Congress, 29 August 2012.

12 The Big MT Research and Development Center serves as the location for the *Fallout: New Vegas* expansion *Old World Blues* (2011).

13 Willis L. Shirk, Jr., "'Atoms for Peace' in Pennsylvania," *Pennsylvania Heritage*, 35, no. 2 (Spring 2009), http://www.portal.state.pa.us/portal/server.pt/community/history/4569/it_happened_here/471309, accessed 21 September 2012.

14 Lewis L. Strauss, *Speech to the National Association of Science Writers*, New York City, 16 September 1954. Reprinted in *New York Times*, 17 September 1954.

15 John Krige, "Atoms for Peace, Scientific Internationalism, and Scientific Intelligence," *Osiris*, 21 (2006), 161–181.

16 Corn and Horrigan, *Yesterday's Tomorrow*, 102

17 An overview of the Manhattan Project is provided in Richard Rhodes, *The Making of the Atomic Bomb*. New York: Simon & Schuster, 1995.

18 LeAnn Erickson, *Top Secret Rosies: The Female Computers of World War II*: Documentary Film, PBS, 2010.

19 Jerome B. Wiesner, *Vannevar Bush: A Biographical Memoir*. Washington, D.C.: National Academies Press, 1979, 98.

20 This and previous quotation from Vannevar Bush, *Science the Endless Frontier*. Washington, D.C.: Office of Scientific Research and Development, 1945, www.nsf.gov/od/lpa/nsf50/vbush1945.htm, Chapter 3.

21 Bush, *Science the Endless Frontier*, Summary of the Report.

22 Bush, *Science the Endless Frontier*, Chapter 4.

23 G. Pascal Zachary, *The Endless Frontier: Vannevar Bush, Engineer of the American Century*. New York: The Free Press, 1997, 369–370.

24 Deborah D. Stine, *The Manhattan Project, the Apollo Program, and Federal Energy Technology R&D Programs: A Comparative Analysis*, Congressional Research Service (Library of Congress) Report for Congress, 30 June 2009, http://www.fas.org/sgp/crs/misc/RL34645.pdf.

25 National Science Foundation, *Science and Engineering Indicators 2012*. Washington, D.C.: National Science Foundation, 2012, 4–10, http://www.nsf.gov/statistics/seind12/.

26 Peter Edson, "Truman's Rosy Plan to Boost Everything—Including Debt,"
       Sedalia Democrat (Sedalia, MO, 6 January 1950). The U.S. national debt in
       2000 was over $5.6 trillion.

27 Richard Pfau, *No Sacrifice Too Great: The Life of Lewis L. Strauss*.
       Charlottesville, VA: University of Virginia Press, 1984.

28 W. Patrick McCray, *The Visioneers: How a Group of Elite Scientists Pursued
       Space Colonies, Nanotechnologies, and a Limitless Future*. Princeton, NJ:
       Princeton University Press, 2012, 4.

29 McCray, *The Visioneers*, 72, 149–150 (in the latter two cases, McCray is
       quoting Eric Drexler).

30 McCray, *The Visioneers*, 153.

31 Corn and Horrigan, *Yesterday's Tomorrow*, 45–56.

Works cited

Avellone, Chris. *The Fallout Bible*. Orange County, CA: Black Isle Studios, 2002.

Bush, Vannevar. *Science The Endless Frontier*. Washington, D.C.: Office of
    Scientific Research and Development, 1945.

Corn, Joseph J. and Brian Horrigan. *Yesterday's Tomorrow: Past Visions of
    the American Future*. Baltimore, MD: Johns Hopkins University Press, 1984.

Edson, Peter. "Truman's Rosy Plan to Boost Everything—Including Debt," *Sedalia
    Democrat* (6 January 1950): A4.

Erickson, LeAnn. *Top Secret Rosies: The Female Computers of World War II*:
    Documentary Film, Indipandant Film Project, Philidelphia, PA: PBS, 2010.

Halberstam, David. *The Fifties*. New York: Villard Books, 1993.

Krige, John. "Atoms for Peace, Scientific Internationalism, and Scientific
    Intelligence," *Osiris*, 21 (2006): 161–181.

National Science Foundation. *Science and Engineering Indicators 2012*.
    Washington, D.C.: National Science Foundation, 2012.

Nukapedia–The Fallout Wiki. URL: fallout.wikia.com

O'Neill, William L. *American High: The Years of Confidence, 1945–1960*. New
    York: The Free Press, 1986.

Pfau, Richard. *No Sacrifice Too Great: The Life of Lewis L. Strauss*.
    Charlottesville, VA: University of Virginia Press, 1984.

Rhodes, Richard. *The Making of the Atomic Bomb*. New York: Simon & Schuster,
    1995.

Shirk Jr, Willis L. "'Atoms for Peace' in Pennsylvania," *Pennsylvania Heritage*,
    35, no. 2 (Spring 2009), http://www.portal.state.pa.us/portal/server.pt/
    community/history/4569/it_happened_here/471309, accessed 21 September
    2012.

Stine, Deborah D. *The Manhattan Project, the Apollo Program, and Federal
    Energy Technology R&D Programs: A Comparative Analysis*, Report for
    Congress. Congressional Research Service (Library of Congress), 30 June
    2009.

Strauss, Lewis L. *Speech to the National Association of Science Writers*. New York City, 16 September 1954. Reprinted in *New York Times*, 17 September 1954.

Wiesner, Jerome B. *Vannevar Bush: A Biographical Memoir*. Washington, D.C.: National Academies Press, 1979.

Woolf, Amy F. *Nonstrategic Nuclear Weapons*, Report for Congress. Congressional Research Service (Library of Congress), 29 August 2012.

Zachary, G. Pascal. *The Endless Frontier: Vannevar Bush, Engineer of the American Century*. New York: The Free Press, 1997.

Games cited

Fallout. Beverley Hills, CA: Interplay Entertainment, 1997.

Fallout 2. Beverley Hills, CA: Interplay Entertainment, 1998.

Fallout 3 (and expansions). Rockville, MD: Bethesda Softworks, 2008.

Fallout Brotherhood of Steel. Rockville, MD: Bethesda Softworks, 2004.

Fallout: New Vegas (and expansions). Rockville, MD: Bethesda Softworks, 2010.

Fallout Tactics. Rockville, MD: Bethesda Softworks, 2001.

20

Irony and American Historical Consciousness in *Fallout 3*

Tom Cutterham

St. Hugh's College, Oxford University

America is a nation with an origin story, a country particularly concerned with its own newness and uniqueness. But the well-defined starting-points in the American narrative generate a particular anxiety: an anxiety about endings. At the Chicago World's Fair in 1893, historian Frederick Jackson Turner put forward the thesis that America's unique history was the product of its frontier—a border with "free land"—that had, at the end of that century, ceased to exist. In other words, he declared with trepidation the end of "the first chapter" of American history.[1] One hundred years later, at the close of the Cold War, Francis Fukuyama announced in a distinctly triumphalist tone the end of history itself.[2] This was an ending-story radically at odds with the fearful expectations of the Cold War era, when American historians and citizens contemplated their role in the shadow of the end of the world. The prospect of nuclear annihilation revived a whole genre, Biblical in origin, of destruction and post-destruction fantasies.

Fallout, a series of games dating from 1997 but exemplified here by its third incarnation, is the descendant of this tradition. The genre as a whole neatly connects with Americans' enlightenment and nineteenth-century historical vision, as historian David W. Noble has described it: the dialectical collision of "progress and primitivism," "savagery and civilization."[3] Cultural scholar Gerry Canavan has suggested that post-apocalyptic fiction can serve almost diametrically opposite motives. It can act as a "reinforcement and justification for the biopolitical power structures that already exist," by presenting the world without them as an "ultra-Hobbesian state of permaviolence and degradation"; or it can fulfill a secret (or not so secret) longing "for the destruction of society in general and/or capitalism in particular."[4] *Fallout* neatly fits this paradoxical dual appeal.

What may be surprising about *Fallout* is that, as November argues in Chapter 19, its post-apocalyptic setting does not offer an ahistorical clean slate. As any work of art must be, it is thoroughly embedded in its own historical moment, and within its own historical consciousness. However much the game consciously distorts and effaces the past, its moral and narrative universe remains grounded in historical meaning. In this way it offers a window on the way we imagine the American past. What is more, the game—partly through its own inherent mechanics, the division between player and character— generates a distance between us and the sense of history it presents. That is, it creates a space for irony. With humor as its main tool, it exploits and exposes the cultural and intellectual forms through which American historical consciousness (and thus, in part, ideology) is reproduced.

Nathan of Megaton

The first place I visited, as a player in *Fallout*, was Megaton. It's hard to miss. Guarded by a wall of scrap metal and a robot programmed to act like a barman in a Spaghetti Western, Megaton is one of the Capital Wasteland's larger towns. Its name comes from the unexploded (at least, at first ...) atomic bomb at its center; but its character comes from a diverse set of residents. One of these is Nathan, an ex-trader living out his golden years in relative comfort with his wife Manya—and waiting for the day when the United States is restored to its former glory by the Enclave, a mysterious and growing force in *Fallout*'s world. He is keen to tell me about it.

"It's your duty, and my duty, to support our country and our president no matter what. Understand?" And for us that means supporting the Enclave, the self-proclaimed remnant of the US government, whose roving drones broadcast the stirring and patriotic speeches of "President Anthony Eden."

Wonder aloud where this duty of loyalty comes from, and Nathan replies, "Where in the constitution does it say that we're supposed to run around questioning the government?" When he tells me that, there is an interesting possible response: "Well, they did give us guns and say, 'If we fuck up, feel free to take us out.'"

Fallout's dialogue here offers up a set of ideas about the US constitution— interpretations that, hackneyed as they are, will be familiar to players living in the twenty-first century. My talk with Nathan even recalls the original debate over the constitution's ratification, in the late 1780s, when Antifederalists (opponents of the constitution) claimed that the central government would become dictatorial if it was given too much power. The second amendment and the rest of the Bill of Rights followed as one of the conditions for ratification in some states, which is why historian Saul Cornell calls the Antifederalists *The Other Founders*.[5]

What interests me most about my encounter with Nathan is what it says about the way Americans use their Constitution, and therefore their history. When it comes to interpreting the constitution, everyone's a historian. Conservative judges and politicians in the twenty-first century defend a doctrine of originalism, which holds that the constitution can mean only what its original authors (and, sometimes, the voters who ratified it) understood it to mean. Even liberals have to engage with the idea that the eighteenth-century authors matter, if only to refute the conservatives. So in this case, history is politics, law, and citizenship—or what school teachers call civics.

The two lines of argument in my conversation with Nathan are both originalist. They are about what the authors of the constitution wanted and meant. They are also both profoundly political: one asks for absolute obedience, the other declares a right to armed resistance. This is the minds of eighteenth-century gentlemen directly informing our basic civic commitments. That Nathan and I are discussing this in a post-apocalyptic wasteland in 2277, five hundred years after the Federalists debated the Antifederalists, is really not much more absurd than the same arguments happening on Fox News today. Is it? The game's setting serves as an exaggeration—a distortion of scale, but not type. Where Thomas Hobbes used the "state of nature" to demonstrate the limits of moral reasoning, *Fallout* uses its post-apocalypse to test the reasonableness of our—of, specifically, Americans'—dedication to the past.

One of the reasons history *is* so important is that it acts as a host for ideology. In fact, the world of *Fallout* strips it of any other function, since the atomic destruction has rendered the patterns of the preceding civilization effectively defunct. We are in the ironic position of entering a new world, but carrying into it the historical forms of the old. "History," wrote Marx, "weighs like a nightmare on the minds of the living." That irony is hauntingly evoked by the ruins of Washington D.C.'s monuments—but my discussion of that comes later. Now I want to look closer at the problem of ideology.

In a recent essay, Adam Kotsko reminds us that "ideology is not to be found in our conscious opinions or convictions but, as Marx suggested, in our everyday practices. Explicit opinions ... serve as symptoms to be interpreted rather than statements to be taken at face value."[6] He goes on to elucidate the philosopher Slavoj Žižek's recommendation that in order to see ideology, we should "look for symptomatic contradictions." We can do the same thing here; in fact, *Fallout* practically does it for us.

Nathan of Megaton is a patriotic American. He goes around whistling "Yankee Doodle"; if he was alive in 2008 he would have voted for McCain and Palin. He believes it is our duty to "support our country and our president no matter what," just as many Republicans did under the Bush presidency. The powerful central state is a principle embedded in the constitution by its Federalist authors, who sought to bring respect to America—and power to themselves—by uniting the separate states under their own strong leadership. But Nathan, like today's Republicans, also believes in the second amendment, and its corollaries as parsed by the National Rifle Association. In other words, he can't disagree when I tell him, "Well, they [the Founders] did give us guns and say, 'If we fuck up, feel free to take us out.'" Instead, his response is predictably defensive, "You're just trying to confuse me with your fancy Vault education and your textbooks ... "

That act of confusion, through the application of thought to culture, is precisely the aim of Žižek's ideological analysis. "The reader should not simply have learned something new. The point is, rather, to make him or her aware of another—disturbing—side of something he or she knew all the time."[7] *Fallout*'s player occupies not only the position of the protagonist, the "Lone Wanderer"; we are also left open to the same confusion as Nathan. It isn't the player that exposes the ideological contradiction here: it's the game. The same can be said for many other episodes in *Fallout*, and more deeply, for our experience of the game as a whole.

Lincoln's legacy

Somewhere in the northeast quarter of *Fallout*'s Capital Wasteland, there's a dilapidated three-storey building known as the Temple of the Union. This temple exists because in this post-apocalypse, slavery is once again prevalent in America. It is a rallying-point—or a hiding-place—for a group of fugitive slaves, and a headquarters for their leader, Hannibal Hamlin (named after Abraham Lincoln's first vice-president). For Hannibal and his followers, the legend of Lincoln is quasi-religious. The victory of Union forces in the Civil War, and the emancipation of slaves in the American south, offers an example of the possibility to win freedom. For the player, the temple presents one of the game's many moral dilemmas. It also allows us to enact a miniature paean to one of America's defining historical moments, and so opens up another symptomatic contradiction in American historical self-consciousness.

The existence of slavery in the world of *Fallout* is revealing in itself, as an evocation of the political and moral tradition of Thomas Hobbes and John Locke, the seventeenth-century English philosophers whose liberal individualism deeply impacted American political thought. Locke, especially, provided the doctrine of just revolution that supported the Declaration of Independence. Both these Englishmen argued that slavery was a natural and justifiable occurrence. In the state of nature where humans would exist without government, the power that one man may hold over the life of another naturally gives him a kind of possession, or dominion. "[T]his dominion," Hobbes wrote, "is then acquired to the victor when the vanquished, to avoid the present stroke of death, [agrees] that so long as his life and the liberty of his body is allowed him, the victor shall have the use thereof at his pleasure."[8] In other words, the sociological prediction depicted in *Fallout* is that if men are free from the restraints of the state, some of them will enslave the others.

America's mythic history entails that it should be the land of individual freedom, the country that threw off the chains of Britain's empire not only for national but also for personal liberty. The problem is that America's story must also be a story of slavery, for slavery must exist in order to be defeated. It should be noted that the republic of Jefferson and Jackson, the republic of the early nineteenth century, is celebrated as the apotheosis of liberty, while at the same time the Civil War that ended that republic—and remade it in blood and fire—is celebrated as its greatest triumph. Lincoln used the power of the industrialized, militarized state to end slavery. But the more basic ironic contradiction is simply that slavery must be an indelible part of American history precisely so that its *ending* can be as well.[9] This is just what happens in *Fallout* too.

We are offered a simple choice: help Hannibal and the fugitive slaves; help the slave-hunters who are tracking them down; or do neither. The quest, as the game scripts it, leads us to the ruins of the Lincoln Monument, where the fugitives will establish a new and more impressive base. The statue of Lincoln is restored by a resourceful stonemason, and Lincoln paraphernalia can be collected from the nearby ruins of the American History Museum. This Lincolnalia, Hannibal believes, will serve as a powerful symbol of hope to slaves all across the Wasteland. There is surely a further irony in the fact that he, a black ex-slave who has fought for and won his own freedom, chooses to idolize a dead white man as freedom's symbol. Of course, he has also relied on the player's help. It is we ourselves, as the player, who play the role of emancipator.

Video games can offer this form of historical identification in a way that text or even films cannot. Which is not to say that the vast industry of Civil War books has nothing to do with the ideological imperative to play out this contradiction over and over again; but video games let us literally *play out* moments of historical fixation (not least, the experience of war). Perhaps this is psychologically necessary because the moments cherished by the ideological mythos are liminal ones: they exist in-between two sites, without the characteristics of either one. So, for example, the American Revolution balances between British colonial rule and the inevitable decline from the Founders' genius. The Civil War is neither the slave society of the antebellum, nor the modern and capitalist world it left behind. These are therefore moments of profound possibility founded on profound lack: they embody a neither/nor, and so they offer a window of withdrawal from the real.

This negative site is just what *Fallout's* post-apocalyptic scenario offers. Here is a world of radical potentiality in which history can be constantly refigured, reshaped, and replayed. The ironic doubling that takes place in American historical identity—the simultaneous existence and destruction of slavery, for example—can be replicated in a narratively satisfying form in the game. It offers us several meanings at the same time; and as cultural theorist Linda Hutcheon has argued, the presence and interaction of multiple meanings creates its own meaning.[10] Here, we are allowed to be more than one thing at the same time (just as video games allow us to *be* someone else while remaining ourselves), we are allowed to embody and enact the ideological contradictions that must be kept under wraps in normal life.

Stealing independence

I am in a bunker underneath the National Archives. To get here I had to fight my way past a dozen robot guards armed with lasers and flamethrowers, and now a malfunctioning tour-guide in a powdered wig is earnestly informing me that he is Button Gwinnett, second signer of the Declaration of Independence. He has appointed himself protector of the document from invading British forces, of whom he is convinced I am one. But what if I can convince him that I am Thomas Jefferson, the Declaration's famous author? There are a few different kinds of reenactment going on here, and none of them is straightforward.

In her book about the modern Tea Party, historian Jill Lepore argues that the political use of history by the American right wing involves a problematic conflation of the present with the past. It is not that they want to go back to the past, she says, it is that they want to bring the past here.[11] But of course, the past is already here. Where else could it be? Writing history, like building museums, is partly about helping the past survive. The question is whether it might be about anything more than that, more than simply the past for its own sake. It is clear that the Tea Party's sense of history is part of a movement that has some clear political goals: to cut taxes, and make the federal government less powerful (except over something like abortion rights). If I take on the voice of Thomas Jefferson in *Fallout*, I am only doing the same thing: using history for my own ends.

Stealing the Declaration of Independence is, in its way, a deeply symbolic act. But what it symbolizes is mostly the failure of symbolism. The paradox of *Fallout*'s post-apocalyptic situation is that history—and thus, the Declaration—both matters, and does not matter. If someone, namely Abraham Washington of Rivet City's "Capitol Preservation Society," wants to pay me to retrieve the document, then it has some value; but Washington's museum, and his whole program, are clearly an eccentric waste of time from the perspective of most wastelanders just trying to survive. That attitude is not so different from how most people see history and museums now. *Fallout*, and this mission in particular, dramatizes this problem.

"I cannot allow you to steal our freedom," declares the robot Gwinnett. "The Declaration must remain here! It is our symbol of hope, the one thing that cries out, 'We are a free nation!'" Listening to this stirring speech has a similar effect of irony and absurdity to our conversation with Nathan in Megaton. Once, we feel, these things may have mattered. But not now. And this must raise the question, when exactly does it stop mattering? Or, what exactly is it that makes it matter? Unlike the Constitution, the Declaration has no legal force in the twenty-first century, let alone the twenty-third. Yet for Gwinnett, "this is no mere document, sir. This is the doctrine laid down by my fellow members of the Second Continental Congress." Abraham Washington, the collector, cannot even get that right: he calls it the "Second Judgmental Congress."

It is clear that the meanings of things, including texts, from the past are created by each user in his or her present context. One of the ironies of historical practice, though, is the almost necessary omnipresence of an intentional fallacy. Readers of novels need not be concerned with the original intentions of the author; most of the time, they recognize that those intentions are irrecoverable anyway. But the idea famously explored by Robin Collingwood in his posthumous *The Idea of History*, that the re-creation or reenactment of the thoughts of past people is the central feature of history-writing, still fits the way audiences approach the past.[12] Video games of course present an opportunity, unimaginable to Collingwood, to re-create past conditions in radically different ways outside the library and the text. Tea Partiers have done that in their own way, too, by donning the costumes and symbols of their historical heroes, however ill-informed about them they might be.

By impersonating Jefferson to get my hands on the Declaration, I share a strategy with those who want to fight originalism (i.e. the idea that "the Founders'" intentions matter, and can be known) with originalism itself. As William Hogeland has argued, left-liberal historians and commentators, whose claims about contemporary law and politics are based on alternate constructions of past texts, events, and characters, are playing the same game as their opponents. "American-history fantasies of the left stand sharply in relation to those of the right," Hogeland writes: but both are fantasies.[13] There is a sense in which such fantasy about American history has been encouraged and developed since the nation's founding. Indeed, any nation by definition relies on a partly imagined construction of its own past to underpin a present identity.[14] In America, the legal force of the Constitution helps reinvigorate those fantasies, both shared and conflicting, through constantly reiterated debate.

Fallout and its post-apocalyptic scenario seem to offer their own kind of independence to the player and the protagonist. In the game's prologue, we learn that life in Vault 101 is governed by a hermetic ideology: "we live in the vault; we die in the vault." Once we escape, we realize this was never true. Escaping from the vault and into the wasteland also represents an escape, for the twenty-first-century player, from a cultural context that is marked by obsessions with imagined pasts—with history. *Fallout* does not just take place after apocalypse: its chronology diverged from our own long before then. So its world is not a mere prophecy, but a different reality altogether: a world in which, once, the world of tomorrow came to pass.

It is a cruel irony then that *Fallout* should be so saturated by the past, and by a particularly American past. Its world, it turns out, shares with our own the key landmarks of a national imaginary: the founding, the Civil War, World War II. There is no escaping, no independence from history. At its most basic, and its most artistically compelling, this point shines through *Fallout*'s passive, background world. Among the crumbled ruins of the Monuments, and on the scorched earth of the open country, the past and its myths stalk us.

Historyscapes

We can distinguish two kinds of interpretation occurring in any work of art. One is interpretation by the artist, in this case the game designers and so on; the other is interpretation by the audience, the player. (Of course, this distinction must be constantly broken down in practice.) A work of art like *Fallout* does not rely on conscious appreciation of historical tropes and allusions for its success as narrative entertainment: perhaps video games even less so than more narrowly intellectual forms. Games do not present themselves as subjects of analysis but as mechanisms of entertainment. *Fallout* relies and plays on already internalized historical knowledge, tropes, allusions; but it also plays *with* these things: like any artwork it reproduces in a distinct form the ideology that informs it. What happens when we play *Fallout* is a creative interaction between the historical consciousness of the game-creators and ourselves, the game players. In other words, to play *Fallout* is to make history.

Landscape is an object of interpretation in various ways, including historical and cultural (not just, for example, strategic). This relies on visual cues/clues taken from cultural context: not least film, but increasingly representations in video games and in other visual media; and also the textual imagery of historical narratives. There are certain images, certain senses of the landscape, which correspond more or less directly to tropes in language and in history. The one most central to *Fallout*'s historical imaginary is the concept of virgin land and the frontier.

Richard Slotkin traces the mythology of the frontier through American history in his trilogy of books culminating in *Gunfighter Nation*, which focused on "Western" films of the twentieth century.[15] *Fallout* could easily be considered part of his corpus. As Frederick Jackson Turner pointed out in his 1893 essay, which stands at the fount of academic historical analysis of the frontier phenomenon, the frontier mechanism applies not only to the Wild West of the mid-nineteenth-century imagination but to all of continental north America. *Fallout*'s sequel, *New Vegas*, might make its Wild West inspiration more obvious, but it is not the specific location that matters so much as its status. To be frontier land is to be uncertain, unsettled, uncontrolled; a space where order and ownership are waiting to be imposed. Thus *Fallout*'s post-apocalyptic Capital Wasteland is very much a frontier.

The same scrubby bushes, the same yellow-baked soil, and the same dust-filtered sunsets characterize *Fallout*'s landscape as we might encounter in any Western film. But it is a frontier landscape with the moral and aesthetic problematics written back in. When we step out of the Vault, are we really setting foot on "virgin land"? As new sets of ruins appear over the crest of each hill, we are constantly reminded of a reality effaced from the traditional Western mythology: this freedom and chaos is built on destruction. Burial mounds, empty fields, and wooded trails were the physical reminders of Native Americans' decimation by European invaders and colonists. In *Fallout*, the detritus of an extinguished consumer culture is far more ubiquitous. Scorched and abandoned children's toys, or "pre-war casual-wear," or wads of bank-notes, proliferate as gravestones to a former America. As Slotkin writes, the myth of the frontier is a story of "*regeneration through violence.*"[16]

Obviously, violence is no mere absent presence in *Fallout*. I have already described encounters with slave-hunters and killer robots, but the paradigmatic antagonist of *Fallout* is something else, with its own ideological underpinnings. "Supermutants" are enormous green men—or anthropomorphic animals—intent on killing the player and any other humans they encounter; they are brutish, slow-witted, inarticulate, single-minded, bestial. Their strongest resemblance is to the orcs, trolls, and giants of popular fantasy. And like those creatures, their narrative and ideological role is to be "Other." Needless to say, there is an equivalent to supermutants in the frontier imaginary of the Westerns: "savages" or "Indians," tomahawk-armed and implacably opposed to the forward march of civilization. They provide the primary conflict, which it is then the player's pleasure to resolve. They frame the experience of the game in terms of warfare, but a fantasized warfare in which the right and wrong sides are clear-cut.

Unlike warfare proper, however, the Western (and *Fallout*) narrative does not hinge on the coordinated effort of large and disciplined groups of people. Precisely the opposite: it is determined by the decisions and struggles of a "Lone Wanderer." This is the genre of rugged individualism *par excellence*. The possibility of engaging a trusty companion, either human or animal (or in-between?) doesn't exactly undermine that; it only serves to highlight the essential nature of the protagonist's own choices. Placed within the narrative structure of the game, we as the player are caught up in a web of moral entanglement with ourselves at the center. We are responsible not only for our own survival and self-improvement, but for the future of the game-world itself. In *Fallout*, you may be a hero or a villain, but you *must* matter. The plot, the world's history, literally cannot move without you.

This trifecta of ideological constructs—the frontier, the savage Other, and the rugged individual—links *Fallout* to the Western genre, and thus to a powerful iteration of the American historical imagination. In case there was any doubt, the first thing anyone said to me outside the vault was "howdy, partner!" And the mayor of Megaton wears a Stetson. Culture has taught us to read these cues and to construct our expectations around them. But it has also given us the tools to read them ironically: that is to critique the ideological assumptions that underpin the frontier myth. Through various techniques of presentation, some of them already described above, *Fallout* seems to encourage the player to pursue an ironic construction. At the very least, *Fallout* harbors an implicit critique of its explicit ideological content. By making us play through the implications of a culturally ubiquitous historical consciousness, *Fallout* effects a Žižekian jolt: it "make[s] [the player] aware of another—disturbing—side of something he or she knew all the time."

Conclusion

When history is translated into myth, the complexities of social and historical experiences are simplified and compressed into the action of representative individuals or "heroes". The narrative of the hero's action exemplifies and tests the political and/or moral validity of a particular approach to the use of human powers in the material world. The hero's inner life—his or her code of values, moral or psychic ambivalence, mixtures of motive—reduces to personal motive the complex and contradictory mixture of ideological imperatives that shape a society's response to a crucial event. But complexity and contradiction are focused rather than merely elided in the symbolizing process. The heroes of myth embody something like the full range of ideological contradictions around which the life of the culture revolves, and their adventures suggest the range of possible resolutions that the culture's lore provides.[17]

Slotkin's analysis of myth here corresponds particularly appositely to the functioning of video games. The difference is that the hero's inner life, his or her code of values, and so on, is (at least inasmuch as we have freedom in our in-game choices) our own. Does this distinction in itself make of video games an inherently ironic medium? *Grand Theft Auto* offers a particularly clear example, because it doubles the player's identity in an extreme way: we happily perform actions that soar absurdly and gleefully beyond our ethical limits outside the game-world. *Fallout* shares similar characteristics, even while it allows more freedom to make ethical choices.

As such, it functions as a critique: it brings into question, in a disturbingly personal way, the kinds of things that the structure and tropes of an American mythology—an American historical consciousness—ask us to do and believe. In this way, perhaps video games have a particular role to play in political, ethical, cultural, and historical conversations. They may have the rhetorical force to help challenge and shift ideological horizons. If that is so, it is something video games share with the genre of history itself. The ability to be, do, and believe different things simultaneously is in the nature of video games. It is also in the nature of historical consciousness. After all, history is the past, but it is also undeniably the work of the present, too.

Notes

1 Frederic Jackson Turner, "The Significance of the Frontier in American History," in *The Frontier in American History*. New York: Henry Holt and Company, 1935.

2   Francis Fukuyama, *The End of History and the Last Man*. New York: The Free Press, 1992.

3   David W. Noble, *Historians against History: the Frontier Thesis and the National Covenant in American Historical Writing since 1830*. Minneapolis, MN: University of Minnesota Press, 1965, 11, 46.

4   Gerry Canavan, "The Past as Anti-Future," blog post at *culturemonkey*, 21 January 2008, http://culturemonkey.blogspot.co.uk/2008/01/past-as-anti-future.html.

5   Saul Cornell, *The Other Founders: Anti-Federalism and the Dissenting Tradition in America, 1788–1828*. Chapel Hill, NC: University of North Carolina Press, 1999.

6   Adam Kotsko, "How to Read Žižek," *Los Angeles Review of Books*, 2 September 2012, http://lareviewofbooks.org/article.php?type=&id=897&fulltext=1&media=.

7   Kotsko, "How to Read Žižek."

8   Thomas Hobbes, *Leviathan*. London, 1651, Ch. XX.

9   James McPherson, *Battle Cry of Freedom: The Civil War Era*. Oxford: Oxford University Press, 1988, 857–862; see also Herman Hattaway and Archer Jones, *How the North Won: A Military History of the Civil War*. Champaign, IL: University of Illinois Press, 1991.

10 Linda Hutcheon, *Irony's Edge: the Theory and Politics of Irony*. New York: Routledge, 1994, 60.

11 Jill Lepore, *The Whites of Their Eyes: The Tea Party's Revolution and the Battle over American History*. Princeton, NJ: Princeton University Press, 2010.

12 R.G. Collingwood, *The Idea of History*. Oxford: The Clarendon Press, 1946.

13 William Hogeland, "Founding Fathers, Founding Villains: The New Liberal Originalism," *Boston Review*, September/October 2012, http://www.bostonreview.net/BR37.5/william_hogeland_founding_fathers_liberalism_originalism.php.

14 Eric Hobsbawm and Terence Ranger, *The Invention of Tradition*. Cambridge: Cambridge University Press, 1983; Benedict Anderson, *Imagined Communities: Reflections on the Origin and Spread of Nationalism*. London: Verso, 1983.

15 Richard Slotkin, *Regeneration through Violence: The Mythology of the American Frontier, 1600–1860*. Middletown, CT: Wesleyan University Press, 1973; *The Fatal Environment: the Myth of the Frontier in the Age of Industrialization*. New York: Atheneum, 1985; *Gunfighter Nation: the Myth of the Frontier in Twentieth-Century America*. New York: Atheneum, 1992.

16 Slotkin, *Gunfighter Nation*, 12.

17 Slotkin, *Gunfighter Nation*, 13–14.

Works cited

Anderson, Benedict. *Imagined Communities: Reflections on the Origin and Spread of Nationalism.* London: Verso, 1983.

Canavan, Gerry, "The Past as Anti-Future," blog post at *culturemonkey*, 21 January 2008, http://culturemonkey.blogspot.co.uk/2008/01/past-as-anti-future.html, accessed 26 January 2013.

Collingwood, R.G. *The Idea of History.* Oxford: The Clarendon Press, 1946.

Cornell, Saul. *The Other Founders: Anti-Federalism and the Dissenting Tradition in America, 1788–1828.* Chapel Hill, NC: University of North Carolina Press, 1999.

Fukuyama, Francis. *The End of History and the Last Man.* New York: The Free Press, 1992.

Hattaway, Herman and Archer Jones. *How the North Won: A Military History of the Civil War.* Champaign, IL: University of Illinois Press, 1991.

Hobbes, Thomas. *Leviathan.* London, 1651, Ch. XX. http://www.gutenberg.org/files/3207/3207-h/3207-h.htm.

Hobsbawm, Eric and Terence Ranger. *The Invention of Tradition.* Cambridge: Cambridge University Press, 1983.

Hogeland, William, "Founding Fathers, Founding Villains: The New Liberal Originalism," *Boston Review*, September/October 2012, http://www.bostonreview.net/BR37.5/william_hogeland_founding_fathers_liberalism_originalism.php, accessed 26 January 2013.

Hutcheon, Linda. *Irony's Edge: The Theory and Politics of Irony.* New York: Routledge, 1994.

Kotsko, Adam, "How to Read Žižek," *Los Angeles Review of Books*, 2 September 2012, http://lareviewofbooks.org/article.php?type=&id=897&fulltext=1&media=, accessed 15 March 2013.

Lepore, Jill. *The Whites of Their Eyes: The Tea Party's Revolution and the Battle over American History.* Princeton, NJ: Princeton University Press, 2010.

McPherson, James. *Battle Cry of Freedom: The Civil War Era.* Oxford: Oxford University Press, 1988.

Noble, David W. *Historians Against History: The Frontier Thesis and the National Covenant in American Historical Writing since 1830.* Minneapolis, MN: University of Minnesota Press, 1965.

Slotkin, Richard. *Regeneration Through Violence: The Mythology of the American Frontier, 1600–1860.* Middletown, CT: Wesleyan University Press, 1973.

Slotkin, Richard. *The Fatal Environment: The Myth of the Frontier in the Age of Industrialization.* New York: Atheneum, 1985.

Slotkin, Richard. *Gunfighter Nation: The Myth of the Frontier in Twentieth-Century America.* New York: Atheneum, 1992.

Turner, Frederick Jackson, "The Significance of the Frontier in American History," in *The Frontier in American History.* New York: Henry Holt and Company, 1935, 1–38.

Games cited

Fallout. Beverley Hills, CA: Interplay Entertainment, 1997.
Fallout 2. Beverley Hills, CA: Interplay Entertainment, 1998.
Fallout 3. Rockville, MD: Bethesda Softworks, 2008.
Fallout: New Vegas. Rockville, MD: Bethesda Softworks, 2010.
Grand Theft Auto IV. New York: Rockstar Games, 2008.

21

The Historical Conception of Biohazard in *Biohazard/Resident Evil*

Robert Mejia
State University of New York, Brockport

Ryuta Komaki
University of Illinois at Urbana-Champaign

The investment of a particular disease with the cultural anxieties and desires of a given population has an effect upon the actual manifestation of the disease in terms of how the dissemination of the "outbreak narrative" promotes or mitigates the stigmatization of "groups, populations, locales, ... behaviors, and lifestyles, and ... change economies," thereby influencing "survival rates and contagion routes."[1] This is particularly evident in the historical response to AIDS, in which the homophobic discourse that has surrounded the transmission of the disease has not only configured the affliction as punishment for homosexual lifestyles but has also obscured the effect it has had on other populations.[2] It seems pertinent, then, that we look to popular histories of disease and contagion if we are to understand how certain populations are marked as worthy of life and others to be expendable.

It is for this reason that we believe the *Biohazard* (Japan)/*Resident Evil* (United States) franchise to be an artifact particularly worthy of historical analysis.[3] This franchise warrants our attention for a variety of reasons: (1) the franchise emerged in the mid-1990s, at the same time that the outbreak narrative was garnering renewed interest and increased significance regarding the Ebola Virus;[4] (2) the franchise has functioned as one of the longest lasting and most prolific of contemporary outbreak narratives, with over nineteen games (and other cultural artifacts) having been produced over the course of nearly twenty years; (3) the franchise operates as an important archive of transnational anxiety and desire, in terms of being produced by a Japanese game company, Capcom, for the intended consumption by Japanese, American, and other international audiences; and (4) the revision of the franchise's internal history during and after the transition from *Resident Evil 1–3 to 4–5* documents the historical effects 9/11 has had on the cultural and political understandings and consequences of epidemiology across the globe. These last two points seem most pertinent, in that, though much work has been undertaken on the significance of outbreak narratives, the scope of analysis has often remained limited to US cultural practices at the very same moment that its global hegemony is undergoing reconfiguration.[5] If we indeed are living in the midst of an epidemic of epidemics, then it seems necessary for us to grasp the operation of this epidemic as it circulates on a global level.[6] Hence, the longevity and popularity of the *Resident Evil* franchise marks it as a rich and compelling archive for understanding the cultural work of the outbreak narrative at a global level. To this end, we argue that the *Resident Evil* franchise documents the transnational fusion of Japanese and US cultural politics around questions of (1) the racialization of anti-capitalist politics; (2) the conception of Africa as being the Heart of Darkness; and (3) the post-9/11 inflection of the outbreak narrative with counterterrorism discourse.

Resident Evil: The anti-capital era (1996–2001)

The early *Resident Evil* franchise was known for both its cinematic and ludic conventions. In terms of cinematography, these early games sought to emulate the claustrophobic camerawork of Hollywood-style horror through the use of a fixed-perspective, surveillance-style camera that conspicuously limited the player's field of view.[7] This added to the unsettling atmosphere of the games in that this perspective made traversing corners and other blind spots nerve-wracking (for fear of an unseen enemy jumping out at the player); moreover, the perspective made combat difficult, and combined with the limited access to resources (e.g. ammo), these game design choices encouraged the player to seek flight over fight. Movement was further restrained by the decision to link the avatar to the controller much like that of a radio-controlled car, with the directional movement always mapped to the physical perspective of the avatar. These three ludic decisions—of fixed perspective, scarce resources, and avatar-centric movement—had the effect of making the early *Resident Evil* games fairly difficult, thereby adding a sense of impending dread to each game's atmosphere. Hence, the franchise, famously known for having popularized the survivor-horror genre, embedded these "horror" conventions not just in the narrative, but also in its ludic elements as well.

The early *Resident Evil* franchise was also known for its explicitly anticapitalist narrative. From *Resident Evil 1* and onward, players come to learn that the series was not really about zombies, but the production of biological weapons by the fictional Umbrella Corporation, a pharmaceutical conglomerate based in Raccoon City. It is revealed via in-game dialogue and other plot devices that this corporation had been conducting experiments in the attempt to manufacture biological weapons, which appear in *Resident Evil 1* as functional zombies, giant spiders, and other—often previously human—creatures. In line with the *daikaiju eiga* (giant monster) and other Japanese horror traditions, the enemy in *Resident Evil 1* is never really the zombie or these monsters, but rather the scientific–military complex run amok.[8]

The monsters—zombies in particular—then, are not necessarily meant to be demonized, but rather sympathized with as potential subjectivities we might ourselves occupy had our luck turned out otherwise; indeed, the game goes to great lengths to provide glimpses of the zombies' former humanity. This sympathy is in stark contrast to conventional Western horror films, in that in the United States monstrosity in and of itself is often conveyed as evidence of one's moral and/or individual failings.[9] Contrarily, monstrosity, in the Japanese horror tradition, is often attempted to be understood, as a means of illustrating not just how someone becomes a monster, but rather why the existence of monsters is punishment for the failings of society.[10] In the case of the early *Resident Evil* franchise's internal history, then, the series establishes that the pursuits of science for the sake of capital carries with them consequences for society, and those consequences are the potential threat of biological catastrophe.

While the franchise positioned the interests of corporate capital and the military–industrial complex in opposition to those of the public, the series also established certain logics regarding who constituted the legitimate victims of biological contamination. This is because *Resident Evil* is informed by the Japanese aesthetic of *mukokuseki*, "literally meaning 'something or someone lacking any nationality'" and was designed to remove Japanese ethnic markers from international cultural products in favor of universal characteristics; in practice, however, the *mukokuseki* style tends to conceive of the universal subject as Caucasian, and *Resident Evil* is no different.[11] In essence, the Raccoon City of *Resident Evil 1* is positioned as an innocent, traditional, "every city," and, along with its protagonists, who are conceived as universal subjects, configured as sympathetic sites and populations: the victims are either predominantly White or unmarked (and hence, presumed to be White), and likewise so too are the protagonists. This particular articulation of whiteness in relation to the outbreak narrative is significant, for, as Priscilla Wald argues, the discourses embedded within epidemics carry with them suggestions as to how to understand who suffers and what must be done in the face of potential epidemic.[12] So though the franchise's biopolitics operates unevenly and at the transnational level, the *Resident Evil* franchise established a particular configuration of the White, gendered, classed, and heterosexual subject as the primary population of concern, as well as primary agents of action.

In essence, the early *Resident Evil* franchises' reliance upon two Japanese cultural practices, the *mukokuseki* and *daikaiju eiga* traditions, results in the entanglement of two competing historical narrative threads, Whiteness and anti-capitalism. On one hand, the early franchise is fairly consistent in its positioning of corporate capital as being antithetical to civil society, as throughout the course of these early games, the player learns that the financial donations made by the Umbrella Corporation to Raccoon City resulted in the corruption of local, state and even national governments. And yet, the conflation of Whiteness as being equated with the universal, in the tradition of the *mukokuseki* style, lends the early *Resident Evil* franchise a "not in my backyard" narrative thrust. The game makes it clear that the Umbrella Corporation is not just in the business of pharmaceuticals but also the production of biological weaponry. The moral focus of the early franchise, however, is not a criticism of biological weaponry in and of itself; it is rather that an outbreak could happen here. What damns the Umbrella Corporation, then, is its failure to adequately respond to the leakage.

Resident Evil: The revisionist period (2002–2004)

At the turn of the century, Capcom was looking to capitalize upon the outbreak narrative it had produced. The ludic and cinematic elements that had been the franchise hallmark, however, were beginning to feel dated by both fans and critics alike.[13] Attempts at updating these conventions, however, met with limited success; *Resident Evil: Survivor*, for instance, which attempted to blend the franchise mythos with the gameplay style of a first-person shooter, was widely criticized and poorly received.[14] This failure may have been due to the conflicting signals between the ludic and narrative elements, for as Irene Chien argues, the horror aspect of the "survivor-horror" video game genre may stem from the ability to reproduce the anxieties of fragmentation through gameplay conventions:

> Rather than gliding into a room towards a cabinet in the corner in a single continuous shot, you first see the doorway to the room from an exterior perspective, then cut to a long shot of one side of the room's interior as you enter, and then cut to another, medium shot of the cabinet as you approach it.... As in horror cinema, a sense of paranoia unsettles every step forward. Navigating through the game becomes a highly anxious experience; the gameplay is hesitant rather than fluid and assertive.[15]

Though operating within the same symbolic universe, the outbreak narrative reproduced through these attempts at expanding the *Resident Evil* series failed to capture the sense of dread that made the franchise so compelling and successful. As a result, Capcom opted to refocus the franchise by returning to its roots with the next installment in the series.[16] This next installment would be the prequel, *Resident Evil 0*. Furthermore, Capcom opted to rerelease *Resident Evil 1–3* and *Code Veronica* as both a moneymaking opportunity and as a means for introducing new fans to the franchise mythos.[17] What is most interesting for our concerns, however, is that the rerelease of the original games was accompanied by several revisions to the internal history of the franchise's outbreak narrative. This was, perhaps, to be expected with *Resident Evil 0*; however, the most significant revisions were those that accompanied the remake of *Resident Evil 1*.

Though the Umbrella Corporation is still held front and center as antithetical to the interests of civil society, the origins of outbreak were rewritten in *Resident Evil 0* and the remake of *Resident Evil 1*. This was done by placing more emphasis on the natural origins of the virus responsible for the epidemic. Meant to operate as a promotional primer for the upcoming release of *Resident Evil 0*, the rerelease of *Resident Evil 1* included new elements that preempted the historical revisions that would take place in the prequel.[18] Most significantly, in conjunction with the rerelease of *Resident Evil 1*, Capcom produced a promotional document entitled "Wesker's Report II." The document was intended to synthesize the outbreak narratives established in the early games in preparation for the prequel. Included in the "Wesker's Report II," however, is a significant treatise on the uses of the Ebola virus as a biological weapon:

> What if a person infected with the Ebola virus could stand up and walk around? And that infected person would have a disrupted chain of thought, and would infect others that weren't infected?

....

The person would be dead from a human's point of view, but would still go around as a human bio-weapon spreading the virus around?

It's fortunate that the Ebola [*sic*] may have features like this.

This conception of the Ebola virus as having the innate potential to transform the infected subject into a "virus bomb" links this revised outbreak narrative with that produced by other cultural artifacts a decade earlier, in the mid-1990s; for instance, note the parallels in language between the above passage from "Wesker's Report II" and Richard Preston's *The Hot Zone*:

> He [Monet] doesn't seem to be fully aware of pain any longer because the blood clots in his brain are cutting off his brain flow. His personality is being wiped away by brain damage.... It could be said that the who of Charles Monet has already died, while the what of Charles Monet continues to live ... Monet has been transformed into a human virus bomb.[19]

Like these other outbreak narratives, then, so too does *Resident Evil* introduce the conception of Africa as the home of biological danger;[20] for even though the Umbrella Corporation is responsible for the production of biological weapons, the "Wesker's Report II" makes it clear that within the franchise's outbreak narrative these biological weapons may already exist within the natural environment.

If the *Resident Evil 1* remake introduced the African Origin Theory of Disease to the franchise, then *Resident Evil 0* subtly crystallized the production of what Lisa Lynch calls "the neo/bio/colonial hot zone"[21]—that is, the legitimation of international intervention upon African countries as a means of combating the threat of global pandemic. In offering insight into how the virus of the franchise was made, *Resident Evil 0* offers parallels between what one of the characters, Billy Coen, has seen during his military service in Africa and the effects of the disease upon US populations. It is never fully articulated, however, whether the bodies he saw in Africa were afflicted with the same condition as those he has seen within the United States. Whether the African victims suffered from the same affliction or not, the link between the experiences is tantalizingly made within the game via a series of flashbacks and plot threads regarding the significance of Billy's military service in Africa. In essence, the connection is this: the Umbrella virus induces a form of madness and suffering that is comparable to that indigenous to Africa.

In conjunction with the revisions made with the rerelease of *Resident Evil 1*, then, *Resident Evil 0* repositions the source of outbreak as ultimately stemming from natural causes—Africa. And yet, even at this point, it was not yet clear what direction the franchise would take. The introduction of the African Origin Theory of Disease did connect the franchise's internal history with that of Western epidemiology; however, the Umbrella Corporation continued to be emphasized as well. The series, then, contained the narrative flexibility to push forward in any number of directions, most notably: further exploring the consequences of finance capital and biological manipulation or continuing to emphasize the natural origins of pandemics. Narratives, however, are never self-contained things and the essence of horror had begun to shift in the period after September 11.[22] So although many narrative possibilities existed regarding the future of the franchise, the constraints of the historical time and place of production made it so that some possibilities were deemed more compelling than others.

Resident Evil: The counterterrorism years (2005 to the present)

If Irene Chien is correct in that the sense of terror experienced within the "survivor-horror" video game genre stems as much from gameplay and cinematography as from the narrative, then which ludic elements are capable of capturing the shift in the essence of horror that had been underway post-9/11?[23] This was the challenge faced by the developer for *Resident Evil 4*, Shinji Mikami, for as Travis Fahs wrote: "If *Resident Evil* [4] was to be scary, it would have to surprise people. A zombie dog jumping through a window just couldn't work anymore."[24] This search for a ludic solution to the shifting definition of terror, however, would affect the narrative thrust of the franchise beyond whether or not a zombie dog jumped through the window.

The ludic framework of the early and middle *Resident Evil* franchise called upon a definition of pandemic horror that had lost some dominance in the aftermath of September 11. Affliction had once meant the transformation of an individual into an unassuming agent of infection (at best) or catatonic "human virus bomb" (at worst).[25] The zombie, the iconic figure of the early and middle franchise, had captured this sense of anxiety well, with its image of a lumbering, passionless—and highly contagious—walking corpse.[26] The sense of paranoia in operation within this particular logic of horror was complemented by the ludic fragmentation indicative of this period of the franchise, with its constant cutting and reframing of action.[27] The zombie of today, however, is "no longer deadpan ... an image of humanity stripped of passion, soul, or spirit [rather] the zombie has become enraged ... a gutted, animalistic core of hunger and fury."[28] Though off-screen movement continues to be an effective tactic for representing this form of zombification, the emphasis on absolute terror, as captured via this form of zombie, calls for the extensive use of long- and medium-shots so that viewers are always aware not just of the horror that remains off-screen, but the horror that is explicitly on-screen as well. As had the franchise before, *Resident Evil 4* would articulate this sense of fear through the implementation of particular ludic conventions; most significantly, through the use of an over-the-shoulder tracking shot.

This new perspective had the effect of radically reconfiguring the outbreak narrative that had been produced throughout the early history of the franchise. In the early games, the zombies were relatively indistinguishable from one another, and this resonated with the sympathy the player was expected to have with those who had become infected; in other words, there was a clear distinction between being human and being infected—being infected had no weight upon the prior character of the individual. In *Resident Evil 4*, however, one cannot help but notice that even prior to infection, these populations were *never* like us: the horror of the conventional zombie narrative is that we might become like them, hence the frequent dilemma regarding when to kill an infected but not-yet-zombified individual; the horror of the *Resident Evil 4* zombie narrative is that while the player characters are clearly differentiated, one cannot distinguish the infected from the uninfected villagers, hence the anxiety that there may be no distinction to be made. The infected, then, do not garner sympathy, for in being unlike us, it is unclear at what moment they came to stand against us. This ambiguity had the effect of revitalizing the terror embedded within the experience of the survival horror.[29] The ambiguity, however, also had the effect of requiring the addition of a narrative thread capable of explaining away the reason one could not distinguish between who was infected and who was not. This plot device would, conveniently, be religion and terrorism.

The reinvigoration of franchise's outbreak narrative through an infusion of post-9/11 counterterrorism discourse suggests that what is most frightening today is not that infection might produce monstrosity, but rather that monstrosity might not need infection. For though *Resident Evil 4* makes it clear through the course of the game that the enemy population is infected with a zombie-like affliction, the distinction between monstrosity and normality is unclear—for the game developers also consistently emphasized that the infected villagers suffered from some far greater affliction than conventional zombification.[30] Near the beginning of the game, for instance, the player as Leon Kennedy observes a scene in which the backwardness of the villagers is associated with the monstrosity of the situation. The non-zombie, zombie-like status of the villagers, then, speaks to the politics of subject formation embedded within representations of monstrosity. If the historical conception of "the monster and the person to be corrected are close cousins," then the contrast between the protagonists and antagonists of *Resident Evil 4* speaks to the contemporary anxieties regarding Islam and bioterrorism that became widespread post-9/11.[31] More to the point, *Resident Evil 4* operates as one site in which the outbreak narrative is rearticulated in accordance with the discourse surrounding contemporary terrorism, in which terrorist populations are always already suffering from affliction—that of an unfamiliar religion or cultural practice.[32] The warning embedded within the definition of the non-zombie, zombie-like villagers is that living the life of a cultural zombie is synonymous with becoming a "real" zombie itself; or rather, the fear for those who believe that national and/or global culture has come to be decadent is that a real zombie apocalypse may be right around the corner.[33] And yet, though *Resident Evil 4* introduced the concept of the cultural zombie to the outbreak narrative of the franchise, it would not be until the production of *Resident Evil 5* that the implications of this entanglement of culture, contagion, and terrorism would raise concern.[34]

Resident Evil 5 revealed the extent of the cultural logic behind the entanglement of the *mukokuseki* style with that of the outbreak narrative and counterterrorism discourse. As Jennifer Robertson writes, in Japan,

> *Minzoku* and *jinshu*, the two Japanese words for "race" in both the social and phenotypical senses, for the most part, were used interchangeably . . . . When prefixed with names, such as Nippon and Yamato, *minzoku* signified the conflation of phenotype, geography, culture, spirit, history, and nationhood. All of these semantic and semiotic inventions were part of the ideological agenda of the Meiji state and were incorporated into the postwar constitution of 1947, which retained the definition of nationality and citizenship as a matter of blood.[35]

This conflation of ethnicity with nation has the effect of conceiving of the ethnic body as an always already national body, regardless of whether or not a given population resides within the "appropriate" national border.[36] The measure of a nation, from this perspective, then, is tied to the ethnic integrity of the nation's rightful population.[37] Hence, *Mukokuseki* speaks not necessarily of the United States, or the West, but rather of the Japanese imagination of whiteness as an obtainable state of racial purity that brings with it certain global privileges.[38] If whiteness is associated with modernity and the universal subject, however, the contemporary formation of whiteness also serves as an allegory for Japanese racial anxieties:[39] in the mid-1980s both former Japanese prime minister Nakasone Yasuhio and prominent

Liberal Democrat Michio Watanabe, on separate occasions, suggested that the economic struggles of the United States were due to the presence of "blacks, Puerto Ricans, and Mexicans."[40]

The point of this aside on the racial politics of Japan is not to paint Japan as more or less racist than the United States—as this would ignore the effect Western hegemony has had on the global circulation of race[41]—but rather to situate the *Resident Evil* franchise as a transnational text embedded with the global anxieties and desires of racial purity. The flexibility of the *mukokuseki* aesthetic means that both Western and Japanese audiences can read themselves into the outbreak narrative presented within the franchise; and hence, it serves as a site for thinking through global biopolitical anxiety and desire. The linkage of the *mukokuseki* style with that of the outbreak narrative and contemporary War on Terror discourse within *Resident Evil 4* and *5*, then, brings to the surface the underwriting logics of race that had been present throughout the series. For though it was not until *Resident Evil 5* that the franchise became a lightning rod for representations of race within video games, the conception of whiteness as the organizational logic of the series had long been present within the series:[42] the citizens of Raccoon City, in *Resident Evil 1–3*, were represented as deserving of sympathy only to the extent that they were racialized as White subjects; in *Resident Evil 4* and *5*, though this sympathy is still there, the rural Spanish (*Resident Evil 4*) and African populations (*Resident Evil 5*) are marked as always already suspect.[43] This is most clearly represented by an early scene in *Resident Evil 5* of three African villagers beating a large human-sized sack with wooden clubs.

Though both the developers of *Resident Evil* and many of the fans of the franchise would argue that the situating of *Resident Evil 5* in Africa was the result of the logical outcome of the internal history of the franchise, these defenses ignore the ideological investment of the *mukokuseki* style within the production of this particular history.[44] Within the *daikaiju eiga* and apocalyptic film traditions of Japanese cinema unbridled scientific research is condemned to the extent that it results in the production of unnatural bodies. When those bodies are already marked as socially and/or physically aberrant or inferior, however, the history of Japan's racial politics, like that of the West, conceives of these populations not as a population to be protected but rather one to be managed, for fear of infecting the rest of us.[45] The ease with which the franchise was able to reposition rural populations and Africa as the original site of infection, moreover, speaks to the cultural logics at play in the global production and consumption of outbreak narratives. Far from the ludic conventions of gameplay draining the abject status of race, then, it would seem that gameplay and cinematic conventions are themselves infused with the politics of biopolitical anxiety and desire.[46] In the post-9/11 world, terrorism offered a compelling narrative thread to understand the source of outbreak. Though the Umbrella Corporation continues to operate in the shadows throughout the later games in the franchise, the real source of affliction, as explained narratively throughout *Resident Evil 4* and *5*, is that participating in an unfamiliar religion and/or harboring anti-Western sentiment opens one's self up to infection: the Spanish villagers of *Resident Evil 4* became infected through their membership of a local religion; the African villagers of *Resident Evil 5* became infected because of their involvement with rebels seeking to rid Africa of Western influence. The later franchise, then, operates as an apologia for contemporary global politics, in that the experience of global suffering is ultimately pinned upon those populations that refuse to and/or are unable to operate within the transnational logics of contemporary capital—the corruption of global capital is not to be found within the logic of capital, but rather those countries that allow these corporations to operate so exploitatively.

Conclusion: Transnational circuits of anxiety and desire

This analysis of the *Resident Evil* franchise suggests that we must understand the contemporary experience of anxiety and desire as operating through transnational circuits of production and consumption. The anxiety and desire surrounding the sense of an impending end of the world that others have recognized as endemic to our historical moment is inflected with the raced, classed, and gendered (amongst other) interests not just of Western, but increasingly of other capitalist populations as well.[47] This is not cause for celebration, as in the destabilization of Western hegemony, and the birth of a new era of a more egalitarian platform for the expression of global anxiety and desire, however; rather, it calls for the increased scrutiny of increasingly global artifacts with a sensitivity to the complex circuits of production and consumption at play in the transnational circulation of these artifacts.

What we have attempted to show through this analysis of the *Resident Evil* franchise, then, is that the fusion of the Western outbreak narrative with that of Japan's *daikaiju eiga* and apocalyptic horror traditions, via the use of the *mukokuseki* style, operates as an important site in which video game players engage with contemporary discourses regarding global terrorism; this particular configuration, as articulated within the franchise, presents a global ecology in which racially pure (that is White, and by extension Japanese) subjects are to be vigilant against the possibility of cultural contamination from others, whether they be corrupt corporations (e.g. *Resident Evil 1–3*) or always already suspect, foreign, populations (e.g. *Resident Evil 4–5*). Hence, the franchise contributes to a conception of the world in which the global disparities in experiences of pleasure and displeasure are explained away as not being due necessarily to transnational political economic exploitation, but rather due to the intrinsic racialized characteristics of regional populations.

Notes

1 Priscilla Wald, *Contagious: Cultures, Carriers, and the Outbreak Narrative*. Durham, NC: Duke University Press, 2007, 3.

2 Wald, *Contagious*.

3 The franchise is known as *Biohazard* in Japan. However, the difficulty of registering this trademark within the United States encouraged Capcom to release the game globally under the name of *Resident Evil*. See GR Asks, "Why" For a fuller explanation of this rebranding. Throughout the rest of this chapter, we will refer to the franchise under its global designation of *Resident Evil*.

4 Cf. Lisa Lynch, "The Neo/Bio/Colonial Hot Zone: African Viruses, American Fairytales," *International Journal of Cultural Studies*, 1, no. 2 (1998).

5 Cf. Lisa Keränen, "Addressing the Epidemic of Epidemics: Germs, Security, and a Call for Biocriticism," *Quarterly Journal of Speech*, 97, no. 2 (2011); Lynch, "The Neo/Bio/Colonial"; Wald, *Contagious*; Priscilla Wald, Nancy Tomes, and Lisa Lynch, "Introduction: Contagion and Culture," *American Literary History*, 14, no. 4 (2002).

6 Cf. Keränen, "Addressing the Epidemic of Epidemics."

7 The cinematography of Hollywood-style horror "corresponds to a temporal structure which raises the anxiety of not being ready, the problem, in effect, of 'too early!'" Linda Williams, "Film Bodies: Gender, Genre, and Excess," *Film Quarterly*, 44, no. 4 (1991), 11.

8 Cf. Jay McRoy, "Introduction," in Ed. Jay McRoy, *Japanese Horror Cinema*. Honolulu, HI: University of Hawai'i Press, 2005.

9 Colette Balmain, "Oriental Nightmares: The 'Demonic' Other in Contemporary American Adaptations of Japanese Horror Film," *At the Interface/Probing the Boundaries*, 57 (2009); Peter Dendle, "The Zombie as Barometer of Cultural Anxiety," in Ed. Niall Scott, *Monsters and the Monstrous: Myths and Metaphors of Enduring Evil*. Amsterdam: Rodopi, 2007.

10 Balmain, "Oriental Nightmares"; McRoy, "Introduction."

11 Koichi Iwabuchi, *Recentering Globalization: Popular Culture and Japanese Transnationalism*. Durham, NC: Duke University Press, 2002, 28–29.

12 Wald, *Contagious*.

13 Travis Fahs, *IGN Presents the History of Resident Evil: Capcom's Gruesome Horror Series Is a Survivor*.

14 Fahs, *IGN Presents the History of Resident Evil.*

15 Irene Chien, "Playing Undead," *Film Quarterly*, 61, no. 2 (2007): 65.

16 IGN Staff, *Capcom Brings the Evil to Cube.*

17 IGN Staff, *Capcom.*

18 Fahs, *IGN Presents the History of Resident Evil.*

19 Richard Preston, *The Hot Zone*. New York: Random House, 1994, 18.

20 Cf. Lynch, "The Neo/Bio/Colonial Hot Zone."

21 Lynch, "The Neo/Bio/Colonial Hot Zone."

22 Colette Balmain, "The Enemy Within: The Child as Terrorist in the Contemporary American Horror Film," in Ed. Niall Scott, *Monsters and the Monstrous: Myths and Metaphors of Enduring Evil*. Amsterdam: Rodopi, 2007.

23 Chien, "Playing Undead."

24 Fahs, *IGN Presents the History of Resident Evil.*

25 Lynch, "The Neo/Bio/Colonial Hot Zone."

26 Dendle, "The Zombie as Barometer of Cultural Anxiety."

27 Chien, "Playing Undead."

28 Dendle, "The Zombie as Barometer of Cultural Anxiety," 54.

29 Fahs, *IGN Presents the History of Resident Evil.*

30 Fahs, *IGN Presents the History of Resident Evil.*

31 Cf. Jasbir K. Puar and Amit S. Rai, "Monster, Terrorist, Fag: The War on Terrorism and the Production of Docile Patriots," *Social Text*, no. 3 (2002): 119.

32 Cf. Puar and Rai, "Monster, Terrorist, Fag."

33 Dendle, "The Zombie as Barometer of Cultural Anxiety."

34 Cf. André Brock, "'When Keeping It Real Goes Wrong': *Resident Evil 5*, Racial Representation, and Gamers," in *Race, Ethnicity, and (New) Media*. College Station, TX, 2009; Eric Freedman, "Resident Racist: Embodiment and Game Controller Mechanics," in Ed. Rebecca Ann Lind, *Race/Gender/ Class/Media 3.0: Considering Diversity across Audiences, Content, and Producers*. Boston, MA: Pearson, 2012.

35 Jennifer Robertson, "Blood Talks: Eugenic Modernity and the Creation of New Japanese," *History and Anthropology*, 13, no. 3 (2002), 195.

36 Jane H. Yamashiro, "Racialized National Identity Construction in the Ancestral Homeland: Japanese American Migrants in Japan," *Ethnic and Racial Studies*, 34, no. 9 (2011).

37 Arnaud Nanta, "Physical Anthropology and the Reconstruction of Japanese Identity in Postcolonial Japan," *Social Science Japan Journal*, 11, no. 1 (2008); Robertson, "Blood Talks."

38 Cf. Iwabuchi, *Recentering Globalization*; Michael Prieler, "Othering, Racial Hierachies and Identity Construction in Japanese Television Advertising," *International Journal of Cultural Studies*, 13, no. 5 (2010); Robertson, "Blood Talks."

39 Iwabuchi, *Recentering Globalization*; Prieler, "Othering, Racial Hierachies."

40 John Russell, "Race and Reflexivity: The Black Other in Contemporary Japanese Mass Culture," *Cultural Anthropology*, 6, no. 1 (1991), 3–4.

41 Nanta, "Physical Anthropology"; Russell, "Race and Reflexivity."

42 Cf. Brock, "When Keeping It Real Goes Wrong"; Freedman, "Resident Racist."

43 Brock, "When Keeping It Real Goes Wrong."

44 Cf. Freedman, "Resident Racist."

45 Nanta, "Physical Anthropology"; Robertson, "Blood Talks."

46 Cf. Freedman, "Resident Racist."

47 Cf. Keränen, "Addressing the Epidemic of Epidemics."

Works cited

Balmain, Colette. "The Enemy Within: The Child as Terrorist in the Contemporary American Horror Film," in Ed. Niall Scott, *Monsters and the Monstrous: Myths and Metaphors of Enduring Evil*. Amsterdam: Rodopi, 2007, 133–147.

Balmain, Colette. "Oriental Nightmares: The 'Demonic' Other in Contemporary American Adaptations of Japanese Horror Film," *At the Interface/Probing the Boundaries*, 57 (2009): 25–38.

Brock, André. "'When Keeping It Real Goes Wrong': *Resident Evil 5*, Racial Representation, and Gamers," in *Race, Ethnicity, and (New) Media*. College Station, TX, 2009. http://resi.tamu.edu/files/draft_program.pdf.

Chien, Irene. "Playing Undead," *Film Quarterly*, 61, no. 2 (2007): 64–65.

Dendle, Peter. "The Zombie as Barometer of Cultural Anxiety," in Ed. Niall Scott, *Monsters and the Monstrous: Myths and Metaphors of Enduring Evil*. Amsterdam: Rodopi, 2007, 45–57.

Fahs, Travis. *IGN Presents the History of Resident Evil: Capcom's Gruesome Horror Series Is a Survivor*, http://retro.ign.com/articles/960/960835p1.html;

Freedman, Eric. "Resident Racist: Embodiment and Game Controller Mechanics," in Ed. Rebecca Ann Lind, *Race/Gender/Class/Media 3.0: Considering Diversity across Audiences, Content, and Producers*. Boston, MA: Pearson, 2012, 285–290.

GRAsks. "Gr Asks: Why Was Biohazard Renamed Resident Evil?" http://www.gamesradar.com/gr-asks-why-was-biohazard-renamed-resident-evil/. GamesRadar, 8 April 2009

IGN Staff. *Capcom Brings the Evil to Cube*, http://cube.ign.com/articles/098/098267p1.html.

Iwabuchi, Koichi. *Recentering Globalization: Popular Culture and Japanese Transnationalism*. Durham, NC: Duke University Press, 2002.

Keränen, Lisa. "Addressing the Epidemic of Epidemics: Germs, Security, and a Call for Biocriticism," *Quarterly Journal of Speech*, 97, no. 2 (2011): 224–244.

Lynch, Lisa. "The Neo/Bio/Colonial Hot Zone: African Viruses, American Fairytales," *International Journal of Cultural Studies*, 1, no. 2 (1998): 233–252.

McRoy, Jay. "Introduction," in Ed. Jay McRoy, *Japanese Horror Cinema*. Honolulu, HI: University of Hawai'i Press, 2005, 1–11.

Nanta, Arnaud. "Physical Anthropology and the Reconstruction of Japanese Identity in Postcolonial Japan," *Social Science Japan Journal*, 11, no. 1 (2008): 29–47.

Preston, Richard. *The Hot Zone*. New York: Random House, 1994.

Prieler, Michael. "Othering, Racial Hierachies and Identity Construction in Japanese Television Advertising," *International Journal of Cultural Studies*, 13, no. 5 (2010): 511–529.

Puar, Jasbir K. and Amit S. Rai. "Monster, Terrorist, Fag: The War on Terrorism and the Production of Docile Patriots," *Social Text*, 20, no. 3 (2002): 117–148.

Robertson, Jennifer. "Blood Talks: Eugenic Modernity and the Creation of New Japanese," *History and Anthropology*, 13, no. 3 (2002): 191–216.

Russell, John. "Race and Reflexivity: The Black Other in Contemporary Japanese Mass Culture," *Cultural Anthropology*, 6, no. 1 (1991): 3–25.

Wald, Priscilla. *Contagious: Cultures, Carriers, and the Outbreak Narrative*. Durham, NC: Duke University Press, 2007.

Wald, Priscilla, Nancy Tomes, and Lisa Lynch. "Introduction: Contagion and Culture," *American Literary History*, 14, no. 4 (2002): 617–624.

Williams, Linda. "Film Bodies: Gender, Genre, and Excess," *Film Quarterly*, 44, no. 4 (1991): 2–13.

Yamashiro, Jane H. "Racialized National Identity Construction in the Ancestral Homeland: Japanese American Migrants in Japan," *Ethnic and Racial Studies*, 34, no. 9 (2011): 1502–1521.

Games cited

Resident Evil 0. Osaka: Capcom, 2002.
Resident Evil 1. Osaka: Capcom, 1996.
Resident Evil 2. Osaka: Capcom, 1998.
Resident Evil 3. Osaka: Capcom, 1999.
Resident Evil 4. Osaka: Capcom, 2005.
Resident Evil 5. Osaka: Capcom, 2009.
Resident Evil: Survivor. Osaka: Capcom, 2000.

22

The Struggle with Gnosis: Ancient Religion and Future Technology in the *Xenosaga* Series

Erin Evans
University of Edinburgh

The *Xenosaga* series is an ambitious space epic, a continuous story over three games with political struggles, corporate intrigue, and military strategies that span entire galaxies.[1] All of these struggles, however, have a foundation deeply rooted in Western esoteric religious traditions—political, military, and even corporate forces are often revealed to be operating in pursuit of goals related to ancient religions founded on Earth in antiquity. Perhaps most striking, however, is the way these religious notions play a vital role in the development of technology. In this future, humanity is technologically extremely advanced, epitomized by the ongoing development of artificial intelligence and humanoid entities with increasingly human traits. In this quest to develop humanlike beings with advanced abilities, mankind approaches a sort of godhood, seeking to create life forms in its own image—but also to control those life forms, creators subordinating the wills of those they create. Furthermore, scientists are continually attempting to harness the limitless energy of the higher dimensions to power new technologies—most often in the form of weapons designed to combat perceived threats also deriving from those higher dimensions. The games abound with subtle and not-so-subtle themes and terminology derived from a wide variety of religious and philosophical backgrounds, blending them together into a future "history" in which the development of human civilization is closely intertwined with both a quest for and struggle against divinity.

This chapter will focus on a narrow subset of historical religious influences, in order to gain a greater understanding of the targeted subjects rather than presenting a broad overview of the symbolism found in this series. Although ideas and images from diverse philosophies and religions, such as Jungian and Nietzschean philosophy, Buddhism, Zoroastrianism, and Hinduism, are utilized to varying degrees in the formation of the physics and future society of this universe, the focus here will be on the appropriation and reinterpretation of terms and concepts from loosely Bible-based texts and traditions from the first few centuries of the Common Era—Jewish mysticism, Christianity, and Gnosticism. While often a character or concept will represent multiple symbols, here the discussion must focus specifically on a small subset of subjects and layers of meaning. Furthermore, although the political and corporate machinations throughout the series are intriguing, the discussion will be restricted to those religious undertones associated with man-made technology and its development. It will examine how ancient esoteric religious ideas are brought to the fore in interpreting technological and weapons development, and the conflict associated with this development. Ultimately it will be demonstrated that the intertwining of future human struggles with actual ancient religious texts and concepts prompts the player to radically rethink certain understood religious histories, particularly relating to Christianity.

Gnosis

Before beginning an examination of the use of technology, a brief explanation of the "monsters" of the *Xenosaga* universe is in order. Entities called the "Gnosis" with monstrous appearances form the core of much of the conflict in the series: they straddle dimensions, existing between the higher/divine and lower/material realms; they cannot be touched by conventional weapons without the use of certain waves or pulses; and if they touch a human being, that human either dissolves, or is eventually transformed into a Gnosis himself. A very small number can be touched and neither dissolved nor transformed.

"Gnosis" is Greek for knowledge; in an ancient religious context, this signified divine knowledge, knowledge of god or true reality.[2] The Gnostic quest was to find this true knowledge and to experience divinity or become divine, sometimes rejecting materiality and the passions of the body in the process; however, not all people were equal in this quest. Some Gnostic groups posited three types of humans: hylic (material), psychic (soul), and pneumatic (spiritual). Those who were hylic could experience none of the divine, and they were doomed to ultimate destruction. The psychics could potentially achieve salvific knowledge, but only through great effort and dedication, being caught between the material drives and spiritual realities. Finally, the pneumatics were predisposed to accept the divine and were guaranteed salvation, although they constituted the smallest group of human beings.[3] In *Xenosaga*, the three potential outcomes of encountering the Gnosis—dissolution, transformation, or acceptance without consequence—may then represent these Gnostic spiritual potentialities. However, in the series' human society at large, there is little understanding and much fear of these entities, and thus the Gnosis are viewed as a major threat. Much of the technology in the games revolves around finding ways to eliminate the Gnosis; ironically, however, most of the research into how to stop them from appearing simply calls more of them into the human dimension. One of the most important factors in attracting these creatures is the use of the most sought-after power source in the universe.

The Zohar

Although the series takes place 4,000 years in to the future, when humanity has migrated into deep space and Earth has been lost for thousands of years—it is here called "Lost Jerusalem," immediately demonstrating the importance of the Abrahamic religions and their influence in this universe—the opening scene roots itself in ancient, Earth-based religion and technology. In the year "A.D. 20XX," an archaeologist makes a dramatic discovery at Lake Turkana, located in modern Kenya at a site extremely important in the study of early human evolution. Reuniting a key with its ancient lock, the ground rumbles, and from the depths of the lake a carefully hewn stone walkway emerges, leading to a giant, floating, glowing object: the Zohar.

The *Zohar*, frequently translated as "The Book of Splendor," is one of the main texts of the Kabbalah, a branch of Jewish mysticism. Although it is now generally accepted by scholars to be a thirteenth-century pseudepigrapha, it is claimed to be the work of the second-century sage Simeon ben Yohai.[4] The fact that it attempts to trace its own roots to the more ancient sage is what is important here. Although it contains interpretations of Torah passages and mythical stories, overall it is meant as a guide to help the already spiritually enlightened person reach a state of spiritual wholeness, exploring the divine process, bringing inner religious experience, and explaining the gradual emergence of God from a state of hiddenness to revelation. Just as God is revealed and then withdraws to himself, so the mystic becomes absorbed in God in religious experience, losing the self, and then in returning from the experience he is reintegrated into his individuality, his own personality.[5]

The Zohar as an object, rather than as a text or teaching, takes a central place in the *Xenosaga* universe. It acts as a portal between two dimensions, real and imaginary space, or the human and divine conscious domains. In the "real" or material universe in which the story takes place, it serves as an almost unlimited power source, a key component in several major technologies. Competing factions struggle to obtain it, to attempt to activate its power for their own purposes. Any living being that *touches* the artifact, however, is immediately dissolved from existence. Direct contact with the divine or its power results in the dissolution of the individual into the infinite divine consciousness. Furthermore, it was experimentation with the Zohar on Lost Jerusalem/Earth in the past that led to humanity's flight to the stars and the loss of the planet. The artifact itself is repeatedly lost and then found again by humanity: the opening scene on Earth unburies it after thousands of years, and in the main body of the game, although several "emulators" that resemble it have been made, the location of the original is often locked away or unknown. This may represent part of mankind's cyclical journey of seeking the divine and the sporadic revelation of true divine knowledge at certain epochs, only to be lost again.[6]

Vessels of Anima and the Zohar Emulators

As mentioned above, there are also a series of emulators of the Zohar in the games. These are man made, and are designed to facilitate the use of the original Zohar. They function by emulating the wavelengths of the Vessels of Anima—another set of ancient relics found on Earth. The Vessels of Anima, in turn, derive their power from the original Zohar. Although Anima plays an important role in Jungian psychology as a representation of the unconscious or true inner self and also as the feminine principle operating in a masculine soul, here it is important through its connection to the Zohar and thus the higher god-principle. It is revealed that the Vessels each contain parts of the original, complete power of Anima, which before it was divided was present in human form in ancient times in a being called Yeshua—the original Hebrew form of the name Jesus.[7] In this case, however, it is not the Jesus of the Bible, the crucified Messiah, who possesses this power—although he was present in the Messiah's circle of followers. This figure, called chaos (with the first letter always lowercase) in the future when the games take place, remains alive and is with the player's party all along, with an air of constant mystery tinged with sadness. The Vessels of Anima, then, combine to form the complete power of Anima in a humanoid being called Yeshua, which is connected with and derives its power from the Zohar, the portal to the higher domain or god-consciousness. This certainly seems to draw from the Christian notion of Jesus as God in human form, both connected with but independent from the Father God in Heaven—but in a more Gnostic than orthodox Christian way, as the Jesus who was crucified was *not* the divine entity.[8] In certain heterodox Christian or Gnostic traditions in the first centuries CE, although the divine savior appears human or might inhabit a human body for a time, he is decidedly not human, and cannot die.[9]

There are twelve each of the Vessels of Anima and Zohar emulators;[10] the former are each named after the offspring of Jacob in the book of Genesis—although Jacob's daughter Dinah replaces one of the twelve sons, Benjamin. The emulators are each named for disciples of Jesus in the New Testament. The twelve disciples are sometimes considered to be representations or counterparts of the twelve sons of Jacob, the foundation of the tribes of Israel.[11] It should also be noted that the name given to the original Zohar is "Marienkind"—Child of Mary, referring to Jesus/Yeshua. The connection of Yeshua to this source of power and portal between the higher and lower realms has been discussed above, and ties the whole system firmly into a Christian-Gnostic perspective. Thus, the emulators (named for the disciples) can only access the power of the Zohar (God) through the mechanism of the Vessels (Yeshua's divine power, split and named after Jacob's offspring), the new emulating and interacting with the old vehicles of divine power in accessing the higher dimension. This also reinterprets important mythic or historical figures of Christianity as tools of human development in a technological light, a rethinking of the accepted religious history of these figures.

Furthermore, human experimentation with one of the emulators, attempting to link it directly with the higher domain or divine consciousness, resulted in the planet on which the experiment took place vanishing. This highlights and reinforces the inability of human constructs or those in the lower realm to *truly* bridge the gap between these domains—only the original Zohar can do that—although it also shows the persistence humans have in attempting to forcibly tap that higher power.

The Vessels of Anima come into play in the realm of human technological development by virtue of their use with piloted mechanical power suits, called AGWS (Anti-Gnosis Weapons Systems). Although AGWS are common in the

Xenosaga universe, when one is fitted with a Vessel of Anima, it becomes an "ES."—an "Ein Sof," a kabbalistic term from the *Zohar* referring to God prior to his self-manifestation, and meaning Infinite, or endless. *Ein Sof* is God eternal and beyond comprehension.[12] By virtue of tapping into the limitless power of the Zohar through the Vessel, these ESs develop much greater freedom than typical suits that must stay close to a power station, as well as enhanced speed, strength, and power. The Vessels of Anima themselves take the form of large human spines, and are referred to in the games as the "body of God" or "power of God"; in a sense, it is granting a lifeless suit an extension of God's unending power, representing his body. Only those with certain types of strong wills or souls can pilot an ES, further showing the connection of technology, divine power, and the individual attempting to bridge the two. The persistent use of this higher power in weapons of destruction is typical of human action, as is to be seen in all of the other major technological developments that utilize the Zohar.

The Merkabah

"Merkabah" means "chariot," and in a mystical context refers to the chariot or throne-chariot of the Jewish god. Although use of the term derives from the account in the first chapter of Ezekiel and there are traces of the Merkabah tradition in early apocalyptic literature, it was most widely used in esoteric literature composed from around 200 to 700 CE, and then later in the medieval period.[13] It became a goal of certain rabbis to undertake a spiritual journey to the Merkabah, to gain comprehension of the heavenly secrets found in the scriptures.[14]

In *Xenosaga*, the Merkabah takes the form of space-going vessels, developed based on information in ancient records, and is extant in two versions: the prototype, "Proto-Merkabah," and the final version, "Tactical Assault Ship Merkabah." The first of these is a space station and research lab, created to discover the true form of the universe, but also designed for the development of a certain type of artificial humans called "Realians"—beings designed for specific purposes, often with abilities superior to humans, and with emotions that can be turned on or off. This is an example of humanity's approach to godhood: having constructed a grand chariot in the heavens, they use it as a base in which the creation of living beings takes place, right down to the decision of whether to give those beings free will in the form of their own emotions or personality. This power of creation can also be abused: certain factions used the station to manipulate certain models of Realian so that they would malfunction and go berserk, exploiting them for political and military gain. This station is designed to incorporate the Zohar, but does not use it as a primary power source. Instead, it uses the medium of the "Song of Nephilim" to attract Gnosis to it, absorbing the Gnosis and converting them to energy. The Tactical Assault Ship Merkabah was created after the Proto-Merkabah was destroyed. It is not used for research, but is now purely a support device for a massive weapons system, again highlighting the human drive to use higher power or energy for destructive purposes. Xenosaga thus re-envisages the historical interpretation of the Merkabah, transforming it from the seat of God into the seat of humanity seeking divinization through creation—while struggling with both itself and the divine.

The Song of Nephilim and the Lemegeton

The Song of Nephilim was designed to dock with Proto-Merkabah and to be used as a control for the Zohar, but is utilized by various factions as a weapon. It emits a song, or wavelength, which is inaudible to normal human ears; however, it attracts Gnosis to it, and for certain beings that *can* hear it—particularly the sabotaged Realians—it drives them into a berserker state. The Song itself is derived from an incomplete or faulty translation of the words of God found in the Lemegeton, a program designed back in the Earth/Lost Jerusalem era to control the Zohar based on the analysis of ancient data. Amongst the human-audible sounds produced by the wave is the word "Nephilim," giving the Song its name. The Nephilim were the offspring of the "sons of god" and "daughters of men" in Genesis 6:4, and the offspring of the fallen angels in the *Book of Enoch* 6:1–7:2.[15] In Jewish tradition, these unholy half-breeds were part of the reason God decided to bring about the flood and wipe out most of his creation. Tying a faulty transliteration of the word of God to the tradition of these demonic entities, the song brings madness and destruction.

The *Lemegeton* is a grimoire, or magical handbook, the full title of which is *Lemegeton Clavicula Salomonis* (the "Lesser Key of Solomon").[16] Although the material is primarily from the medieval period stretching into the seventeenth century, containing exhortations to Jesus as Lord, it presents itself as deriving from ancient times, claiming to originate from the wise King Solomon's dealings with good and evil spirits. As such, it purports to detail the ritual arts of commanding or controlling these beings, which derive from the higher realm. It contains prayers, incomprehensible names, or magical words and images possessing power over certain divine or otherworldly beings and powers. It is as mystical words or divine commands that the Lemegeton is ultimately presented in *Xenosaga*, although instead of particular spirits or invocations, the waves derived from its "words"—unutterable by and inaudible to most humans—work to control the Zohar, the device connecting to the power of the higher dimension, the divine god-consciousness. The games take fringe elements from Abrahamic traditions—a piece of the mythic history of the Old Testament and related documents, and a popular grimoire with historical claims—and again transform them from distant myth into literal tools in humanity's struggle for power and dominance.

KOS-MOS and T-elos

Arguably the most vital hybrids of religion and technology in the series, these two figures are female androids designed to combat Gnosis: KOS-MOS being the prototype and T-elos the ostensibly superior final version. They are humanoid and look very similar, but with different color schemes and weapon efficiencies—and rather different personalities.

KOS-MOS is one of the central characters in the series, and is composed entirely of mechanical parts. In addition to her arsenal of weapons, she has the ability to bring the Gnosis from imaginary into real space—making it so that weapons can hurt them, because as noted above, under normal conditions Gnosis can touch humans, but physical weapons cannot harm Gnosis. She is also programmed to protect employees of the company that created her—but more specifically Shion, the series' main character and one of the lead figures on her development team. However, the person primarily responsible for her main design and implementation has vanished, and no one else in the development team knows the extent of her programming or capabilities that are sealed away in her black box. She occasionally reveals knowledge and abilities that Shion was completely unaware she possessed; furthermore, occasionally in times of great duress, her eyes change color and she develops a more caring, human persona from her usual emotionally devoid logical interface.

Kósmos, or "cosmos," is Greek for "order." In classical Greek philosophy it applied not only to the universe, but also to society, household life, and generally all levels of existence. Man was also a microcosm of the universe, further reflecting that perfect order. In Greek thought this concept held a prominent place, associated with the highest nature of the divine: all in the universe is ordered as it should be. Indeed, the cosmos was accepted as the finest and most perfect offshoot of the highest god or being in existence, and could itself be considered divine.[17] It is the counterpart to chaos, the formless state of the universe prior to creation from which order emerges.[18] By creating a humanoid entity called KOS-MOS, her creators were again reaching for divinity: re-creating order, the universe, in the microcosm of human form. Not only this, KOS-MOS is a vessel for a soul—the empathetic personality that emerges in times of danger to protect her charge and those around her.

Beyond this connection to Hellenistic religion and philosophy, KOS-MOS has still more overt ties to a Christian Gnostic background. Although her true purpose is only fully revealed in the final chapter of the series, this purpose plays a major role in the entire perspective of religious history and the connection of the holy relics and technology. As noted above, she is the vessel of a soul—but not just any soul. The soul of Mary Magdalene sleeps within KOS-MOS's form, as the misguided ruler of this dimension manipulates events to awaken her. This is the same Mary Magdalene of the Bible and Gnostic Gospels, described in the game as being the companion of "the Messiah," the crucified Jesus; and in fact there are scenes explicitly placing her in the Messiah's presence on Lost Jerusalem. At the entrance to the sealed room where Mary finally awakens within KOS-MOS, there is an inscription from Matthew 28:5–6, depicting Mary Magdalene as the first to discover that Jesus had risen: "And the angel said unto the women, Fear not ye: for I know that ye seek Jesus who was crucified. He is not here, for he is risen, as he said."

Certain Gnostic groups placed a great deal of importance on Mary Magdalene, sometimes believing that she was married to Jesus, but more often simply asserting her spiritual superiority and her great powers of wisdom.[19] There was also a notion of the importance of male–female balance among the universal principles or deities; when a male entity came into being, a female also had to arise to maintain the balance.[20] The same is true of the power of Anima discussed above: it required its counterpart, the Animus— the masculine principle in the female soul—which in the *Xenosaga* universe dwelled in Mary Magdalene. Mary's companion was not the Jesus of the Bible, but rather Yeshua, the possessor of Anima. This balance is reflected further in their character names in this future setting: chaos, the formless state of preexistence, is the counterpart of KOS-MOS, the reasoned order of creation. As noted above, the Anima was divided into parts in ancient times—this was because for various reasons, its continued existence would eventually result in the destruction of the universe. To counteract this, Mary Magdalene/Animus split it into the Vessels, even though this act necessitated her own death or dissolution to maintain the balance. She thus sacrifices herself to save the universe. Although it is apparent that the prevailing militant religious group of the series is of Christian descent, utilizing New Testament quotes throughout the series and believing in the crucifixion of the Messiah, the one who saves mankind and is resurrected here is not the crucified Jesus but Mary Magdalene. The technologically advanced, artificial vessel that is KOS-MOS was intended by its original creator to house Mary's will, or soul, retrieved from the collective consciousness of the universe, until such a time as it had awakened—at which point it was meant to be transferred into the "superior" model, T-elos.

T-elos appears only in the final installment of the series, and like her predecessor, she is also designed as a weapon; however, rather than being purely mechanical, she is formed with the preserved bodily remains of Mary Magdalene. *Télos* is Greek for "consummation" or "completion"; it is the final end of a process. By transferring the awakened consciousness of Mary into T-elos, it was meant to bring about her true resurrection, joining her physical body and immaterial will/soul. However, as a construct with more base, biological components, T-elos is overcome with passion, full of pride and anger. In order to achieve her completion, T-elos seeks to destroy KOS-MOS, but ultimately it is KOS-MOS who destroys T-elos, absorbing part of her instead.

We thus see a radical reinterpretation of Christian myth: the Jesus of the Bible is a human teacher whose message of hope and love is supported by a pair of divine powers, called Mary Magdalene and Yeshua, Animus and Anima. After her self-sacrificial death, it is Mary who is resurrected in the future to continue the process of preserving the universe she began in the time of Jesus. There is a notion of the separation of body and soul, with both being thought necessary for a true resurrection by the followers of the crucified "Messiah" attempting to affect Mary's reincarnation. Mary rejects her physical "resurrected" body, however, preferring to remain in the mechanical construct, separate from the passions that encompass the more biological T-elos before finally returning to an incorporeal form. This reinforces the Gnostic motif of rejecting the material body to strengthen the soul or spirit, and continues the theme connecting divine powers or conscious elements to technological controls or devices.

Conclusions

Ultimately all of the key technologies in *Xenosaga*, from space stations to battle robots, derive power or inspiration from a higher dimension, the divine consciousness. Much of the data or materials used to create or attempt to control these devices derive from thousands of years in the past—the time of Jesus on Earth. Their names show their connections to actual mystical texts and concepts, each of which claims to have come from the ancient sages, and to grant the one who rightly utilizes their contents with contact with the divine realm in the form of spiritual enlightenment, controlling the angels or spirits, or encountering God. By taking ancient Jewish and Christian esoteric fringe concepts and embodying them as physical artifacts with true power, it has sweeping consequences in terms of viewing humanity's development as a sometimes unconscious interaction with the divine, and demonstrates humanity's tendency to misuse power. The advanced technology of this universe is largely utilized in ways that reveal both humanity's fear of the higher dimension and its offshoots—weapons designed to destroy the Gnosis or combat the god-consciousness—and humanity's struggle to become godlike itself—the creation of sentient artificial beings, with or without a soul or free will.

Furthermore, the series features a radical re-envisioning of religious history: it transforms the Christian myth of a dying and resurrecting god-man into a Gnostic vision of spiritual male–female balance, self-sacrifice, resurrection of the will or soul, and rejection of the passions of matter—while still incorporating the blending of divinity and technology in the final result, in keeping with the theme found in all the devices discussed above. The fact that the primary religious practitioners in the *Xenosaga* universe clearly utilize the New Testament and blindly believe in a system akin to orthodox Christianity shows that this is a deliberate and explicit turning of the myth on its head, meant to be a shocking reinterpretation both to the player and to the characters in the game world.

Notes

1 The three games are all for Playstation 2, developed by Monolith Soft and published by Namco Bandai: *Xenosaga Episode I: Der Wille zur Macht* (2003); *Xenosaga Episode II: Jenseits von Gut und Böse* (2005); and *Xenosaga Episode III: Also sprach Zarathustra* (2006).

2 For a brief introduction to gnosis and Gnosticism as a religious phenomenon in a popular cultural context, see Frances Flannery-Dailey and Rachel Wagner, "Wake up! Gnosticism and Buddhism in *The Matrix*," *Journal of Religion and Film*, 5, no. 2 (2001); and more briefly in "Stopping Bullets: Constructions of Bliss and Problems of Violence," in Eds. Matthew Kapell and William G. Doty, *Jacking in to the Matrix Franchise: Cultural Reception and Interpretation*. New York: Continuum, 2004, 97–114. For a broader introduction to early Gnostic traditions and their texts, see Birger A. Pearson, *Ancient Gnosticism: Traditions and Literature*. Minneapolis, MN: Fortress Press, 2007.

3 This is a much-simplified interpretation, embraced more by detractors of the Gnostics; the Gnostic texts themselves suggest less that individuals were

predetermined for destruction, but rather that some mobility between states was possible. See Elaine Pagels, *The Johannine Gospel in Gnostic Exegesis: Heracleon's Commentary on John*. Atlanta, GA: Scholars Press, 1989, 52–57.

4 See Gershom G. Scholem, *Zohar: The Book of Splendor*. New York: Schocken Books, 1963, 12–21.

5 Arthur Green, *A Guide to the Zohar*. Stanford, CA: Stanford University Press, 2004, 78–79.

6 The Zohar, even if it was composed in the second century, was lost or underground until Moses de Leon revealed it again in the twelfth century. The Christian New Testament presents itself as a new revelation clarifying and revising the past prophesies and laws of the Old Testament; and the Koran presents itself as the correction of both these flawed histories or revelations. Certain Christian Gnostic groups held that a divine savior would descend to the world to present the truth at three points in history, the final one heralding the coming of final redemption. Amongst the Nag Hammadi Coptic Gnostic treatises, see, for example, the *Apocryphon of John* (long recension), the *Trimorphic Protennoia*, the *Apocalypse of Adam*, the *Gospel of the Egyptians*, and the *Hypostasis of the Archons*. On the shared salvific descent motif in Sethian Gnosticism, see also John D. Turner, *Sethian Gnosticism and the Platonic Tradition*. Québec: University of Laval Press, 2001, 93–108.

7 Jesus is the Greek transliteration of the earlier Hebrew name Yeshua—although the earliest extant forms of the Gospels are in Greek, Jesus was a Jew and would have had a Hebrew name.

8 One of the major factions in the series is a religious organization aspiring to return to Lost Jerusalem, the land of their crucified Lord and Messiah—but in the end, it is revealed that this goal was only a front to motivate the followers for the founder's true purpose of managing the words and artifacts of God, the technologies of power and divinization of mankind discussed here. Thus, a radically militant Christian organization is shown to be guilty of blind faith in a lie—a criticism of organized Christian religion in the face of individual mystical quest?

9 See Pearson, *Ancient Gnosticism*, 35, 37–38; Hans Jonas, *The Gnostic Religion: The Message of the Alien God and the Beginnings of Christianity*, 2nd ed. Boston, MA: Beacon Press, 1963, 78, 195. This is an extreme simplification of the situation, in which there were numerous different groups or sects with slightly differing interpretations of the Savior, his entry into the world, and how he operated.

10 There is also a thirteenth, inferior emulator made by a different scientist out of spare parts; it is unnamed, and not part of the main body of emulators.

11 See Matthew 19:28 and Luke 22:30.

12 *Zohar* ii. 42b; see Scholem, *Zohar*, 79; *Kabbalah*. Jerusalem: Keter Publishing House Jerusalem Ltd., 1974, 88–90.

13 Andrei A. Orlov, *From Apocalypticism to Merkabah Mysticism: Studies in the Slavonic Pseudepigrapha*. Leiden: Brill, 2007, 224n4.

14 Dan Cohn-Sherbok and Lavinia Cohn-Sherbok, *Jewish and Christian Mysticism: An Introduction*. New York: Continuum, 1994, 4.

15 E. Isaac, "1 Enoch," in Ed. James H. Charlesworth, *The Old Testament Pseudepigrapha, Vol. 1: Apocalyptic Literature and Testaments*. London: Darton, Longman & Todd, 1983, 15–16.

16 There are many editions; for one example, see Joseph H. Peterson, Ed. *The Lesser Key of Solomon: Lemegeton Clavicula Salomonis*. York Beach, ME: Weiser Books, 2001.

17 Jonas, *The Gnostic Religion*, 241–243.

18 James A. Arieti, *Philosophy in the Ancient World: An Introduction*. Lanham, MD: Rowman & Littlefield, 2005, 106.

19 The position she held varied from group to group. For examples of Mary Magdalene's prominent role in noncanonical texts, the *Gospel of Mary* and the *Pistis Sophia* feature her in an enlightened position. See also the *Gospel of Philip*, 63, 33–64, 10, for her close relationship to the Savior. Epiphanius mentions texts called the *Greater* and *Lesser Questions of Mary* (*Panarion* 26.8.2), which also seem to suggest a place of high esteem for her.

20 See, for example, Einar Thomassen's discussion of pleromatology among the Valentinians (*The Spiritual Seed: The Church of the Valentinians*. Leiden: Brill, 2008, 193–247).

Works cited

Arieti, James A. *Philosophy in the Ancient World: An Introduction*. Lanham, MD: Rowman & Littlefield, 2005.

Cohn-Sherbok, Dan and Lavinia Cohn-Sherbok. *Jewish and Christian Mysticism: An Introduction*. New York: Continuum, 1994.

Ephriam Isaac, E. "1 Enoch," in Ed. James H. Charlesworth, *The Old Testament Pseudepigrapha, Vol. 1: Apocalyptic Literature and Testaments*. London: Darton, Longman & Todd, 1983, 5–89.

Flannery-Dailey, Frances and Rachel Wagner. "Wake up! Gnosticism and Buddhism in The Matrix," *Journal of Religion and Film*, 5, no. 2 (2001. http://www.unomaha.edu/jrf/gnostic.htm, accessed 25 May 2013.

Flannery-Dailey, Frances and Rachel Wagner. "Stopping Bullets: Constructions of Bliss and Problems of Violence," in Eds. Matthew Kapell and William G. Doty, *Jacking in to the Matrix Franchise: Cultural Reception and Interpretation*. New York: Continuum, 2004, 97–114.

Green, Arthur. *A Guide to the Zohar*. Stanford, CA: Stanford University Press, 2004.

Jonas, Hans. *The Gnostic Religion: The Message of the Alien God and the Beginnings of Christianity*, 2nd ed. Boston, MA: Beacon Press, 1963.

Orlov, Andrei A. *From Apocalypticism to Merkabah Mysticism: Studies in the Slavonic Pseudepigrapha*. Leiden: Brill, 2007.

Pagels, Elaine. *The Johannine Gospel in Gnostic Exegesis: Heracleon's Commentary on John*. Atlanta, GA: Scholars Press, 1989.

Pearson, Birger A. *Ancient Gnosticism: Traditions and Literature*. Minneapolis, MN: Fortress Press, 2007.

Peterson, Joseph H., Ed. *The Lesser Key of Solomon: Lemegeton Clavicula Salomonis*. York Beach, ME: Weiser Books, 2001.

Scholem, Gershom G. *Kabbalah*. Jerusalem: Keter Publishing House Jerusalem Ltd, 1974.

Scholem, Gershom G. *Zohar: The Book of Splendor*. New York: Schocken Books, 1963.

Thomassen, Einar. *The Spiritual Seed: The Church of the Valentinians*. Leiden: Brill, 2008.

Turner, John D. *Sethian Gnosticism and the Platonic Tradition*. Québec: University of Laval Press, 2001.

Games cited

Xenosaga Episode I: Der Wille zur Macht. Tokyo: Monolith Soft, Namco Bandai, 2003.

Xenosaga Episode II: Jenseits von Gut und Böse. Tokyo: Monolith Soft, Namco Bandai, 2005.

Xenosaga Episode III: Also sprach Zarathustra. Tokyo: Monolith Soft, Namco Bandai, 2006.

23

Conclusion(s): Playing at True Myths, Engaging with Authentic Histories

Matthew Wilhelm Kapell
Sierra College

Andrew B. R. Elliott
University of Lincoln

[T]he future of things past has never been more promising.

WILLIAM URICCHIO[1]

When historians stop writing histories and turn to writing about the writing of history, they go back to the basics. They have, of late, found themselves with certain problems concerning what "history" is understood to mean. Often this leads to inevitable ideological positions less about what history *is*, but about what it is *for*. The British scholar Richard J. Evans is often cited when these questions are raised because his *In Defence of History* offers an attempt to answer both the *is* and *for* questions.[2] For Evans history

---

John Shelton Lawrence offered insightful readings of this conclusion and helped improve it immeasurably. Part of the improvements were conceptual, but they also included help in changing what can only be termed, with appropriate upper-case emphasis, some of the "Most Horrible Sentences in the History of the English Language." He has our thanks.

offers many ways of trying to be useful in both understanding the past, and using that understanding as a way of supporting ideas current in the cultural milieu of the working historian's present. "But," Evans concludes eventually about such a perspective,

> history can only provide reliable support for social and political empowerment in the present if it can convincingly claim to be true, and this in turn demands a rigorous and self-critical approach to the evidence on the part of the historian, who must be willing to jettison political ideas if they prove unworkable without distorting or manipulating the reality of the past.[3]

To put that another way: whatever the use of history might be, it can only be useful if the facts and events organized by the historian can be widely accepted as "true." Leaving aside the philosophical issue of what "true" might mean, at the very least the "facts" used by a historian must be *perceived* by the reader of a work of history to be "correct," which is what leads us to separate *accuracy* from *authenticity* in the current volume.

Playing with the Past is an analysis of historical ideas found in computer and console games that feature "the past" in one fashion or another. But at almost no point do those games feature a factually correct past—even when they allow the player the option of attempting to adhere to a "correct" past, gameplay often requires the inclusion of errors in favor of, simply, a satisfying experience for the player. In any number of the games discussed here it is possible to offer an analysis that says, "That's not the way it happened." To be blunt, *Playing with the Past* could have easily been a work of how these games misrepresent the past in an effort to prove what the games, so often, "get wrong." In other words, this book could be nothing more than a series of statements about how ridiculous it is to suggest Queen Victoria's Royal Army invading and conquering ancient China with high-tech tanks and jet fighters, or a twenty-first century based on ideas of the future located in the pre–computer chip era of 1950s America.

This would make for a book in which history is simply a series of facts, organized in a correct chronological order, and thus the games under discussion could be faulted for both "getting the facts wrong," and for "getting the chronology wrong." It would have been a relatively simple process for the contributors, and it could easily have been done as an extended PowerPoint presentation rather than as a series of chapters.

We do not believe this would have made for a particularly useful—or even *slightly* interesting—book.

Imagining the past

The American historian Lloyd S. Kramer has made a general point about history that we believe can apply to the games that engage with the past under discussion here. While Kramer is interested in exploring the traditional ways history is understood—that is, through the writing of historical narratives—his position is intentionally open and thus easily applied here. "The fictive, imaginary dimension in all accounts of events does not mean that the events did not actually happen," he has offered, "but it does mean that any attempt to describe events . . . must rely on various forms of imagination."[4] Now, of course, Kramer is a historian and he remains committed to "events" that did "actually happen." And, again, it is a relatively simple task to note that the Aztecs did not ever succeed in throwing off the yoke of the Spanish Conquistadors or that Abraham Lincoln never declared an American communist nation, and these are both things possible within the game space of various games discussed in this book.

But Kramer also notes that, "one cannot write history without both philosophy and fictional narratives,"—that is, without a philosophy of what the past "is" and how fictional narratives change the perception of that past.[5] In short, history is a story about the events of the past, that is told by a historian, and when read by someone it engages with the imagination of the reader to create an *idea* or series of *ideas* about what occurred in that past. As we will suggest below, the notion of history being a narrative about what happened in the past is a key to both understanding this book—and understanding why we consider digital games to be an important way of representing that past.

But, there is a difference between a traditional historical narrative and a game narrative, too—obviously. When a person reads a work of history the only active role they are allowed—the only time they are allowed to do something other than passively receive the text provided by the historian—is when they imaginatively envision the story presented to them. Yes, it is possible for a reader to engage with a work of history on a factual level, of course. The reader, as they read, may think "I do not believe this historian is emphasizing fact *x* enough," or, "This would be a better argument if the historian were to mention the events of *y*." Such an activity is largely confined to other professional historians, though, or perhaps highly engaged and informed students. The rest of their activity in the process can only be described as, for lack of a better term, passive.

History is not the only human activity to engage with the past, however. Novelists writing historical fiction, scholars of religion exploring the past of the faith they are analyzing, even marketing professionals referencing the past of products they are selling are all engaging with previous events. For the editors and contributors of this work, though, it is the American global historian William H. McNeill who has offered the insight necessary to understand what historical games are actually undertaking. McNeill, in his Presidential Address to the American Historical Association in 1985, put it succinctly:

> Myth and history are close kin inasmuch as both explain how things got to be the way they are by telling some sort of story.[6]

Historians have never taken McNeill's position particularly seriously—nor even with much professional respect. They tended to agree too much with his next statement: "But our common parlance reckons myth to be false while history is, or aspires to be, true."[7] This distinction, that myth is false while history aspires to truth, has long been seen as the defining difference that makes history—whatever else it may be—a social science. As McNeill continues:

> To become history, facts have to be put together into a pattern that is understandable and credible; and when that has been achieved, the resulting portrait of the past may become useful as well—a font of practical wisdom upon which people may draw when making decisions and taking action.[8]

This volume does agree with McNeill about how "the resulting portrait of the past may become useful," but, as may be obvious in a book about digital games, we do not necessarily believe that to be "useful" in the present there is a requirement that all the "facts" are correct—perhaps, as we have seen, "playable" is a better term. Yet, this remains a driving goal of the professional historian's project: to get the facts right.

We could offer a series of quotes from historians and philosophers to make this *desire for truth* claimed by historians more evident. The one most often used has long been the line from the philosopher George Santayana whose claim that "those who cannot remember the past are condemned to repeat it" has been so long a standard for historians that it is almost a ritual when quoted.[9] Even taken out of context (it is from a section not about the actual past, but about the need for continuity of ideas in order to achieve progress), it is a statement that offers an elegant summary of what historians aspire to accomplish. This is why, regardless of the quote's context, it is almost impossible to attend a professional meeting of historians without hearing it quoted by someone.

But it remains a quotation that begs an important question that is significant for this book: What, exactly, does it mean to "remember the past"? Is the remembrance of the past something that requires the correct facts? If those facts are in error, is the remembrance, then, also erroneous? As editors we have both attempted to answer precisely these questions in different ways in our past work, and it is worth a quick recap of our own perspectives, here.

One of us (Elliott), writing on the way films represent the Middle Ages, has argued, simply, that for films depicting this period, historical accuracy is perhaps less important than historical *authenticity*. That is to say, "a film [or a game] need not conform to the historical reality (whatever this might have been), but only to what audiences think the period looked like."[10] Like such films the digital games under consideration in this book are important not because of what they get "right" or "wrong" when compared to the known historical record, but in the way they make a game player interact with a past that feels "authentic." There is an obvious problem with such a statement, though—at least for a historian who believes the discipline of history is an empirical undertaking. From this perspective the historical significance of the digital games considered here are not—and should not be—about their historical accuracy. They are, instead, to be viewed as attempts to approach historical *authenticity*. Or, more directly, it is not and cannot be about "getting the historical facts correct," but is about getting the experience and expectations of the past "right."

That is to say, the veracity of games that engage with history is less about their ability to represent an accurate past and more about their ability to present what "feels" like an authentic one. This, it should be noted, is really a mythic perspective and not a historical one. The other editor of this volume (Kapell), explaining the emergence of myths of the American West in relation to the vast narrative of *Star Trek*, has argued that history becomes merely a subcategory of the larger category of myth. This, we think, is a useful perspective for understanding the digital games concerned with history in this work. Such games offer a "process [that] involve[s] much more than simply history—and [is] usually wholly contradictory to history."[11] But, at the same time, such narratives—be they films representing the Middle Ages, television shows representing the future exploration of space, or digital games with historical themes—the important factor is not adherence to historical fact. It is a feeling for historical *authenticity*. This, as William H. McNeill suggests, is more the purpose of myth than it is that of history—but it is really the purpose of both.

And it is bound to anger some professional historians.

A playable past

The games under discussion in *Playing with the Past* tend to follow William Uricchio's categorization of such games—being either quite narrow and specific (such as being about aircraft in World War I or individual events) or more concerned about broad historical sweeps (such as *Three Kingdoms* or *Age of Empires*). Uricchio claims that it is the second type that "tend[s] to be more evidently structured by unspoken historical principle (or better, ideology)."[12] As editors, though, we find the ideological underpinnings inherent in all historically minded games one of their key components. It is the examination of such ideologies that this work concerns itself and, moving somewhat away from Uricchio's categories as a result, we find those ideologies to be not just historical, but also mythical. This is simply because ideology is a major component of all myths—indeed, ideology is their *point*.

Myth, as American myth scholar Bruce Lincoln has put it, is largely "ideology in narrative form."[13] That is to say, it is a story that offers, also, a worldview for those who accept it as "true." As editors we would argue that an "ideology in narrative form" or a story that contains a worldview is largely the purpose of not just myth, but of history as well. Also, it is precisely what digital games exploring historical periods, topics, or ideas also offer the player—the opportunity to work at creating a new narrative with a new ideology. As one of us (Kapell) previously suggested about the *Civilization* franchise, "It is further a myth that is individualized *to* their desires, and individualized *by* those desires, while still reinforcing the very mythological structure through which it operates."[14] Yet unlike "history," in which the reader is mostly a passive recipient of the historian's narrative (and, importantly, the historian's ideology inherent within that narrative), the player is capable of interacting with an authentic historical past in any way she or he may choose. The player thus is able to play within the narrative and reimagine history in any way that might be desirable.

What does that active role afforded the player really amount to? Or, for that matter, what of the gameplay engagement with a past that, if not factually correct, does at least "feel authentic"? That has been long seen as a traditional function of myth.

The myth scholar William G. Doty has put this very idea quite plainly, claiming that myths "determine and shape ideals and goals for both individual and society."[15] While digital games are less about such a role for society (other than within the game, itself), they very much capture for the player— the individual—a way to experiment with ideals and goals for themselves as they engage with and shape an imagined society. It is, in very mythical terms, what Josh Call, Katie Whitlock, and Gerald Voorhees can call in their edited volumes on digital games, a "grand adventure"—surely not a phrase that finds itself often in historical texts, but quite often in the descriptions of mythic ones.[16]

Using historical games to create one's own ideology in narrative form is precisely what is offered to the player. Simply: this is using history for mythic purposes. And, perhaps more importantly, that active use of history is important because it affords a player of such games an education on how historians think. Thus, while the facts of any specific game may be erroneous, the experience may enable the player's engagement with more traditional historical narratives increase by virtue of their exposure to some of the most important parts of the historians' toolkit. In play they must deal with historical contingency and the broad effects of such contingency on the shape of historical change.

Such contingency explains the organization of *Playing with the Past*. Traditional issues recognized by historians, such as worries over teleology and various deterministic models, are offered in Part One. In Part Two we question the well-established issues of what the anthropologist Eric R. Wolf once called *Europe and the People without History*, in which the ideology of Western historians largely determined how they would offer the history of non-Western peoples.[17] Part Three considers ways in which the past can be remade by the players themselves—an activity that historians have long claimed that historians have long claimed falls within their unique province. their unique province and pertain to their competence. Part Four distills from that topic the issues surrounding authentic—if not correct—representation of the past in digital games. Finally, Part Five moves forward into a utopian or dystopian space to examine how ideas of "the past"—as they vary—may affect "the future."

That is quite a lot to cover! But, if considered from another perspective it is the same long path trodden by professional historians as a group in the last 150 years or so. *Playing with the Past* offers one history of historiography—or one narrative of seeing how "thinking about the past" has changed over time among professional historians. From the teleology of the nineteenth century, to the grand Western histories written in the early and middle of the twentieth, to a willingness to expand the very notion of what an "historical text" might be beginning in the 1960s, to postmodern questions of representation of the 1980s and counterfactual experiments of the 1990s and beyond, *Playing with the Past* offers a history of historiography written between the lines throughout.

Or, put another way, this book offers both a new way of thinking about the past alongside studies of new ways of engaging with the past, but also offers a very general overview of previous ways of thinking about the past.

At the same time, however, it does so through a continual acknowledgment of the simple fact that, in each case, the player remains active and not passive in the process. And such an active role is, simply, far more in tune with myth than it ever has been with history. This also undermines the traditional status of the professional historian in interpreting the past—or at least in one of the historian's traditional roles, namely the active generation of meaning and interpretation of facts. This cannot be discounted.

The problems of a mythical past for the historian

The ongoing project that is professional history, however, is one that at times cannot easily allow such an active role for a non-professional historian. This is, as William H. McNeill once claimed, part of the historians' attempt to forge a "desacralized ... past," which could not help but view a mythic—and individualized—interpretation as both a sacred and non-empirical vision.[18] Of course, it would be a ridiculous argument to suggest that the playing of historical games is a sacred pastime. But it does still grant the player a level of agency that is more in tune with myth than it could ever be with traditional ideas of "history."

The relationship between cultural myth and individual agency has long been a topic for anthropologists. Dorothy Eggan, in an examination of the Native American Hopi culture and the individual's use of myth among the Hopi, captured what we believe is a possibility for individual game players as well. For Eggan, a member of the Hopi was able to negotiate a position through dreams as they relate to broader myths of that culture to "fuse his personal problems to those of his culture's heroes," and thus relate his individual story to the stories of his people.[19] We would not ascribe such an important and significant role to digital games, of course. But we would suggest it is an option that is available.

It is also a supremely important option.

As an available option such a relationship offers the game player something that simply is not available to the traditional reader of a historical work. While advanced students or professional historians are able to infuse their reading of a history with their own (hopefully learned) opinions, the average reader is expected to merely *receive* the historian's words—which must also force upon that reader a disconnect from the past events about which she or he is reading. This is the key position that establishes a professional justification of the work of any historian and it is also the key in how game players are able to undermine that justification as well. A work of history can, at its best, offer a way for the reader to find coherence in their own culture's current status, but myth offers a way for the *individual* to find coherence in their place *within* that culture.

In other words, the playing of a game that centers on history—whether factual or counterfactual—offers the possibility of the individual player discovering a greater relevance within her or his culture. Digital games that simulate history are important because they recognize the agency of the individual and they do so by specifically undermining the professional status traditionally afforded to the historian. In allowing a player to achieve what the psychologist Dan P. McAdams terms a "generative integration" between the individual and the stories common in the society at large, historical games offer a way for those who play them to become *part* of a narrative that, previously, they could only examine from the outside.[20] Professional historians, with a jealous desire to maintain control over their historical narratives, have long policed access to the past and its interpretation by virtue of their perceived professional status. Historical games, however, allow the player to work around the professional historians' control of such content and, at the same time, also provide the player with agency in interacting with that past.

We are not suggesting that the simple act of playing a game of historical content makes the individual player more relevant to the player's culture. We are suggesting, however, that in granting the individual greater access to the historical narrative they are also granted the psychological benefit of feeling more connected to those historical events—and thus more connected to their own *present*.

In allowing individual access to the historical narrative through games, the individual player is able to *feel*, as a single person, connected to those past events in ways that no traditional reader of a historical tome can be.

Democratizing the narrative of the past through play

When the game under consideration is a single-player activity, of course, the access to historical narratives is primarily a personal activity. Like the Hopi, however, that play also allows for a connection with the traditional stories of the many cultures of the past. When the game becomes multiplayer, the activity becomes slightly more dispersed and with the addition of massive, multiplayer online games the narrative's scope is still greater. Modding offers an even more expanded position on the ideology in narrative form that is offered: no longer is the player consigned to interacting and changing the narrative within that narrative's original breadth. Now the entire narrative is open not just to interpretation, or gentle tweaks, or even somewhat major adjustments. Now the narrative, itself, has become part of the activity of the player/modder.

While contemporary historians are more open, today, to the inclusion of non-professional opinions about the interpretation of the past than ever before they still retain a veto power over what is considered acceptable and what is not. Ultimately, it is the professional opinion of an academic historian or group of historians that finalizes how the "ideology in narrative form" will be cemented into what is an acceptable interpretation of the "historical record." In the games analyzed in *Playing with the Past*—and a host of other games as well—that veto power is removed from the equation. The player is offered a chance to interpret the narrative, experiment with counterfactual positions, or alter the narrative wholesale. In this sense the games considered here— and in *all* digital games, period—offer the possibility of a democratization of the process of creativity, of the control of the narrative, and of allowing the individual player, group of players, or modders to take part in the shaping of both history and myth. As Dorothy Eggan described the use of myth and dreams among the Hopi as one of "introduce[ing] new emphases and directions into Hopi lore," the digital gamer is allowed the same option during play.[21]

Unlike the more traditional historical activity of professionals, this is, indeed, both historical *and* mythic. Also, unlike traditional histories, these narratives are uniquely the province of ... well, the province of any person who wishes to play.

The past has always been available to all who wish to discover it. Historians have long labored to offer a narrative of the past that would—at least for a time—be stable and unchanging. Each new generation of historians has retold their story of the past, in the words of one famous American historian, "with reference to the conditions uppermost in its own time."[22] In historical games such examples of new narratives of the past need not wait upon a new generation of professional historians, however. As editors we agree with the statement by anthropologist Claude Lévi-Strauss about myth—and would also apply it to history and to historical games as well:

> Myths do not consist in games finished once and for all. They are untiring;
> they begin a new game each time they are retold or read.[23]

Or each time the player simply reboots.

In *Playing with the Past* (not only in terms of this book, but also more generally) we see, for the first time perhaps, that a *narrative* of the past—once the purview mainly of professional historians—is now also available to everyone who wishes to *play* with it.

Everyone.

Notes

1 William Uricchio, "Simulation, History, and Computer Games," in Eds. Joost Raessens and Jeffrey Goldstein, *Handbook of Computer Game Studies*. Cambridge, MA: MIT Press, 2005, 336.

2 Richard J. Evans, *In Defence of History*. London: Granta, 1999. Originally published in the United Kingdom, this spelling of "defense" is correct in British English.

3 Evans, *In Defence of History*, 222–223.

4 Lloyd S. Kramer, "Literature, Criticism, and Historical Imagination: The Literary Challenge of Hayden White and Dominick LaCapra," in Ed. Lynn Hunt, *The New Cultural History*. Berkeley, CA: University of California Press, 1989, 101.

5 Kramer, "Literature, Criticism, and Historical Imagination," 101.

6 William H. McNeill, "Mythistory, or Truth, Myth, History, and Historians," in *Mythistory and Other Essays*. Chicago, IL: University of Chicago Press, 1986, 3.

7 McNeill, "Mythistory, or Truth, Myth, History, and Historians," 4.

8 McNeill, "Mythistory, or Truth, Myth, History, and Historians," 5.

9 George Santayana, *The Life of Reason: The Phases of Human Progress, Volumes One Through Five*. New York: Dover, 1905, http://www.gutenberg.org/files/15000/15000-h/15000-h.htm, accessed 15 March 2013.

10 Andrew B.R. Elliott, *Remaking the Middle Ages: The Methods of Cinema and History in Portraying the Medieval World*. Jefferson, NC and London: McFarland, 2011, 215.

11 Matthew Wilhelm Kapell, "Conclusion: The Hero with a Thousand Red Shirts," in Ed. Matthew Wilhelm Kapell, *Star Trek as Myth: Essays on Symbol and Archetype at the Final Frontier*. Jefferson, NC and London: McFarland & Co, 2010, 214.

12 Uricchio, "Simulation, History, and Computer Games," 328.

13 Bruce Lincoln, *Theorizing Myth: Narrative, Ideology, and Scholarship*. Chicago: University of Chicago Press, 1999, 207.

14 Matthew Kapell, "Civilization and Its Discontents: American Monomythic Structure as Historical Simulacrum," *Popular Culture Review*, 13, no. 2 (2002): 130. Emphasis in the original.

15 William G. Doty, *Mythography: The Study of Myths and Rituals*, 2nd ed. Tuscaloosa, AL: University of Alabama Press, 2000, 26.

16 Joshua Call, Katie Whitlock, and Gerald A. Voorhees, "From Dungeons to Digital Denizens," in Eds. Gerald A. Voorhees, Joshua Call, and Katie Whitlock, *Dungeons, Dragons, and Digital Denizens: The Digital Role Playing Game*. New York: Continuum, 2012, 23.

17 Eric R. Wolf, *Europe and the People Without History*, 2nd ed: University of California Press, 2010.

18 William H. McNeill, *The Changing Shape of World History*, Conference Presentation presented at the History and Theory World History Conference, 25 March 1994, http://www.hartford-hwp.com/archives/10/041.html.

19 Dorothy Eggan, "The Personal Use of Myth in Dreams," in Ed. Thomas A. Sebeok, *Myth: A Symposium*. Bloomington, IN: Indiana University Press, 1955, 107.

20 Dan P. McAdams, *The Stories We Live By: Personal Myths and the Making of the Self*. Guilford Press, 1993, 112.

21 Eggan, "The Personal Use of Myth in Dreams," 118.

22 Frederick Jackson Turner, "The Significance of History," in Ed. Ray Allen Billington, *Frontier and Section*. Englewood Cliffs, NJ: Prentice Hall, 1961, 17.

23 Claude Lévi-Strauss, *The Story of Lynx*, trans. Catherine Tihanyi: University Of Chicago Press, 1996, xii.

Works cited

Call, Joshua, Katie Whitlock, and Gerald A. Voorhees. "From Dungeons to Digital Denizens," in Eds. Gerald A. Voorhees, Joshua Call, and Katie Whitlock, *Dungeons, Dragons, And Digital Denizens: The Digital Role Playing Game*. New York: Continuum, 2012, 11–24.

Doty, William G. *Mythography: The Study of Myths and Rituals*, 2nd ed. Tuscaloosa, AL: University of Alabama Press, 2000.

Eggan, Dorothy. "The Personal Use of Myth in Dreams," in Ed. Thomas A. Sebeok, *Myth: A Symposium*. Bloomington, IN: Indiana University Press, 1955, 107–121.

Elliott, Andrew B.R. *Remaking the Middle Ages: The Methods of Cinema and History in Portraying the Medieval World*. Jefferson, NC and London: McFarland, 2011.

Evans, Richard J. *In Defense of History*. London: Granta, 1999.

Kapell, Matthew. "Civilization and Its Discontents: American Monomythic Structure as Historical Simulacrum," *Popular Culture Review*, 13, no. 2 (2002): 129–136.

Kapell, Matthew Wilhelm. "Conclusion: The Hero with a Thousand Red Shirts," in Ed. Matthew Wilhelm Kapell, *Star Trek as Myth: Essays on Symbol and Archetype at the Final Frontier*. Jefferson, NC and London: McFarland & Co, 2010, 213–219.

Kramer, Lloyd S. "Literature, Criticism, and Historical Imagination: The Literary Challenge of Hayden White and Dominick LaCapra," in Ed. Lynn Hunt, *The New Cultural History*. Berkeley, CA: University of California Press, 1989, 97–128.

Lévi-Strauss, Claude. *The Story of Lynx*, trans. Catherine Tihanyi, Chicago: University Of Chicago Press, 1996.

Lincoln, Bruce. *Theorizing Myth: Narrative, Ideology, and Scholarship*. Chicago, IL: University of Chicago Press, 1999.

McAdams, Dan P. *The Stories We Live By: Personal Myths and the Making of the Self*. New York: Guilford Press, 1993.

McNeill, William H. "Mythistory, or Truth, Myth, History, and Historians," in *Mythistory and Other Essays*. Chicago, IL: University of Chicago Press, 1986, 3–22.

McNeill, William H. *The Changing Shape of World History*, Conference Presentation presented at the History and Theory World History Conference, Wesleyan University, Middleton, CT. 25 March 1994, http://www.hartford-hwp.com/archives/10/041.html, accessed 28 May 2013.

Santayana, George. *The Life of Reason: The Phases of Human Progress, Volumes One Through Five*. New York: Dover, 1905, http://www.gutenberg.org/files/15000/15000-h/15000-h.htm, accessed 15 March 2013.

Turner, Frederick Jackson. "The Significance of History," in Ed. Ray Allen Billington, *Frontier and Section*. Englewood Cliffs, NJ: Prentice Hall, 1961, 2–27.

Uricchio, William. "Simulation, History, and Computer Games," in Eds. Joost Raessens and Jeffrey Goldstein, *Handbook of Computer Game Studies*. Cambridge, MA: MIT Press, 2005, 327–338.

Wolf, Eric R. *Europe and the People Without History*, 2nd ed, Berkeley, CA, and Los Angeles: University of California Press, 2010.

About the contributors

Tom Apperley, Ph.D., is a researcher of digital media technologies and is currently Senior Lecturer at the Journalism and Media Research Centre, the University of New South Wales, Sydney, Australia. His previous writing has covered broadband policy, digital games, digital literacies and pedagogies, mobile media, and social inclusion. He is the editor of the open-access peer-reviewed journal *Digital Culture & Education*. His open-access print-on-demand book *Gaming Rhythms: Play and Counterplay from the Situated to the Global* was published by the Institute of Network Cultures in 2010. He spends most of his spare time mining obsidian.

Emily Joy Bembeneck is a Ph.D. candidate in Classics at the University of Michigan. She works on storytelling in both traditional and digital forms and has a keen interest in the relationship between video games and identity. In 2012, she designed a game platform called *Storydeck* and a mobile game for iOS called *Ella* that explores possible tellings of the Cinderella story through the power of cards. She is a contributor at playthepast.org, where she writes on the intersections of games, history, and cultural identity. You can find her online at adaplay.wordpress.com and on Twitter as @adarel. Expect to see many pictures of cats, none of which can compare to the greatest of the species, her own Grim M. Cuddlesworth.

Jonathan M. Bullinger is currently a doctoral candidate in media studies at Rutgers University's School of Communication and Information. His area of focus is the intersection between collective memory and political economy or the selling of history with a particular emphasis on the role of branding. He has presented regularly at national conferences including Popular Culture Association and currently has articles published in *Reconstruction: Studies in Contemporary Culture* and *JASIST*, and an article is currently under revision at the *Journal of Communication Inquiry*. Previously fulfilled in his life as an international playboy and raconteur, he nonetheless gave it all up in order to contribute to this present volume.

Adam Chapman is a Ph.D. student in his final year at the University of Hull. Adam's research focuses on the video game as a historical form and seeks to weave existing historical theory and analysis with game-focused research that emphasizes the unique qualities of games and play, as well as, more recently, Gibsonian ecological psychology. Accordingly, he is attempting to develop an analytical framework for historical video games that includes understanding both action/agency and narrative/representation and the interplays between these aspects. He is also believed to be the only person in the known universe that claims to understand the entire transmedia storyline of the *Halo* series. He can be contacted at achapman593@me.com and @Woodlandstaar.

Gareth Crabtree is an independent researcher and writer. He holds a Ph.D. from the University of Manchester in UK. His thesis, "Playing at War: Games Technology and British Military Imaginings 1870–2010," maps the creation, production, and consumption of war games in British society from the Victorian period to the present day. He is currently turning his thesis into his first monograph and writing an article on how Prussian-inspired military war gaming acted as a forum for military-civic exchange in late nineteenth-century England. He is dedicated to utilizing games, their play, and the communities they form as a way to engage with present and historical culture. He spent the entirety of Ph.D. insisting that he was not just playing games all day. He is not entirely sure that he was believed.

Tom Cutterham is a doctoral student in US History at St. Hugh's College, Oxford. His thesis, "Gentlemen Revolutionaries: Power and Ideology in the 1780s," looks at American elites in the decade following the Revolution. He holds the Rothermere American Institute's Three Year Studentship, and is also an Associate Lecturer at Oxford Brookes University. His writing on history and politics has appeared online in places like *Prospect* and *Jacobin*, and he is also a senior editor at the *Oxonian Review*. Addiction to *Civilization III* is probably more responsible than anything for turning him into a historian.

Douglas N. Dow has recently completed a book on apostolic iconography and Florentine confraternities at the end of the sixteenth century. He is currently an assistant professor of art history at Kansas State University and has published articles on Benvenuto Cellini and the art patronage of Florentine confraternities. His next project marries his interest in the urban fabric of that city with his work on lay corporate groups, and explores how those organizations used their real estate portfolios to establish an urban presence outside of their small chapels. The chapter in this volume stems from his interest in video games and post-modern theory, both of which provide an escape from reality.

Andrew B. R. Elliott is Senior Lecturer in Media and Cultural Studies at the University of Lincoln, UK. His research focuses on the representation of history in popular culture, having published on a range of topics from accuracy and authenticity to Vikings and violence. His first book, *Remaking the Middle Ages*, analyzes the reconstruction of the medieval period in modern cinema, and his forthcoming edited collection *The Return of the Epic Film* (EUP, 2014) analyzes the resurgence of the sword and sandal film in the twenty-first century. Given that it is the only video game he has ever been able to complete, he still fervently insists that *The Secret of Monkey Island* on the Amiga 500 counts as a historical video game.

Erin Evans recently completed her Ph.D. in Religious Studies at the University of Edinburgh. Her research has related to ancient Gnosticism, particularly the group represented by the Coptic texts *The Books of Jeu* and the *Pistis Sophia*. With a publication pending on the use of astrology in these texts, more recently she is turning toward examining the use and movement of astrological motifs in esoteric religion from the ancient Near East to the Far East. She collects badger-related goods, and has a set of stuffed badgers named Sophia, Renaldo, Piyo, Deathstriker, and Hermes the Pocket Badger of Esoteric Wisdom.

Sean Joseph Fedorko is currently pursuing a Ph.D. in Political Science at Indiana University, Bloomington, and participating at the Ostrom Workshop in Political Theory and Policy Analysis. He spent the preceding two years as project manager for the Mercyhurst Center for Applied Politics, where he enjoyed training student-researchers in social science research ethics and interview skills, as well as contributing to survey instrument design. He holds B.A.s in Political Science and Philosophy with interests in environmental policy, environmental philosophies, political theory, and existentialism. When not advertising himself in short paragraphs, Sean can be found building models of mobile suits, watching anything with the word "star" in the title, or walking without rhythm so as not to attract the worm.

Kazumi Hasegawa is a Ph.D. candidate in the Graduate Institute of the Liberal Arts, Emory University. She teaches Japanese history at University of

Georgia. Her dissertation examines the creation of modern Japanese identity within an international context, through the life history of Oyabe Zen'ichirō. Oyabe's multiracial experiences in the United States from 1888 to 1897 and interests in race even after his return to Japan made him unique among the Japanese intellectuals. His various life enterprises such as providing education for the Ainu and producing historical myths and legends in Japan centered on the remaking of modern Japanese identity. Kazumi finally discovered a good Chinese restaurant in Athens after numerous attempts, which she believes, will bring lots of good fortune this year.

Joshua D. Holdenried is a student at the University of Mississippi's Sally McDonnell Barksdale Honors College, pursuing a B.A. in Public Policy Leadership with a minor in Intelligence and Security Studies. He is currently working on his senior thesis, entitled "Generation Collaboration: Measuring the Propensity of Generation Y to Information Sharing in the Post-9/11 Intelligence Community." Along with his passion for public policy and defense studies, Joshua is also a history enthusiast and had the opportunity to take an honors course that focused on interpretations of history through video games. His term paper was eventually edited and its publication made possible by his professor, Nicolas Trépanier. Joshua is 22 and has a 5-year-old brother, who many people mistake as his son.

Matthew Wilhelm Kapell has edited volumes on *The Matrix*, *Star Wars*, *Star Trek*, and the films of James Cameron. With M.A. degrees in anthropology and history he holds a Ph.D. in American Studies from Swansea University in Great Britain and has taught extensively both there and in the United States. He has published on subjects as diverse as human genetics, Utopian fiction, and African colonial history. Further professional details can be found at matthewkapell.com. A native of the not particularly violent city of Detroit, he has tattoos for each of his book projects and is very much looking forward to the new one for editing this volume.

William M. Knoblauch is Assistant Professor of History at Finlandia University in Hancock, MI. He received his Ph.D. in American History from Ohio University and was a fellow of the Contemporary History Institute in Athens, Ohio. His research examines the interplay between twentieth-century popular culture, politics, and foreign policy. He has forthcoming articles set to appear in collections by the German Historical Institute and Michigan State University Press, and is currently working on a manuscript of his dissertation: "Selling the Second Cold War: Antinuclear Cultural Activism and Reagan Era Foreign Policy." Perhaps more impressive than these teaching and writing achievements, he can still knock out Mike Tyson in the NES game *Punch Out*.

Ryuta Komaki studies immigration, migration and digital media, race, ethnicity and digital media, and global circulation of media products. He has just completed his doctoral dissertation research on Japanese-Brazilian return migrants in Japan and their new and traditional media use, and is receiving his Ph.D. from the Institute of Communications Research at the University of Illinois at Urbana–Champaign. Previously he has presented his works at media and communication studies, science and technology studies, and East Asian studies conferences. The scene where a zombie dog jumps in through the window in the first *Bio Hazard/Resident Evil* title still traumatizes him, and he is glad his coauthor did not make him re-play the game or play the sequels.

Josef Köstlbauer is a historian working and teaching at the University of Vienna, Austria. Having studied in Vienna, Berlin, and New Orleans, he holds a Ph.D. in History. He has published on a wide variety of subjects including early modern Atlantic history, comparative frontier studies, and digital humanities, and he has been employed in various hypermedia projects exploring the challenges and possibilities of acquiring and disseminating historical knowledge within rapidly converging media environs. When not teaching or writing he is way up in the border country with his horses and his hounds.

Hyuk-Chan Kwon is Assistant Professor in the Department of Chinese, Translation, and Linguistics at the City University of Hong Kong and has previously taught in both Korea and Canada. In multiple languages he has published in *Acta Koreana*, *Rivista Italiana Di Geopolitica*, and *Chungguk Sosol Nonch'ong*, among others. He is revising his dissertation, "From *Sanguo yanyi* to *Samgukchi*: Appropriation and Domestication of *Three Kingdoms* in Korea," for publication. While working on *Three Kingdoms* for the past decade, his favorite historical simulation game of all time is *Age of Empires* series.

Robert Mejia is Assistant Professor with the Department of Communication at the State University of New York, Brockport. He received his doctorate from the Institute of Communications Research at the University of Illinois at Urbana–Champaign. He is a media and cultural theorist specializing in cultural studies, gender and women's studies, historiography and memory studies, media history, technology studies, and game studies. His work has appeared in *Explorations in Media Ecology*, *Personal Relationships*, and *Race/Gender/Class/Media 3.0*. His latest teaching evaluation mentioned that he reminded one of his students of a character from *The Big Bang Theory*. This was meant as a positive comparison.

Andrew Justin Miller is a public librarian and Federal Depository Coordinator for the Erie County Public Library System. He holds a B.A. in history from Westminster College, Pennsylvania, where he translated sections from the tenth-century Byzantine court manual *De Ceremoniis* for his honors thesis. He also holds an MLIS from the University of Pittsburgh. He currently develops programs that advance use of technology and gaming in library settings. As a resident of Northwestern Pennsylvania, Andrew prides his beard and his tolerance of cold temperatures above all his earthly possessions. He currently lives in Erie with his lovely wife and newborn daughter.

Rebecca Mir works as an Educator in the Education Division of the New-York Historical Society and holds an M.A. in Decorative Arts, Design History, and Material Culture from the Bard Graduate Center, where she discovered her passion for object-based learning. She is a contributing author for playthepast.org, where she writes about how (and why) artifacts and cultures are (mis)represented in games, as well as how museums utilize games to engage audiences. Rebecca is dedicated to using social media for educational good, and can be found on Twitter as @mirseum. Her cats are named Tiberius and Jean-Luc, implying that, obviously, she would relinquish her current positions for a post at Starfleet Academy.

Joseph A. November is Associate Professor of History at the University of South Carolina, where he teaches courses on the history of science, medicine, and technology. His recent book, *Biomedical Computing: Digitizing Life in the United States* (Johns Hopkins University Press), shows how computing and biomedicine shaped each other. He received his Ph.D. in History from Princeton University in 2006. His fascination with history has been intertwined with his fascination with computers. He has been an avid video-gamer since he was five years old, when his father brought home a TRS-80. The skills, patience, and ambitions he developed as a gamer during the 1980s led to some interesting programming work (and his career as a historian of computing) but also to his vulnerability to Dwarf Fortress.

Trevor Owens is a historian, archivist, and blogger in Northern Virginia. He works as a Digital Archivist in Office of Strategic Initiatives at the Library of Congress and occasionally teaches a digital history graduate seminar for American University. He blogs about games and history at playthepast. org, about digital preservation for the Library of Congress, and various and sundry other things related to digital history at trevorowens.org. You can find him on Twitter @tjowens. He and his wife Marjee are the proud humans/ tamers of two small dogs, a chocolate-brown Pomeranian named Bowser and a black-and-white mismarked Japanese Chin named Zelda.

Rolfe Daus Peterson is Assistant Professor of Political Science at Mercyhurst University. His recent research on politics and social media has been published in the *Social Science Journal* and *American Politics Research*. Born in Southeastern Idaho, he received his B.A. from the University of Idaho and his Ph.D. from the University of California at Davis. When not impressing upon his American Government students the intricacies of *The Big Lebowski*, he enjoys reading science fiction and inhabiting virtual realities both historical and fantastical in nature.

Clemens Reisner is a Ph.D. student with the department for Media Sudies at the University of Vienna and a research assistant for the Austrian Society for the Study of Historical Sources. His areas of interest include the (global) history of the Cold War, historical culture, and media theories. He holds a Bachelor in Japanese studies and an M.A. in Global History, both from the University of Vienna. Currently he is working on his Ph.D. thesis about "The Cold War in computer games, 1980–2010." In doing so he faces the everyday challenges of a part-time student life and the sweet uphill struggle of sorting (and playing) through around 160 games that are to be used for his thesis.

Daniel Reynolds is Assistant Professor in the Department of Film and Media Studies at Emory University in Atlanta, Georgia. He holds a Ph.D. in Film Studies from the University of California, Santa Barbara, where he was a founding editor of *Media Fields Journal*, which can be found at mediafieldsjournal.org. Recently, he has contributed essays to *The Routledge Encyclopedia of Film Theory*, edited by Edward Branigan and Warren Buckland, and to the journal *Fibreculture*. Reynolds is currently co-chair of the Video Game Studies Scholarly Interest Group of the Society for Cinema and Media Studies. This may all be out of date soon, as his copy of *Ni No Kuni* arrives tomorrow and he will probably never show up for anything again.

Andrew J. Salvati is a doctoral candidate in media studies at Rutgers University's School of Communication and Information. His research interests fall at the intersection of media, memory, and history. His work has examined how we engage with and represent the past in various media contexts including television, film, and video games. In addition to his work in the present volume, he has coauthored a work of critical/cultural studies on branding and the political economy of World War II media. In addition, Andrew studies historical play: parody, satire, games, and fantasy in popular representations of the past.

Marcus Schulzke is Research Director of the Project on Violent Conflict at the University at Albany. He received his Ph.D. in Political Science from the University at Albany in 2012 with a dissertation on how soldiers make ethical decisions during counterinsurgency operations. His research interests include political violence, game studies, applied ethics, contemporary political theory, and new technologies. When he is not doing research, Marcus is an avid gamer, though he always finds that even casual gaming raises innumerable issues for future research.

Nicolas Trépanier is Assistant Professor of History at the University of Mississippi, where he teaches an Honors Seminar on representations of history in video games, as well as a variety of courses on Middle Eastern history. He holds a Ph.D. in History and Middle Eastern Studies from Harvard University (2008) and is currently completing a book on food, daily life, and worldviews in medieval Anatolia. He is from Québec, and will make sure you know it.

Andrew Wackerfuss is a historian with the United States Air Force Office of Historical Studies in Washington, DC. He holds an M.A. in German and European Studies and a Ph.D. in History from Georgetown University, where he continues to teach courses in European history. He is currently finishing two forthcoming books: a work on USAF prisoners of war in North Vietnam, and the revision of his dissertation, "Stormtrooper Families" (the Nazis, not the galactic). In addition to these and other article-length publications, he has published what he hopes to be an essential philosophical guide for a post- apocalyptic world: "Thus Spoke Zombiethustra: A Book for the Living Undead."

Index

Page numbers in bold type refer to main entries and definitions.

Made in the USA
Middletown, DE
04 February 2023

23939805R00225